WERTHEIM FELLOWSHIP PUBLICATIONS

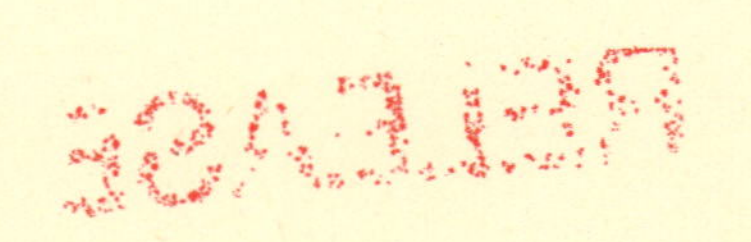

The Danish System of Labor Relations

A Study in Industrial Peace

WALTER GALENSON

Associate Professor of Industrial Relations

University of California at Berkeley

HARVARD UNIVERSITY PRESS
CAMBRIDGE, MASSACHUSETTS
1952

DISTRIBUTED IN GREAT BRITAIN BY

GEOFFREY CUMBERLEGE
OXFORD UNIVERSITY PRESS
LONDON

Library of Congress Catalog Card Number 52-5029

PRINTED IN THE UNITED STATES OF AMERICA

WERTHEIM FELLOWSHIP PUBLICATIONS

In 1923 the family of the late Jacob Wertheim established the Jacob Wertheim Research Fellowship for ". . . the support of original research in the field of industrial coöperation . . ." The Fellowship was intended to enable men and women ". . . who already have expert knowledge of this subject, to pursue research that may be of general benefit in solving the problems in this field . . ." Fellowships are awarded annually by the President and Fellows of Harvard College on the recommendation of the Wertheim Committee.

The Committee undertakes to provide general supervision to the program of research of the Wertheim Fellow. When that research yields findings and results which are significant and of general interest, the Committee is authorized by the terms of the grant to Harvard University to recommend publication. The Jacob Wertheim Research Fellow alone has responsibility for the facts, analysis, and opinions expressed in this volume.

WERTHEIM FELLOWSHIP PUBLICATIONS

Walter Galenson, *The Danish System of Labor Relations: A Study in Industrial Peace*, 1952

John T. Dunlop and Arthur D. Hill, *The Wage Adjustment Board: Wartime Stabilization in the Building and Construction Industry*, 1950

Ralph Altman, *Availability for Work: A Study in Unemployment Compensation*, 1950

Dorothea de Schweinitz, *Labor and Management in a Common Enterprise*, 1949

Walter Galenson, *Labor in Norway*, 1949

Leo C. Brown, S.J., *Union Policies in the Leather Industry*, 1947

Paul H. Norgren, *The Swedish Collective Bargaining System*, 1941

Johnson O'Connor, *Psychometrics*, 1934

William Haber, *Industrial Relations in the Building Industry*, 1930

Wertheim Lectures on Industrial Relations, 1929

J. D. Houser, *What the Employer Thinks*, 1927

FOREWORD

The trade union movements of different countries are the products of conditions in those countries, and each of them exhibits distinctive characteristics that reflect the differences in their environments. Careful case studies are needed to produce a reliable basis for generalizations about why men organize and why different trade union movements develop different objectives, policies, and methods. The accumulation of the necessary case studies is bound to take years. For a second time, Professor Galenson has placed students of industrial relations and economic history deeply in his debt by providing them with a well-informed, comprehensive, and judicious study of the trade union movement of a country.

Trade unionism has developed in Denmark with less storm and stress than probably in any other country. Partly this is attributable to the absence of serious ideological differences between workmen and employers (though most workers are nominally Socialists) and within the trade union movement, and partly to the fact that the collective tradition has been strong both among Danish employers and among the skilled crafts of the country. Hence, almost from the beginning, Danish employers' organizations were conciliatory rather than combative. The collective tradition, however, did not prevent the employers from fearing the strength of organized workers, so that the early history of trade unionism in Denmark saw several large and prolonged lockouts — the lockout in the Copenhagen metal trades in 1885, and the great lockout of 1899. It is significant, however, that the lockout of 1899 produced an agreement that has been a sort of "constitution" governing union-employer relations in Denmark ever since.

Industrial relations in Denmark are highly organized and are orderly. All agreements expire on the same date, there is a uniform procedure for negotiating renewals, great importance is attached to the observance of agreements, and there is a Labor Court to hear complaints of noncompliance. In no other country are individual workmen held responsible for living up to the terms of agreements as strictly as in Denmark.

Probably the most interesting part of Professor Galenson's study is his discussion of the evolution of methods of settling labor disputes. Danish experience highlights the difficulties of settling the most important disputes by collective bargaining alone. Conditions in Denmark, superficially at least, seem to have been most favorable for collective bargaining. Unions are well-established, employers are organized, both sides are represented by expert negotiators, and both sides strongly desire to make collective bargaining work. And yet conditions beyond the control of the two parties have been bringing about an evolution that neither the trade unions nor the employers have particularly desired. Collective bargaining has come more and more to be supplemented by "mediation," the nature of mediation itself has gradually changed, and in recent years mediation has frequently been supplemented in important cases by government intervention — usually in the form of a vote of Parliament enacting into law the recommendations of the mediator. The evolution in the methods of handling industrial disputes has been partly caused by the reluctance of trade union officers to accept the responsibility for recommending negotiated settlements to their members (a condition that has manifested itself in other countries) and partly by the inability of the country to tolerate the loss of output that would result from widespread stoppages. The methods of settling industrial disputes in Denmark still seem to be changing and it is not clear what next developments will be.

An important part of Professor Galenson's study is his analysis of the fundamental economic conditions within which the trade unions of Denmark operate. One important economic fact is the collective tradition which has helped to make industrial relations orderly. This tradition, however, has not been conducive to industrial efficiency and expansion. There has been a lack of strong competition of employers for markets and an addiction of employers to price and market agreements. Professor Galenson calls attention to the fact that real hourly earnings in Denmark have not kept pace with real hourly earnings in Sweden or Norway since 1932, and he asks, "Why?" He thinks that part of the explanation is the slower growth of productivity in Denmark, which may in turn be due to the lower proportion of the national income devoted to domestic capital formation in Denmark. The main reason, however, probably is the unfavorable shift in the terms of Danish trade — the result of the fact that Danish exports consist more largely of agricultural products than do the exports of Sweden or Norway. With the recovery of industrial production in Germany, perhaps the terms of trade will change in favor of Denmark.

During recent years the most important fact about the Danish economy has probably been the chronic deficit in her balance of payments. This condition obviously creates special problems for trade unions. Professor Galenson points out that the economic condition of the country has stimulated the interest of unions in problems of production. In 1947, the Federation of Labor and the Employers' Association concluded an agreement providing for the establishment of labor-management production committees which have been taken more seriously by the Danish trade unions than is true of the unions in some other countries where similar bodies have been set up. The Danish unions have been active in spreading information about the problem of production among their members.

The possibility that the deficit in the balance of payments will continue suggests that the government may be compelled to intervene rather frequently in the settlement of important industrial disputes, and Professor Galenson asks whether the intervention can be kept sufficiently uncertain so that the efforts of employers and unions to settle their differences by bargaining will remain unimpaired. Thus, as Professor Galenson points out, the evolution of the institutions of industrial relations in Denmark may well depend upon what happens to the Danish terms of trade.

No student of industrial relations and indeed no student of modern economic history can afford not to study thoroughly Professor Galenson's incisive and richly documented book.

Sumner H. Slichter

CONTENTS

TABLES

APPENDIX

CHARTS

AUTHOR'S PREFACE

THIS VOLUME was warmly supported from the start by the two organizations whose story it tells, the Danish Employers' Association and the Danish Federation of Labor. The chairmen of the organizations, Mr. Hans L. Larsen and Mr. Eiler Jensen, placed much valuable material at my disposal, provided me with working facilities, and taught me the true meaning of Danish hospitality. However, this is in no sense an official history. There is much in it to which neither organization would subscribe.

The many friends who gave generously of their time facilitated my task immeasurably. I am particularly indebted to Mr. Allan Rise, director of the Danish Employers' Association, who took an active interest in the project from start to finish; to Mr. Einar Nielsen, vice-chairman of the Federation of Labor; and to Mr. Oluf Carlsson, secretary of the Social Democratic Party. Among the others whose assistance it is a pleasure to acknowledge are Messrs. Walter Elmquist and Henning Nielsen of the Employers' Association; Oluf Bertolt and A. Kocik of the Federation of Labor; Professor Knud Illum of the University of Aarhus; Professor F. Zeuthen of the University of Copenhagen; Mr. Henning Friis of the Ministry of Labor; and Mr. Jørgen Paldam of the Workers' Economic Association. Professors Sumner Slichter and John T. Dunlop of Harvard University were kind enough to read the manuscript and give me the benefit of their advice. A grant from the Penrose Fund of the American Philosophical Society enabled me to spend the summer of 1949 in Denmark. An award from the Wertheim Committee of Harvard University and financial assistance from the Rockefeller Foundation to a series of studies at Harvard University on foreign labor movements have also supported this research project.

My wife contributed to what is really a joint venture by reading the manuscript critically for both form and content and by cheerfully assuming more than her share of our domestic obligations.

Cambridge, 1951 WALTER GALENSON

CHAPTER I

INTRODUCTION

IT IS A REMARKABLE FACT that Danish industrial relations have hitherto gained so little international attention. During the last half century Danish employers and trade unions have fashioned what has a strong claim to be the most detailed and complete system of collective bargaining in existence. The rich body of accumulated experience provides an invaluable source of information for practitioners of labor relations in government, industry, and labor who are seeking new ideas and techniques in the cause of industrial peace.

The unique aspect of Danish labor relations is that as long ago as 1899, after a devastating labor dispute, organized employers and workers sat down together and worked out a comprehensive approach to collective bargaining. This was embodied in a document popularly known as the "September Agreement," which is still in full force and is rightly considered the constitution of the labor relations system. Like any constitution, it has required interpretation by tribunals established for the purpose. But the essential guarantees of the September Agreement remain unchanged, and to a greater extent than any other single factor, it is responsible for the present stability of Danish industrial relations.

The Danish collective bargaining system can be understood only against the background of the organizations that have been instrumental in its development. The Danish Federation of Labor and the Danish Employers' Association, representing the great majority of the nation's industrial workers and employers, respectively, came into existence in the same year, 1898, after a decade of effort to achieve centralization. Together, these organizations created not only the September Agreement, but every major piece of labor legislation subsequently enacted in Denmark. There was no Taff Vale decision or Taft-Hartley Act to exacerbate industrial relations. Rather, the two central organizations have been endowed with a quasi-public status, and Parliament has deferred to their views in formulating labor policy. Every element in the complex of rules and regulations governing the operation of the system grew out of actual experience and represents a response to a jointly acknowledged need. Neither side has attempted through the use of political power to impose its will upon the other in matters relating to the bargaining system.

The history and problems of labor and employer organization, the subject of Part I of this volume, provide fascinating material for the student of comparative labor problems. Unlike the British development, in which the demise of the medieval gilds and the foundation of a permanent labor movement were separated by almost a century of *laissez faire* in the labor market, or the American, in which modern industry developed in a milieu largely devoid of restrictive economic institutions, the Danish gilds played a significant role in the evolution of that nation's contemporary labor market organization. Not until 1862 were the gild monopolies abolished in Denmark, and within two decades of the introduction of free trade, lasting organizations of workers and employers had been established. The extent to which there was an organic connection between the masters' gilds and the employer associations on the one hand, and between journeymen gilds and trade unions on the other, is a matter of some controversy among Danish historians. But it is quite clear that the corporate spirit of the gilds has continued to permeate the labor market, and explains much of the organizing propensity to be observed among workers and employers.

The gilds also had a critical influence on the structure of the labor movement, which is organized along horizontal lines. A single national union represents the unskilled and semiskilled workers of the country, comprising 40 per cent of total membership in the Federation of Labor, while the skilled workers, all of whom have undergone formal apprenticeships of from four to five years, are divided among some 70 smaller craft unions. The internal rivalry between the skilled and the unskilled for shares of the national wage bill and allocation of the job market has created knotty problems both in collective bargaining and in trade union government. This aspect of the labor scene is developed in Chapter IV.

Considerable interest also attaches to the organization and operation of the Danish Employers' Association, the most efficient of the three Scandinavian employer associations. Danish employers have delegated virtually their entire bargaining function to professional negotiators, who in turn provide their constituents with representation of a very high order. The Employers' Association is well financed and is endowed with financial sanctions that have helped to maintain organizational discipline. While there have been serious policy differences within the Association, arising from the conflicting interests of the industrial groups that comprise it, they have always been resolved internally. Indeed,

Danish employers have manifested a greater degree of solidarity than the workers.

Part II deals with the methods and results of collective bargaining over new agreements, that is, disputes over interests. Based on the September Agreement, an elaborate set of bargaining rules has been developed, partly through further agreement and partly through legislation. Notable is the system of mediation, in which a government mediator, if the parties fail to reach agreement through direct bargaining, prepares a draft agreement which must be submitted to both the employers and workers concerned for referendum vote by secret ballot. This proposal of the mediator has come to occupy a focal position in the bargaining process. The way in which the mediation proposal is formulated and the rules governing the subsequent referendum provide an instructive chapter in the problems faced by a responsible trade union leadership armed with insufficient authority finally to conclude agreements.

The two final chapters of Part II are concerned with some economic aspects of collective bargaining: methods of wage payment, the movement of wage rates, and the effects of the collective bargaining system on wage structure. Relatively good Danish labor statistics permitted examination of a few specific problems of interest to the economist: the relationship of labor disputes to the movement of wages, both money and real; the varying impact of piece and time rates upon earnings; and the effects of productivity and changes in the terms of foreign trade upon the level of real wages.

The next portion of the volume, Part III, deals with the conduct of labor relations under a collective agreement, that is, disputes over rights. Success in the avoidance of open conflict during the periodic negotiation of new agreements is of little avail if controversy over interpretation and administration of the agreements is permitted to result in work stoppages, which in the long run may prove even more costly to the economy. The pivotal position in the scheme of assuring the observance of collective agreements is occupied by a tripartite Labor Court. This tribunal, established in 1910 on the initiative of the two central bargaining organizations, has dealt with more than 4,000 cases. Its decisions constitute the real corpus of Danish labor law, for the ordinary courts have played an insignificant role in labor relations. One of the extraordinary attributes of the Labor Court is its ability to enforce its decisions by levying fines, not only upon employers and trade unions, but upon individual workers as well. The fact that fines against the latter are often collected through check-off from the weekly pay envelope has endowed the Court with great respect among workers, and in many ways facilitated the work of trade unions leaders concerned with the administration of agreements. Supplementing the Labor Court is a network of industrial arbitration boards, to which contract disputes that are primarily technical in character are referred. The line between the respective jurisdictions of the Labor Court and the arbitration boards is not easy to draw from the standpoint of legal theory, but in practice there is a satisfactory division of labor, which on the one hand prevents overcrowding of the Labor Court docket with minute problems that are best dealt with by technical specialists, and on the other hand provides a speedy and effective means of enforcing arbitration awards.

The problems arising out of labor-management relations in so small a country as Denmark naturally do not compare in complexity with corresponding problems in the United States. Yet the Danish experience carries many lessons of value. Certain aspects of the Danish system, both in collective bargaining and in the adjudication of contract disputes, may be of direct application to the American scene. Proponents of an American labor court, for example, would do well to study the structure and operation of the Danish labor court. Advocates of fact-finding or emergency board procedures will find much of interest in the Danish system of mediation. The fact is that even by comparison with their Scandinavian neighbors, the Danes have been remarkably successful in averting labor conflict. There are both intellectual satisfaction and practical ideas to be gained from perusal of the experience of a people who have found a road to industrial peace.

PART ONE

HISTORY OF LABOR AND MANAGEMENT ORGANIZATIONS

CHAPTER II

THE ORIGINS OF THE LABOR MOVEMENT

MANY CONTEMPORARY DANISH LABOR PROBLEMS can be traced back to the social and economic environment prevailing when trade unionism was in its infancy. Two related groups of factors in particular left a permanent imprint upon the labor movement: the character of the Danish industrial revolution and the persistence of the medieval gilds until the middle of the nineteenth century. In the light of these and other aspects of Denmark's economic history, the origins and growth of the modern labor movement will appear in clearer perspective.

EARLY ECONOMIC DEVELOPMENT

The growth of modern Danish industry was hampered by the lack of fuel and industrial raw materials. Coal and iron ore are not to be found in the country, and wood is available only in limited quantities. On the credit side of the ledger, however, was a favorable geographical position and soil and climatic conditions that could support a prosperous agriculture.

Early attempts by the state to create a factory system failed as the result of an inadequate internal market and the reigning mercantilism of the day, which prevented the development of foreign markets for Danish goods. The home market suffered from the handicap of an inefficient agriculture; during the eighteenth century an enclosure movement had concentrated land ownership into large manorial estates, the labor being provided by a poor peasantry which was reduced to virtual serfdom in 1733.[1] This group, comprising the majority of the population, could not absorb the surplus product of the urban communities. Peasant demand for manufactured commodities was largely satisfied by farm industrial production and by small workshops scattered throughout the countryside.[2]

[1] Under the so-called *stavnsbaand,* male farm tenants between the ages of 14 and 36 could not leave the parishes in which they were born without permission of their lords. The purpose of this arrangement was partly to facilitate military recruitment and partly to protect the agricultural labor supply.

[2] In 1787, out of a total population of 842,000, there were only 28,000 persons engaged in handicrafts in Copenhagen, and 25,000 in provincial cities. However, 67,000 persons were

State support to industry was withdrawn after 1766, and the Tariff Act of 1797 marked the final ascendancy of *laissez faire.* A government commission established in 1787 to study trade problems concluded that Denmark was not "naturally" an industrial nation, but should rather rely upon the more advanced industrial countries for its manufactured commodities. The Napoleonic Wars provided industry with a temporary shelter, but after 1820 foreign competition wiped out the remnants that had managed to survive.[3]

The impulses to reconstitution of Danish industry came from changes that were taking place in the structure of agriculture. Beginning with the abolition of the *stavnsbaand* in 1788, there was a gradual transition from the manor to a system of small freeholds. This process was facilitated initially by rapidly rising agricultural prices, although temporarily halted by the price decline of 1818. By 1865, however, Danish agriculture was predominantly capitalist and relatively prosperous. There were 2,000 large farms, 70,000 medium holdings (from 25 to 120 acres) and 70,000 small holdings, and an additional 70,000 landless laborers.[4]

Not only the structure, but the type of agriculture was changing. Until the middle of the nineteenth century, the chief product was grain, which was exported in sizable quantities. Increasing American grain exports, however, forced farmers to turn to animal products; after 1885 Denmark became a net grain importing country. The new agriculture was accompanied by considerable technological development, dairying in particular becoming mechanized. The result of the agricultural transformation was the creation of a growing domestic market for both capital and consumer goods. The primitive self-sufficiency of the manor gave way to specialization; farmers produced cash crops and required fabricated goods that they could not produce themselves. A money economy replaced the system of barter that had been common in rural Denmark.

From 1820 to 1870, Danish industry and handicrafts[5] retained their traditional workshop character. There were 1,400 factories in 1872, but most of them were merely enlarged workshops. The average number of

---

engaged in handicraft production in rural communities. Sven Henningsen, *Studier Over Den Økonomiske Liberalismes Gennembrud i Danmark* (Göteborg, 1944), p. 140.

[3] See Max Kjaer Hansen, *Industriens Udvikling i Danmark* (Copenhagen, 1925), pp. 12–17.

[4] Einar Jensen, *Danish Agriculture* (Copenhagen, 1937), pp. 95, 122.

[5] The categories "industry" and "handicrafts" commonly employed in Danish statistics are not conceptually pure. Originally "industry" included manufactures characterized by establishments of relatively large size and employing mechanical power. In time this distinction became blurred. Thus, tobacco processing plants operated entirely by hand are considered "industry," while mechanized shoe factories and printing shops are included in "handicrafts." In general, that portion of manufacturing with gild antecedents tends to be called "handicrafts," while new industries are considered "industry." See Georg Nørregaard, *Arbejdsforhold Indenfor Dansk Haandvaerk og Industri* (Copenhagen, 1943), pp. 112–113.

workers per factory in Copenhagen in 1872 was 30.7; for the entire country, 21.9. In the factories founded after 1864 average employment was even lower, 15.6 and 13.3 respectively, reflecting slow growth rather than sudden expansion.[6]

This half century was not entirely devoid of industrial progress. An event of considerable importance was the foundation in 1829 of a polytechnical institute in Copenhagen, laying the basis for Denmark's future engineering preëminence. The Industrial Society, established in 1838, became the spearhead of the drive for industrialization. Some firms that originated during this period, and managed to survive, were destined to play a significant role in the Danish economy.[7]

THE INDUSTRIAL REVOLUTION AND LATER INDUSTRIAL DEVELOPMENT

After 1870 events moved more quickly, influenced, among other things, by agricultural improvements and by new means of transportation, the steamship in particular. Whereas from 1857 to 1871 only a single industrial corporation was chartered, 86 charters were granted between 1872 and 1875.[8] By 1897 there were 77,300 industrial establishments in existence, employing 272,500 workers.

Notwithstanding the considerable change that had occurred, the Danish industrial revolution was neither rapid nor structurally thoroughgoing. In 1897, the date of the first reliable census of manufactures, there were only 3.5 employees per establishment, and barely 4,000 of the 77,300 enterprises used mechanical power.[9] The great majority of the enterprises were little more than the old gild workshop. Average employment per establishment rose very slowly, and in 1948 had reached only 5.8.

While the small average unit size of Danish industry is a factor that requires emphasis, it would be erroneous to conceive of manufacturing as composed exclusively of specialized workshops employing only a few skilled artisans each. In 1935 half the workers in textiles were employed in establishments with over 100 workers, and sizable fractions of the labor force in the metal, chemical, and paper industries were in establishments of similar size. The American industrial giant is unknown in Denmark, but many establishments are sufficiently large to pose indus-

[6] Henry Bruun, *Den Faglige Arbejderbevaegelse i Danmark Indtil Aar 1900* (Copenhagen, 1938), p. 119. These data are not comparable with the census data cited in the following section.

[7] A detailed account of industrial development from 1820 to 1870 may be found in Axel Nielsen, *Industriens Historie i Danmark* (Copenhagen, 1944), vol. III.

[8] Bruun, p. 119.

[9] Plants with mechanical power had an average employment of 20 workers.

trial relations problems quite different from those arising under the older master-servant relationship.[10] To ascribe Danish industrial peace, as Danes often tend to do, exclusively to the unit size of enterprise constitutes an oversimplification.

The importance of the city of Copenhagen in the industrial life of the country should be mentioned. In 1935, 21.8 per cent of the nation's industrial establishments, employing 40.4 per cent of the industrial labor force, were located within the Copenhagen urban area. These establish-

TABLE 1

GROSS NATIONAL PRODUCT OF DENMARK, 1948, AT FACTOR COST
(*In current kroner*)

Sector of the Economy	Billions of Kroner	Per Cent of Total
Agriculture, forestry, fishing	3.937	21.4
Industry, handicrafts, building, public utilities	6.815	37.1
Trade, finance, hotels and restaurants, entertainment	3.248	17.7
Transportation and communications	1.336	7.3
Utilization of housing	.833	4.5
Professions and domestic service	.777	4.3
Government services less adjustments	1.430	7.7
Total	18.376	100.0

Source: *Economic Survey of Denmark, National Budget for 1949*, p. 102.

TABLE 2

GAINFUL EMPLOYMENT IN DENMARK, 1948, BY MAJOR SECTOR OF THE ECONOMY

	Self-employed	Employees	Total	Per Cent of Total
Agriculture, forestry, fishing	299,700	240,100	539,800	29.1
Industry and handicrafts	122,000	389,200	511,200	27.6
Building and construction	26,600	99,000	125,600	6.8
Transportation	17,900	91,100	109,000	5.9
Finance, commerce, professions	106,200	214,500	320,700	17.3
Other	8,200	239,300	247,500	13.3
Total	580,600	1,273,200	1,853,800	100.0

Source: *Economic Survey of Denmark, National Budget for 1949*, p. 61.

[10] For example, the shipbuilding firm of Burmeister & Wain employs over a thousand skilled workers in one of its plants. A number of additional metal firms are fairly large — Lauritz Knudsen, the Ford Motor Company, the Danish Airlines, to name a few.

ments were thus larger on the average than those located in provincial communities; while 37.8 per cent of the Copenhagen workers were employed in plants with more than 100 employees, only 22.9 per cent of the provincial workers were in plants of that size.

Tables 1 and 2 show statistically the relative importance of agriculture, industry, and other economic activities to the Danish economy. Industry, building, public utilities, and transportation and communications contributed 44 per cent of gross national product in 1948. Denmark's reputation as an agricultural nation is derived from the role of agriculture in the export trade rather than in the economy as a whole; while agriculture, forestry, and fishing provided only 21 per cent of gross national product in 1948, 70 per cent of total commodity exports in that year were derived from such activities. With respect to employment opportunities, agriculture provided 29 per cent of total jobs in 1948,[11] while industry, building, and transportation provided 44 per cent.

The relative importance of various industries to the Danish economy can be seen from Table 3. The metal trades and shipbuilding play an

TABLE 3

PRODUCTION IN THE MAJOR DANISH INDUSTRIES, BY VALUE OF OUTPUT AND VALUE ADDED, 1948

(*In millions of kroner*)

	Value of Output	Value Added
Food and beverages	2,013	834
Textile	731	303
Clothing	634	280
Wood	303	169
Paper	551	282
Chemical and rubber	894	304
Stone, earthenware, glass	304	189
Metal	1,316	706
Transportation, rolling stock, ships	537	282
Leather	264	142
Total	7,547	3,491

Source: *Economic Survey of Denmark, National Budget for 1949*, p. 131.

important role, and in particular the manufacture of marine Diesel engines, in which Denmark pioneered. The production of cement and cement machinery, and food processing, are other major industries.

[11] This compares with approximately 50 per cent for the Soviet Union, 14 per cent for the United States, 38 per cent for Norway, and 24 per cent for Sweden.

ORIGINS OF THE WORKING CLASS

The character of a labor movement is determined to a large extent by the social and economic milieu from which its members are drawn and by the rate of speed with which the transition from the old to the new way of life is accomplished. While there are undoubtedly other important factors, some of them of a random character and others rooted in the peculiarities of national temperament and psychology, the working habits of an industrial group prior to its induction into the factory system and the manner in which assimilation takes place exert a powerful influence upon its temper, upon whether an almost inevitable revolt against the discipline of the machine and changed (often unfavorably) living conditions will express itself in violent rebellion or orderly, organizational protest.

The ideology and structure of the Danish labor movement were profoundly affected by the contiguity of city and farm, the tardy emergence of industrialism, and the relatively slow tempo of industrial growth. When trade unionism first began to take root, about 1870, 52 per cent of total employment was in agriculture and only 26 per cent in industry. A majority of the industrial workers were craftsmen rather than factory workers, and their living standards were protected to a certain degree by unofficial continuance of gild practices. Many of them, moreover, were scattered in small towns and hamlets.

From 1870 to 1890 the share of agriculture in total employment fell from 52 per cent to 41 per cent. Industry's share increased by 4 per cent and that of trade by 5 per cent of total employment. The increasingly urban character of Danish society is reflected in the growth of Copenhagen and the larger provincial cities: whereas in 1880 the respective shares of the two in relation to total population were 13 and 15 per cent, by 1901 they had increased to 19 and 20 per cent.

The urban trend was pronounced, but there was no parallel to the explosive population changes that occurred in England after 1770,[12] nor was there similar pauperization of the workers. Denmark was still predominantly rural in 1901; some 61 per cent of the population lived in rural communities, and perhaps half the remainder in small cities with close ties to the land. The rate of urban expansion did not create undue pressure upon living standards. Careful investigations of the period 1870 to 1900, when Danish industrialization was taking place, have revealed that economic conditions of the urban worker improved rather than de-

[12] See J. L. and Barbara Hammond, *The Town Labourer 1760–1832* (London, 1925), pp. 4–6.

teriorated.[13] Even urban housing standards were bettered, despite the influx of new workers. "Housing conditions in Copenhagen were much improved during the eighties and nineties. More and more the workers moved out of the old city, and no longer were buildings put up without regard to light and air, as often happened in the seventies." [14] In part, this favorable development derived from late industrialization. The spread of humanism in Scandinavia rendered impossible exploitation of labor such as might have occurred a century earlier. The new philosophy was reflected in social legislation and improved building codes, as well as in benign social regard for worker organization.

A large proportion of the increment to the industrial labor force from 1870 to 1900 was supplied by the farms. Between these years the urban population increased by 494,000, of which 220,000 represented net migration from rural areas.[15] The peak of the rural-urban migration was reached during the decade 1880 to 1890, coinciding with a sharp drop in agricultural prices, when 15,000 people left the land each year, 8,000 going to the cities and 7,000 emigrating. The economic lever that produced this movement was a sharp differential between the real incomes of farm and factory workers.[16]

The industrial recruits came not from an independent yeomanry (as they did in Norway) but rather from among the cottars and agricultural laborers who constituted 70 per cent of the agricultural labor force in 1870. Both of these groups earned their living by working for others, either for wages or payment in kind. Thus the young men and women who entered the factories were not farm-owners fallen upon hard times, nor the surplus children of independent farmers, but rather a dependent group inured to exceedingly unfavorable economic circumstances,[17] attracted to the cities by the lure of economic betterment. They were conditioned, if not to the rigorous discipline of the factory, at least to severe restrictions upon freedom in allocating their time.

These people, entering upon an improved though by no means com-

[13] Nørregaard, p. 536; Even Marstrand, *Arbejderorganisation og Arbejderkaar i Danmark* (Copenhagen, 1934), p. 145; Jørgen Pedersen, *Arbejdslønnen i Danmark* (Copenhagen, 1930), p. 218; Knud Dalgaard, "Arbejderklassens Økonomiske Kaar i Danmark," *Nationaløkonomiske Tidsskrift*, 1926, p. 179.

[14] Marstrand, p. 142.

[15] Pedersen, p. 230. This represents a larger farm contribution than comparison of the two figures would suggest, since most of those who migrated to the cities were of working age and entered the labor force immediately, while the remainder came primarily from natural increase in the urban population which was not immediately reflected in the labor force (to the extent that it was due to increasing longevity, very little).

[16] From 1901 to 1905 rural-urban migration was completely halted as a result of industrial depression, but it resumed after 1906, though at a lower rate than previously.

[17] See, for example, Bryn J. Hovde, *The Scandinavian Countries* (Boston, 1943), pp. 289*ff*.

fortable status in the cities, would hardly be likely recruits for extremist political movements preaching violent revolution, and this would be even more true of the workers of urban origin, most of whom had craft backgrounds. The absence of a large, impoverished proletariat, cast suddenly and involuntarily into a milieu for which there was no precedent in their personal experience, goes a long way in explaining the consistent moderation of Danish labor ideology.

THE GILD SYSTEM

In their celebrated essay on trade unionism, the Webbs were at considerable pains to refute the then current notion, originating from Brentano's work on the gilds, that British trade unionism was a lineal descendant of the medieval craft gilds.[18] They made out a strong case against organic connection between either the masters' or journeymen's gilds and modern trade unionism, though a somewhat less convincing one with respect to the influence of the spirit of gild corporatism upon later worker association. In Denmark, however, the relationship between the two systems appears to be much closer. Perhaps the most important reason is the persistence of the Danish gild monopolies almost into a period which provided favorable conditions for trade union organization. Not until January 1, 1862, were the legal privileges of the gilds abolished in Denmark, and twenty years later a permanent union movement had been founded.

The Danish gilds, often modeled after their German counterparts, were much more important economically than those of the other Scandinavian countries. They had been dissolved in 1613 when the Crown, under the influence of mercantilist doctrine, was endeavoring to promote trade and industry, but were restored in 1621 with little change in power or function. Not until 1800 was there any diminution of their monopolies; in that year legislation was enacted permitting journeymen of four years' standing to set themselves up as "freemasters" without completing the master-work, although such freemasters were restricted to the employment of wife and children, and could only take on apprentices at the end of an additional ten years. In 1822 the obligatory master-work was restored and other liberalizing concessions introduced in 1800 repealed.

Danish students are not in full agreement upon the forces which led to the ultimate dissolution of the gilds. The most common explanation is that the rising industrialists found the gild monopolies increasingly irksome, and led the movement for their abolition. A painstaking analysis of industrial development during the first half of the nineteenth century, however, yielded the conclusion that through a policy of liberal exemp-

[18] Sidney and Beatrice Webb, *The History of Trade Unionism* (London, 1911).

tion from gild regulations, the government prevented undue friction between the gilds and the new factory industry, accounting in part for the survival capacity of the gilds.[19] The author of this study places great emphasis upon the increasing use of homework as a factor in the loosening of the gild bonds, since this practice increased the difficulty of controlling quantity and quality. There were many complaints after 1820 that journeymen were working for their own accounts, and competing unfairly with the masters. Nevertheless the practice of homework spread, for the growth of commerce and expanding markets made it possible for masters to handle the product of a greater number of journeymen. The increasing ratio of journeymen to masters introduced a fundamental change in the gild concept, and hastened the final victory of free trade.

Whatever the actual causes of gild demise, the growing cleavage between the two groups within the gild framework was of paramount significance. A certain amount of internal differentiation had always existed, by the very logic of gild organization. As early as 1403 the Copenhagen journeymen bakers had formed their own association. But as the Webbs have pointed out, the probability that all journeymen would some day be masters forestalled any basic antagonism arising out of differences in status.[20] Only when the opportunities for journeyman advancement were limited by increasing capital requirements for independent mastership, and by the growing size of the enterprise unit, did permanent differences develop. In this respect there was a good deal of variation among the Copenhagen crafts. In 1840, Copenhagen master masons averaged 20 journeymen each, building timberers 17 to 18, sailmakers 8, bakers, painters, and joiners, 3 to 4. By 1850, however, the number had grown; the mason ratio, for example, had risen to 23.[21]

The average journeyman's age increased, as well as the number of married journeymen. At the height of the gild system it was unusual for a journeyman to marry until he had completed his master-work and opened his own shop. In 1843, however, one-third of the Copenhagen journeymen were married, the percentage being particularly high in the crafts with a high ratio of journeymen to masters. Marriage increased

[19] "The red thread running through the concession system was that new developments should not be hindered by existing law, particularly the gild regulations, and one can undoubtedly say that through the concession system the gilds, in the decades under consideration, lacked what were ordinarily their most significant disadvantages, and did not have the rigid character they retained in other countries. One must certainly agree with Otto Müller when he says that there are not many instances when a profitable industry was prevented from coming into being or from expanding for want of dispensation from the authorities. It is therefore hardly correct to say that the gilds hindered industrial development, thus leading to economic freedom, or to maintain that industry destroyed the gilds." Axel Nielsen, p. 85.

[20] Sidney and Beatrice Webb, pp. 24–25.

[21] Nørregaard, p. 32.

the difficulty of attaining the status of master by reducing the journeyman's ability to accumulate capital and by tying him more closely to a particular locality.

The results of the increasing stratification within the gilds have been well summarized as follows:

Increasingly more journeymen gave up the hope of securing their own workshops in time, so that the wage question assumed a sharper form than had theretofore been true. The young and unmarried journeymen in the small crafts still received board and lodging from their masters, and for them money wages constituted a less significant supplement, determined by the cost of clothing and entertainment; but for an older journeyman, who had rent to pay and a family to support, it was of vital importance to secure an income which covered his urgent needs and which was received regularly and certainly. Though the desire for regularity had a dampening influence on the demand for higher wages, there is no doubt that the change in the composition of the journeyman class sharpened the opposition to the masters and furthered the development of a class mentality. The generation of journeymen which first resigned itself to not completing the master-work, and still more, their children and grandchildren, who became employees of workshops and factories, sensed to a much greater extent than the eighteenth century journeyman that they had separate economic interests to defend . . .[22]

The journeyman gild, like the British friendly society, concerned itself primarily with sickness insurance and burial payments. Another function, though of diminishing significance, was the maintenance of lodging houses for wandering journeymen, and the provision of small sums of money to help them on their way. But alongside these activities there was a growing preoccupation with wages and other conditions of labor. Beginning in 1750 there were occasional journeymen strikes, particularly in the building trades, the most important one coming in 1794 when a strike of Copenhagen building timberers spread to other trades. This strike, which aroused a good deal of public attention, led to the establishment of a government commission to investigate gild conditions and resulted eventually in the gild reforms of 1800, which were mentioned above. Through strike action the notion of collective negotiation with masters gained currency. Although wage schedules were always imposed unilaterally by the master gilds, there is evidence that by 1850 the journeymen in a number of trades had gained some influence over wage levels.[23] No collective agreements, in the modern sense, existed, but the tendency so marked in later years to settle labor disputes within the

[22] Bruun, pp. 38–39.
[23] Nørregaard, p. 34.

trade without recourse to outside authority can be traced back to the gild practices developed during this period.

GILDS AND TRADE UNIONS

Dissolution of the gilds in 1862, on the basis of an Act of Parliament passed in 1857, left a vacuum in the labor market. The liberal proponents of free trade had envisioned the installation of the labor market of classical economic theory, in which wages would be fixed by direct bargaining between the employer and the individual worker. Instead, many gild organizations continued in existence, though with modified functions, until they either merged with or were supplanted by unions and employer associations.[24]

There appears to have been little *organic* connection between the journeyman gilds and the trade unions (the antecedents of modern employer associations are dealt with in Chapter V). Many journeyman gilds continued as sick and burial societies, though weakened by their inability any longer to check off dues payments into the funds.[25] Some of them sought to advance the more general economic interests of their members, but the majority confined themselves to "friendly" activities, and finally ceased to exist because the workers who entered the labor market after 1862 were not attracted to them. "Examples of connection between the journeyman gilds of 1862 and the modern trade unions are rare. True enough, the 1862 gilds on several occasions during the rise of trade unionism participated in industrial relations and represented the journeymen against the masters; but often there was enmity between the two groups of unions." [26]

Of much greater significance was the organizational tradition left by the gilds. Eighty per cent of the 65 local trade unions established in Copenhagen from 1870 to 1880 were in trades in which a gild monopoly had existed, although at most 65 per cent of the city's workers were in those trades. The most stable and best disciplined of the early trade unions — the masons, timberers, carpenters, plumbers, and shoemakers — had been preceded by strong gild organization. By 1875 almost all of the former gild crafts of any size had achieved trade union organization, though not all survived the depression of 1877–1879. The only important

[24] The majority of the journeymen were opposed to dissolution of the gilds. They feared that their trades would be overrun with untrained workers who could compete with them on the basis of low standards. Bruun, p. 86.

[25] It was estimated that in 1874 three-fifths of the journeymen who had belonged to these organizations in 1860 still retained their membership. Nørregaard, p. 73.

[26] Nørregaard, p. 76. In a few instances the journeyman gilds were captured by socialists and reorganized. See Bruun, pp. 475–480.

unions in the non-gild trades were those of the printers and cigar makers, the printers for the reason that led them to be among the first to organize the world over, the cigar makers largely because of their close relations with the strong German unions in the same trade.

Some of the attributes of contemporary Danish unionism can be traced to the gild influence. The great interest displayed by trade unions in welfare schemes stemmed initially from the necessity of competing with the journeyman gilds. Socialist theorists originally opposed linking mutual benefits to trade unionism; in 1876 the Social Democratic Federation adopted the following resolution: "The congress states its conviction that the free trade unions, by establishing sick funds, are departing from their social-political purpose." [27] But doctrinaire pronouncements could not prevail against the desire of the workers for a modicum of security, and the new unions were obliged to continue the traditional benefit schemes. For many years some trades continued the old custom not only of paying burial expenses, but also of providing a union delegation to escort the body of the deceased members to the grave; the glaziers' union required all members to attend funerals under penalty of fine.

Another gild legacy was the attitude of craftsmen to non-craftsmen. Danish labor history has never witnessed a Knights of Labor or an I.W.W. seeking membership among all workers, regardless of craft or trade. Not only have the skilled workers been uninterested in promoting organization of the unskilled, but there has been a deep seated hostility between the two groups. The significance of this fact will appear below, when the structure of the trade union movement is examined.

THE FIRST TRADE UNIONS

From 1862 to 1871 there was little new organization among workers. The journeyman gilds continued as voluntary benefit societies, and some new associations were formed under the slogan of "help to self-help," designed primarily to assist workers in raising their cultural standards. There were a few spontaneous strikes, but lack of organization rendered them ineffectual.

A bitter dispute at the Burmeister and Wain shipyard in Copenhagen in 1871 enabled a few socialists to gain a foothold among the city's workers. In October 1871 they established the International Labor Union of Denmark, the most important single unit being that of the cigar makers. The leaders of this organization, which was as much political as economic in character, were a young intellectual, Louis Pio, and two equally young associates, Harold Brix and Poul Geleff, all of them strongly influenced

[27] Bruun, p. 470.

by Marx's First International. Immediately following its establishment the new body managed to gain about 850 adherents, but it was not destined to have a long life. In April 1872, after having sponsored an unsuccessful masons' strike, it was dissolved by the police, and the three leaders sent to prison.

The International was succeeded by a number of local craft unions, some of which arose out of the remains of the dissolved organization. From June 1873 to February 1874, twenty locals were formed in Copenhagen, mainly under socialist influence. The upward trend in the business cycle, which continued until 1875, provided propitious organizational conditions. During 1875, twelve unions were formed. The reversal of the economic trend in 1876 slowed organization, however, as the following data indicate: 1876, six unions formed; 1877, three unions; 1878, two unions; 1879, two unions.[28] Loose national associations were formed among the tailors, printers, tobacco workers, and masons.

In 1874 a new central organization, the Free Trade Union Central Committee, was established under the leadership of E. V. Klein, a socialist, and a barber by trade. At its height, during the winter of 1876–1877, it embraced 32 locals. When Pio was released from prison in 1875, he was immediately installed as chairman of the Central Committee. However, he displayed greater interest in political than in trade union work, and strong opposition to his policies developed within the organization. The resolution of these differences came in dramatic fashion: on March 25, 1877, the socialist newspaper issued a laconic statement to the effect that Pio and Geleff had emigrated to the United States.

Pio's desertion, which was later revealed to have been caused by police pressure and bribery, and the severe economic crisis of 1877 to 1879 almost destroyed the infant labor movement. Collective agreements were no longer respected by employers; wages were reduced. The Central Committee went out of existence in 1879. In sum, the labor movement of the seventies was an intermediate step between the gilds and permanent trade unionism. This was in many ways an experimental period, not unlike the period in the United States when the National Labor Union and other predecessors of the American Federation of Labor played their brief roles on the American scene.

FOUNDATION OF A PERMANENT LABOR MOVEMENT

Only 24 locals in Copenhagen, and seven in the rest of the country, survived the crisis of 1877–1879. But the upward cyclical turn in 1880, and a sharp reduction in unemployment, gave new impetus to organiza-

[28] Bruun, p. 264.

tion. The course of trade union membership during the following decade is illustrated by the membership figures for 22 Copenhagen craft locals:[29]

1881	4,301	1886	8,201
1882	5,432	1887	7,551
1883	7,471	1888	8,074
1884	9,412	1889	9,165
1885	9,491	1890	10,257

The membership decline after 1885 was again due to poor economic conditions, which persisted until 1888, when the upward course of trade union membership was once more resumed.

The decade from 1890 to 1900, particularly the last five years, was characterized by a rapid expansion of trade unionism that placed the labor movement on a secure footing. The first few years were not overly auspicious. While good economic conditions in 1889 and 1890 strengthened the unions, a decline began in 1891 which was more marked during the following year. By the end of 1892, unemployment among Copenhagen trade union members had reached 44 per cent.[30] Beginning with 1895, however, prices began to rise, ushering in more favorable conditions for trade union growth.

While there are no comprehensive data on trade union membership from 1890 to 1900, the following membership data for the Metal Workers' Union[31] illustrate the course of development during this period:

1890	1,106	1896	4,657
1891	1,067	1897	5,028
1892	1,162	1898	6,728
1893	1,204	1899	7,342
1894	1,883	1900	7,444
1895	2,955		

The rapid growth of trade union membership after 1895 was paralleled by the formation of many new local unions. Prior to 1890, the greatest number of local unions established in any one year was 28, in 1885 and 1887. The number of local unions established in 1890 and the subsequent years was:[32]

[29] The figures are from J. Jensen og C. M. Olsen, *Oversigt over Fagforeningsbevaegelsen i Danmark 1871–1900* (Copenhagen, 1901), p. 170.

[30] Pedersen, p. 41.

[31] *Dansk Smede og Maskinarbejderforbunds 25 Aar Jubilaeum* (Copenhagen, 1913), p. 341.

[32] Jensen og Olsen, p. 79.

1890	76	1895	104
1891	53	1896	163
1892	57	1897	113
1893	53	1898	136
1894	51	1899	168

Why after several decades of struggle for mere existence the Danish trade unions should suddenly have achieved a very rapid rate of growth from 1895 to 1900 cannot be explained simply in terms of any single factor. While the industrial labor force was increasing, its growth was nothing like that of trade union membership;[33] the peak of the migration of the farm labor force to the city had been reached during the preceding decade. A growing degree of acceptance of trade unionism by employers, as well as increasing social tolerance of union activities and the rising political power of labor, certainly facilitated organization. Above all, however, it appears to have been the conjuncture of six years of relatively good employment conditions and the existence of a hard core of trade unionists with considerable organizational experience that created the circumstances favorable to rapid trade union growth. The associational propensity of the Danish worker had been frustrated by the rapidly alternating cycles of employment, and when a modicum of stability was achieved, the workers flocked to the trade unions. Both economically and politically, the time was ripe for consummation of the organizational endeavors which had extended over the preceding 25 years with indifferent success.

The Copenhagen locals generally took the initiative in expanding the scope of organization. They were the first and the strongest of the local unions, and possessed the resources to send traveling organizers about the country. They also had strong economic motives for national organization: protection of their wage standards from provincial undercutting, and prevention of the importation of strikebreakers from the small towns. Unification was furthered by continuation of the gild custom of journeyman wandering. There was no serious competition to the rising national unions from regional organizations, for the dominance of Copenhagen and strong intercity craft ties rendered the national craft union the most natural structural form.

Among the national unions there were a few that were industrial in character, taking in skilled and unskilled workers alike. Of this type were the organizations in such non-gilded industries as paper, tobacco,

[33] Exact labor force figures prior to the first census of manufactures in 1897 are lacking. The conclusion that labor force expansion was not very rapid during this decade was reached by Nørregaard (pp. 357–360) on the basis of an analysis of population censuses.

textiles, and ceramics. The great majority of the unions, however, set completion of apprenticeship and advancement to journeyman status as a condition of membership. The same craftsmen who displayed so much energy in the organization of their fellow craftsmen were quite indifferent to the organizational status of the unskilled. The handicraft character of much of the manufacturing and the strength of working traditions removed most of the danger of the use of unskilled workers as strikebreakers. An old gild term, *fuskeri* (bungling), was applied to the employment of unskilled workers for work that belonged to a craft, and employers who indulged in this practice were frowned upon not only by the unions but by fellow employers as well, since they were potential price cutters.[34] The possibility of substitution was greatest in the newer industrial establishments, and there were numerous strikes by the craftsmen to prevent the hiring of unskilled labor.

Also contributing to keep the two groups of workers apart was the medieval social barrier. "From the gild days a disgraceful and unfortunate tradition lasted well into modern industry, that journeymen regarded laborers as far beneath them. On building sites, in shipyards and other places there was a gulf between the groups. They could not sit and have lunch at the same table. A laborer could not hold a plumb line together with a journeyman. He could bring beer to the journeyman, but could not drink with him. In a craft such as that of the pavers the journeymen worked by the piece and paid 'their' laborers by the day, while they reaped the extra piece earnings of both for themselves." [35]

Excluded from the craft unions and lacking organizational traditions, the unskilled workers were relatively late in forming trade unions. When they finally organized, however, they substituted for the ties of craftsmanship a fierce, defensive solidarity, based upon antipathy to the exclusive crafts and a belief in the dignity of common labor, a restricted class consciousness that made them the problem children of the labor movement. Their organization, the Danish Laborers' Union (*Dansk Arbejdsmands Forbund*), came into being in 1897. It was composed of workers from almost every branch of industry, the principal groups comprising longshoremen, dairy, cement, shipyard, and heavy construction workers. The union was handicapped not only by the indifference of the workers, but by the considerable hostility displayed by employers toward

[34] "In most cases employers and workers were quite helpful to one another when questions of exclusive craft jurisdiction arose. The result was that by 1900 in some areas there were as many craft boundaries and as large a proportion of exclusive jurisdiction as the members of the master and journeyman gilds had enjoyed before the introduction of free trade." Nørregaard, p. 455.

[35] Oluf Bertolt, *M. C. Lyngsie* (Copenhagen, 1944), p. 27.

organization of the unskilled.[36] At its head was a man who had been the driving force behind unification of the unskilled local organizations, the most controversial and one of the most interesting figures in Danish labor history, Michael C. Lyngsie.

In his philosophy, in his union tactics, and in the results he achieved, Lyngsie resembles no one so much as John L. Lewis. This identity is not entirely fortuitous. Both men were the spokesmen for depressed groups of workers who occupied increasingly strategic positions in the economy. Both were determined to raise the relative standards of their constituents, if necessary at the expense of other workers. Neither was a political radical; their horizons were of necessity bounded by the intense controversy which their union policies engendered. A contemporary judgment of Lyngsie's role in Danish labor history, rendered by a man who had engaged in collective bargaining with him for many years, has many parallels with the valedictory that Lewis may well receive:

> No one in this Assembly will deny that Mr. Lyngsie is a great agitator, and that the Danish Laborers' Union is a product of the almost superhuman energy he has displayed during a generation of activity. He wanted to raise the unskilled workers above the level of the proletariat — an aim which has our full sympathy as long as it is pursued with judicious regard to economic conditions and to business capacity . . . He raised a storm, he lived in incessant struggle, and he has left the country in alarm behind him year after year. With a disturbed world situation for company, he has been able to force unheard of concessions from employers. But his life work constantly reveals a weak sense of reality, and his uncontrollable energies, which have cost the economy incalculable amounts, have in the final analysis not yielded the Laborers greater results than a more moderate policy might have achieved, without paying for them by the unreasonable sacrifices that resulted from a war leader like Mr. Lyngsie.[37]

The two major economic goals of the Laborers' Union were to increase unskilled relative to skilled wages[38] and to prevent the crafts from en-

[36] "Yes, that the craftsmen, the smiths, carpenters, etc., formed trade unions, let that pass, when nothing could be done about it. It was unfortunate that these unions were socialist and 'sowed discontent among the lower classes and misunderstanding and hatred toward the well to do' . . . But that day laborers also wanted to join trade unions, that was unheard of, that was truly not permissible. They had no trade. For that matter, there were those among the skilled workers who felt the same way about it. The good old gild days were not so far in the past. Gild cooperation and craft pride had not given way to a general, wider feeling of class solidarity, let alone national feeling." Bertolt, p. 27.

[37] *Referat af Dansk Arbejdsgiverforenings Generalforsamlinger*, 1924–25, p. 221.

[38] Lyngsie said on this score: "When a laborer's wage is set, no one asks what his labor is worth, but only: what does the craftsman or the foreman get, and *how much less* shall the laborer have. That a laborer shall have less than the other is taken for granted, regardless of the fact that what the other gets is already too little for a human being to live on. To eradicate this wage principle to the greatest possible extent is the most important job of the Laborers' Union." Bertolt, p. 96.

croaching upon the job area of the unskilled worker when employment was slack. Both aims were pregnant with potentialities of conflict, and friction with the crafts was not long in coming. Within a few years of the establishment of the Laborers' Union, the expansionist tendencies of craft unions and the formation of new unions catering to non-craft workers in railroad and municipal employment presented grave problems to the labor movement.

One other organization is worthy of special note. In 1901 the Women's Labor Union was founded, with its membership mainly among unskilled women workers.[39] This union, now the fourth largest in Denmark, has members in a variety of industries, including the manufacture of matches, tin products, oleomargarine, and in the metal trades.

At the turn of the century, 76 per cent of all adult male workers and 22 per cent of female workers in Danish industry and handicrafts were organized,[40] a remarkable achievement for the relatively young labor movement. The percentage of organization was generally higher in Copenhagen than in the provinces. It is very doubtful whether this degree of organization could have been attained had it not been for the associative philosophy of the gild tradition, which both increased the propensity of the workers to organize and diminished employer resistance to unionism.

FOUNDATION OF THE DANISH FEDERATION OF LABOR (DE SAMVIRKENDE FAGFORBUND)

The demise of the Free Trade Union Central Committee in 1879 marked only a temporary halt of centralization efforts. For the next five years the newly formed Social Democratic Party, under the chairmanship of Peter Knudsen, a glovemaker, functioned as a coördinating body for the socialist trade unions. In 1886, some 54 socialist locals formed the Copenhagen Federation of Trade Unions, the major purpose of which was to afford the members mutual strike support. At first the larger unions were opposed to any systematic scheme of strike benefits, fearing that they would be called upon to make the bulk of financial contributions. After years of intermittent negotiation, a formal system was established in 1895. It was provided under the rules then adopted that as a condition for receiving strike assistance from the central body: (a) each individual union would have to set aside 4 øre per week per member in a special fund which it could use only to finance strikes; (b) at least 5 per

[39] Of the 72 national unions affiliated with the Danish Federation of Labor in 1948, 44 admitted women and 28 were confined to men.

[40] Jensen og Olsen, pp. 173–174. These data refer only to a limited sector of the Danish economy, and should not be taken as global organizational percentages. *Cf.* Table 4 below.

cent of the individual union's total membership would have to be affected by the strike; and (c) the strike would have to be approved by at least a two-thirds' majority of the affiliated unions. To finance the benefits, the central body was empowered to levy special assessments upon non-striking unions in amounts not to exceed 25 øre per week per member. Although the large unions objected that the scheme discriminated against them on two grounds — namely, that the maximum limit restricted too severely the assistance they could expect from the small unions, and that the minimum participation qualification reduced the likelihood of their receiving benefits at all — they yielded to the argument that strikes in the major crafts, when they did occur, were likely to place the greatest strain on the resources of the Federation, so that they would secure an equitable share of the combined protective fund.

This was the first application of the principle of compulsory strike insurance in Denmark. Of equal importance was the fact that the system envisioned the accumulation of separate strike funds in each affiliated union, rather than a single central fund. The extension of this principle to nationwide federation later proved a deterrent to trade union centralization.

The next step was the extension of federation to the country as a whole. A national convention was held in 1898 to create the basis for national trade union unity. The only unanimity, however, was on the desirability of federation; on almost every practical issue there were two and sometimes more factions. The committee established to prepare a draft constitution had recommended that it be made incumbent upon affiliated unions to submit to the executive committee of the proposed federation for counsel in advance all new contract demands, and that approval of such demands be made a condition of future strike assistance. The large unions opposed the grant of central authority thus implied, and proposed instead that an affiliated union which believed that it could finance the cost of a possible conflict without outside assistance be exempt from the duty to consult the federation. Along similar lines, the drafting committee proposed that where the federation rendered financial assistance to affiliates, it should be empowered to conduct all further negotiations with employers, whereas the dissenters insisted upon preserving the autonomy of the national union under all circumstances.

The statutes of the federation represented a victory for the proponents of decentralization. Affiliated unions were required to notify the federation in advance of the presentation of new demands to employers, but they retained complete freedom of action. The federation was empowered to withhold strike benefits where it disapproved of the strike, but this negative control was vitiated in part by decentralization of the strike funds among the affiliates. Federation assistance was to be financed entirely by *ad hoc* assessments.[41]

With the resolution of these and other differences,[42] the Danish Federation of Labor formally came into existence.[43] Its initial strength was 61,000 members in 38 national and 25 separate local unions. While the degree of authority vested in it was disappointing to many, particularly the socialists, its establishment nevertheless represented considerable concessions on the part of the crafts. The initial failure to define more precisely the obligations of affiliated unions has since been lamented by several generations of Federation officials, but few would maintain that this was too high a price to pay for unity.

FOREIGN INFLUENCES

In a country the size of Denmark, astride important land and sea routes and an active participant in international trade, it was inevitable that foreign thought and practices should have influenced the development of its institutions. And if one looks at a map, it is not at all surprising that the principal contributions were made by Germany.

The chief source of contact between the early Danish and German labor movements was through interchange of journeyman labor as a result of continuation of the wandering tradition of gild days. Between 1870 and 1890 some six to eight thousand Germans worked in Denmark each year. On the other hand, it was the unusual Danish journeyman who had not spent a year or two in Germany or Austria. Many early leaders of the Danish labor movement were Germans who had served their apprenticeships in Germany and later settled in Denmark.

Some crafts had direct ties to the German trade unions. For example, in 1873 the Danish printers concluded an agreement with the Germans providing for mutual travel assistance to journeymen. Each of the movements attempted to use the wage gains secured by the other to support its own claims. There was a further mutual interest in preventing the movement of strikebreakers across the frontiers.[44]

While fraternal relations with the German trade unions continued close until their dissolution by the Nazis, personal contact among workers declined after 1890. The rise of German industry provided greater opportunities for steady employment, which, combined with several depres-

[41] *Protokol for De Danske Fagforeningers Iste Delegeretmøde*, 1898, appendix.

[42] For a full discussion of the differences, see *Under Samvirkets Flag* (Copenhagen, 1948), pp. 227–300.

[43] No one played a greater role in the creation of the Federation than Jens Jensen, a painter, the very prototype of the conservative Danish skilled worker. For a brief account of his career, see *Folkestyrets Maend* (Copenhagen, 1949), pp. 301–313.

[44] See Bruun, pp. 286–290.

sions in Denmark, reduced German wandering into Denmark. After 1900 only specialists accompanying machinery produced in Germany came in any number. A certain amount of Danish wandering to Germany continued, but this too was curtailed as the gild traditions receded.

The influence of British trade unionism was considerably less. Pio and other pioneers of the Danish labor movement had been greatly interested in the British trade union model, but there was little interchange of workers. The predominant factory system of Great Britain offered few employment opportunities for wandering craftsmen during the last half of the nineteenth century.

Since Denmark was the first of the Scandinavian countries in which trade unionism was established, the early impulses were outward rather than inward. Inter-Scandinavian coöperation became increasingly important, however, and after 1900 it represented for each of the three countries the most fruitful source of outside influence. The first inter-Scandinavian labor congress was held in 1886. Since that time not only has the Danish Federation of Labor met periodically with the Norwegian and Swedish federations, but many individual unions have established joint assemblies. It is the exception for a Danish trade union leader not to meet with his Norwegian and Swedish counterparts at least once a year. Trade union collaboration, as well as collaboration among employers, has given the three countries many similar industrial relations institutions, so much so that the casual observer is often misled into the belief that the differences among them are insignificant. Actually, each movement emerged out of peculiar economic and social circumstances, and these peculiarities are reflected in many aspects of their experience. For example, Danish trade union structure is closer to that of Britain than to either Norway or Sweden. It is undoubtedly true that the Scandinavian labor movements have tended to converge in recent years, particularly on the political side. But the trade union movements, perhaps because they are more closely tied to the economic environment, have retained their respective identities to the extent of rendering *Scandinavian* trade unionism a somewhat misleading term.

CHAPTER III

THE DANISH FEDERATION OF LABOR: STRUCTURE AND POLICIES

THE DANISH FEDERATION OF LABOR celebrated its fiftieth birthday in 1948. During the half century it had become the most powerful economic organization in the country. Through its political ally, the Social Democratic Party, it had exercised great influence over the government of Denmark for two decades. So completely did the Federation become an integral part of Danish social structure that not even five years of German occupation greatly affected its functions and structure, a situation unique among the occupied nations of Europe.

There were of course a great many problems, of both an internal and an external character, during these years. In general, political dissension led to less internal difficulty than it did in Norway and Sweden. Nor was the employers' challenge to extension of trade union influence very potent, while the government, if not always friendly, rarely displayed hostility. The Federation's major difficulties have arisen rather from within, out of the sharp division between the skilled and the unskilled worker. Much of the present chapter will be devoted to an account of the many facets of this internal struggle, which has had a decisive influence upon the Danish system of industrial relations.

Table 4 shows the course of trade union membership in Denmark from 1898 to 1949, by five-year periods.[1] During only two periods, 1901 to 1903 and 1920 to 1922, did trade union membership decline, in both cases as a consequence of business recession. Actually, the latter decline was much less severe than that suffered by most European labor movements after 1920. The holding power of Danish unionism is further demonstrated by the continued membership advance during the great depression of the 1930's.

The proportion of organized workers affiliated with the Federation of Labor is also shown in Table 4. The decline after 1910 was due to the defection of several syndicalist affiliates. A more serious loss was suffered when the Laborers' Union withdrew in 1925, but since reaffiliation

[1] For the year-to-year membership changes, see Table A3.

of this union occurred in 1929, the five-year intervals of the data in Table 4 hide the effect. By 1949, 96 per cent of all organized workers were Federation members, leaving outside seven independent unions, the largest of which were the Brewery Workers, the Telephone Workers, and the Musicians. Repeated attempts to secure affiliation of the remaining holdouts have failed. In 1948, the executive committees of the brewery and telephone unions recommended affiliation, but the membership, satisfied with their relatively high pay and stable employment, and unwilling to pay per capita dues to the Federation, overruled them in referenda.

TABLE 4

TRADE UNION MEMBERSHIP IN DENMARK, 1898–1949

Year	Membership in Danish Federation of Labor (*Thousands*)	Membership in Independent Unions (*Thousands*)	Total Trade Union Membership (*Thousands*)	Federation Membership as a Percentage of Total Union Membership
1898	51.0	27.8	78.8	65
1900	77.1	19.3	96.4	80
1905	68.8	19.2	88.0	78
1910	101.6	21.3	122.9	83
1915	131.9	41.1	173.0	76
1920	279.3	83.1	362.4	77
1925	239.7	70.8	310.5	77
1930	259.1	80.2	339.3	76
1935	381.3	56.8	438.1	87
1940	515.8	28.2	544.0	95
1945	604.3	26.2	630.5	96
1949	635.8	27.8	663.6	96

Source: *Under Samvirkets Flag* (Copenhagen, 1948), pp. 558–559.

There were two periods of particularly rapid trade union growth: 1914 to 1918 and 1933 to 1939. During the former period the chief cause lay with the skyrocketing price level, which affected real wages adversely. For the first time agricultural workers were organized, some 32,000 of them becoming trade unionists by 1915. However, the postwar recession affected their union, and to a lesser extent the Laborers' Union, adversely. By 1922 membership in the Agricultural Workers' Union had fallen to 13,000, while the Laborers' membership fell to 80,400 from a peak of 86,500. The craft unions displayed much greater stability; for example, from 1919 to 1922, membership in the Typographical Workers' Union

TABLE 5

ESTIMATED PERCENTAGE OF TRADE UNION ORGANIZATION IN MAJOR ECONOMIC SECTORS, 1948

Industry	Employment, 1948	Estimated Trade Union Membership	Percentage of Organization
Manufacturing	389,200		
Building and construction	99,000	519,200	89.6
Transportation and communication	91,100		
Commerce	129,500	49,600	38.3
Hotels and restaurants	35,000	17,000	48.6
Government	87,300	25,400[a]	29.1[a]
Agriculture (excluding independent farmers)	240,100	38,900	16.2
Total	1,071,200	650,100	60.7

Sources: Employment, *Economic Survey of Denmark*, 1949, p. 61; membership, *Beretning om De Samvirkende Fagforbunds Virksomhed*, 1948, Tables V a, c.
[a] The percentage of organization in the government service is understated by virtue of the inclusion of substantial numbers of government workers in trade unions predominantly in manufacturing, transportation, and communication.

TABLE 6

STRUCTURE OF THE SCANDINAVIAN FEDERATIONS OF LABOR, 1948

	Denmark	Norway	Sweden
1. Total membership	623,000	455,000	1,239,000
2. Number of national union affiliates	72	40	45
3. Average number of workers per affiliated national union	8,700	11,400	27,500
4. Percentage of total federation membership in the single largest affiliated national union	38	12	10
5. Percentage of total federation membership in the three largest affiliated national unions	54	31	33
6. Percentage of total federation membership in the smallest affiliated national unions, comprising 50 per cent of the total number of affiliates	4	10	15

Sources: Denmark, *Beretning om De Samvirkende Fagforbunds Virksomhed 1948*, Appendix; Norway, *Fri Fag bevaegelse*, March 15, 1949, p. 78; Sweden, *L O Verksamhets Berättelse*, 1948, pp. 302–303.

remained unchanged, while that of the Metal Workers rose from 20,400 to 22,600.[2]

The membership increase from 1933 to 1939 was again accompanied by rising prices and declining real wages. The unskilled workers registered the greatest gains, membership in the Laborers' Union rising by 77 per

[2] The data are taken from *Beretning til De Samvirkende Fagforbunds Repræsentantskabsmøde*, 1914, 1920, 1924.

cent, and in the Female Workers' Union by 70 per cent. The Metal Workers' Union, on the other hand, registered a membership increase of only 23 per cent, due to the high degree of organization prevailing in this trade at the beginning of the period. White-collar workers showed an interest in unionism for the first time.

During and subsequent to World War II, trade union membership continued to rise at an even rate, and by 1950 had reached a level that made the rate of further expansion problematical. A rough estimate of the degree of organization prevailing in 1948 is shown in Table 5. It should be noted that the percentage of organization in government employment is understated, and that in manufacturing, building, and transportation overstated, due to the impossibility of dividing trade union membership accurately between these two categories. While the data may be subject to other qualifications, they do demonstrate the high degree of organization prevailing in industries traditionally subject to unionism, as contrasted with fairly poor organization in agriculture (which here includes forestry and fishing). Further trade union membership gains will have to come from the white-collar and agricultural sectors of the labor force, which are as difficult to organize in Denmark as in the United States.

PROBLEMS OF UNION STRUCTURE

Some quantitative aspects of Scandinavian trade union structure are shown in Table 6, from which it is seen that the distribution of membership among the Danish national unions is relatively skewed. A single national union, the Laborers' Union, encompassed 38 per cent of total Federation membership in 1948, with the two next largest unions, the Office and Commercial Workers and the Metal Workers, contributing an additional 16 per cent between them. At the opposite end of the scale, the 36 smallest national unions contained only 4 per cent of total membership. By contrast, the Norwegian and Swedish national unions were larger, on the average, than the Danish. This is natural in the case of Sweden, with its larger global membership, but the fact that it is also true for Norway attests to the extreme dispersion of Danish trade union membership among small craft unions.

Membership concentration or dispersion, in this sense, is an element to be considered in evaluating trade union centralism. A priori, it is reasonable that the coexistence within a federation of a single powerful union and numerous small ones would make for a weak central body (unless the dominant union gained absolute control, in which event the degree of central power would tend to reach the opposite extreme). For if the smaller unions can combine to gain a majority within the federation, they can protect themselves against unpalatable central policies, but cannot on the other hand force through policies unacceptable to the large minority union without endangering the continued existence of the federation, since secession of the large union would mean a great numerical membership loss. It seems an almost necessary, though not sufficient, structural condition for workable trade union centralism that there be some normality of membership distribution among affiliated unions, so that no one or a few giant unions can dominate, or disrupt the central body by secession.

Of the three Scandinavian labor federations, there is least concentration of union membership in Norway and most in Denmark, with Sweden in an intermediate position. Membership concentration is inversely correlated with the degree of central authority enjoyed by the federation, the Danish Federation of Labor being the weakest of the three, and the Norwegian the strongest, relative to affiliated national unions. There are historical circumstances that help to account for the differences in central power, but there is no doubt that the accident — or design — of national union structure has been a factor of some importance.

Most of the national unions that constitute the Danish Federation of Labor are collateral, if not lineal, descendants of the gilds. For example, there is a coopers' union with 320 members; a gilders' union, 117 strong; a glovemakers' union of 144. Between these and the Laborers' Union there are a few industrial or semi-industrial unions, such as the organizations in ceramics, tobacco, textiles, and printing. The large union of skilled workers covering most of the metal trades is essentially a composite craft organization, including within its ranks locksmiths, blacksmiths, boilermakers, pipe fitters, and auto mechanics. Because of its size and strategic industrial position, it has attained a position of leadership among the craft unions.

There has never been in Denmark a strong drive for industrial unionism comparable to the successful ones in Norway and Sweden.[3] The strength of the craft tradition and the offsetting separate organization of the unskilled created vested interests among both groups, no less among the unskilled than the skilled workers. In 1904, when several craft unions were beginning to display an interest in expanding their jurisdictions to the unskilled workers in their industries, the chairman of the Laborers' Union remarked: "This is an honor for the laborers. Not so many years ago the craftsmen considered it beneath their dignity to be together with laborers . . . It is very kind of them, but the matter has another side,

[3] For accounts of the rise of industrial unionism in Norway and Sweden, see: Gunnar Ousland, *Fagorganisasjonen i Norge* (Oslo, 1949), II, 147–191; Ragnar Casparsson, *L O Under Fem Årtionden* (Stockholm, 1947), I, 438–450.

namely, whether the laborers are well served by losing influence over the determination of their own conditions of labor, for it has been demonstrated time and again that small industrial organizations are incapable of securing good wages for the laborers as a whole." [4] The craft unions, while willing to "industrialize" at the expense of the Laborers, did not show equal enthusiasm for craft mergers.

There were attempts at structural reform in the direction of industrial unionism, principally under syndicalist and communist, and to a lesser extent under socialist, auspices.[5] In 1912, after several years of incessant syndicalist agitation, the Federation of Labor established a committee to investigate the desirability of structural change. The report of the committee, adopted by the 1913 congress with only four dissenting votes, was largely negative in tone, urging only the establishment of intercraft associations to promote related interests.[6] Even this mild expression of the desirability of greater craft coöperation was opposed at first by the Laborers' Union, which feared possible hostile craft combinations.

Two so-called "cartels" of related trades had been founded prior to the 1913 resolution: the Woodworkers' Secretariat in 1904, and the Central Organization of Metal Trades in 1912. Not until 1938, when the Building Trades National Association was formed, was there another cartel. The 1913 resolution fell on barren ground.

Some of the craft unions, however, continued to be interested in craft amalgamation in order to eliminate the numerous minute unions. The

[4] Bertolt, *Lyngsie,* p. 97.

[5] The following observation on the failure of industrial unionism to make headway in Denmark appears in the official socialist party history: "There is so much conservatism in the Danish worker that he does not like to alter a form once adopted. This is sometimes regrettable. At the same time the Danes have shown a strong practical sense and an ability to adjust, so long as they are free from commands." E. Wiinblad og Alsing Andersen, *Det Danske Social Demokratis Historie* (Copenhagen, 1921), II, 226.

[6] The committee report said, among other things: "All trade organization rests upon voluntary combination to protect common interests. Experience has always shown that the most suitable forms of organization lie in organized coöperation. The Danish trade unions have progressed through just such pragmatic experimentation; and the fact that in most cases they are organized along craft lines indicates that up to the present this form of organization has been the correct one. Trade unions are living organisms, which must *grow* out of actual conditions. They cannot be *constructed* through constitutional provisions or in any other way. The predominantly craft character of Danish organization cannot be transformed into an industrial form by a resolution of the Congress . . . Any attempt to do so would only cause boundless confusion and weaken the organizations' strength.

"Rapid changes within certain industries . . . render increasingly desirable, where it has not already been effected, more intimate coöperation among related trades. However, this cannot be formalized, but must as heretofore be permitted to develop out of conditions within each industry and organizational willingness within each trade.

"The Congress urges affiliated unions to give their attention to this matter, and urges that craft cartels or groups of related trades be established whenever possible . . ." *De Samvirkende Fagforbund, Protokol over Generalforsamling* (23–26 April, 1913), p. 20.

leader of this movement was I. A. Hansen, chairman of the Metal Workers' Union, who had been instrumental in creating the metal trades cartel to achieve what he regarded as a first step toward industrial unionism. As the largest of the crafts, the Metal Workers' union had nothing to fear and much to gain from amalgamation.

The issue was raised anew at the 1922 congress of the Federation of Labor. There was a constitutional provision to the effect that no local union which had seceded from an affiliated national union, or which was eligible to join a national union, could be admitted to the Federation. It was proposed that the following amendment be added: "The provisions of the present paragraph shall not prevent workers, when they so desire, from combining in cartels and industrial unions." The amendment was fought vigorously by the Laborers' Union, which looked upon it as an invitation to the crafts to engage in raiding expeditions. Adoption of the amendment led the Laborers to threaten secession, which was avoided only when they were given an explicit guarantee by the Federation that locals seceding without permission would not be accepted into any other union.[7]

In the final analysis, "the amendment had no practical results, and there have since been no noteworthy changes in union structure, which may be said to have become static, although the possibility of merger of related trades has been discussed from time to time among the interested organizations and the question of organizational form made the subject of debate."[8] In 1922 there were 51 national unions affiliated with the Federation; by 1948, far from contraction having occurred, the number had risen to 72. Informed observers agree that industrial unionism is hardly a possibility in Denmark. The rock upon which a campaign to that end is almost certain to founder is the adamant refusal of the Laborers' Union to abate its jurisdiction; even if by some miracle this were achieved, there would still be the forbidding shoals of craft separatism to navigate.

Apart from the basic skilled–unskilled division, Danish trade union structure does not present unique characteristics. At the base of the organizational pyramid is the local union, with jurisdiction over a carefully specified geographical area, varying in size from five to several thousand members.[9] The local is governed by an executive committee which averages nine members. Larger locals are often subdivided into clubs, one for each factory within its jurisdiction or for each trade subdi-

[7] *Beretning om De Samvirkende Fagforbunds Virksomhed* (1923–1924), p. 4.

[8] *Under Samvirkets Flag*, pp. 233–234.

[9] In 1948 there were 3,514 locals in the Federation. The Laborers' Union averaged 184 members per local; the Metal Workers, 495. At the opposite end of the scale were the Locomotive Engineers with 9.

vision, whichever is appropriate. Associated with most locals are branches of the national union unemployment insurance societies, which are generally governed by the local officers. Formally, the law requires that they be administered as distinct entities. Many locals also operate employment exchanges in conjunction with the insurance branches, making for a considerable administrative burden.

All local unions are affiliated with the Federation of Labor through national unions, there being no counterpart to the federal union of the American Federation of Labor. Relationships between the national and local unions are considered below; suffice it to say here that the principal power resides in the national union, which receives the bulk of dues payments (the 80 per cent going to the Metal Workers' Union from its locals is typical), and administers the various union funds.[10] The national union is governed by its congress, meeting at intervals of from three to five years, by an intermediate central board which convenes several times a year, and by a small executive committee.

The structure of the Laborers' Union is unique. Originally, it was based upon the usual geographical pattern, but with growth this form became unwieldy, and in 1935, after many years of internal agitation, a structural reform was undertaken.[11] At the present time the union is a federation of four major semi-autonomous groups, covering (a) factory work, (b) building and heavy construction, (c) agriculture, and (d) transportation (longshoremen, teamsters, warehousemen). Each group is governed by its own council, and has nine representatives on the central board of the Laborers' Union, while the chairman of each group sits on the union executive committee.

Collective agreements with the Laborers' Union cover all or a fraction of a group, so that the chief bargaining unit on the trade union side is the group. There are elaborate constitutional provisions covering the relative authority of group and national union; while the groups have a good deal of freedom, the chairman of the national union is a member ex officio of all negotiating committees, and exerts considerable influence on group agreements. The central strike fund, moreover, is administered by the national union rather than the groups.

The Federation of Labor is governed by a triennial congress, a representative council of about 350 members meeting annually, and an executive council which includes the elected officers. The Federation is rela-

[10] The Federation constitution requires only that all affiliates set aside 10 kroner per annum per member into a fund limited to the payment of strike benefits. Many unions have set up additional special funds, providing for old age assistance, burial insurance, sick help, educational assistance, and others.

[11] For the history of the efforts at reorganization, see Axel Olsen, *Dansk Arbejdsmands Forbund Gennem 50 Aar* (Copenhagen, 1947), pp. 112*ff*.

tively poor. It receives regularly for administrative purposes 1.52 kroner per member per annum from affiliated unions. However, extra assessments are often levied for special purposes, while strike benefits are financed by levies on the individual union strike funds.

The "cartel," which has already been mentioned, is an organization similar to the department of the American Federation of Labor. By far the most important of the existing "cartels" is the Central Organization of Metal Trades, which includes members of eleven unions working in the metal industry. The metal "cartel" bargains collectively with an association of metal trades employers, and concludes a single master agreement with the latter, covering the entire industry. Largely because of the dominance of the Metal Workers' Union, there has not been undue difficulty in securing agreement among the 55 members of the "cartel" negotiating committee on bargaining policy, but the accession of the Laborers' Union to the "cartel" in 1949 may create future problems in this respect.

The remaining "cartels" are of less importance. There is one for the wood trades, which has confined itself to determining jurisdictional boundaries, facilitating the transfer of working cards, and promoting pre-collective bargaining conferences in the interest of uniformity of approach. It does not bargain on behalf of its members, or conclude agreements. A building trades "cartel" was organized in 1938, but it too has proved to be merely an informational and advisory center. Finally, there is a unique body, the Central Organization of Danish Civil Servants, including 28 separate unions, some of which are not affiliated with the Federation of Labor.

The city central trades councils occupy a relatively minor place in trade union government. They perform a variety of functions peripheral to the chief trade union purposes, including the management of coöperatives, the provision of union halls and the organization of demonstrations and festivals such as that held on the first of May each year.

NATIONAL-LOCAL UNION RELATIONSHIPS

The majority of Danish workers are covered by collective agreements regional or national in scope, which are negotiated by the national union on behalf of its locals. Local influence is exercised in the formulation of policy and in referendum voting on proposed agreements, but ordinarily local officers do not participate in collective bargaining. However, in the case of the numerous small agreements with employers who are not affiliated with the Employers' Association, the local unions may actually conduct the negotiations, but they are required to adhere to national policy on the terms to which they may agree.[12]

A local union may not on its own initiative call a strike without the express permission of the national union. Failure to secure permission results in forfeiture of the right to strike benefits, a serious penalty in view of the weak financial situation of most locals. On the other hand, the national union may generally order a local to call a strike in support of fellow unionists, regardless of the immediate interests and desires of the local membership.

There are numerous additional restrictions upon the freedom of action accorded to local unions. For example, they are generally forbidden to close their rolls to transferees from other local or national unions, either by unilateral action or by agreement with employers. Their right to expel members is usually subject to national review.[13] Even in the handling of local grievances the national union typically becomes involved at an early stage in the procedure.

The highly centralized collective bargaining system in Denmark renders close national control of local unions a practical necessity. National agreements would mean little if locals were permitted to offer more favorable terms to unorganized employers outside the main agreement. The high degree of financial liability for breach of contract imposed upon trade unions requires a correspondingly high degree of internal union discipline. The pattern of national-local relationships resulting from these requirements has been summed up as follows:

National collective agreements presuppose a central organ which can negotiate and agree on behalf of the membership. The national union has become such an organ. This is not to say that the local union has no influence upon

[12] For example, the constitution of the Ship Carpenters' Union provides: "No local union or individual member may enter into an agreement covering hours of work and wages or agree to a mediation proposal or an arbitration award without the approval of the national executive committee. Breach of this rule may lead to a maximum fine of 50 kroner per member." *Love for Dansk Skibstømrerforbund*, 1945, Section 10. The Laborers' Union constitution provides: "No local union may make general or far reaching demands for wage increases or shorter hours of work or terminate existing collective agreements with employers until the national executive committee or the appropriate national officials have given their consent. By general and far reaching demands are meant demands which cover all members of a local union or all workers at a place of work or factory. However, local unions may themselves adjust minor differences, but they shall, if time permits, seek advice and guidance of the national office." *Love for Dansk Arbejdsmands Forbund*, 1948, Section 39.

[13] The Laborers have a constitutional provision whereby a member expelled from a local union for failure to obey a strike order may be permanently excluded by that local, but after a year has elapsed he may be accepted into another local upon payment of a fine. This rule is a compromise between the reluctance of workers to accept "traitors" back into their ranks and the practical problem of finding employment for the erring worker in a highly organized labor market.

collective agreements. On the contrary, the national union is not an independent entity, but rather a federation of locals, each of which influences the union's leadership and policies through the congress, while the locals and their members also influence the terms of agreements through referendum voting on the results of negotiation. But the national union is the legally contracting party, which implies that the local's everyday influence upon the national agreement must be limited.[14]

OBLIGATIONS AND RIGHTS OF UNION MEMBERSHIP[15]

It has been established by the Danish courts that as a concomitant of the right of workers to organize, "anyone who belongs to a group of individuals which has general access to trade union membership has the right to be accepted as a member, unless in the opinion of the courts there are satisfactory grounds for denial of membership." [16] This view conforms to the consistent Danish tendency to endow trade unions, and employer associations, with the character of public institutions. Implicitly, their social position is recognized, and the individual is afforded legal protection against abuses of monopoly power.

It follows that reasonable membership requirements may be imposed. Most skilled trades require successful completion of an apprenticeship as a prerequisite to union membership; this is considered justifiable if it is reasonably related to the maintenance of craft standards. Organized workers who act as strikebreakers may thereafter be excluded, but unorganized workers who simply remain at work when a strike is called may not be permanently excluded after the conclusion of the strike.

Initiation fees are generally low, rarely going above 5 kroner, while the incidence of dues payments varies considerably among unions. In 1948, average weekly dues payments were 1.06 kroner, ranging from 0.40 kroner for the Laborers to 9.25 kroner for the Printers.[17] This amounted to 0.3 per cent of the laborer's wage and 5.7 per cent of the printer's wage, a difference reflected in the more liberal benefit payments offered by the latter organization. In addition, the member must contribute to the unemployment insurance fund of his union, the average payment being 2.83 kroner per week in January 1948. The precise amount of the unemployment insurance levy also varied with the scale of benefits and the experience of the individual club.[18]

[14] Kaj Bundvad and others, *Tillidsmands Kundskab* (Copenhagen, 1946), pp. 67–68.

[15] The legal aspects of this subject are treated in detail in Knud Illum, *Den Kollektive Arbejdsret* (Copenhagen, 1939), pp. 22–76.

[16] Illum, p. 35.

[17] *Beretning om De Samvirkende Fagforbunds Virksomhed* (1947), Appendix, Table V.

[18] Unemployment insurance contributions by workers averaged slightly more than 2 per cent of the full-time wage. A member of the Ship Carpenters' Union paid 0.6 per cent of his earnings, a member of the Pavers' Union, 3.5 per cent.

A member of a trade union has the right to participate in general meetings of his local and to vote in all referenda, including those on new collective agreements which affect him. He is entitled to share in the many benefit funds which Danish trade unions have established. An inquiry conducted in 1949 revealed that 11 unions maintained sick help funds, 25 had burial funds, and 33 had old age and invalidity funds, all supplementary to the regular (and very liberal) government social security system.[19]

Welfare funds, while they cement the bonds of loyalty between a worker and his union,[20] are designed primarily to further individual security. The system of strike benefits, on the other hand, is intended to augment union bargaining strength. In the event that a national union has satisfied the Federation requirements for strike assistance — that is, that it has secured the approval of the Federation for the strike and has more than one per cent of its membership on strike — its striking members receive from the Federation 15 kroner per week, the funds being raised through special assessments levied on the other unions.[21] Most unions pay liberal supplements to these basic benefits,[22] and a worker often receives what he would have been paid in unemployment insurance benefits for the same period.

Failure of a trade union member to subordinate himself to decisions taken by competent bodies of the organization may lead to fine or expulsion, the most common violation being failure to pay dues and assess-

[19] *Arbejderen*, April 1, 1949, p. 78. To take a specific example, a member of the Metal Workers' Union of 25 years' standing may apply for help to the union pension fund upon attaining the age of 60 years. The amount to which he is entitled varies with a number of factors. Funeral benefits are proportional to union seniority, with a maximum limit of 500 kroner. The union's unemployment insurance fund, in addition to regular payments per day of unemployment, pays out the following benefits: (a) one krone per day for each dependent child under 17 years; (b) house rent to a maximum of 60 kroner per month; (c) per diem allowances while the member is in travel status in search of work; (d) reimbursement for train fare expended in search of work; (e) in the event of permanent change of residence to obtain employment, travel expenses of the family and the cost of moving the household; (f) if unemployed for 12 days between November 25 and December 22, Christmas benefits to a maximum of one week of regular unemployment benefits.

[20] Tying of unemployment insurance to the individual trade union has undoubtedly been an element in furthering union solidarity. Under present law, nonunion workers must be admitted to the state supported fund for their trade, though they may be charged higher rates, justified by the fact that they represent a greater unemployment risk in so highly organized a community. There are reciprocity arrangements among the funds so that a worker who changes his trade does not lose his right to benefits.

[21] From 1898 through 1938 Federation assessments for strike benefits were 16 million kroner, about 4 kroner annually per member. Some 55 per cent of the total was levied during the period 1921 to 1925 inclusive. *Beretning om De Samvirkende Fagforbunds Virksomhed* (1938), p. 214.

[22] The relative importance of Federation and individual union strike benefit payments may be gaged from the following data showing total benefits paid out from 1898 to 1922:

ments (the checkoff is not practiced in Denmark). Refusal to obey a strike order is a universal cause for expulsion. More generally, there are constitutional provisions to the effect that "a member who acts dishonestly, disloyally or against rules adopted by the workers to protect and further their interests, may be expelled by the general meeting (of the local union) by a two-thirds majority of the votes cast." [23] However, there does not appear to have been any great abuse of the power conferred by such clauses, and in particular, there has been little use of them to stifle free expression of opinion within the union hostile to the current leadership. The courts, moreover, have insisted that there must be a reasonable interpretation of the general power to discipline; that, for example, while public criticism of union policy to the detriment of the union may constitute a valid ground for expulsion, private criticism does not justify the imposition of penalties.[24] Local votes of expulsion are ordinarily appealable to the central board of the national union and to its congress.

The constitution of the Federation of Labor guarantees every union member the right to transfer from one union to another when he changes his trade, provided he has fulfilled his obligations to the union he is leaving and that he satisfies the entrance requirements of the new union. However, no union may accept a transferee unless he has been given a release by his previous organization, a provision that has occasioned numerous jurisdictional disputes.

On the whole, the constitutional rights of Danish workers are amply protected by union process and through recourse to the regular law courts. There have been very few court appeals in recent years. Opposition to union leadership is taken for granted by virtue of the strong political minorities that exist in most unions, and is not generally regarded by the membership as directed against the union itself. The strong sense of solidarity and craft loyalty that pervades the movement has tended to reduce the problem of discipline to one of minor proportions.

TRADE UNIONS AND POLITICAL ACTION

Danish trade unionism has been politically minded since its inception. The first unions, organized in opposition to the journeyman gilds, were

---

by the Federation of Labor, 6.7 million kroner, 30 per cent of the total; by individual unions, 15.7 million kroner, 70 per cent of the total. *De Samvirkende Fagforbund i Danmark 1898–1923* (Copenhagen, 1923), pp. 240–245. During the same period the Danish trade unions paid out three million kroner in strike assistance to foreign labor movements (mainly those of Sweden, Germany, and Austria) and received 1.7 million in reciprocal aid.

[23] *Love for Dansk Smede og Maskinarbejderforbund*, 1947, Section 10 (C).

[24] It may be noted that the Swedish courts have not imposed similar limitations upon Swedish unions, and in consequence Swedish unions enjoy greater disciplinary power than the Danish.

led by socialists with more interest in politics than in economic activities. Only after strong objection by the craftsmen that blending the two tended to hinder the growth of the unions was an organizational schism effected with the formation of the Social Democratic Party in 1878.

The founders of Danish social democracy were not Marxists, though they felt a certain kinship with the First International. It was considered that the way to worker emancipation was through producer cooperation rather than social revolution.[25] When the original leaders, Pio and Geleff, fled to the United States, they left the political labor movement in the hands of a group of craft unionists who were more interested in building an organization than in socialist theory. For three decades after 1878 the principal party leaders were Peter Knudsen, a glovemaker by trade, and Emil Wiinblad, a printer. Knudsen was succeeded in 1910 as party chairman by Thorvald Stauning,[26] who had been chairman of the cigar makers' local in Copenhagen from 1896 to 1908, and Stauning in turn was succeeded in 1939 by Hans Hedtoft, who although his career began in the socialist youth movement, had served his apprenticeship as a lithographer.

The common social origins and outlook of party and trade union leadership prevented in large measure the sharp policy differences that often characterized the labor movements of countries in which intellectuals controlled the party side.[27] What friction there was arose out of the unskilled workers' distrust of party domination by the skilled workers. Lyngsie, the first chairman of the Laborers' Union, resented what he regarded as unfair treatment at the hands of the party in allocating parliamentary seats and in its support of candidates; he ascribed loss of his parliamentary mandate in 1906 to "skilled worker chicanery." [28]

[25] Wiinblad og Andersen, p. 27. One of the earliest socialist programs, that of 1876, was closely modeled upon the German Gotha program of 1875.

[26] This brief reference hardly does justice to one of the most remarkable personalities in European labor history. From 1910, when he became chairman of the Social Democratic Party, until his death in 1942, Stauning was undisputed leader of the Danish labor movement. From 1929 until 1942 he served as prime minister of Denmark. Robust and cheerful, he personified the ideal Danish personality. At the same time he was a shrewd and careful politician who built the Social Democratic Party into one of the strongest political machines in Europe. Although a socialist, it was rightly said of Stauning that "an increase in the fuel allowance of old age pensioners interested him to a much greater extent than a whole library of Marx and Engels." Stauning was social reformism incarnate, and he left an indelible stamp upon the character of the Danish labor movement.

[27] Until recently, few intellectuals occupied positions of influence in the Social Democratic Party. The chief exception was F. J. Borgbjerg, who joined the party in 1890 and later became minister of labor under Stauning. However, since the rise of social democracy to governmental power, it has been necessary to enlist the services of an increasing number of intellectuals to man the technical posts at the party's disposition. Among the most prominent of these have been K. K. Steincke, C. V. Bramsnaes, Vilhelm Buhl, and Hartvig Frisch — all of whom occupied high government positions and figured prominently in party councils.

[28] Bertolt, *Lyngsie*, p. 75.

Danish socialism was nurtured in a political milieu devoid of state repression, and derived its support primarily from relatively well situated craftsmen who had achieved substantial economic results through the method of collective bargaining. Their economic gradualism was reflected in their political views. Although officially committed to eventual socialism, there has been little interest in concrete nationalization measures.[29] The 1945 party program emphasized the desirability of economic controls, but advocated state ownership of only a very limited list of industries.[30] Emphasis has been placed on limited, realizable goals that would redound to the immediate political and economic advantage of the workers: free education in non-confessional schools, progressive income and inheritance taxation, a legal maximum working day, accident and sickness insurance, "more, better and cheaper" houses, and, not least, extension of the franchise.[31] The contemporary socialist party is anything but a doctrinaire advocate of socialism, but it is committed to such state regulation of the economy as it deems necessary to maintain full employment.[32]

Dictatorship of the proletariat is a concept that has always been alien to Danish labor mentality. It has been assumed that progress would have to be achieved primarily through collective bargaining, supplemented by parliamentary means. Consequently, the energies of the party have been focused on the problem of increasing its parliamentary representation. The success of this endeavor may be judged from Table 7, in which the socialist vote is shown for all general elections between 1895 and 1950. These figures show the remarkably steady extension of socialist political influence for half a century. The first real setback suffered by social democracy came in 1945, as a result of communist inroads into the socialist electorate.[33]

[29] Even the statements of party principle have been watered down through time. Compare the 1919 program (*Protokol for den 18 Socialdem. Partikongress*, 1919, p. 44), and the 1939 program (*Protokol for den 23 Socialdemokratiske Partikongress*, 1939, p. 85).

[30] These were production of sugar, oleomargarine, munitions, equipment for the state owned railway and telephone systems, asphalt, matches, paper, and sulphuric acid (the last four on the basis of already existing private monopolies), the banks, and some branches of insurance. See *Fremtidens Danmark, Socialdemokratiets Politik*, 1945.

[31] Abolition of the upper house of the parliament, in which for many years the socialists were grossly underrepresented, was a long standing socialist aim. While this was never achieved, the socialists obtained a working majority there in 1936. The voting age for the lower house still is an issue. It remains fixed at 25 years, with the socialists advocating a reduction to 21 years.

[32] It is perhaps well to remark that the generic term "socialism" covers a wide spectrum of political and economic beliefs. From the point of view of fundamental change in the form of society, Danish socialism has always occupied one of the most conservative positions in this spectrum, well to the right of Austro-Marxism and Norwegian syndicalism, and even British Fabianism.

[33] The communist vote in 1945 was 38 per cent of the social democratic vote, against 5 per cent in 1939. However, the percentage fell to 12 in 1950.

TABLE 7

SOCIAL DEMOCRATIC VOTE AS A PERCENTAGE OF MAJOR PARTY[a] VOTE IN GENERAL ELECTIONS, 1895–1950

Year	Percentage	Year	Percentage
1895	11.2	1924	37.8
1901	18.7	1926	38.1
1903	22.6	1929	42.9
1906	25.2	1932	44.7
1909	28.8	1935	50.8
1910	28.3	1939	48.5
1913	29.5	1943	47.9
1918	29.3	1945	39.3
1920 (Sept.)	33.4	1947	45.9
		1950	45.5

Sources: 1895–1943, Kjeld Winding, *Den Danske Arbejderbevaegelse* (Copenhagen, 1943), p. 98; 1945–1950, *Socialdemokratiske Noter, passim.*

[a] Includes Conservative, Agrarian, Liberal, and Social Democratic parties.

However, because of the relative overrepresentation of the rural districts, the social democrats have never attained an independentp arliamentary majority, nor do the possibilities of their gaining it within the ascertainable future appear strong. While Denmark has been governed by socialists for most of the period since 1929, it has always been a minority government, dependent for support upon political parties committed to the retention of capitalism. This minority status has had significant repercussions upon socialist psychology, policy, and relations with the trade unions.

The day to day parliamentary struggle absorbed the energies of the party bureaucracy. The problem of obtaining parliamentary majorities for each successive legislative proposal left the party leadership with little time and inclination to interfere in trade union affairs. Those who gravitated to the important posts in the party tended to be political tacticians rather than political theorists. The party's political precepts were mainly imported from Germany, and actually played but a minor role in organizational life.

The inability of the first generation of socialists to gain a free hand in the national state stimulated an early interest in municipal affairs, particularly in Copenhagen. In 1917 they gained a majority in the Copenhagen city council, and have since similarly captured every city of any size in the country. The wide scope of municipal activities in Denmark[34]

[34] Public utilities and urban transportation facilities are almost entirely municipally owned in Denmark. In addition, municipal governments operate a wide range of social services, many of which, such as hospitals, are largely in private hands in the United States, and have financed a considerable amount of apartment building.

made this a fruitful avenue for the exercise of the strongly pragmatic bent of Danish socialism. It is in municipal policy that the creative abilities of the Danish labor movement are best demonstrated. Only superlatives can be applied to the hospitals, schools, nurseries, housing, homes for the aged, and other public institutions of the modern Danish city, that are to a large extent the work of social democracy.[35]

Open friction between party and trade unions has been confined to the few occasions on which trade union policy came into conflict with the party's governmental responsibilities. There has been no issue of principle between the two, such as the appropriate use of the general strike which rent the German labor movement for many years.[36] However, there are many day to day problems that cut across the boundary line between political and economic activities, involving joint interests and requiring joint decision. To adjust differences that may arise, there is close collaboration between the two organizations on both an institutional and personal level.

Formally, party and trade unions are completely separated. There is not even the collective affiliation of local or national trade unions, which is practiced in England and the other Scandinavian countries.[37] The socialist party is a federation of some 1,360 local clubs, with 316,000 members (1949), the majority of whom are also trade union members. At the local level, institutional coöperation is secured through affiliation of the socialist club with the central trades and labor council. Nationally, the Federation of Labor has as one of its constitutional purposes "to coöperate with the Social Democratic Party in order jointly to further labor legislation"; in addition, the party elects two members to the executive committee of the Federation.[38] In reciprocation the Federation elects one member to the executive committee and one to the small and powerful council of the party.[39] The Federation provides the party with

[35] The interested reader is referred for details to *Social Denmark* (Copenhagen, 1945), and Orla Jensen, *Social Services in Denmark* (Copenhagen, 1948).

[36] Only on one occasion did the party call upon the trade unions to exercise the strike as a political weapon. That occurred in 1920, when as a result of the perennial Schleswig question King Christian X dismissed a ministry without a prior parliamentary vote of nonconfidence. Before the effective date of a general strike called jointly by the party and trade unions, the King bowed and accepted a new ministry satisfactory to the Socialists. It may be noted in this connection that prior to its rise to power, the Socialist Party favored a republican form of government. See *Protokol for den 18 Socialdem. Partikongress*, 1919, p. 99. This has now ceased to be a political issue, however. The socialists politely refrain from any mention of the monarchy in their political program, and have established friendly personal relations with the present monarch, Frederick IX.

[37] Collective trade union affiliation currently provides the Norwegian Labor Party with 45 per cent of its total membership, and the Swedish Social Democratic Party with 66 per cent.

[38] *Love for De Samvirkende Fagforbund i Danmark*, 1946, Sections 2, 30.

[39] *Love for Socialdemokratiet i Danmark*, 1945, Sections 15, 18.

considerable financial assistance. In 1947, it contributed 1.4 million kroner to *Social Demokraten*, the Copenhagen daily socialist newspaper, and 50 thousand kroner to the party campaign fund. Certainly not without significance is the joint occupancy by the two organizations of an office building in Copenhagen, affording daily personal contact between the leadership.

The growth of a career bureaucracy in the party has given rise to some difficulty in allocating parliamentary seats and ministerial posts, which is usually smoothed over behind closed doors but occasionally receives open expression. Thus, one delegate at the 1937 congress of the Federation said in support of trade union members of parliament: "We have enough school teachers in the parliament, we ought rather to see some of our own people there." [40] Not many individuals who came up through the trade union side have held cabinet posts, among other reasons because they prefer the authority and permanence of their union positions to the less stable prestige afforded by a ministry. Normally, a trade union leader can count on remaining in union office until he retires, but if he resigns to go into the government, he may have some difficulty regaining his union post when the government falls. It is customary, however, to afford the most prominent union leaders the opportunity of joining the cabinet, and occasionally one is drafted for work in which close trade union coöperation is critical to the success of a government program. The remaining positions are filled from the various sections of the party bureaucracy: the labor press, the economic research association, the coöperatives, and from among the organizers. Long parliamentary experience may also be taken into consideration.

It is virtually impossible for one who has not participated in the decision making process to determine conclusively whether in the last analysis it is the party or the trade unions that will have the final say on disputed issues that cannot be compromised. To an outsider, there are reasons for believing that the preponderance lies with the party. The split within trade union ranks between the skilled and unskilled workers means that the party faces two groups rather than one, groups that are often widely separated on matters of economic policy. On the personal level Thorvald Stauning, the party chairman from 1910 to 1939, overshadowed all other labor leaders in terms of prestige and popularity among the workers.

Perhaps the most important factor in party dominance, however, is that it is the party and not the trade unions that is confronted with the more basic policy problems. The wage decisions of the trade unions are

[40] De Samvirkende Fagforbund, *Protokol over Generalforsamling*, 1937, pp. 74–75.

only part of the economic data with which the party must deal, but the converse is not true: many party decisions are outside the range of trade union competence. It seems almost inevitable that the accession of a labor party to political power entails increasing supremacy over its allied trade unions.

The alliance between Danish trade unionism and social democracy has not gone entirely unchallenged. Syndicalism, which captured the Norwegian trade unions and made deep inroads in Sweden,[41] also spread to Denmark after 1910. In that year the Federation of the Trade Union Opposition was established by syndicalists, who captured three national unions — masons, seamen, and maritime engineers — which withdrew from the Federation of Labor. Some progress was also made in the Laborers' Union, mainly among the longshoremen. A number of illegal strikes were called during World War I under syndicalist auspices, in line with the advocacy of "direct action" to achieve economic demands. But Danish labor did not provide fertile ground for the growth of syndicalism. The skilled crafts were devoted to collective bargaining and impervious to the alleged advantages of more militant procedures. The unskilled workers had also benefited from collective bargaining and were, moreover, staunch opponents of the industrial unionism advocated by the syndicalists.

Fundamentally, Danish economic development was much less favorable to the spread of syndicalist influence than that of either Norway or Sweden. The Danish working class grew at a relatively slower rate — that is, there was a less rapid induction of farmers into the industrial labor force, during the crucial years when syndicalism was on the rise in Europe, largely as a consequence of earlier and slower Danish industrialization.[42] Better labor conditions in Denmark and the absence of those frontier industries in which syndicalist strength has tended to center because of the large proportion of rootless, non-family men engaged in them — heavy construction (particularly in newly opened areas), lumbering, and mining — also contributed to the conservatism of Danish labor. Moreover, Danish trade unionism was much the strongest when syndicalism made its bid for power in Scandinavia;[43] it had achieved a

[41] See Walter Galenson, *Labor in Norway* (Cambridge, Massachusetts, 1949), chaps. ii, iii; Valter Åman, *Svensk Syndikalism* (Stockholm, 1938). An independent syndicalist trade union center has been in existence in Sweden since 1910. Its membership has never exceeded 36,000, however.

[42] From 1890 to 1910 the number of persons dependent upon industry for their livelihood increased by 26.9 per cent in Denmark, 37.9 per cent in Norway, and 95.5 per cent in Sweden.

[43] Membership in the Scandinavian labor federations in 1910 was: Denmark, 102,000; Sweden, 85,000; Norway, 46,000. Ten years later the figures were, respectively, 279,000, 280,000, and 143,000. (The relative sizes of the three countries should be kept in mind in this connection.)

stability of collective bargaining relationships which the other two movements required several more decades to obtain.

Danish syndicalism, which lost all its influence after the recession of 1921, was replaced by communism as the chief opponent of social democracy within the labor movement. Unlike Norway, however, where the majority of the socialist party voted for affiliation with the Third International, the proponents of communism were a tiny minority within the Danish socialist party, which remained a firm adherent of the Second International.[44]

The Danish Communist Party originated in 1919, with its base in the socialist youth movement. It gained few adherents, however, and was weakened by the same pattern of fissions that affected world communism in 1922 and 1929–1930. During the 1920's its maximum voting strength at general elections was 6,200. The depression of 1930 enabled the party to expand, its vote rising to 17,000 in 1932, 27,000 in 1935, and 41,000 in 1939, the last sufficient to send three communist deputies to the parliament. Communist influence was strong among the maritime workers, but in general it constituted more a source of annoyance than a threat to the socialist trade union leadership.

It was only after World War II that the Communist Party lost its sectarian character and became a major political force. Socialist participation in government under the German occupation, communist martyrdom through suppression of the party and imprisonment of several hundreds of its leaders, and war weariness and discontent among the workers combined to give the Communist Party 255,000 votes and 18 parliamentary seats in the general elections of 1945. Even more serious was communist capitalization on an accumulation of wartime grievances among workers to sponsor numerous strikes, including one among the Copenhagen printers which forced most of the press of the city to suspend publication for four months in 1947.

The 1947 general elections, in which the communist vote dropped to 140,000 and its parliamentary mandates to nine, marked a return to a more normal state of affairs. Improved economic conditions and strenuous efforts by the socialist party machine had succeeded in wresting all but a few local unions from communist control.[45] By 1950 Danish communism had reverted to substantially its prewar position, that of a numerically inconsequential minority capable only of capitalizing upon crisis conditions.

[44] See *Protokol for den 18 Socialdem. Partikongress*, 1919, p. 81, for a record vote on the issue of international affiliation.

[45] A survey in June 1949 revealed that of 205 local unions in Copenhagen, with a total membership of 220,000, the communists controlled only 23 locals with a membership of 37,600. *Socialdemokratiske Noter*, vol. 20, no. 8, p. 584.

THE TRADE UNIONS AND THE COÖPERATIVE MOVEMENT

An account of Danish trade unionism would not be complete without reference to its participation in the coöperative movement. There are several distinct branches to the movement, namely, agricultural coöperatives, consumer coöperatives, producer coöperatives, and such miscellaneous coöperative institutions as banks and insurance companies.[46] The labor movement has been directly interested in all branches but the first.

Ferdinand Lassalle, who was in many ways the intellectual precursor of the Danish labor movement, had advocated trade union sponsored producer coöperation as a means of freeing the worker from his dependence upon capitalists. The Danish trade unions early embraced this notion, made attractive by the prevailingly small unit scale of enterprise which permitted the establishment of competitive coöperative workshops with small initial investments. Angered by the failure of bread prices to follow the downward price of wheat in the 1880's, workers in many towns founded coöperative bakeries, which were later drawn together into the Associated Joint and Coöperative Bakeries and proved a successful venture. Unemployment in the building construction industry around 1900 led a number of the building trades to set up coöperative building associations, which have become important sources of apartment building financing. Other circumstances, often lengthy strikes or lockouts, caused trade unions to embark upon other enterprises, including a dairy,[47] a brewery, insurance societies, and a hairdressing establishment. All of these enterprises were formed into a loose federation in 1922, the Coöperative Union.[48]

The importance of coöperation to the trade unions transcends the economic benefits which individual workers derive from it. Some of the coöperatives provide the unions with important sources of income. For example, a coöperative brewery owned by the Copenhagen trade unions did a gross business of 23.7 million kroner in 1947–48, and its profits financed union expenditures for educational and cultural work.[49] In emergencies, funds can be secured from the reserves of coöperative enterprises.

Union wage policy with respect to the coöperatives has been the source

[46] See Henning Ravnholt, *The Danish Cooperative Movement* (Copenhagen, 1947).

[47] For an account of the Laborers' experience with a coöperative dairy, see Bertolt, *Lyngsie*, pp. 49–65.

[48] In 1947 there were associated with the Coöperative Union 40 bakeries, 13 fuel concerns, 35 canteens, 53 building contracting firms, 157 building coöperatives, and 60 consumer coöperatives.

[49] Arbejderbevaegelsens Erhvervsraad, *Økonomisk Oversigt 1947 og 1948*, p. 136.

of some difficulty. The coöperatives have often complained that trade unions were using them as levers for raising wages in private enterprise, thus endangering their competitive position. In 1949 an agreement was reached between the Federation of Labor and the Coöperative Union stating that "the trade union movement is in full accord that broader demands with respect to wages and working conditions should not be made upon the coöperatives than upon those private establishments which, within each trade, are among the best from the point of view of operation and profitability." The last clause has been interpreted as meaning the establishments within the "best third" of private industry. Despite this agreement, it is hardly to be expected that individual unions will refrain from attempting to gain special concessions from the coöperatives, reflecting a problem that has arisen in the nationalized industries of other countries.

CHAPTER IV

THE DANISH FEDERATION OF LABOR: INTERNAL PROBLEMS

THE RELATIONSHIP BETWEEN SKILLED AND UNSKILLED WORKERS

THE ORGANIZATIONAL DIVISION between skilled and unskilled workers arose out of the peculiar social and economic circumstances that attended the foundation of the Danish labor movement. The division, once achieved, was maintained partly through institutional inertia. But other environmental factors contributed to its perpetuation, the exploration of which will be the purpose of this section.

The most important continuing source of conflict between the two groups of workers lies in the competition for available employment opportunities, arising out of what Perlman calls "the scarcity consciousness of the manualist." [1] The craft unions inherited from the gilds control over sharply delineated job areas, and have had to defend them against encroachments by non-craftsmen, for the substitution of machinery for handwork provided the latter with technical means to perform formerly skilled work. However, the unskilled workers have by no means been the sole aggressors; the craftsmen have on occasion endeavored to acquire control of the unskilled workers within their industries, where the two were working side by side.

Both these expansionist proclivities manifested themselves at an early date. Efforts to substitute unskilled for skilled workers after the general work stoppage of 1899 led to sharp protests by the craftsmen.[2] On the other hand, the attempted transformation of craft into industrial unions (for example, the Journeyman Shoemaker Association changed its name to the Shoe Workers' Union) was protested vigorously by the Laborers'

[1] Selig Perlman, *A Theory of the Labor Movement* (New York, 1949), p. 239.

[2] The chairman of the Metal Workers' Union declared at that time: "With regard to the introduction of laborers into our trade, we recognize that the modern development of machine technique makes it possible to use unskilled labor to a greater extent than previously, and we are willing to take that into consideration; but if the employers are going to interpret the agreement to the effect that they can quite arbitrarily set the skilled worker aside and hire unskilled workers because they are cheaper, that will be a source of much strife, because it is a matter of our daily bread, and we must assert to the limit what we consider to be our natural right." Ernst Christiansen, *Danske Smede* (Copenhagen, 1948), p. 51.

Union in 1904.[3] A controversy typical of this early period arose when machine molding, a new technological process, was assigned to foundry laborers, threatening the continued existence of the Molders' Union. The jurisdictional disputes board of the Federation of Labor[4] held for the Molders, arguing that it was in the interest of the workers concerned to be covered by Molders' agreements, since they contained higher wage rates.[5] Secession of the Laborers' Union over this decision was narrowly averted.[6]

In the numerous subsequent disputes of a similar nature between the skilled and the unskilled, when it appeared that either the Laborers' Union[7] on the one hand, or craft[8] or industrial unions[9] on the other had no historical claim to the work in question, but were merely raiding, the *status quo* was maintained. Generally, however, there had been industrial innovations for which no direct precedent existed. Where the work involved required any considerable degree of skill, even in the absence of formal apprenticeship, as a condition precedent to its performance, the jurisdictional board tended to assign it to the skilled crafts,[10] unless there was a well-established practice to the contrary in which the skilled unions had acquiesced.[11] Some weight was given to the type of materials

[3] Bertolt, *Lyngsie*, p. 97.

[4] See below, p. 63.

[5] De Samvirkende Fagforbund, *Graensesager*, 1943, Cases No. 11, 12 (1913). This citation refers to a compilation of the decisions of the jurisdictional board of the Federation of Labor. Cases decided subsequent to 1943 have been secured from the annual reports of the Federation, but will be cited similarly for convenience.

[6] Bertolt, *Lyngsie*, p. 104. The two unions eventually agreed to arbitrate future disputes.

[7] *Graensesager*, Case No. 57 (1937), involving work that had been assigned to the Stone Workers' Union by previous agreement; Case No. 103 (1946), in which the Laborers attempted to take over the construction of aerial power lines from the Electrical Workers; Case No. 109 (1947), involving paper workers clearly within the jurisdiction of the industrial union in that field; Case No. 126 (1948), same as No. 57 above.

[8] *Graensesager*, Case No. 46 (1937), in which the Leather and Fur Workers' Union endeavored to expand its craft structure on the basis of technological change.

[9] *Graensesager*, Case No. 118 (1947), where the Textile Workers' Union demanded exclusive jurisdiction over laundry workers.

[10] *Graensesager*, Case No. 88 (1945), in which the following observations were made: "The fact that one or more unskilled workers in an establishment learn and are engaged in work of a special character cannot afford them any preference over skilled workers, to whose trade the work in question generally belongs, even though such work is characterized by the peculiar circumstances of the work place and requires some training of skilled workers as well. There is a real question whether the craft union could not raise the issue of whether laborers may rightly engage in work which, though of a special nature, is of a craft character." See also Case No. 71 (1942) where the operation of printing machinery was assigned to the Typographical Union even though the work was performed by unqualified printers. The fact that skilled workers spend part of their time doing unskilled work was held not to justify the Laborers' Union's claim to jurisdiction in Case No. 120 (1948).

[11] *Graensesager*, Case No. 48 (1934), where the board, though conceding that the disputed work was of a craft character, decided nevertheless that "a definite custom has been established under which unskilled workers are trained to perform metal pressing, and the Metal

used [12] and to the desires of the workers involved,[13] in the assignment of jurisdiction. Though these criteria, in general, favored the craft unions, the board often leaned over backward to avoid undue damage to established interests of the Laborers,[14] and on occasion cut the Gordian knot by dividing the work more or less arbitrarily.[15]

That jurisdictional conflict between the skilled and unskilled workers has not assumed more serious proportions may be ascribed to the fact that a large proportion of the unskilled work lies in distinct job areas quite separate from the handicrafts — for example, dock and agricultural work — as well as to the cohesiveness and strength of the craft unions, which are reflected in the maintenance of a formal apprenticeship system. The apprenticeship, which averages 4½ years, provides an objective test of skilled status that has served as a bulwark for the maintenance of craft prerogatives. Employers, partly through fear of union reaction and partly through sheer habit, are little disposed to substitute unskilled for skilled labor even though job content may have changed.[16] Occasional concessions are made by the skilled unions when economic pressure becomes too great to resist entirely, but when the pressure slackens, the traditional system is restored in all its pristine purity.[17]

Pressers' Union has not objected to their membership in the Laborers' Union. Moreover, the Laborers' Union has been able to secure for them hourly and piece rates that are significantly in excess of average factory rates . . ." The same decision was rendered in a dispute over pipe repair work in a chemical plant between the Plumbers and the Laborers, Case No. 106 (1947).

[12] The introduction of rockwool insulation in building led to a dispute between the Laborers and Carpenters. The latter had been using this material in the insulation of pipes and boilers, and were awarded jurisdiction largely on that basis. *Graensesager*, Case No. 63 (1939). Jurisdiction over the manufacture of pipes (for smoking) was awarded to the Woodworkers' Union on the ground that "it is a job area which is largely of the same nature as light wood fabrication." Case No. 121 (1948).

[13] *Graensesager*, Case No. 32 (1926): "The board is unanimous in deciding that the workers involved in the dispute belong to the Woodworkers' Union, with particular weight being given to the fact that there is a written declaration from the workers themselves expressing the desire to be transferred to that union."

[14] In *Graensesager*, Case No. 107 (1947), where the Laborers had held contracts covering a ceramics manufacturing plant for two years, the board ruled that while "the workers involved are classified under the Ceramic Workers' Union, because of the existing contracts the case must be referred to negotiation between the two unions." See also Case No. 123 (1948).

[15] *Graensesager*, Case No. 47 (1933); Case No. 54 (1936).

[16] In some trades employers owe their monopoly positions to the craft union monopoly, and oppose changes in the labor force that might permit new employers to enter the trade. Cf. John T. Dunlop, "Jurisdictional Disputes," *Proceedings of the New York University Second Annual Conference on Labor*, 1949, p. 486.

[17] During World War II the demand for workers in the job area of the Metal Workers' Union outran the supply of skilled labor, and necessitated the employment of non-craftsmen for such work as ship welding. The Metal Workers' Union thereupon decided to permit unskilled workers who had reached the age of 18 years and had been employed for at least two years in a metal shop to fulfill the apprenticeship requirements in two years instead of the customary five, to prevent the Laborers' Union from gaining entrance to the trade. Only a

The problem is by no means a settled one, however. Unemployment among unskilled workers concurrent with shortages of labor in the skilled trades has produced a mounting demand for abrogation of the craft monopolies and job rationalization. The fact that on this issue the Federation of Labor supports the craft unions[18] is not designed to mollify the Laborers.

A second major cause of dissension between skilled and unskilled workers springs from differences in the wage systems under which they work. The Laborers' agreements, in general, stipulate standard wage rates, either on a time- or piece-rate basis. In the metal trades, on the other hand, a so-called "elastic" wage system is employed, whereby only minimum rates are fixed by collective bargaining, the effective rates being determined by individual bargaining between the employer and each employee. This distinction is reflected in collective bargaining strategy; the skilled workers are apt to be relatively conciliatory, for although changes in their minimum contract rates do affect earnings (though not proportionally), errors in the assessment of cyclical movements can be corrected during the contract period through the presentation of individual wage demands to their employers.[19] The unskilled workers have no such opportunity, for their wages are fixed for the duration of the agreements.

Traditionally in collective bargaining, agreement in the metal trades has been the signal for a general settlement among the crafts, creating a wage pattern which the Laborers have found it difficult to resist, no matter how reluctant they were to accept the same terms.[20] The Laborers

---

few hundred workers came into the union this way, however, for diminishing employment in the postwar period resulted in return of the work to regularly apprenticed metal workers.

[18] A recent editorial in the journal of the Federation of Labor read, in part: "It is thought by some . . . that the present limitations upon what work may be done by unskilled workers do not suit current needs, and become less suitable with technological change. To this it may be said that it is completely erroneous to believe that the unemployment problem can be solved merely by admitting a certain number of unskilled workers to the various trades. The lack of skilled manpower which characterized the past few years has diminished of late and prevails in only a minor degree. Removal of craft lines would meet with the opposition of the skilled workers, who have a natural right to preserve the work they have sacrificed years to learn. It is possible to train unskilled workers for some of the less skilled jobs in certain industries, but that does not solve the problem, if skilled workers are thereby rendered superfluous." *Arbejderen,* April 1, 1949, p. 74.

[19] This wage system is discussed in greater detail below, pp. 146–150.

[20] "It was Lyngsie's and the Laborers' belief that the Metal Workers had placed serious obstacles in the way of their efforts to improve wage conditions . . . The principal allegation is that the Metal Workers were not interested whether their minimum wages were a few øre higher or lower, for they were not paid the minimum; but the employers used those same minima as a barrier over which they would not permit the Laborers to pass." Bertolt, *Lyngsie,* p. 100. See also Axel Olsen, p. 335: "There was also a desire to put an end to the negotiating tactics followed by the metal trades for many years, whereby negotiations took place first with the Central Organization of Metal Workers, thereafter with the skilled crafts in the

could have taken the lead and attempted to set the pattern themselves, but this would have involved abandonment of their basic wage strategy, which was to whittle down wage differentials by securing a little more than the skilled workers each year. They were thus on the horns of a dilemma: if they acted as the spearhead in general wage movements, their agreement would almost certainly have had wide application, leaving relative wages undisturbed; but if, as it was once characterized, "they played their traditional role, which consisted of using the other trades as shock troops and cannon fodder," [21] employer resistance to concessions over and above those contained in the skilled trades agreements was certain to be fierce.

In choosing, until recent years, to adopt the latter bargaining alternative, the Laborers were bound to antagonize not only the employers, but the skilled crafts as well. Their reputation as the stormy petrels of the Danish labor movement grows out of their rejection of a fixed ratio between the wages of skilled and unskilled workers.[22] And there is no doubt that they have secured a narrowing of this differential. In 1914, average hourly earnings of male laborers were 75 per cent of the average skilled earnings; by 1948, they had reached 83 per cent. The crucial question, however, is whether this was due, as is sometimes claimed, to the independent organization of the laborers, and to their bargaining tactics, or whether it simply reflects underlying changes in the supply and demand for various types of labor.

One approach to a solution of this problem lies in a direct comparison of Danish wage differentials with those prevailing in Norway and Sweden, where trade union organization is along industrial lines.[23] Unfortunately, the available wage data do not lend themselves to a general comparison of this sort, for the Danish statistics alone consistently distinguish

metal trades, so that those who followed were faced with a *fait accompli* with respect to what could be obtained . . ."

[21] *Beretning om Dansk Arbejdsgiverforenings Virksomhed*, 1921–1922, p. 52.

[22] The literature is replete with specific references to this policy. A chairman of the Laborers' Union wrote, for example: "Regardless of how low a laborer's wages are, regardless of the fact that thousands of laborers perform work which is fully as skilled as that of the craftsmen, notwithstanding that the laborer's work is often as wearing and in many ways more disagreeable and dirty, there must be a wage differential, perhaps even a very great differential, between laborers and craftsmen. But that is a traditional belief which does not square with practical developments, since the difference between skilled and 'unskilled' work has become more and more blurred; but nevertheless forced attempts are made to retain the old time, gild division lines, as far as wages are concerned, whereas in other aspects of production, machine techniques and rationalization have condemned all the traditional and mouldy gild meditations." Axel Olsen, pp. 340–341.

[23] The value of this comparison is enhanced by the institutional similarities among the Scandinavian countries. Job titles and content are relatively uniform, for example, and industrial structure contains fewer differences than would ordinarily be found in making international comparisons.

between skilled and unskilled wages. Table 8 compares skilled and unskilled wage differentials for a few trades in Denmark and Norway (comparable wage data for Sweden are lacking), confined to the capital cities of each,[24] since dissimilarities in urban-rural employment patterns might prove a seriously distorting factor. These data do not support the hypothesis that separate organization in Denmark has brought the unskilled workers relatively nearer the skilled level, for out of the three trades studied, the Danish differential was less in one (printing), greater in a second (metal working), and approximately equal to the Norwegian in

TABLE 8

WAGE DIFFERENTIALS BETWEEN SKILLED AND UNSKILLED MALE WORKERS IN COPENHAGEN, DENMARK, AND OSLO, NORWAY, 1946

	Denmark			Norway		
	Average Hourly Earnings of Skilled Workers (*In øre*)	Average Hourly Earnings of Unskilled Workers (*In øre*)	Unskilled as a Percentage of Skilled Earnings	Average Hourly Earnings of Skilled Workers (*In øre*)	Average Hourly Earnings of Unskilled Workers (*In øre*)	Unskilled as a Percentage of Skilled Earnings
Printers, newspaper }	303[a]	251[a]	82.8	418[b]	331[b]	79.2
Printers, book..... }				323[b]	235[b]	72.8
Masons..........	378[a]	336[a]	88.9	393[b]	353[b]	89.8
Metal workers....	314[a]	260[a]	82.8	315[c]	281[c]	89.2
				290[d]	248[d]	85.5

[a] Third quarter 1946. Source: *Beretning om Dansk Arbejdsgiverforenings Virksomhed*, 1946–1947, pp. 69–73.
[b] Third quarter 1946. Source: *Norges Offisielle Statistikk* X, vol. 159 (1946), pp. 54–55.
[c] Fourth quarter 1946. Includes all workers in Akers Shipyard in Oslo. Source: Mimeographed data compiled by Norwegian Metal Workers' Union.
[d] Fourth quarter 1946. Includes all workers in Norwegian shipyards. Source: *See* note c.

a third (masonry). The reader is cautioned, however, that this conclusion is highly tentative, and requires verification by intensive recourse to unpublished wage statistics.

An alternative approach to the same problem, avoiding the conceptual differences in the wage statistics of the Scandinavian countries, entails a comparison of relative wages for those industries in which the Danish Laborers' Union is substantially represented among the employees, with

[24] No figures are available for the Oslo metal trades, and instead the data represent wage differentials in the largest shipyard in Oslo, and in Norwegian shipbuilding as a whole. Since in both Denmark and Norway the shipyards are the principal employers of metal trades workers, the comparison has more validity than might appear at first thought. However, it should be kept in mind that in the metal workers category the groups of workers compared in Denmark and Norway are not identical.

the level of wages for all industry. If it were found, for example, that the wage level of such industries in Denmark was closer to the all-industry average than was true in Norway and Sweden, it could be argued that the separate organization of unskilled workers in Denmark was significant in producing the observed difference.[25] The principal obstacle to this procedure arises again from the nature of the published wage statistics. Comprehensive wage data by industry are not available for Denmark, since all skilled work is broken down by craft, with industrial categories including only the non-craftsmen. In Norway and Sweden,

TABLE 9

AVERAGE HOURLY EARNINGS IN SELECTED INDUSTRIES COMPARED WITH AVERAGE HOURLY EARNINGS IN ALL INDUSTRY, FOR DENMARK, NORWAY, AND SWEDEN, 1946

	Denmark		Norway		Sweden	
	Average Hourly Earnings in Designated Industry (*In øre*)	Ratio to Average Hourly Earnings in All Industry (*271 øre = 100*)	Average Hourly Earnings in Designated Industry (*In øre*)	Ratio to Average Hourly Earnings in All Industry (*266 øre = 100*)	Average Hourly Earnings in Designated Industry (*In øre*)	Ratio to Average Hourly Earnings in All Industry (*215 øre = 100*)
Cement	257 (Cement and Cement products combined)	94.8			188	87.4
Cement products					206	95.8
Brick manufacture	243	89.7	246	92.5	179	83.3
Glass products	249	91.9			185	86.0
Peat	262	96.7			185	86.0
Fats and oils	242	89.3	244	91.8	211	98.1

Sources: Denmark: Calculated from *Beretning om Dansk Arbejdsgiverforenings Virksomhed*, 1946–1947 (data are for third quarter of 1946); Norway: Calculated from *Norges Offisielle Statistikk* X, vol. 159, *Arbeidslønninger* 1946; Sweden: Calculated from *Lönestatistisk Årsbok för Sverige*, 1946.

on the other hand, the wages of both skilled and unskilled workers are combined in an industry average, with the result that such an average would tend by its composition to exceed the Danish. However, this discrepancy is partly offset by the choice for comparison of industries in which the skilled crafts, in the Danish sense, are in a small minority.

Table 9, which shows the results of such a comparison, is inconclusive. The relative wage levels of the predominantly unskilled industries tend

[25] There are of course other factors that might influence the comparison. Among them may be listed industrial location, the varying extent of dependence upon the export trade, differences in the composition of the labor force, and the varying influence of particular industries upon the all-industry average among the three countries. An attempt to adjust for these factors is out of proportion to the significance of this point.

to be somewhat higher in Denmark than in Sweden, but lower than those in the two industries shown for Norway. Again, however, the nature of the data calls for caution in drawing conclusions. It is to be hoped that more intensive work will provide a definitive answer to this interesting problem.

Over the years there has been a good deal of personal recrimination between the leaders of the two major factions in the trade union movement, which was regarded as causative rather than merely symptomatic. Strained relationships existed, for example, between Lyngsie and I. A. Hansen, chairman of the Metal Workers' Union, which had its climax in 1909 when the two defeated one another for the chairmanship of the Federation of Labor. The feud was continued when Johannes Kjaerbøl succeeded Hansen; in 1931, Lyngsie publicly accused Kjaerbøl of having taken the initiative in proposing a general wage reduction, and when the latter stigmatized the charge as "lying, mean, and unworthy," Lyngsie brought suit for slander. The Metal Workers' Union forbade Kjaerbøl to defend the suit, and Lyngsie collected 200 kroner in damages.

The ill feeling on the part of the Laborers extended to the Social Democratic Party. Lyngsie had a long standing complaint that his union was not given adequate parliamentary representation. In 1925, when Stauning, in his capacity as prime minister, was endeavoring to bring to an end a paralyzing general strike, Lyngsie showed his resentment when he declared to the press: "If only the prime minister would stop his perpetual prophecies of peace. What sort of garrulous talk is that for a prime minister? He has nothing to do with it, and knows nothing." [26]

With the lessening intensity of the economic sources of conflict, personal relationships between the skilled and unskilled workers have improved. This is not to say that there are no longer any problems. But the wages of unskilled workers are now at a point where further relative wage increases can hardly be expected, a fact that is reflected in the increasing tendency of the Laborers to set the pattern in collective bargaining. And while technological advance continues to raise new jurisdictional issues, the respective rights of the two groups are so well delineated by custom and board decision that further change will probably be of a marginal character. Symptomatic of the current atmosphere was the election in 1943 to the chairmanship of the Federation of Labor, for the first time, of a member of the Laborers' Union, Eiler Jensen.[27]

[26] Bertolt, *Lyngsie*, p. 141.

[27] The previous Federation chairmen were Jens Jensen (1898–1903), a painter; Martin Olsen (1903–1909), a carpenter; Carl Madsen (1909–1929), a shoemaker; Vilhelm Nygaard (1929–1936), a cigar maker; Christian Jensen (1936–1938), a tobacco worker; Knud V. Jensen (1939), a woodcarver; and Lauritz Hansen (1939–1942), a stationary engineer. No member of the Metal Workers' Union has ever held the post.

THE PROBLEM OF TRADE UNION CENTRALISM[28]

The allocation of authority between the Federation of Labor and the constituent national unions has been a constant source of controversy since the foundation of the Federation. Every gain achieved by the proponents of centralism has been fought by a strong minority group, in which the Laborers' Union was the principal element. In general, the Federation has been given additional powers only when the practical need for them was convincingly demonstrated. The prevailing inclination in the Danish trade union movement has been and remains centripetal.

The chief advocates of increased central power have been the skilled crafts, with the Metal Workers' Union at their head. The attitudes of the skilled and unskilled workers stem from the situations of the two groups; the Metal Workers, secure in their jurisdictional area and generally able to muster a majority vote within the Federation, have little to fear from a strong Federation, while the Laborers, in a minority against the combined forces of the skilled crafts and suspicious of craft encroachment upon their prerogatives, are reluctant to cede any of their autonomy.

The scheme of representation prevailing in the Federation is not designed to allay the fears of the unskilled workers. In the congress, the small crafts are overrepresented and the Laborers underrepresented. At the 1946 congress the Laborers had one delegate for each 2,034 members, as against one delegate for each 27 gilders, for each 41 coopers, and for each 1,637 metal workers. The Laborers' and Female Workers' Unions represented 44 per cent of total Federation membership at the 1946 congress, but had only 13 per cent of the total delegates present.

The constitution of the Federation permits the congress to take decisions on all but "wage questions" by simple or stated majorities of the delegates present; but voting on "wage questions" is proportional to membership represented. It is not strange, under the circumstances, that congress decisions are almost always the result of previous agreement, where conflicting union interests are involved. Coercion of minorities would long since have led to severance of the oft precarious organizational bonds.

The strongest allies of the proponents of greater central power have been the organized employers. Once collective bargaining was accepted and a strong employer association established, it was in their interest to deal with a federation that could commit its affiliates. As early as 1899,

[28] For an excellent analysis of this problem, see the article by A. Kocik and Henry Grünbaum in *Under Samvirkets Flag*, pp. 243–293.

in its draft of a proposal to settle the great dispute that occurred in that year, the Employers' Association made the following point: "Future agreements which may be concluded between the central organizations must not hereafter be dependent upon approval by subordinate or local organizations, and the respective central organizations shall assume responsibility for the loyal fulfillment of agreements by local organizations." [29]

Though this provision was deleted before the final draft, in substance it continued to be a goal of the employers. Repeatedly, they refused to conclude agreements involving large numbers of workers when small crafts were holding out, insisting on a joint settlement as the only means of assuring equity among the crafts. General settlements could be negotiated most readily with a powerful Federation of Labor; therefore, there are many statements from employer sources, such as the following, indicating the desirability of structural reform within the labor movement:

If the Federation of Labor were in a position to adjust its organizational structure so as to centralize the power to decree and conclude disputes to a greater extent, in conformance with the prevailing situation in the Employers' Association, we would be able to deal as equals, and it would be possible to make the contribution of the central organizations to collective bargaining far more significant than it is today.[30]

There has been some progress in the direction of trade union centralization since 1898. In 1900, for example, the following provision was inserted into the constitution of the Federation:

When an actual or contemplated work stoppage has assumed, or threatens to assume, such dimensions that it endangers the peaceful continuance of work in other trades, the trade involved in the dispute, when the Representative Council [of the Federation of Labor] requires it by a three-quarters majority vote, shall seek to conclude or prevent the stoppage.[31]

This authority, however, has rarely been employed. It was last applied in a shoemakers' strike of 1931, resulting in vehement protest by that trade.

The September Agreement of 1899 empowered the Federation of Labor and the Employers' Association to call sympathetic strikes (or lockouts) against one another. To implement this authority on the labor side, the congress of the Federation was empowered by a constitutional amendment adopted in 1900 to declare sympathetic strikes binding upon

[29] *Arbejdsgiverforening Gennem 25 Aar* (Copenhagen, 1921), p. 97.
[30] *Beretning om Dansk Arbejdsgiverforenings Virksomhed*, 1946–1947, p. 97.
[31] *Lov for De Samvirkende Fagforbund i Danmark*, Section 10.

constituent unions, by a three-fourths majority vote. The power thus granted was employed in 1902, disastrously for the trade unions, leading to a demand by the Laborers' Union that no affiliated union thereafter be required to engage in a work stoppage contrary to its wishes. This change was incorporated into the statutes of the Federation, and at the present time no union need become involved in a sympathetic strike unless its own congress or other competent body has agreed to do so.

Scarcely a Federation congress went by without debate on the issue of centralism versus autonomy, but not until 1921 was there any concrete change in the *status quo*. In 1918 the Federation had entered into an agreement with the Employers' Association providing for cost of living supplements to wages to prevent deterioration of workers' living standards as a result of rapidly rising prices. This agreement, binding upon all workers, was followed by another in 1919 providing for the eight-hour day. As long as wages were going up, there was little disposition to question the competence of the Federation to deal with such "general" problems. In 1921, however, the congress voted by a close margin to accept a reduction in the wage supplements in order to avoid a threatened lockout. This action was promptly repudiated by several unions, and resulted in a lockout of six weeks' duration.

In consequence of this experience, a committee was established to consider the future role of the Federation in wage movements. The committee majority proposed that when wage movements involved more than one union, the Federation should be empowered to make decisions binding upon the unions affected. A minority of the committee wanted to limit the function of the Federation to polling the individual unions on agreements, the outcome to be determined by a majority of the votes cast, regardless of craft lines. Lyngsie, representing the Laborers, objected to any extension whatever of Federation power.[32]

The committee's report was debated at an extraordinary congress held in 1922. The executive committee of the Federation, Lyngsie excepting, argued that each union should have freedom of action except on "questions of vital significance to workers generally, when a joint decision must be adopted under certain circumstances." The Laborers' Union moved the following clause in opposition: "The congress [of the Federation] cannot conclude agreements involving wages and other conditions of labor on behalf of affiliated organizations or against their desire, and the executive committee cannot participate in negotiations over such agreements unless the craft concerned is represented." [33]

By the vote of 287 to 235 the Laborers' resolution was adopted, and a

[32] *Beretning om De Samvirkende Fagforbunds Virksomhed*, 1921–22, pp. 14–15.
[33] De Samvirkende Fagforbund, *Protokol over Generalforsamling*, October 9–10, 1923, p. 54.

split in the ranks of the Federation, threatened by the Laborers if they were defeated, averted. While the craft unions largely voted with the executive committee, some of the industrial unions, apparently sharing the Laborers' fear of craft domination, either cast their votes entirely for the Laborers, or were divided. However, the congress, in rejecting efforts at centralization, did make specific the range of "general" questions on which the Federation was empowered to act. In this category were placed agreements on the maximum working day, vacations, and the socialization of industry, to which custom has added the negotiation of cost of living supplements to wages.

The issue of centralization was laid to rest for a decade by the verdict of 1922. A new phase began in 1931, when the State Mediator, in setting forth a proposed collective agreement covering several trades jointly, decreed that if the majority of any single union voted against it, the entire proposal would be regarded as rejected by all the unions. This policy, designed to force the unions into a more rational ratification procedure, led to renewed pressure for greater centralization of authority. The difficulty was surmounted by an amendment to the Mediation Act providing for ratification or rejection of a mediation proposal on the basis of a majority of all votes cast, disregarding union lines, thus depriving the small unions of the ability to defeat agreements to which they were insignificant minority parties. While this amendment did not directly augment the power of the Federation, it undoubtedly gave the Federation greater latitude in promoting general settlements, since it was no longer necessary to secure the assent of each individual union. The change was not made without considerable opposition from the unions, and it required the prestige of Prime Minister Stauning to ensure its acceptance by the Federation.[34]

There had always been some consultation among related crafts preliminary to the formulation of specific demands, particularly in the metal trades, where the joint collective agreement customarily negotiated made inter-union collaboration mandatory. With little discussion, the 1939 congress of the Federation adopted more general rules for union coöperation, according to which three representatives of each national union were to meet prior to the expiration of the principal collective agreements to explore general policy lines. Thereafter, related crafts were "to coöperate as far as possible to reach agreement on the contemplated demands of the several organizations, in order that lack of agree-

[34] Stauning told the 1934 Federation congress: "Perhaps it is something new, but it was necessary *to increase centralization*. It must not happen again, as it has happened before, that a little group objects to a mediation proposal and forces 100,000 to 200,000 workers to remain out on strike. If we go on strike together, we should go back together, *on the basis of a majority vote*." De Samvirkende Fagforbund, *Protokol over Generalforsamling*, 1934, p. 18.

ment shall not hinder effectuation of the desired results in negotiations with employers." [35] These rules have thus far proved of little practical importance.

The proponents of centralism within the Federation of Labor have not yet given up hope. At the 1946 congress, the chairman remarked, apropos of criticism that the Federation had failed to act decisively: "You cannot favor joint action and joint decision and at the same time demand that each union be absolutely sovereign in judging its own position. You must take one or the other approach, for every experienced organization man knows that the Federation cannot go both ways at once." [36] He received warm support from the Metal Workers, but the Laborers warned against any expansion of the central power "that might lead to the adoption of agreements not satisfactory to all trades." [37] It is apparent that progress toward centralization is contingent upon further rapprochement between the skilled and the unskilled workers.

While the Danish Federation of Labor has lagged behind the other Scandinavian labor movements in terms of the degree of authority exercised over affiliates, it is incorrect to assume that it is an impotent organization. In fact, the Federation is functionally much stronger than, for example, the American Federation of Labor, as the following summary of the tasks it actually performs clearly indicates:

1. The Federation is the representative of affiliated unions in proceedings before the State Mediator. While it cannot commit them, except on "general" questions, the expertness of its negotiators affects the outcome of negotiations to a considerable degree.

2. The Federation can recommend that sympathetic strikes be called. Although each union decides for itself whether to honor a call, in fact this has almost always been done in major disputes.

3. The Federation represents all unions before the Labor Court. The importance of this function will become clearer when the role of the Labor Court in industrial relations is considered.

4. The Federation may withhold strike assistance from an affiliate if it disapproves of the strike. However, this right is rarely exercised.

5. Preliminary collective bargaining conferences among related crafts are held under Federation auspices. This may yet be the principal avenue for extension of Federation influence.

6. The Federation represents the trade union movement in the formulation of policy with respect to other than purely trade union questions.

[35] *Beretning om De Samvirkende Fagforbunds Virksomhed*, 1939, p. 22.
[36] De Samvirkende Fagforbund, *Protokol over Generalforsamling*, 1946, p. 39.
[37] *Ibid.*, p. 29.

JURISDICTIONAL DISPUTES

The jurisdictional struggle between the skilled and unskilled workers has been described above as part of the pattern of relationships between the two groups. But this by no means exhausts the subject. The solution of the more orthodox types of jurisdictional disputes has been a major problem of the Federation of Labor, and the nature of the adjudicatory mechanism and the results achieved will now be considered.

A joint committee of employers and trade unions, established in 1909 under government auspices to draft new labor legislation and rules for collective bargaining, weighed the question of whether the settlement of jurisdictional disputes was an appropriate subject for joint employer-union action. While the unions indicated a willingness to accept a joint board, the employers refused for the following reasons:

1. They feared that trade unions might attempt to shift the responsibility for jurisdictional strife to employers.

2. A joint board would constitute indirect recognition of the monopoly right of individual crafts to specified work areas.

3. A joint committee would tend to be guided by previous practice, the effect of which would be to place restraints upon industrial development.[38]

With employers unwilling to become involved, the Federation of Labor turned to the alternative of self-adjudication. The problem could no longer be neglected, for the spread of machine techniques was undermining job stability. Those crafts which were being rendered redundant,[39] faced with shrinking employment opportunities and growing unemployment rolls, both sought new job areas and were exceedingly zealous to protect those they still retained. In 1911 the Federation established a board with authority to mediate and, if necessary, to arbitrate jurisdictional disputes, which were divided into the following categories:

1. Disputes over the craft to which work belongs.
2. Disputes over the mutual fraternal obligations of crafts and branches, both under peaceful conditions and during labor disputes.
3. Disputes over which organization workers should appropriately join.
4. Other intercraft disputes which the unions agree to submit for judgment.[40]

The jurisdictional board was originally composed of seven members, four elected by the congress and three by the Federation's executive com-

[38] *Beretning om Dansk Arbejdsgiverforenings Virksomhed*, 1909–1910, p. 99.

[39] From 1900 to 1910, for example, the Tawer's Union suffered a membership decline of 50 per cent; the Glove Makers of 43 per cent; the Ship Carpenters of 40 per cent; the Coopers of 18 per cent. At the same time, total Federation membership increased by 33 per cent.

[40] *Beretning til De Samvirkende Fagforbunds Repræsentantskabsmøde*, 1912, pp. 11–12.

mittee. In 1949, under pressure from the Laborers' Union, it was altered in composition, and now consists of three permanent members selected by the executive committee and four *ad hoc* members for individual disputes, two selected by each of the contending parties.

All jurisdictional disputes are first brought before the executive committee, which may attempt to mediate. In the ordinary course of events, failure of mediation results in submission to the jurisdictional board for further mediation and arbitration, but occasional disputes involving basic principles may be referred to a special committee or to the representative council of the Federation, and even to the congress.[41] From its establishment in 1911 to 1948 the jurisdictional board rendered 128 formal decisions, half of them since 1940. The secular increase in the number of disputes appears to be due to increased competition among unions for the diminishing pool of unorganized workers, to increasing pressure of the unskilled workers upon the craft domains, and to the rise of the municipal and white-collar unions, which cut across industrial and craft lines.[42]

Formal decisions, however, by no means represent the full case load of jurisdictional disputes in Denmark. During the eight-year period 1941 to 1948, the executive committee of the Federation handled 131 disputes, as against 62 formal board decisions, a ratio of 2.1 to 1. There are undoubtedly other disputes that are settled directly between the parties without recourse to the Federation machinery.

On the whole, securing compliance with board decisions has not been a major problem.[43] This is not to say that all unions acquiesce in unfavorable decisions without protest; on the contrary, there have been threats to secede, and a few actual secessions from the Federation, over jurisdiction.[44] But there is a tradition of compliance that has prevented the frequent migration in and out of Federation ranks that might have been anticipated in view of the relatively slight disabilities involved in secession. Work stoppages over jurisdictional disputes have been almost

[41] A long standing controversy between the Laborers and the Municipal Workers' Union was referred to the representative council in 1930; a dispute between the Laborers and the Carpenters over insulation work went to a special committee in 1940.

[42] Of the jurisdictional cases decided since 1940, the two major unskilled unions, the Laborers' and Female Workers' Unions, were involved in 40 per cent, the Municipal Workers' and Commercial and Office Workers' Unions in 30 per cent.

[43] It should be noted that the Employers' Association does not regard the decisions of the jurisdictional board as binding upon its members. In most cases, however, the employer will not be disposed to question the jurisdictional assignments of the Federation of Labor.

[44] The most recent involved a dispute between the Laborers' Union and the Tanners in 1947. When the latter refused to abide by an executive committee award, it was ordered to comply on pain of expulsion.

nonexistent, due in large measure to the financial penalties that employers could have exacted through the Labor Court, since such stoppages would usually have involved breach of collective agreements.[45]

Substantively, the most difficult jurisdictional problem arose out of the expansion of the Municipal Workers' Union, which was involved in 20 per cent of all awards rendered. This organization caters to all permanent employees of municipal and other local governmental units, and thus comes into conflict with other unions whenever craftsmen secure such employment. Because of the regularity of employment among its members, the level of unemployment insurance and other benefit assessments required by the Municipal Workers' Union is significantly below that of other unions,[46] which gives it a competitive advantage in the quest for membership. Workers in municipal employment have been reluctant to finance the unemployment of private employees.

Growth of the Municipal Workers' Union was resisted strenuously by the standard unions, not least by the Laborers, who feared the rise of a rival general workers' organization in what was obviously an expanding area of employment. The early decisions of the jurisdictional board, almost uniformly against the Municipal Workers, expressed the determination of the dominant crafts to curb its growth. The very first award of the board assigned jurisdiction over stationary engineers in the employ of the municipality of Copenhagen to the craft union on the ground that the workers had benefited from the union's efforts to raise wages in the trade and should therefore bear their share of the burdens.[47] Nonetheless, the Municipal Workers' Union continued to extend its influence, and in 1918 the Federation was obliged to recognize its jurisdiction over all classified employees, though reserving jurisdiction over day or weekly labor to the standard unions.

This by no means terminated the strife, however, since there were disputes over the interpretation of the term "classified," as well as attempts on both sides to cross the line that had been drawn. After years of wrangling, the representative council of the Federation of Labor, in 1930, awarded the Municipal Workers explicit jurisdiction over classified employees working in gas and electric works, hospitals, schools, and other public buildings, but reserving "laborers, craftsmen, stationary engineers employed by municipalities for work of the same character as that

[45] Illum, p. 235; Knud V. Jensen, *Arbejdsretten i Danmark* (Copenhagen, 1946), p. 87.

[46] In 1947, members of the Municipal Workers' Union paid 0.26 kroner a week to the union's unemployment insurance fund and 0.35 kroner in dues, compared with average insurance contributions of 2.56 kroner and dues of 0.94 kroner.

[47] *Graensesager*, Case No. 1 (1911). See also Case No. 6 (1911); Case No. 9 (1912); Case No. 18 (1920).

performed by their colleagues in private employment" to the standard unions.[48] Since this meant a substantial loss of membership for the Municipal Workers' Union, it refused to comply, and was ordered to do so by the 1931 congress on pain of expulsion.[49] However, neither side wanted to precipitate an action which would have led to chaotic competition for members, and after further negotiation, during which concessions were made to the Municipal Workers' Union, agreements were finally reached which resolved the controversy satisfactorily.[50] Subsequent jurisdictional disputes involving the Municipal Workers entailed primarily the interpretation of these agreements. Out of eighteen such cases, the Municipal Workers won eleven, indicating that its newly defined jurisdiction is receiving protection from the Federation.

A minor source of conflict from parallel causes arose from the organization of unions of civil servants, with jurisdiction over the classified employees in the employ of the national government. Ordinarily there is a clear dividing line, but in several instances borderline groups such as probationers were involved, in which the jurisdictional board adopted the rule of affording the individuals concerned the option of choosing between the contesting unions.[51]

Apart from the foregoing types of disputes, which have their origin in the peculiarities of Danish union structure, the jurisdictional board has had to deal with matters familiar to the student of American industrial relations, arising out of changes in machinery,[52] materials,[53] occupations[54] and products and processes.[55] Greatest weight has been accorded to

[48] *Beretning om De Samvirkende Fagforbunds Virksomhed*, 1930, p. 10.

[49] De Samvirkende Fagforbund, *Protokol over Generalforsamling 1931*, pp. 12–14.

[50] *Beretning om De Samvirkende Fagforbunds Virksomhed*, 1935, pp. 28–32.

[51] *Graensesager*, Case No. 90 (1945); Case No. 110 (1947); Case No. 122 (1948).

[52] The replacement of steam by Diesel power brought into conflict the Stationary Engineers and the Metal Workers. *Graensesager*, Case No. 24 (1921). Electrification of the railroads heightened the interest of the Electrical Workers' Union in mechanics who had always belonged to the Metal Workers' Union, and caused the board, which in 1932 (Case No. 41) had rejected the claims of the former, to reverse itself four years later (Case No. 53) on the ground that the rapidity of the technological change and the consequently great new demands for electricians on the railroads was decimating the Electrical Union membership.

[53] Wartime production of stainless steel eating utensils in silver factories, because of the unavailability of silver, resulted in a dispute between the Grinders and the Silver Workers. *Graensesager*, Case No. 75 (1942).

[54] There was a question as to whether watchmakers were entitled to repair instruments at airline repair shops, which had been the exclusive domain of the Metal Workers. *Graensesager*, Case No. 111 (1947).

[55] Among those that have given rise to jurisdictional disputes were book matches (*Bookbinders* v. *Tobacco Workers*, Case No. 20, 1921); automobile bodies (*Carpenters* v. *Carriage Makers*, Case No. 36, 1926); domestic tanning of hides (*Tawers* v. *Hat and Fur Workers*, Case No. 104, 1946).

traditional jurisdiction, where clear parallels existed.[56] On occasion, a doctrine of *laches* was applied against unions with "legal" claims to work which had permitted other crafts to perform the work for considerable periods of time without protest.[57] A union that allowed a related craft to work within its jurisdiction during a period of labor stringency, but refused to accept such craftsmen into membership, was later precluded from objecting to an agreement signed by the rival union,[58] and eventually lost all claim to exclusive jurisdiction.[59] Other criteria have been employed where tradition or custom did not provide suitable standards. Among them have been the desires of the workers concerned,[60] the relative wage levels of the competing unions,[61] and the collective bargaining situation.[62] Where the equities were evenly balanced, the board sometimes apportioned the work between the claimants,[63] or left assignment to the discretion of the employer.[64]

It is interesting to speculate on the contrasting histories of the jurisdictional dispute in the United States and Denmark. On a priori grounds, a greater incidence of jurisdictional strife could have been anticipated for Denmark, due to its minute craft stratification, the higher degree of trade union organization that prevailed, limited opportunities for expansion, and the linking of unemployment insurance to the individual union, which placed an additional economic premium on the maintenance of job opportunities. Yet the problem has been a more stubborn one in the United States, and far more costly to the economy.

[56] For example, ". . . the disputed work is decidedly building carpentry, and the workers employed thereon must transfer to the Carpenters' Union." *Graensesager*, Case No. 39 (1928). See also Case No. 62 (1939); Case No. 99 (1946); Case No. 104 (1946).

[57] *Graensesager*, Case No. 58 (1938); Case No. 59 (1938); Case No. 64 (1940). However, in Case No. 93 (1946), with a minority in dissent, the board assigned work to the Painters despite the fact that "for many years the work has been done by the Laborers."

[58] *Graensesager*, Case No. 74 (1942).

[59] *Graensesager*, Case No. 124 (1948).

[60] *Graensesager*, Case No. 33 (1926); Case No. 110 (1947).

[61] Craft unions have often argued that they were in a better position to improve wage conditions than the industrial or general unions. *Graensesager*, Case No. 12 (1913); Case No. 99 (1946).

[62] The existence of a collective agreement counted heavily in favor of the contracting union. "The fact that the Metal Workers' Union has the collective bargaining agency leads to the Board's inability to sustain the position of the Electrical Workers." *Graensesager*, Case No. 41 (1932). Also, Case No. 33 (1926); Case No. 36 (1926).

[63] *Graensesager*, Case No. 68 (1941); Case No. 69 (1941); Case No. 78 (1942); Case No. 127 (1948).

[64] "The price lists of both unions contain prices for the construction of moldings, so it is assumed that the workers of both trades [carpenters and electricians] can (and should) perform the disputed work, and since custom shows a division of the work between the two crafts, no one craft can be given exclusive jurisdiction, but the work must — as appears to have been done hitherto — be regarded as a sphere of employment which, on the basis of individual circumstances, particularly the determination of the architect, can be performed by either craft or divided between them." *Graensesager*, Case No. 85 (1944).

While there seems to be no simple explanation of the differences observed, a few factors that appear relevant may be cited. For one, the concept of exclusive craft jurisdiction has been much stronger in Denmark, where it was a legacy of the gild system, and survived transplantation to the trade unions without loss of rigor. American trade unions, on the other hand, evolved the principle of exclusive jurisdiction out of their immediate economic environment, and had both to establish and maintain it by force. To the Danes, invasion of jurisdiction was tantamount to transgression of recognized property rights, which could be protected by "law." But in the United States the property right in jurisdiction has been much less well developed, and "extralegal" means, principally the strike, had to be employed in its protection.

Even in Denmark, however, there would probably have been more open conflict had it not been for two things: the jurisdictional board in the Federation, and the Labor Court. Initial agreement to the establishment of a jurisdictional board with broad authority reflects the well settled nature of jurisdictional rights. Once in being, the board undoubtedly made an independent contribution to maintenance of peace by providing a forum for quick adjudication of conflict. The deterrent effect of the Labor Court has already been noted.

Though the greater ideological unity that prevails among workers in Denmark, and in Europe generally, is often overemphasized in its effect upon the economic practices of trade unions, it should not be neglected entirely. Acceptance of socialism by Danish workers by no means eliminated or even dampened internecine strife when important economic interests were involved, but it did contribute to prevention of the gross breaches of labor solidarity sometimes witnessed in American rival union warfare.

CHAPTER V

THE DANISH EMPLOYERS' ASSOCIATION

A REMARKABLE FEATURE of the Danish labor market is the extent of organization that prevails among employers. The central bargaining agent for employers, the Danish Employers' Association, is vested with a degree of authority in representing its members far exceeding that enjoyed by the Federation of Labor. The impact of this circumstance upon the techniques and results of collective bargaining is one of the most interesting aspects of Danish industrial relations. The present chapter will be concerned primarily with the internal organization and the process of policy formation within the Employers' Association, while its role in the labor market will be dealt with in the later chapters on collective bargaining.

EARLY ORGANIZATION

With the abolition of the gild system in 1862, many of the master gilds continued as voluntary organizations with their chief function the administration of accumulated benefit funds. They were also interested in preserving intact the apprenticeship system, motivated in part by the desire to keep their trades from becoming overcrowded and competitive. However, their membership declined, largely as a result of inability to recruit new entrants to their trades; between 1860 and 1870, membership in 22 Copenhagen master gilds fell from 2,620 to 1,597.[1] The voluntary gilds retained the patriarchal attitude of their predecessors, and were not disposed to enter into collective bargaining relations with the journeymen. But the organization of trade unions forced them to modify their views. While the pioneers in modern employer organization were not the gilded trades, but rather the newer industries which faced more militant labor organization, the former demonstrated a greater capacity for organization when trade union pressure in the handicrafts became severe.[2]

[1] Henry Bruun, "Arbejdsgiverforeningen i Danmark i Aarene 1862–1898," *Skrifter Udgivet af Institutet for Historie og Samfundsøkonomi* (Copenhagen, 1931), p. 355.

[2] By 1897, complete organization prevailed among the baking, timbering, painting, and masonry employers in Copenhagen, while the butchers, carpenters, and hatmakers were more than 80 per cent organized. On the other hand, such non-gild trades as book printing (27 per cent), tobacco fabrication (66 per cent), and the metal trades (72 per cent) were less well organized. Nørregaard, p. 361.

The connection between the master gilds and the employer association movement is a matter of some controversy. Bruun writes: "To regard the Copenhagen gilds . . . as the real predecessors of the employer associations is not possible; one may safely say that there was in the former no germ that could of itself develop in the latter direction. Danish employer associations (in the narrow meaning of the term) developed only because trade union attack forced their formation." [3] But this appears to be an unduly restricted view, for there are numerous examples not only of master gild initiative in the establishment of employer organizations, but of the actual transformation of gilds into employer associations. The historians of the Employers' Association have more accurately stated that when "the labor movement forced the employers into similar organization, the old gilds provided an organizational base and experienced a renascence as employer associations." [4] The experience of the Master Carpenters' Gild is instructive. In 1879 a group of its members established a separate organization to bargain with the Carpenters' Union, in deference to the disinclination of other members to involve the Gild in this type of activity. Ten years later, however, the Gild itself became an employer association, the separate body being dissolved.[5]

The early employer movement took on a bifurcated aspect. The newer industrial establishments, particularly in the metal trades, provided the original impetus to organization; the handicraft masters, with the building trades in the lead, constituted the other wing. When the two were united in 1898, the modern Danish employer movement was born. But to a certain extent the original differences in outlook, due in part to real divergences of economic interest and in part to varying traditions, persisted, and constituted at times a serious internal problem for the Employers' Association. As in the case of the labor movement, the gild system cast long shadows upon employer organization in the twentieth century.

The first permanent employer association of importance was the Association of Manufacturers in the Copenhagen Metal Trades, formed in 1885. In the very year of its organization it conducted a five-month lockout aimed at forestalling the organization of workers. At the conclusion of the lockout the trade union was greatly reduced in strength, but the employers were forced explicitly to recognize the right of workers to organize. This episode brought home to employers generally the realization that trade unionism had become a permanent feature of the

[3] Bruun, *Arbejdsgiverforeningen*, p. 371.

[4] Sophus Agerholm og Anders Vigen, *Arbejdsgiverforeningen Gennem 25 Aar* (Copenhagen, 1921), p. 3.

[5] Bruun, *Arbejdsgiverforeningen*, pp. 379–380.

labor market, and while it was not the final effort of employers to stop the expansion of the unions, it hastened the conversion of the organized employer movement from anti-unionism to collective bargaining. Unlike their American counterparts, Danish employer associations were almost from the beginning conciliatory rather than combative organizations.

It may be wondered, in the light of American conditions, why the Danish employer has been willing to delegate to an association so important a part of his managerial prerogatives. Certainly the unit size of industry had something to do with it; the small employer, faced with the rising power of labor, was prone to organize early in self-protection, while some of the larger firms, which could fight back unaided, remained independent until relatively late. The informal type of employer organization represented by price and wage leadership was not a feasible alternative in most industries due to the absence of real leaders, and formal organization proved necessary as a means of maintaining discipline. But of even greater importance was the strength of the collective tradition among Danish employers. Under the gilds, wages had not constituted a competitive cost factor, but were quite uniform among employers. Nor was price cutting looked upon with favor by entrepreneurs, some of whom endeavored to expand the function of employer associations to include price fixing. In short, relegation of the wage-setting function was deemed not too high a price to pay for the establishment of neo-gild monopolies, particularly by employers who were not faced with foreign competition.

The insularity and limited economic horizons of Danish entrepreneurs also contributed to their organizational potential. There were no great fortunes to be made from exploitation of domestic resources or an expanding internal market. Quality rather than price appeal contributed to the growth of many of the leading contemporary firms,[6] and the competitive spirit has never been as pervasive as in the United States. Moreover, the immobility of the Danish population, small community size, and the great stability of social structure have meant that business competitors and social acquaintances are mutual categories, enhancing the likelihood of coöperation.

As in the case of the trade unions, the period in which employer association was perfected and established on a permanent basis was the decade from 1890 to 1900. While the formation of several employer associations from 1885 to 1890 reflected increased employer interest in organization, the principal purpose of those associations was the promo-

[6] The concerns which have established an international reputation for Danish goods — Georg Jensen for silverware, Royal Copenhagen and Bing and Grøndahl for porcelain, Burmeister and Wain for marine engines, the Carlsberg Brewery for beer — are all manufacturers of quality goods.

tion of trade interests rather than collective bargaining or anti-union activity. The chief exception was the association in the Copenhagen metal trades, which had carried on a lockout against the Metal Workers' Union in 1885.

Even after 1890, most of the newly formed employer organizations had predominantly mercantile rather than labor purposes, although there were numerous instances of collective bargaining, particularly in the building trades. It was not until 1895 that the majority of the employer organizations emerged as genuine bargaining agencies, while the older gild aim of restricting competition lost in importance. Organizational talk was in the air during these years, and each strike augmented the feeling that formal arrangements for mutual help were essential. A great deal was written in the Danish press about German employers' associations, which were held up as models for the Danish employers. More than anything else, however, it was the rapid growth of the trade unions that led to more effective employer organization after 1895. Beginning in 1890, efforts had been made to promote inter-industry coöperation on labor matters, paralleling centralization in the labor movement. A milestone was reached with the formation of the Employers' Association of 1896, the work of two energetic men, Niels Andersen, a general building contractor, and Vilhelm Køhler, a mason contractor. This organization had its base in the Copenhagen building trades. Largely because of friction between building and metal trades employers, which had occurred during a strike in 1889, the employers in the metal trades at first refused to join the new organization, but as a consequence of a serious metal labor dispute in 1897, they were induced to join the Employers' Association of 1896.

The organization of the Danish Employers' Association was finally completed in 1898, when the Joint Council for Danish Industry and Handicrafts affiliated with it. The latter was an older organization, with its main strength outside Copenhagen, and it had evolved slowly from a pure trade association into a collective bargaining organization. The principal obstacle to its affiliation with the Copenhagen employers was the fear that the favorable wage differential long enjoyed by provincial employers would be eliminated. The Joint Council was brought in under a compromise regional plan of organization, with each region enjoying considerable autonomy.

What hastened the organization of employers, in the last analysis, was increasing trade union pressure during the prosperous years prior to the turn of the century. Strikes solved all internal organizational problems by creating a mood of compromise. The motives of the employers were mixed: some, particularly in the old gild trades, wanted merely to come to terms with the unions on a plane of equality, while others, largely in the metal trades and the newer industries, still had hopes of weakening the unions.

DETERMINANTS OF GEOGRAPHICAL STRUCTURE

The Danish Employers' Association is a federation of employers' associations, some of which embrace entire industries within the country, while others are confined to geographic segments of industries. In the latter case, the usual pattern is one association for that portion of an industry located in Copenhagen, and another for the rest of the industry (the longshore and local trucking industries are exceptions in being organized on a local market basis). The question considered in this section is: Was the national or regional pattern of employer organization a matter of chance, or can structure be rationalized with reference to particular economic factors?

Table 10 compares average hourly earnings for workers in and outside Copenhagen, by type of employer organization, for major occupations in which the available wage data lend themselves to classification by type of employer organization. Several things are immediately noticeable from the table. (a) In general, the regionally organized trades and industries (with reference to employers) tend to be those of a handicraft character, the lineal descendants of the gild workshop, whereas the nationally organized industries are those in which a factory system arose at the time of the Danish industrial revolution. (b) The markets for which the regionally organized industries produce are narrower than those for which the nationally organized industries produce. (c) The absolute wage levels, both for Copenhagen and the provincial cities outside Copenhagen, are higher for the regionally than for the nationally organized industries.

A wage differential between Copenhagen and the provinces has been noted as far back as wage statistics go. This difference has been attributed to an overrepresentation of the middle-aged, high earning groups in Copenhagen, and of the younger and older age groups in the provinces; and to the greater intensity of labor and the finer quality of the product in Copenhagen. The differential has been less for unskilled than for skilled workers, due to the lesser significance of those factors in the unskilled trades.[7] Differences in the cost of living between Copenhagen and the provinces must also have played a role in the determination of wage differentials.[8]

[7] Knud Dalgaard, "Arbejderklassens Økonomiske Kaar," *Nationaløkonomisk Tidsskrift*, 1926, pp. 175–176.

[8] For a good discussion of differences in living costs around 1900, see Jens Warming, *Danmarks Statistik* (Copenhagen, 1913), pp. 495–505.

TABLE 10

GEOGRAPHIC WAGE DIFFERENTIALS IN DENMARK, THIRD QUARTER 1948, BY TYPE OF EMPLOYER ORGANIZATION (MALE WORKERS)

	(1) Average Hourly Earnings in Copenhagen (*In øre*)	(2) Average Hourly Earnings outside Copenhagen (*In øre*)	(3) Ratio of (2) to (1) (*Per Cent*)
A. *Employers organized nationally*			
Cigar manufacture	314	316	100.6
Brewing	264	254	96.2
Stereotypy	357	335	93.8
Dyeing and bleaching	265	248	93.6
Textiles	292	273	93.5
Lime products, bricks	293	274	93.5
Ceramics	350	325	92.9
Paper products	289	268	92.7
Tanning	354	322	91.0
Sugar products	290	248	85.5
Conserves	326	259	79.4
Gold and silversmiths	427	330	77.3
Average, 12 trades and industries	318	288	90.6
B. *Employers organized regionally*			
Warehousemen	265	246	92.8
Woodworking	274	250	91.2
Printing	355	319	89.9
Tailoring	339	300	88.5
Longshoremen	356	312	87.6
Metal trades	366	318	86.9
Cabinetmakers	348	298	85.6
Plumbers	369	315	85.4
Upholsterers	375	315	84.0
Bakers	305	256	83.9
Electrical installation	346	288	83.2
Painters	368	303	82.3
Bookbinders	362	289	79.8
Shoe manufacturing	372	297	79.8
Building carpenters	388	297	76.5
Masons	464	342	73.7
Building timberers	429	309	72.0
Average, 17 trades and industries	358	297	83.0

Source: *Beretning om Dansk Arbejdsgiverforenings Virksomhed, 1948–1949*, pp. 56–60.

Wage differences for all industry between Copenhagen and the provinces, for the same period as that covered by Table 10 (third quarter, 1948), were as follows:

	(1) *Average hourly earnings in Copenhagen (øre)*	(2) *Average hourly earnings outside Copenhagen (øre)*	(3) *Ratio of (2) to (1) (per cent)*
Unskilled and semiskilled workers	304	272	89.5
Skilled workers	369	313	84.8

Source: *Beretning om Dansk Arbejdsgiverforenings Virksomhed*, 1948–1949, p. 55.

To the extent that there is an identity between unskilled labor and nationally organized employers on the one hand, and skilled labor and regionally organized employers on the other, geographic wage differentials between nationally and regionally organized employers may be attributed to the skill and earnings factor. Comparing the all-industry differentials with the data in Table 10, it appears that the absolute wage level for nationally organized employers *exceeds* that for unskilled and semiskilled workers, while the wage level for regionally organized employers is *less than* that for skilled workers. One would therefore expect to find, assuming that the geographical wage differential is a function of skill and level of earnings, a greater difference in the geographical wage differentials between skilled and unskilled workers (all industry) than between regionally and nationally organized employers. Since the reverse is true (the differences are, respectively, 4.7 and 7.6 per cent), it follows that the wage differentials between the two types of employer organization are not due to the skill and level of earnings alone.[9]

It is possible only to conjecture at the other origins of the relatively greater geographical differentials in the handicrafts compared with the newer factory industry. There has been a constant trend toward geographical wage equality, and it may be that the institutional conservatism of gild organization in the handicrafts prevented the same free play of economic forces as in the non-gild factory industry. The nature of the product market may also be a factor: large wage differentials may prevail between noncompeting local markets, such as those for which most of the handicrafts originally produced, whereas in the case of the na-

[9] The argument may be expressed symbolically as follows: assume that the geographical wage differential G is a unique function of level of earnings (skill) L. G_1, G_2, G_3, and G_4 represent, respectively, the geographical wage differential between skilled workers, unskilled workers, regionally organized employers, and nationally organized employers; L_1, L_2, L_3 and L_4, respectively, the level of earnings for the same groups. Then $G_1 - G_2 = G_3 - G_4$ if $L_1 = L_2$, $L_3 = L_4$. However, if $L_1 > L_3$ and $L_2 < L_4$, $G_1 - G_2 > G_3 - G_4$. In actual fact, however, $G_1 - G_2 < G_3 - G_4$; therefore, $G \neq f(L)$.

tional market, to which factory industry catered, large wage differentials would not be likely to persist in a country the size of Denmark.

Given the existence of geographical wage differentials, however, the employers in the low wage areas have a vested interest in their retention, particularly when local market monopoly barriers begin to crumble. The firms in those areas are enabled, with the competitive advantage afforded by lower wages, to hold their own markets against more efficient outsiders, and if they are the relatively efficient producers, to capture new markets.

If organization of employers is viewed as a reaction to trade union organization, the national employer association would be a logical corollary of the national trade union. However, national employer organization, with the entire industry as the collective bargaining unit, tends to produce geographical wage equality. Therefore, we may expect that where there are sizable geographic wage differentials, the low wage employers will forego the bargaining strength vis-à-vis their workers attendant upon national organization, and bargain in smaller units, to protect their wage advantage. Moreover, to the extent that local product market monopolies continue to exist, it is the local rather than the national wage level that is of importance to the employers concerned, and the unit of employer organization (and of collective bargaining) is likely thereby to be determined.

In sum, differences in geographical wage differentials in Denmark between the older handicrafts and the newer factory industry, in part a function of the varying skill and earnings composition of the two groups and in part resulting from historical factors, have led to differences in the geographical scope of employer organization. The pattern of organization has in turn influenced the differential, reinforcing differences where they were large and strengthening the equalization tendencies where they were small.[10]

[10] There are some exceptions to this theory, based upon special circumstances, but not as many as a glance at Table 10 might seem to indicate. All of the trades and industries listed under part A produce predominantly for a national market, and it is interesting to note that the only trade in this group that emerged from a gild trade, the gold and silversmiths, had the largest differential in the group. The six building trades listed in part B, all with gild antecedents, cater primarily to local markets, as do the bakers, upholsterers, cabinetmakers, tailors (custom), and printers (newspaper, but not book). Of the six remaining trades in part B, two, warehousemen and longshoremen, have been subject to special equalization pressures due to their organization by the Laborers' Union; while the woodworkers and shoemakers, who produce for a national market, are to a large extent the successors of gild trades, with inherited wage structures. The metal trades in reality belong with the nationally organized employers, for although they are formally organized along regional lines, they are united in the powerful Metal Trades Employers' Association, which bargains for the national metal trades as a single unit. The bookbinders, too, have a single collective agreement for the entire country.

This is not to say, however, that employer organization has arrested the basic trend toward geographical wage equality. Trade union wage policies, provincial labor shortages, and the breakdown of market barriers have counteracted the efforts of provincial employer associations to maintain their wage advantage, as the following data for the high differential building trades indicated:[11]

Percentage of Provincial to Copenhagen Hourly Earnings

	1914	*Third quarter 1948*
Plumbers	74.2	85.4
Painters	71.5	82.3
Building carpenters	67.9	76.5
Masons	66.8	73.7
Building timberers	62.3	72.0

Sources: 1914, *Beretning om Dansk Arbejdsgiverforenings Virksomhed 1921–1922*, p. 70; 1948, Table 10.

ORGANIZATION OF THE EMPLOYERS' ASSOCIATION

The Danish Employers' Association, the parent organization, is a federation of industrial and regional employer associations, and individual firms not eligible for membership in any existing employer association. On July 1, 1950, there were 251 employer association and 314 individual firm affiliates. Table 11, which compares the membership

TABLE 11

MEMBERSHIP IN THE SCANDINAVIAN EMPLOYER ASSOCIATIONS, 1945 AND 1946

	Number of Member Associations	Number of Member Establishments	Number of Workers Employed by Members
Denmark (1945)	246	19,658	222,000
Norway (1946)	16	4,400	160,000
Sweden (1945)	41	7,700	470,000

Sources: Denmark: Danmarks Statistik, *Statistisk Aarbog*, 1946; Norway: Walter Galenson, *Labor in Norway;* Sweden: Svenska Arbetsgivareförening, *A Survey of Social and Labor Conditions in Sweden*, October 1945.

That geographic wage equalization has not been due entirely to national collective bargaining, but preceded the full development of industry-wide bargaining, is indicated by the existence of substantial equalities in the national market industries when the collective bargaining system was still in its infancy. In 1914, the first year for which comprehensive statistics are available, the wage difference between Copenhagen and the provinces was only 6.4 per cent for textile workers, 9.7 per cent for cigar makers, 10.7 per cent for workers in margarine producing plants, and 17.8 per cent in papermaking. At the same time, there was a difference of about 33 per cent in the building trades. *Beretning om Dansk Arbejdsgiverforenings Virksomhed, 1921–1922*, pp. 72–73.

[11] It is interesting to note that the ranking of the crafts in respect to their geographical differentials remained unchanged from 1914 to 1948.

structure of the Scandinavian employer associations, would appear to indicate a lesser degree of centralization in the Danish association than in its Norwegian and Swedish counterparts. This is not the case, however, for the Danish Employers' Association is probably the most centralized of the three, in terms of the power wielded by the central organization over its affiliates.

The structural dispersion of the Danish Employers' Association is overcome to a certain extent by the grouping of individual associations into large subassociations for collective bargaining and administrative purposes. The most important of the subassociations is the Metal Trades Association, founded in 1902, which bargains for 29 separate employer associations and a number of individual establishments. The members of the Metal Trades Association pay out about 30 per cent of the total wage bill of the Employers' Association.

In 1907, a number of employer associations in factory industries producing primarily for a national market, and having as a common bond collective relationships with the Laborers' Union, endeavored to emulate the bargaining centralization achieved by the metal trades. However, the organization which they established, the Industrial Trades Association, which now includes about 25 separate associations, never developed into a single bargaining unit because of the diversity of the interests represented. Its activities have largely been confined to the provision of technical assistance during collective bargaining, to the representation of its affiliates in arbitrations under collective agreements, and to the performance of ministerial functions.

The Textile Industry Employers' Association provides the best example of a true industrial association. It negotiates a basic collective agreement for the entire industry with the Textile Workers' Union, one of the few industrial unions in the country. Although average earnings tend to be uniform throughout the industry, piece rates are negotiated factory by factory, the association policing the wage structure to prevent individual firms from getting out of line.

There are other subassociations, but they are of lesser importance from the point of view of collective bargaining. Among them may be mentioned the Clothing Industry Association, the Graphic Trades Association, the Association of Harbor and Wholesalers' Associations (which unites about 65 local associations), the Ceramics Industry Association, and the Association of Truckers in Copenhagen and Vicinity. The Copenhagen building crafts took the initiative in 1910 in the formation of a Handicraft Trades Association, which it was hoped would parallel the Metal Trades Association. However, unlike the situation in the metal trades, where shipbuilding was the predominant industry and the unit of enterprise large, the diversity of conditions prevailing in the several trades among numerous small contractors proved too great an obstacle to the evolution of joint bargaining, and the projected handicraft organization lapsed.[12]

When the Employers' Association had been in existence for two decades, the distrust and antipathy between Copenhagen and provincial employers that had dictated the original geographic division diminished sufficiently to permit reorganization of the Association's scheme of representation along functional lines. There are now three broad departments: the handicrafts, industry, and commerce (a fourth, agriculture, was dropped when the Employers' Association failed to make any appreciable headway among agricultural employers).[13] Each department is assured of a minimum voice in the representative bodies of the Employers' Association.

The highest constitutional body in the Employers' Association is a general assembly of 600 members; of these, 514 are elected by affiliated associations or individual firms in proportion to dues payments, while the remaining 86 are selected by the three functional departments in proportion to the number of firms within each one. In providing for the election of 14 per cent of the delegates on the basis of the number of firms, a concession was made to the smaller employers, but nevertheless the large industrial employers, by virtue of their dues payments, dominate the general assembly.[14] However, there is a better balance in the central committee, a 54-member body which meets three or four times a year and exerts a greater policy influence than the large, unwieldy general assembly. Each department elects members to the central committee in proportion to its representation in the general assembly, with the proviso that no department may have more than 27 members. In 1948 the central committee included 26 representatives of the industrial department, 20

[12] Agerholm og Vigen, p. 264.

[13] There was a movement at one time to build these functional groups into full-fledged administrative units. The proponents of this change were motivated chiefly by the desire to augment solidarity among the handicrafts, since there had been repeated complaints that factory industry, through the Metal Trades and Industrial Trades Associations, were dominating the Employers' Association. However, the movement failed because handicraft employers were more fearful of one another than of the industrialists. The difficulties were summarized as follows: "The fact is that in the handicrafts the provinces are on one side and Copenhagen on the other, and since the two could not agree, nothing could come out of the plan . . . Their interests differ. First and foremost there is a tradition that Copenhagen is one thing and the provinces another. Moreover, Copenhagen is on piece work and the provinces have a time rate system that they want to continue." See *Beretning om Dansk Arbejdsgiverforenings Virksomhed 1927–1928*, pp. 117–128; *idem, 1928–1929*, pp. 76–79, 121–131.

[14] There have been many changes in the scheme of representation over the years, usually in response to the complaint of small employers that they had no effective representation. See Agerholm og Vigen, pp. 151, 153, 359; Anders Vigen, Sophus Agerholm, og Carl Plum, *Arbejdsgiverforeningen Gennem 50 Aar* (Copenhagen, 1946), pp. 315–317.

of the handicraft department, and 8 of the commercial department, the latter two thus being overrepresented in proportion to employment and financial contributions to the Association, but underrepresented on the basis of the numbers of member firms.

The central committee elects from among its members an executive committee of fifteen, which is actually the effective policy-making instance. Although there is no predetermined representation by department, custom dictates that every major interest group be given representation in the executive committee. The committee holds regularly scheduled meetings biweekly, and can act authoritatively in view of the fact that its members are the executives of the larger subassociations.

The influence exerted by the secretariat of the Employers' Association, headed by a chairman and vice-chairman elected by the executive committee, is not to be minimized. Although major decisions are made ultimately by the elected representatives, a large share of the day-to-day load in collective bargaining, with regard to conflicts of both rights and interests, is borne by the permanent officials, who, through their specialized knowledge of bargaining techniques, inevitably play a major role in policy formation. The importance of this concomitant of employer bargaining organization cannot be overemphasized; the most impressive aspect of the employer bargaining apparatus is the breadth of knowledge possessed by the professional employer representatives with respect to labor law, the strategy of bargaining, the personalities on the union side of the bargaining table, the internal politics of trade unions as they bear upon union policy formation and industrial wage structure. Permanent staff members of the Employers' Association of necessity develop a different attitude toward trade union leaders with whom they have almost daily contact than do the individual employers they represent. The chief work of the secretariat is the amicable adjustment of labor disputes; it is the executive committee and the higher representative bodies that are called upon to conduct industrial warfare.

The Employers' Association has a large statistical department for the collection and processing of wage data, which are then published as the official government statistics. This provides an interesting example of the manner in which the Employers' Association (and the Federation of Labor as well) has been evolving toward the status of a quasi-public institution.

Each member firm pays to the Employers' Association annual dues equal to 0.5 per cent of the amount it paid out in wages during the previous calendar year, while initiation fees are fixed at one per cent of the same base. The money thus collected is allocated by the executive committee among the following funds:

(1) The administrative fund, which is used to meet the administrative expenses of the Association. The expenses of affiliated associations must be covered by assessments levied separately by each.

(2) The "disposition" fund, which can be used for purposes "connected with protection of the special interests of employers."

(3) The reserve fund, out of which work stoppage benefits are paid.[15]

Employer Association members employed 285,000 workers in 1949, compared with concurrent trade union membership of 636,000. This, however, does not reflect a true measure of the relative organizational strength of the two organizations. While few employers in agriculture and commerce are associated with the Employers' Association, the trade unions have substantial memberships in those fields. Moreover, labor organization in the municipalities, railways, postal and communications service, and civil service finds no counterpart among employers.[16] In manufacturing, while there are many unaffiliated employers, those affiliated with the Employers' Association are generally the larger ones; in 1944, the affiliated establishments averaged 13 workers each compared with 3.1 workers for manufacturing generally.[17] In any event, the influence exercised by the Employers' Association on the Danish labor market is far in excess of its formal organizational strength.

BARGAINING POLICY FORMATION

The scope of Employer Association authority may be judged from the constitutional provision[18] which forbids affiliates from entering into collective agreements, without permission of the Association's executive committee, on the following subjects:

(1) reduction of working time,
(2) general wage increases,
(3) new minimum wages,
(4) paid or unpaid vacations in excess of those stipulated by law,
(5) accident or sickness compensation in excess of legal requirements,
(6) union shop provisions,
(7) apprenticeship restrictions,
(8) union hiring halls, and
(9) provisions that may interfere with participation in a lockout declared by the Employers' Association.

[15] The Employers' Association does not make public the magnitude of its financial resources. There is no doubt, however, that it is a wealthy organization.

[16] The number of organized workers in these categories may be estimated roughly at a minimum of 115,000, reducing the trade union organizational magnitude comparable with Employer Association organization to roughly 500,000.

[17] K. Vedel-Petersen, *Danmarks Statistik* (Copenhagen, 1946), p. 444.

[18] *Love for Dansk Arbejdsgiverforening*, Section 20.

Contract changes covering any of the enumerated points, proposed either by employers or trade unions, must be submitted to the Employers' Association before bargaining with a union may ensue, and the Association's express approval obtained before they are finally incorporated into new agreements. Where disputes over new contract terms or over the interpretation of existing agreements cannot be resolved directly between the parties involved, representatives of the Employers' Association conduct further negotiations with higher instances on the union side.

The question crucial to an understanding of the Employers' Association and its role in collective bargaining is the extent to which the broad constitutional authority vested in the Association actually results in centrally determined employer wage policy. While the question cannot be answered in absolute terms, it seems clear that there has been a consistent trend in this direction, resulting in a much greater degree of central policy formation than that which prevails in the Federation of Labor. In 1931, for the first time, the Employers' Association made mandatory upon all its affiliates a uniform bargaining policy,[19] and although this practice has not always been effected explicitly in subsequent years, it is generally believed that the Association's policy "recommendations" [20] are followed more or less literally by its affiliates.[21]

While the formulation and execution of collective bargaining policy constitute the principal functions of the Employers' Association, it is also engaged in subsidiary activities relating to industrial relations. It is the spokesman for employer interests before government agencies; it selects the employer members of the Labor Court. Internally, the Association maintains an arbitration commission to deal with disputes between member firms or associations. The jurisdiction of the commission,

[19] Vigen, Agerholm, og Plum, p. 208.

[20] A typical "recommendation," made in 1947, read in part as follows: "When employers, in the near future, prepare proposals for changes in existing agreements, we do not believe that . . . we can advise demands for a general wage reduction. On the other hand, there can be no doubt that during the war 'camels' have crept into agreements, so that both in the case of fixed price schedules and piece rates there are provisions that yield unreasonably high earnings. Such provisions provide an opportunity for employers to demand contract changes, and we therefore urge you to review your agreements and prepare your demands as soon as possible." *Beretning om Dansk Arbejdsgiverforenings Virksomhed 1947–1948*, p. 16.

[21] The Federation of Labor has complained that this practice impedes collective bargaining: "Recognizing that the results obtained in one trade would sooner or later spread to others, the Employers' Association sought at an early date to take wage developments in hand in order as far as possible to forestall concessions by affiliated organizations or member firms that could affect other trades . . . the Federation of Labor has on numerous occasions pointed out that this jeopardizes labor peace. Such objections have never been given consideration, despite the fact that limitations upon the freedom of affiliated employer associations constitute a serious obstacle to amicable adjustment of differences within the trade, without intervention of the central organizations." *Under Samvirkets Flag*, pp. 156–158.

which has not been very active, is coterminous with that of the Employers' Association — that is, it is confined to employment relationships and does not extend to commercial disputes.

SANCTIONS AGAINST TRADE UNIONS

Work stoppages resulting from the breakdown of collective bargaining may take the form of either strikes or lockouts, depending upon which party is seeking contract changes, which in turn largely depends upon the phase of the business cycle. It is apparent from a review of Danish labor history that the Employers' Association has followed an aggressive policy in promoting what it deemed to be the legitimate interests of its constituents.[22]

Lockout procedure is defined precisely by the constitution of the Employers' Association. If an affiliated organization by a three-fourths vote of its general assembly, or an individual enterprise, desires to effectuate a lockout, the executive committee of the Employers' Association is authorized to approve such action if it is unanimous. Otherwise, the central committee may approve the action by a three-fourths vote. If both of these bodies deny permission to lockout, approval may be sought of an extraordinary general assembly. The central committee may, on its own initiative, order employers to lock out their workers if the total number of workers involved does not exceed 10 per cent of the number employed by members of the Association; in excess of that number, a three-fourths majority of the general assembly is required. The customary procedure, however, is for an extraordinary general assembly called to consider a contemplated lockout to delegate its authority to the central committee, which then makes the ultimate decision.

Every member employer who is ordered to do so must lock his workers out, whether or not he is immediately involved in a dispute with them. A sympathetic lockout is lawful in Denmark even in the presence of a valid collective agreement, and no action for breach of contract may be brought against an employer who obeys a properly authorized instruction from the Employers' Association. The central committee may exempt individual employers from the lockout, but it is ordinarily reluctant to do so unless great inconvenience to the general public may result.[23]

[22] In its own accounts of labor relations history, the Employers' Association referred to the general work stoppages of 1899, 1921 and 1936 as lockouts. Agerholm og Vigen, pp. 40, 382; Vigen, Agerholm, og Plum, p. 57. Many other disputes can be classified as lockouts, both technically and realistically.

[23] During the great 1925 work stoppage there were 145 requests for "dispensations" from the lockout order, 86 of which were granted and 59 denied. However, most of those granted were for shops employing a very small number of workers. A more liberal policy was adopted in some cities in South Jutland, where the employers were poorly organized, in order not to

Employers who are not involved in the work stoppage are under the duty not to act against the interests of those affected "by undertaking to perform work, the delivery of materials, transportation, etc., which had been begun or contracted for by firms involved in the work stoppage, or to take over deliveries or performance of any character which the latter might have undertaken before the inception of the stoppage." [24] Violation of this obligation is a serious breach of discipline, and may subject an offender to a fine not exceeding 100,000 kroner and expulsion.[25] While there have not been many instances of breach of discipline, the few that occurred were met with prompt and severe punishment by the Employers' Association.

A problem faced by the Employers' Association, particularly in its earlier years, was the danger that unaffiliated employers might attempt to win over the customers of member employers shut down because of a strike or lockout.[26] As a counter measure, member employers may be ordered to break off all commercial relations with "lockout breakers" during and even subsequent to the stoppage of work. In 1922, for example, the Association successfully opposed the election to the board of directors of a bank a nonmember factory manager who had doubled his output during a work stoppage by putting on an extra shift, by threatening to boycott the bank if he were elected. The chairman of the Association stated publicly that "among the members of the Employers' Association it would be regarded as a slap in the face if so uncollegial a person were made a member of the board of the Farmers' Bank, and it is quite clear that in consequence many would withhold their patronage from the bank." [27]

Affiliated employers may not escape the obligations of membership by resigning from the Association during a labor dispute, for the constitution provides that there may be no resignations during a labor dispute,

---

jeopardize the competitive position of the affiliated employers. See *Referat af Dansk Arbejdsgiverforenings Generalforsamlinger, 1924–1925*, p. 255. A good discussion of the "dispensation" problem is to be found in *Arbejdsgiverforenings Haandbog, 1911*, pp. 143–151.

[24] *Love for Dansk Arbejdsgiverforening*, Par. 26.

[25] For example, during the work stoppage of 1925 a member firm which had a contract to do nickel plating for the Ford Motor Co. (a nonmember), after having locked out its workers, leased its plant to Ford, which continued to operate with substantially the same work force. The member firm was fined 5,000 kroner, twice the amount it received for the lease of its property. *Referat af Dansk Arbejdsgiverforenings Generalforsamlinger, 1924–1925*, pp. 255–258.

[26] "Time and again one witnesses unaffiliated employers, during work stoppages, seeking to usurp the work of members, hiring striking or locked out workers, etc. With respect to such employers, who lack the simplest understanding of the significance of organization, there is no need to mince matters; they have taken a stand, and elected not only to remain *outside*, but to stand *against* the Employers' Association." *Arbejdsgiverforenings Haandbog, 1914*, p. 23.

[27] *Beretning om Dansk Arbejdsgiverforenings Virksomhed, 1922–1923*, p. 57.

or for a period of two years after an employer has received financial assistance from the Association. In ordinary circumstances, a firm may withdraw as of July 1 of any year, provided it has given six months' notice of its intent.

WORK STOPPAGE BENEFITS

The Employers' Association has developed a comprehensive system of benefits as a positive means of assuring member solidarity. No regular system was in effect during the first decade of its existence, although occasional grants were made to hard-pressed members. In 1911, motivated by the experience of the Swedish Employers' Association, a committee was appointed to look into alternative schemes.

The proponents of regular benefits were aware that payments could not be expected to cover the entire economic loss which an employer might suffer during a stoppage of work. Benefits were conceived rather as a means of providing liquid funds for meeting continuing overhead costs. The method of calculating the incidence of such costs proved a matter of some controversy; the ideal method would have been to determine separately for each employer the amount of continuing expenses, and to reimburse him for a certain percentage. However, this was administratively impossible, and it was decided instead that wages paid by an employer in the corresponding quarter of the previous year should be used as an arbitrary index of loss. A proposal to follow the Swedish model, whereby employers who were subject to relatively severe strike loss could secure higher benefits by paying higher dues was rejected in order to make the initial scheme as simple as possible.[28]

More controversial was the question of the locus of the strike insurance funds. By 1911, the Employers' Association had accumulated a general purpose fund of one million kroner, while some of the trade associations had sizable funds of their own. The committee proposed the transfer of a large portion of the individual funds to the central fund, a proposal which was resisted strenuously by the trades with the larger funds, notably such crafts as the painters and masons. In addition to the desire to retain their own money, the handicraft employers were fearful that a single central fund would place too much power in the Employers' Association, and subject them to the domination of the larger industrial employers. They also argued on the basis of experience that the lion's share of benefits would go to industrial employers.

Despite the opposition of the handicrafts, the committee proposal was adopted and became effective January 1, 1913. But dissatisfaction with

[28] *Arbejdsgiverforeningens Haandbog, 1912*, pp. 45-46.

it continued among the original opponents, and in 1922, after severe drains on the central fund necessitated increased dues payments, the centralized system was replaced by one more to the liking of the craftsmen. Under the new scheme, which is still in effect, every affiliated association is required to maintain a fund reserved exclusively for the payment of work stoppage benefits. The annual contribution to each fund must be at least 0.25 per cent of total wages paid out by the membership of the affiliated association during the previous calendar year.[29] When the amount in a fund exceeds 2.5 per cent of the average annual wage bill of the three previous calendar years, further contributions may be suspended until the fund again falls below the 2.5 per cent level. Affiliated associations may pool their funds, a practice followed by the Metal Trades and Industrial Trades Associations.

Benefit payments vary from fund to fund in respect to amount and duration. The amount is generally fixed at a percentage of the employer's wage bill, with a week's waiting period not uncommon. No benefits may be dispensed, without permission of the Employers' Association, if a fund has not reached a minimum of 0.5 per cent of the previous year's wage bill.

Contrary to what might have been expected, the decentralization of work stoppage funds did not seriously impair the authority of the Employers' Association. This may be attributed to two principal causes:

1. Some degree of centralization has been retained in the provision that after a work stoppage has been in effect for 24 working days, the central committee of the Employers' Association, at the request of an affiliate, may provide further financial assistance which is normally equal to one-quarter the average daily wages paid out in the previous calendar year. Moreover, in the event of a lockout decreed on the initiative of the central committee of the Employers' Association, Association benefit payments start immediately. These benefits are drawn from the Reserve Fund, built up out of regular dues to an amount determined annually by the central committee. To ensure its adequacy, no benefits may be paid from it until it has reached a minimum of 2 per cent of the Association's total wage bill in the previous calendar year. If necessary, the general assembly of the Association, by a majority of three-quarters, may levy extra assessments upon members not affected by a current work stop-

[29] In Sweden, contributions are based upon the numbers of employed workers rather than upon the wage bill, thus softening the downward cyclical impact upon the amounts paid in. It was the necessity of raising the rate of contribution in Denmark, caused in part by the money wage declines in 1921 and 1922, that led to the final and successful revolt of the handicrafts. In times of rising wages and prices, however, the Danish system maintains the real value of contributions without requiring rate adjustment, whereas the Swedish system entails eventual rate increases to prevent reductions in real income.

page. Statistics are lacking on the relative importance of the central and individual strike funds in financing work stoppage benefits, but the relatively long duration of a number of major work stoppages in the last few decades implies considerable central fund participation.

2. Work stoppage benefits do not have the same importance for employers as for workers, so that decentralization of the funds in the Employers' Association does not have the same organizational significance as in the Federation of Labor. Benefits at the level provided in the Danish scheme are not likely to be of critical importance to employers in determining labor dispute strategy. Therefore the specific statutory powers of the Employers' Association with respect to collective bargaining, combined with custom and tradition, are sufficient to offset any tendencies on the part of affiliates with large treasuries to follow independent policies. The loss of the political and moral assistance entailed by defiance of the Employers' Association is a more serious matter than the pecuniary considerations.

Strike fund decentralization met, in part at least, the desire of the handicrafts to be relieved of the obligation of financing work stoppages in the large industrial establishments. Since payments to the individual strike funds may cease when a minimum level has been reached, the level being a function of stoppage experience, there is a closer relation of contributions to benefits than was true under the original scheme. The central assistance provides a sort of reinsurance, the plan thus representing an interesting compromise between an equitable relation of cost to benefit on the one hand and financial security on the other.

"ANNOTATION 2"

A resolution adopted by the Employers' Association and known as "Annotation 2" sets forth the mutual obligations of members in the following terms: "It is an obligation of honor for each member of the Employers' Association, in order to further cooperation within the Association, to give members preference in all commercial relations, in the performance of work and in the purchase of materials and other goods."

When the Employers' Association was founded, a resolution substantially similar to the one currently in effect was adopted. However, some groups of members, particularly those in the building trades, wanted to make preference a legal as well as a moral obligation. In 1907, therefore, Annotation 2 was amplified and divided into two parts, the first applying generally and the second only to the Copenhagen building trades. The general provisions read:

It shall be deemed an uncollegial act

1. To fail to observe Annotation 2. Note: The obligation to give preference

to members in commercial relations, work or purchases presupposes that preference does not involve significant additional costs than would be entailed in dealing with a non-member, all other things being equal with respect to quality and the ability of the member firm to deliver . . .[30]

This obligation found stronger expression in the special rules governing the Copenhagen building trades:

1. No member of the Employers' Association, in the capacity of a general contractor or in any other capacity, may accept competitive bids from non-members, unless the craft concerned is not organized under the Employers' Association.

2. Every member, before finally accepting a job on which he is not the general contractor, shall undertake to investigate with which employers he will be obliged to work.

3. If, during the performance of a job, a non-member is assigned to some work, each member shall endeavor, with the assistance of the Employers' Association, to be released from his obligations. This is based upon the assumption that the new contractor in question will not or cannot be accepted into membership.[31]

This resolution constituted a clear expression of the desire of the former gild groups within the Employers' Association to restore the old trade monopolies. The industrial employers were dubious of the wisdom of this policy, but they acceded to it in the limited area in which it was applicable. It soon became apparent, however, that extension of Association functions into the sphere of trade and price regulation might jeopardize its primary collective bargaining activities, and a committee was established in 1913 to review the experience under the 1907 resolution. The committee came to the following conclusions:

1. Even within the building trades there was dissatisfaction with the operation of the resolution. Some contractors felt that it had the effect of maintaining prices at an uneconomically high level and reduced the amount of work undertaken. The greatest difficulty was experienced with the clause requiring contractors to withdraw from jobs already under way.

2. Minimum price regulation based upon the resolution rendered difficult the organization of unaffiliated firms.

3. The committee distinguished, for purposes of price regulation, between two major types of enterprise: those producing goods, and those engaged in the sale of services. With respect to members in the first category, it was deemed unnecessary to forbid affiliates to require as a condition of membership adherence to a fixed price schedule, on the

[30] Agerholm og Vigen, p. 155.
[31] Agerholm og Vigen, p. 156.

theory that competition from unaffiliated employers and from foreign trade would prevent the maintenance of artificially high prices. But for the firms selling services, and the building trades in particular, the danger of monopoly pricing was considered sufficiently acute to warrant the outlawing of compulsory price fixing.

4. It was suggested that the *moral* obligation to prefer members in business be extended to consumer relationships as well.[32]

Although there was an indicated majority against compulsory price regulation at the 1913 session of the general assembly, it was agreed to hold the question over for another year because of the sharp differences that prevailed. In 1914, the previous resolution was replaced by one in which the crucial section read as follows:

> Members should refuse to accept competitive bids from non-members, unless particular business or technical conditions, time of delivery, etc., render it necessary or natural to accept bids from non-members.
>
> In general, where there are bids both from members and non-members, members should be given preference, other things being equal . . .[33]

The revised resolution provided a slender reed for the support of price regulation, which declined in importance thereafter. When a decade later a few crafts again proposed that adherence to Annotation 2 be made compulsory, the chairman of the Employers' Association remarked:

> Obligatory adherence to Annotation 2 would signify that the Employers' Association could be regarded with justification as a great monopoly which might wield a certain amount of power but in return would lose its authority (to represent employers) . . . In my opinion the Danish economy cannot be maintained on a free basis without legislative control in the absence of free competition.[34]

Precisely what Annotation 2 has meant, in its voluntary form, is difficult to assess. Certainly some price fixing has been accomplished under its aegis. But this has probably been confined to trades in which there would have been price fixing in any event. A few trades have used the resolution as an organizing device. Window cleaning employers have with some success induced Association members to give them preference, and thus forced nonmembers to join. The upholsterers have promoted product differentiation on the basis of a label, and increased their membership substantially thereby.

It is the general consensus that the present economic significance of

[32] The text of the committee report may be found in *Arbejdsgiverforeningens Haandbog 1913*, pp. 95–110.

[33] *Arbejdsgiverforeningens Haandbog, 1914*, p. 131.

[34] *Beretning om Dansk Arbejdsgiverforenings Virksomhed, 1922–1923*, p. 77.

Annotation 2 is not great. In part, the growth of the Employers' Association has removed the rationale for its enforcement. But perhaps the decisive factor was a growing realization within the Employers' Association that an admixture of two essentially different economic functions was not compatible with the satisfactory performance of either. The continuance of price regulation would have provided the trade unions, which already had socialist goals, with additional ammunition for government regulation and ownership of business, and rendered the Employers' Association vulnerable to political attack. The Danish experience makes it clear that associations of employers formed for collective bargaining purposes can function most effectively if they refrain from auxiliary price regulation.[35]

UNAFFILIATED EMPLOYERS

The "free rider" among employers is the subject of obloquy much as is his counterpart among the workers. "Unaffiliated employers profit from the fact that they live in a country with an Employers' Association which regulates and controls relations with workers, particularly regarding wages, and the unaffiliated employers shabbily take advantage of this activity by getting it free." [36] This animosity does not arise solely from the fact that nonmembers do not bear an equitable share of the cost of administering the collective bargaining system. Of greater importance is the constant threat to the combative potential of the Employers' Association and the viability of the organized wage level.

The trade unions have not been reluctant to profit by division in the ranks of employers. Agreements were often concluded with unaffiliated employers providing for their continued operation during strikes or lockouts, with the understanding that wage provisions eventually concluded with the Employers' Association would be applied to them with retroactive effect.[37] Independents have been encouraged to expand output during labor disputes both as a means of providing income to workers and to threaten the markets of the affiliated employers.

Until recently, it was the low wage competition of unaffiliated employers that was the principal concern of the Employers' Association. There was constant complaint in the building trades, for example, that unaffiliated employers used their status as an advertisement to attract business. Some unaffiliated employers were also nonunion, but in many instances they employed union labor, the trade unions being forced by

[35] Many of the affiliated employer associations continue to perform functions which are essentially mercantile in character. The Textile Employers' Association, for example, has devoted much of its energies to the problems of textile supply and rationing since 1940.

[36] *Arbejdsgiverforeningens Haandbog, 1914*, p. 98.

[37] *Ibid.*, pp. 84–85.

economic necessity to accept lower wage scales. In 1933, at the depth of the depression, the Employers' Association charged that the wage level of unaffiliated employers lay 40 to 60 per cent below that of its members.[38]

Spurred by the magnitude of this differential, the Employers' Association demanded that the Federation of Labor assist it in combating "unfair" wage competition. The following agreement was reached in 1934:

> 1. There shall be established for each trade, upon demand, a committee consisting of three representatives of each of the two central organizations, with a chairman appointed by the Labor Court. The purpose of the committee is to determine to what extent unfair wage competition prevails . . . Where such competition is found to exist, the committee shall seek to take steps to prevent undermining of the contractual wage level . . .
>
> 2. The Federation of Labor pledges itself and its members not to work for or conclude agreements with non-members of the Employers' Association for less wages or poorer labor conditions than those contained in collective agreements between the Employers' Association and its affiliates on the one hand and the Federation of Labor and its affiliates on the other.[39]

This agreement, however, was never of great practical importance. The improvement in business conditions served to reduce the wage advantage of unaffiliated employers; and the Employers' Association was by no means interested in an absolute equality of wage levels, which might create pressure on the general level of wages and promote unionization of unorganized employers. Since independents tended to be the smaller, marginal firms, a wage difference was not dangerous, provided it did not become too large. The trade unions plaintively noted the lack of employer interest in enforcing the agreement.[40]

From 1945 to 1947 the problem took a novel turn. Owing to the high level of employment, many unaffiliated employers offered higher than the contractual wage level. To curb the breach of agreements, some employer associations ordered their members to refrain from pirating workers from fellow members, and the Employers' Association established a commission to hear complaints of such practices. The trade unions insisted upon the right of their members to accept above-contract wages from unaffiliated employers, but the matter was rendered academic by the return of a normal labor market in 1948.

[38] Vigen, Agerholm, og Plum, p. 222.

[39] *Beretning om Dansk Arbejdsgiverforenings Virksomhed, 1933–1934*, pp. 42–43.

[40] "The agreement was in accord with labor's desires, and there was reason to expect that employers and workers would fight unfair competition hand in hand as good friends. This did not happen, for when it came to the test, the Employers' Association flatly refused to participate." Axel Olsen, p. 269.

INTERNAL POLICY DIFFERENCES

Of the many policy differences that have arisen within the Employers' Association during the fifty years of its existence, one deserves special note: the conflict over wage policy between large-scale factory industry, producing primarily for export, and the handicrafts, producing for the domestic market. The economic basis of the conflict is clear. Some years ago the historians of the organized employer movement wrote:

> Much is said in the press about the *war party* within the Employers' Association, and it is assumed that this party has its stronghold in large-scale industry and its leader in Alexander Foss. This much is true, that time and again, Foss, for economic reasons, advised unconditional opposition to increases in the wage level which would place us in an unfavorable competitive position compared with high-tariff neighboring countries with lower wages.[41]

The wage policy of the Employers' Association has represented a compromise between the views of the two major groups. During the years 1921 to 1926, when a severe price deflation accompanied upward valuation of the Danish crown, both complained of the line adopted by the Association: the export trades charged that the wage cuts demanded were not sufficiently drastic,[42] the domestic trades that the cost of wage reductions, in terms of industrial peace, was too great.[43] But these differences were in degree only, and not in basic wage attitudes. While producers for the domestic market had more leeway than exporters, the elasticity of demand for most manufactured goods provided a strong incentive to keep wages down. Even in the building trades, the "peace at any price" attitude was tempered by the presence of unaffiliated and unorganized contractors.

[41] Agerholm og Vigen, pp. 218–220.

[42] "One should say to the leadership of the Employers' Association that it is following too weak a wage policy . . . Every time there have been new wage negotiations, the Employers' Association has been too compliant. In negotiating for a reduction in proportion to the price level, we have steadily encountered demands from the trade unions for an increase or a lesser reduction, and when it came to the Employers' Association for final settlement, we did not receive the support we should have had, but had to give in under pressure of the Association leadership. The Employers' Association prides itself on its will for peace, but this can be carried too far . . . there is need for a central organization which can say: thus shall the line be, that is correct — and which can help those who really demand a wage reduction, and force those who for selfish reasons, because they do not suffer from foreign competition and are not interested in making sacrifices to do things right, to go along." *Beretning om Dansk Arbejdsgiverforenings Virksomhed, 1926–1927*, p. 123.

[43] "When [it is said] that it would have been cheaper to engage in a struggle than to acquiesce in the demand for half an øre in one or another instance, I disagree. It can be much cheaper and less dangerous to make concessions, even if it costs a half or quarter øre . . . than to have a work stoppage." *Ibid.*, p. 125.

The picture of the Employers' Association that emerges from the foregoing pages is that of a powerful collective bargaining agency, representing a degree of employer organization to be found in few other countries. Its bargaining techniques and its position in the labor market will be considered in the following chapters.

PART TWO

METHODS AND RESULTS OF COLLECTIVE BARGAINING

CHAPTER VI

THE FRAMEWORK OF COLLECTIVE BARGAINING

COLLECTIVE BARGAINING between employers and employees emerged in Denmark with the abolition of the gild system. Although there were instances of informal negotiation between masters and journeymen, the gild spirit was opposed to any division of authority, and at most the journeymen were successful in securing price lists that were promulgated unilaterally by the masters. But within five years of the demise of the gilds, many of the lineal successors of the journeyman gilds had concluded collective agreements with their former masters. The shoemakers were the first to secure a written agreement, the carpenters the first to sign a contract providing for a joint committee to adjudicate disputes over contract interpretation. Although the extension of collective bargaining suffered a setback during the depression of 1877–1879, the next decade saw a resumption of the movement. For the first time collective agreements were signed in the non-gild trades, although the majority continued to be confined to the gild handicrafts. The recession of 1885 again brought to a halt the upward trend in collective bargaining, but when the cycle turned in 1888, the network of collective agreements once more expanded.

The last decade of the nineteenth century witnessed the final establishment of collective bargaining as the normal method of determining wage and working conditions in Denmark. By 1899 virtually every trade in Copenhagen and the more important trades in provincial cities were governed by collective agreement. In some industries, particularly those characterized by large-scale production, the scope of agreements encompassed large portions or all of the country.

But the termination of open hostility between organized employers and trade unions and the inauguration of the contemporary collective bargaining system were not achieved without a final dispute of severe dimensions. The "great lockout of 1899" arose out of a trivial incident, a strike of carpenters in seven provincial cities. The Employers' Association seized upon this strike as an excuse to present to the Federation of Labor a set of demands which it could hardly have expected to gain peacefully.[1] As nearly as can be discerned, the organized employers, aroused by the increasing trade union aggressiveness occasioned by favorable employment conditions, decided to wage a preventive war before their opponents grew too strong.[2] It does not seem likely that any large number of employers hoped to crush trade unionism; rather, it was the growing union challenge to traditional management prerogatives, coming half a century earlier in Denmark than in the United States, that provoked this vigorous reaction by employers who previously had displayed pacific proclivities.

The details of the lockout of 1899, which lasted over three months and entailed a loss of three million working days, need not concern us.[3] As the stoppage continued, it became increasingly evident that the employers had miscalculated their own strength and the powers of trade union resistance. For one thing, only about 20 per cent of the nonagricultural labor force of the country was involved, since the majority of employers had not yet become affiliated with the Employers' Association. Then, the trade unions were able to secure substantial financial assistance from neighboring countries, and many of the locked out workers took temporary employment abroad. The major strategic error of the employers, however, was in timing the lockout to coincide with the peak of the business cycle.

[1] The principal demands were (a) acceptance by the Federation of Labor of full responsibility for the observance of collective agreements by its affiliates; (b) explicit recognition of the employer's sole responsibility for managing the enterprise and employing labor; (c) guarantee of nonunion status for foremen; and (d) a uniform expiration date of January 1 for all collective agreements. The Employers' Association itself later termed these demands a "declaration of war." Agerholm og Vigen, p. 63.

[2] At least this is the conclusion of Nørregaard, p. 514, whose analysis of the situation is careful and objective. The trade unions have charged that the purpose of the lockout was "destruction of labor organization or, if this could not be accomplished, weakening their economic resistance so that in the future, employers could hope by threat of general lockout to be the sole masters in determining labor conditions . . . " Jensen og Olsen, p. 131. The employers have offered the following justification for their action: "The general assembly [of the Employers' Association] assumed leadership when struggle became necessary, for it is in agreement with the nation's employers, who for a number of years had felt the pressure of no longer possessing the necessary authority to run their own enterprises; things have come to the pass that workers regard it as their right to come and go at will; employer criticism of work is met by the threat to leave and take the remaining workers along, yes, in some trades there is encouragement to leave in the workers' right to receive support as 'unemployed.' Workers determine the division of labor, the number of workers employed, etc.; if the employer's wishes do not meet with the approval of the workers, he gets no labor . . . The employer's influence over wages has almost disappeared; if there is no agreement, the work is not performed, and when there is agreement, the workers often force higher wages by unilateral action." Agerholm og Vigen, pp. 67–68.

[3] See H. L. Bisgaard, "Den Store Lockout," *Nationaløkonomisk Tidsskrift*, XXXVII (1899), 497.

THE SEPTEMBER AGREEMENT[4]

The lockout was brought to a conclusion by an agreement that proved of paramount importance for the future of Danish industrial relations. When compared with the original employer demands, it might appear to represent a considerable victory for employers. However, there were provisions that conferred benefits upon trade unions, and what is more important, some of the pro-employer clauses proved, through subsequent interpretation, to be less advantageous than originally anticipated. Since Danish collective bargaining hinges to so large an extent upon the September Agreement, a brief review of its major provisions is in order.[5]

1. *Strike authorization and notice.* Paragraph 2 of the September Agreement contains the following points: (a) mutual recognition of the right to effect work stoppages; (b) the requirement of a three-fourths majority vote by a representative union or employer association body as a preliminary to the calling of a strike or lockout; (c) fourteen days' notice to the other party of intention to bring a work stoppage proposal before the competent representative body, and seven days' notice of the decision to strike or lock out; (d) a mutual pledge not to support a work stoppage in violation of these conditions.

It was decided early that the notice requirements applied not only to the central organizations, but to all affiliated organizations as well, so that with few exceptions no legal work stoppage can take place without a preliminary warning of at least 14 days. Although there has been some grumbling among workers that the requirement of notice deprived unions of the weapon of surprise,[6] this rule has been received with general satisfaction and is observed punctiliously. On the other hand, the

[4] For the text of this agreement, see Appendix B.

[5] The application of the Agreement has largely been a function of the Labor Court (*Den Faste Voldgiftsret*), the work of which is the subject of Chapter XI. Fortunately, it has not been necessary to undertake the almost impossible task of delving into the thousands of cases decided by this tribunal, since there are several excellent commentaries upon its decisions. See Knud Illum, *Den Kollektive Arbejdsret* (Copenhagen, 1939); Knud V. Jensen, *Arbejdsretten i Danmark* (Copenhagen, 1946); W. Elmquist, *Septemberforliget* (Copenhagen, 1930); Hjalmar V. Elmquist, *Den Kollektive Arbejdsoverenskomst* (Copenhagen, 1918).

[6] One of the most prominent trade union leaders once commented upon this point as follows: "Most people would agree that the strike notice . . . has never operated against workers — on the contrary. It is clear that under pressure of a strike notice we have often been able to obtain more than would otherwise have been possible. The strike warning has certainly saved our membership from numerous lost strikes by yielding results before a sentiment for *war at any price*, which is easily aroused by strikes called without warning, could develop . . . In my opinion, the strike called without warning, as a tactic, absolutely prevents a purposeful wage policy, the gains from which far outweigh what can be realized by a coup in any single instance." De Samvirkende Fagforbund, *Protokol over Generalforsamlingen*, 1919, p. 21.

ratification requirement has proved to be a formality, with little deterring effect upon the calling of work stoppages.

2. *Central organization responsibility.* Each of the signatories assumed responsibility for the effectuation of agreements concluded directly *between them,* both on their own account and by affiliates. The limited subject matter upon which the Federation of Labor may contract rendered this clause of comparatively minor importance, falling far short of the employers' hope of making the Federation responsible for collective agreements entered into by affiliated national unions.

3. *Management prerogatives.* Paragraph 4 of the September Agreement, guaranteeing to employers the right to direct and distribute work, subject to certain limitations in the case of piece work, represented labor's most substantial concession to employers. Trade union critics of the Agreement charged that this clause would permit employers to favor unorganized workers and thus weaken labor organizations. But the Labor Court has established in numerous decisions that the right conferred upon employers may not be used to discourage membership in trade unions, on the ground that the entire rationale of the September Agreement, which is based upon mutual recognition of rights by the two central organizations, would thereby be contravened. Wage favoritism to unorganized workers and threats of discharge designed to hinder organization have thus been condemned as breaches of the September Agreement.[7]

In other respects, Paragraph 4 has been of considerable assistance to employers. For example, trade unions have been prevented thereby from instituting work sharing arrangements by unilateral action during periods of unemployment.[8] Employers have been permitted to install time clocks and initiate time studies, to adopt reasonable precautions against thievery, including search of the worker's person, to establish the precise hours of work and rest, and to determine other working rules without first bargaining with the union. In the case of hourly rated workers, the employer's right of intra-plant transfer has been construed broadly, although he may not effect unreasonable increases in the intensity of labor without recourse to the collective agreement. However, in the case of piece work, changes in work that reduce earnings must be negotiated. The Labor Court has also interpreted the Agreement to mean that an employer may not arbitrarily assign work traditionally

[7] This clause implicitly guarantees the right of employers to maintain the open shop; however, the strength of trade union organization has made this right of little value. See De Samvirkende Fagforbund, *Protokol over Generalforsamling,* 1919, p. 22.

[8] Bilateral work sharing agreements, however, are perfectly legal. In 1940, a national work sharing scheme was adopted by law as a means of combating unemployment caused by the German occupation.

performed by one craft to another craft, a matter of particular importance in the building trades.

Recent trade union sentiment for greater worker participation in management may raise Paragraph 4 to a position of even greater prominence.[9] Certainly, employers intend to use it as a bulwark against any invasion of their prerogatives. But like the rest of the September Agreement, this provision is flexible, and the Danish genius for compromise may prevent its becoming a source of friction.

4. *The status of foremen.* The September Agreement guarantees foremen "full liberty not to become members of a trade union." This has been held to give employers the right to insist that their foremen refrain from joining the standard trade unions, and except among commercial firms, where the September Agreement has been superseded by a special agreement in this respect, foremen are not union members.[10]

The trade unions have been chiefly concerned with the prevention of the use of foremen as strikebreakers, and there has been considerable litigation over the correct designation of particular groups of employees. The September Agreement itself contains only two conditions for foreman status, namely, that the individual concerned shall have a fixed salary and shall not participate in piece work; but additional guides have been added by the Labor Court. Authority to hire and fire, to allocate work, to set piece rates, and to inspect work may constitute indicia of the foreman status in appropriate circumstances.[11] But the Labor Court has made it clear that employees may be disqualified as foremen if during labor disputes they perform work outside of their regular duties, unless imperative to preserve property from destruction.

5. *Termination of the September Agreement.* Paragraph 13, which stipulates that only the central organizations can terminate the Agreement, and that unions and employers withdrawing from the central organizations continue to be bound by its terms, has been of inestimable value in preserving the integrity of the Agreement. The Labor Court has gone so far as to declare that an independent local union, formed from among the members of a dissolved union which had been affiliated with the Federation of Labor, remained subject to the Agreement. Only the few trade unions that have never joined the Federation and unaffiliated

[9] The 1947 congress of the Metal Workers' Union called for revision of this paragraph on the ground that it is incompatible in its present form with the aims of the labor-management production committees established in Denmark since the war.

[10] However, there are strong foremen's associations that in some cases bargain collectively. See below, pp. 255–257.

[11] While plant guards have not been accorded the status of supervisors, the Labor Court has upheld the right of employers to forbid their membership in the plant union, though not in separate unions of their own. Illum, p. 197.

employers, steadily diminishing groups, are exempt from its coverage.

The significance of the September Agreement as a whole is far greater than the sum of its individual provisions. In innumerable ways the Labor Court has premised basic regulatory decrees upon the spirit of the Agreement, with results that probably would have confounded the original signatories. Moreover, the September Agreement has had a symbolic value exceeding its practical, day to day operation. Originating from the last great noneconomic test of strength between the two labor market adversaries, it represented a treaty of peace and a promise of mutual coöperation. In a symposium on the occasion of its fiftieth anniversary, the chairman of the Federation of Labor declared that "the most significant aspect of the September Agreement is that it contains mutual recognition of rights and rules for coöperation," while the chairman of the Employers' Association agreed that "in the very first interpretations it was made clear that the September Agreement presupposes recognition of the right of the employer as well as the worker to organize." [12] It is fair to say that it was in removing the troublesome issue of the right to organize from the Danish labor arena that this unique document made its greatest contribution to industrial peace.

THE "STANDARD RULES" FOR NEGOTIATING COLLECTIVE AGREEMENTS[13]

The September Agreement covered both major phases of collective bargaining, the conclusion of new agreements (interests) and the interpretation of existing agreements (rights). Thereafter the two were carefully distinguished. Following the Danish scheme, this and the following two chapters will deal with collective bargaining over interests, after which the methods of adjusting disputes over rights will be considered.

In 1925, a joint committee representing the Employers' Association and the Federation of Labor was established to examine the desirability of codifying the negotiation practices that had developed in piecemeal fashion over the years. The principal desiderata of a bargaining system, as envisioned by the employers, were:

1. Nationwide agreements for uniform and related work.

2. Worker rejection of agreements negotiated by their representatives only by large majorities.

3. Collective bargaining through representatives armed with mandates to conclude final agreements.

4. Greater emphasis upon direct bargaining and less upon government mediation.[14]

[12] *Arbejdsgiveren*, October 1, 1949, pp. 249, 252.
[13] For the text of these rules, see Appendix C.
[14] *Beretning om Dansk Arbejdsgiverforenings Virksomhed*, 1925–1926, pp. 23–24.

The purpose of the employer proposals was to concentrate bargaining responsibility in the central organizations, a process that had gone quite far on the employer side of the bargaining table, but had made little headway on the labor side. Given the strong separatist tendencies in the Federation of Labor (the Laborers' Union had just seceded), points 2 and 3 in particular had little chance of adoption. The trade union counterproposals were designed mainly at speeding up the bargaining procedure by providing specific time periods for the various phases of negotiation.[15]

The time was not propitious for agreement, for the country was still in the grip of deflation, placing great strain upon labor relations. It was not until 1936, when the great depression had given way to an inflationary trend, that a decade of intermittent negotiation was finally consummated in the standard negotiation rules. The rules are divided into two major sections, the first setting forth general principles regarding future agreements, the second mainly of a procedural character. The principal provisions of the first part were four in number, as follows:

1. The conclusion of nationwide agreements is set forth as a goal of collective bargaining.[16] Actually, such agreements were common even prior to 1936, as Table 12 shows (the years 1915 and 1928 are the only two for which comprehensive contract statistics are available). By 1928, 74 per cent of all workers covered by agreement were subject to agree-

TABLE 12

COLLECTIVE AGREEMENTS IN DENMARK, 1915 AND 1928, BY SCOPE OF COVERAGE

	1915		1928	
Unit of Coverage	Number of Agreements	Number of Workers	Number of Agreements	Number of Workers
Entire country	48	53,822	152	104,844
Copenhagen	} 353	42,604	73	26,805
Provinces			41	33,257
Single city			237	22,003
Single employer	726	24,512	691	36,955
Total	1,127	120,938	1,194	223,864

Source: *Arbejdsoverenskomster i Danmark, Statistiske Meddelelser*, vol. 81, no. 1 (1928), p. 287.

[15] *Beretning om De Samvirkende Fagforbunds Virksomhed*, 1926–1927, pp. 12–13.

[16] This represented a concession in principle by some trade unions which had traditionally employed variation as a tactic in whipsawing employers. For example, it was said of Lyngsie, the founder of the Laborers' Union, that "he was long an opponent of nationwide agreements with their uniformity of conditions. It was difference and instability that he could use so excellently as a lever." Bertolt, *Lyngsie*, p. 114.

ments covering either Copenhagen or the remainder of the country as a single unit, leaving only 26 per cent in single city or single employer units.

The absence of more recent statistics makes it impossible to evaluate the precise influence of the standard rules upon the scope of agreements. It is the consensus, however, that there has been little consolidation of agreements since 1936. The industries currently operating under national agreement, mainly manufacturing, had already achieved that status by 1936, while the service and local transport industries remain predominantly under local agreement. Apparently the decades of free collective bargaining prior to 1936 had produced an optimum adjustment of agreement coverage which the predilections of the central organizations have been powerless to alter.

2. March 1 was made the common expiration date for all collective agreements. The Employers' Association had been working toward this goal ever since 1899, motivated by the desire to effect a common settlement of all disputes rather than to permit unions to use agreements negotiated at the beginning of a year as a stepladder for subsequent wage demands. For the same reason, as well as because they were better off with a series of small strikes rather than a single large one, the trade unions had resolutely opposed common expiration. Moreover, the individual craft unions feared that a common expiration date for all agreements would augment the power of the Federation of Labor and curb their ability to make separate bargains.

There were several factors instrumental in overcoming the trade union opposition. Regardless of craft separatism, the economic problems arising out of the great depression and the rise to power of a socialist government led the Federation of Labor increasingly to take the lead in collective bargaining. If the trade unions were not to impede government action designed to restore a reasonable level of employment, an integration of union wage policy was required. Moreover, despite the theory of craft self-determination, in actual practice there had been a secular trend toward centralization and uniformity. In 1928, some 44 per cent of all collective agreements, covering 27 per cent of the workers under agreement, expired in April, while 80 per cent of the agreements, covering 86 per cent of the workers, expired during the four months February to May inclusive.[17] Therefore, a uniform expiration date did not mark as sharp a break with previous practice as might have been expected.

The March 1 date was reached as the result of a compromise. The employers would have preferred an expiration date in midwinter, when employment was slack, particularly in construction, whereas the unions

[17] "Arbejdsoverenskomster i Danmark," *Statistiske Meddelelser*, vol. 81, no. 1, p. 295.

preferred summer expiration. Failure to agree upon a single date until the last minute almost prevented the consummation of the standard rules agreement, the employers insisting to the end that they could not go beyond February 15, while the unions were equally adamant on April 1 as the earliest date acceptable to them.[18]

It is instructive to note that both with respect to widening the scope of agreements and to uniform expiration provisions, the initiative came from employers rather than trade unions, contrary to the general rule in the United States. However, where medium or small-sized American employers have had to deal with powerful unions, they have not been at all reluctant to accept standardization of agreements.[19] On the other hand, had there been dominant individual corporations in Danish industry, the road to uniformity would probably have been much rockier. As for the trade unions, if Danish unions had been as poorly organized and as insecure as most American unions were until recently, their enthusiasm for diversity in employment conditions would undoubtedly have been much less.

3. The parties agreed upon the desirability of collective agreements of more than a single year's duration, with interim reopening in the event of large price fluctuations. The agreement term in Denmark has been sensitive to cyclical fluctuations. Price stability from 1900 to 1914 led to the conclusion of two- and three-year contracts, climaxed by a general five-year term in 1911. However, wartime inflation resulted not only in shortening the average term to one year, but even to the inclusion of reopening clauses within this period. Not until 1936, when the memory of the initial fall in real wages occasioned by long duration contracts during World War I had faded, was the general term of agreement lengthened to two years. The maintenance of price control during and since World War II has facilitated the continuance of this practice.

The recent desire for agreements of longer duration has grown out of the increasing complexity of collective bargaining and the desire on both sides for longer periods of labor peace. From beginning to end, general wage movements require from five to six months. If negotiations were required each year, the officials of the central organizations would not have sufficient time to deal with the myriad non-wage problems which have devolved upon them.

4. The parties agreed to urge upon their affiliated organizations the inclusion in all collective agreements of specified procedures for negotiating changes in piece rates necessitated by new work or altered meth-

[18] *Beretning om Dansk Arbejdsgiverforenings Virksomhed*, 1935–1936, p. 8.

[19] For example, see Clark Kerr and Roger Randall, *Multiple Employer Bargaining in the Pacific Coast Pulp and Paper Industry* (Berkeley, 1948).

ods of production. In fact, many trades had long followed the procedures suggested, but the object of the standard rules was to make them universal.

Two alternative rules were suggested, though neither was made mandatory. Under the first, disputes over new rates which could not be settled by direct bargaining were to be submitted to arbitration at the request of either party, the arbitrator to be guided by the piece earnings prevailing for comparable work in the trade. The second formula provided that until the parties could agree upon new piece rates, the work was to be performed on an hourly rate basis, each worker to receive the equivalent of his average piece earnings over the previous three-month period, less 20 per cent. The reduction in earnings was intended to stimulate the interest of both parties in reaching agreement, the worker because of the drop in his take-home pay, the employer because he could expect a more than proportional fall in output, in view of the customary time rate–piece rate differential of from 25 to 33 per cent.[20]

The second portion of the standard rules of 1936 relates chiefly to the collective bargaining timetable, which will be dealt with in the next chapter. However, a few preliminary comments may be made:

1. The September Agreement had required notice of three months for the termination of collective agreements. While this requirement was a mere formality, the press often interpreted it as the beginning of a crisis, creating unrest among the workers. It was therefore decided to reduce the term of notice to 14 days. That this was a change in form rather than in substance is indicated by the fact that a rule was simultaneously adopted stipulating that "the party desiring amendments to an agreement currently in force shall submit proposals for such amendments not later than three months prior to the date of expiration of the agreement. If proposals are not submitted in due time, the agreement shall remain in effect for another year." [21] The new rule thus accomplished the original purpose, that of affording the parties adequate notice of projected contract changes, and at the same time avoided the disquieting features of formal notice of termination.[22]

[20] The first formula was better adapted to trades with fixed price lists that might afford adequate bench marks to arbitrators, the second formula to trades in which work was usually done on the basis of a local agreement for each new job (shipbuilding). See Kaj Bundvad, *Afstemnings, Samarbejds og Forhandlingsregler* (Roskilde, 1940), p. 39.

[21] The force of this rule has been augmented by a Labor Court decision requiring the new proposals to be fairly concrete. A union had simply served notice that it reserved the right to make specific demands concerning wages and other conditions of labor at a later date, and the Court ruled that this was insufficient. See Knud V. Jensen, pp. 207–209.

[22] Section 8 (d) of the U. S. Labor-Management Relations Act of 1947 requires a 60-day notice of termination or modification. The wisdom of this provision is questionable in the light of the Danish experience.

Professor George Taylor has questioned the desirability of having demands specified in detail in advance of negotiation:

> If exact and complete demands have to be precisely spelled out and filed with the other party to a labor agreement sixty days prior to contract expiration, a considerable restriction upon the "give and take" characteristic of negotiations may be introduced. Nor will bargaining be facilitated if the size and variety of demands thrown into collective bargaining by both parties are increased as a protective measure. After all, a demand not placed on the table within the deadline date can be introduced later only with extreme difficulty. The procedures can easily tend to make big disputes out of little ones.[23]

This point is well taken, in the light of the Danish experience. During the 1949–1950 bargaining sessions, for example, considerable difficulty was caused by the fact that some of the unions involved had not specifically requested certain concessions which constituted part of the general settlement, a fact which the mediator had to ignore in granting them the same terms anyway. In negotiations looking toward revision of the bargaining rules that commenced in 1950, one of the principal demands of the Federation of Labor was elimination of the strict requirement that all demands be specified by December 1. In support of this position, the Federation argued with considerable justification that the requirement tended to increase the volume of bargaining subject material, since each national union tended to follow the practice of looking around and adopting all the demands of fellow unions, lest it receive less in the final settlement.

2. In an effort to lighten the burden of collective bargaining, a rule was adopted advocating voluntary submission to arbitration of minor issues in dispute. Arbitration boards established to decide such issues are enjoined from handling "questions of a general nature . . . such as a general change in the hours of work or a general demand for a change in the wage level." This rule has had little application, partly because of the difficulty of segregating minor from major issues.

GOVERNMENT MEDIATION

The Danish system of governmental mediation is much more precise and elaborate than current practice in the United States. It is based upon legislation first enacted in 1910, and subsequently amended in several important particulars, each time on the basis of joint labor-management recommendations to the parliament. In 1908, as a stipulation in an agreement ending a serious stoppage of work, the Employers'

[23] George W. Taylor, *Government Regulation of Industrial Relations* (New York, 1948), p. 286. For evidence of awareness of this danger by the Danish Labor Court, see its Cases No. 2603 and 2604.

Association and the Federation of Labor agreed to participate in a joint commission, headed by an impartial chairman, to examine the existing system of collective bargaining and make suggestions for its improvement. The commission held 29 plenary sessions and numerous informal meetings during the following year, and out of its deliberations emerged a report which is second in importance only to the September Agreement in its impact upon Danish industrial relations.[24] On the basis of this report the parliament enacted the fundamental labor laws of the country, establishing the mediation institution and the Labor Court.

The mediation act,[25] which is the concern of the remainder of this chapter, is conveniently divided into three major headings for analytical purposes: the mediation personnel, the functions of the mediators, and the rules for voting upon collective agreements.

1. *The mediation personnel.* Initially, there was a single mediator, appointed by the government for a term of two years upon recommendation of the public members and either the labor or employer members of the Labor Court. In the event of the Court's failure to make a recommendation within a specified time, the appropriate government ministry was to make the appointment on its own. In actual practice, the mediators have always been designated after unanimous approval of the Labor Court.

After some years of experience, another joint industrial commission recommended enlargement of the number of mediators to three, since the increasing number of collective agreements, the shortening of the contract term, and the trend toward a common expiration date had placed an intolerable burden upon the single mediator. By an act of December 21, 1921, this was done, and at the same time the term of office was raised to three years, with one term expiring at the end of each year.

The three mediators now select a chairman from among them, and apportion the work as they see fit. While mediation in concert is specifically permitted by law, it is rarely employed. The annual or biennial general wage movements are in fact handled by the chairman of the mediation institution alone, with the other mediators specializing in particular disputes not included in the general movements (for example, agricultural labor disputes).

Another change in personnel was introduced in 1945. The trade unions

[24] *Beretning Fra Faellesudvalget af 17 August 1908* (Copenhagen, 1910).

[25] The text of the act, in its 1950 form, is given in Appendix D. For earlier versions, see International Labor Office, *Legislative Series,* 1921, Part II, Den. 2; 1927, Part I, Den. 1; 1934, Part I, Den. I.

had long complained that with the increasing centralization of collective bargaining, there was a tendency for issues which were important to particular crafts but which did not loom large in the total picture to become lost in the final stages of mediation.[26] On their insistence, a panel of submediators was added to the mediation institution, with the duty of participating in the early stages of collective bargaining at the request of either party. In the event that no agreement is reached, the submediator prepares a report setting forth the original demands, those that are dropped, and any points upon which agreement is reached, which is transmitted to the principal mediator who will next intervene in the proceedings. Modeled after the successful Swedish practice, the purpose of submediation was to further collective bargaining at levels below the final stage involving the central organizations. Submediation was employed effectively for the first time in the 1950 negotiations, but it is still too soon to tell whether it will remain a permanent feature of the Danish bargaining system.

2. *The power and functions of the mediator.* The role of the government mediator in collective bargaining has been a controversial issue in Denmark. The trade unions, on the whole, have been in favor of permitting him to play an active part, whereas the employers would have preferred that he restrict his activities to pure conciliation. This difference of opinion was first manifested in the report of the joint industrial commission of 1908. The public chairman and the unions advocated then that the mediator be empowered to perform the functions, bordering on arbitration, that he now performs, but the employer representatives took exception with respect to the following significant potential powers of the mediator:

(a) They objected in principle to the inclusion of a provision making it incumbent upon the parties to meet at the call of the mediator, taking the position that he should have the power only to invite. However, the legal obligation to meet was included nonetheless, though without penalty for refusal.

The original act did not confer strike-delaying authority upon the mediator, although it was implied in the obligation to meet at his call.

[26] "The principal task of the mediator is to ensure real bargaining over all the many detailed questions which are contained in collective agreements and price lists. Hitherto, these special problems, when the parties themselves could not agree on them, were put aside for further negotiation during mediation; but since the mediator lacked the time and the knowledge to examine all these technical problems, they were shelved in favor of the more general problems, and as a result obviously unreasonable provisions are found in collective agreements and should be eliminated." *Beretning om De Samvirkende Fagforbunds Virksomhed* 1945, p. 25.

At the recommendation of the government representatives on the Industrial Relations Commission of 1925,[27] the law was amended by the insertion of a provision permitting the mediator to require the parties, *as a condition of his intervention*,[28] to refrain from commencing an impending stoppage of work until he has declared his intervention terminated, with a maximum time limit of one week. Thus, the mediator does not have an absolute legal right to delay strikes or lockouts; his power in this respect is conditional upon acceptance by both parties of his mediatory services. But this limitation has been of no practical importance, for not only have both parties always accepted his intervention, but except under extraordinary circumstances they have readily extended negotiations beyond the legal limit of one week when requested to do so by the mediator.

(b) The employer representatives on the 1908 commission also expressed concern over the authority of the mediator to formulate specific terms of settlement for submission to the parties, in what has come to be known as the *mediation proposal*. They feared that this document would tend to mold public opinion and create irresistible pressure upon the parties to accept it, thus producing settlements that lay midway between the bargaining positions of the parties, regardless of their economic effects.[29] Although the employers did not succeed in this attempt to reduce the status of the mediator to that of conciliator,[30] a proviso was inserted into the law forbidding publication of the mediation proposal "without permission of both parties, [and] unless a work stoppage has occurred and the mediator has concluded his activities in the matter."

But in 1921, after several turbulent years, it was agreed that the position of the mediator should be strengthened by permitting him to publish his proposal at any time and without the consent of the parties, subject only to the restriction that he discuss it both as to form and substance with representatives of both parties before preparing a final draft. It is now the normal procedure for him to withhold publication until both parties have replied formally to the proposal, after balloting upon it, as required by law. The only instances in which the penal sanctions of the mediation act have been employed were in the imposition of fines upon newspapers which printed information about mediation proposals without the consent of the mediator.

[27] Arbejdskommission af 1925, *Betaenkning Vedrørende Maegling og Voldgift* (Copenhagen, 1926), Minority Report III.

[28] The mediator is not obliged to intervene in a labor dispute. In fact, the statute permits him to do so only when he finds that it threatens vital social interests and "where negotiations have already been carried on by the parties in accordance with the rules agreed upon between them and have been declared by either party to be closed without arrival at a settlement."

[29] *Beretning om Dansk Arbejdsgiverforenings Virksomhed*, 1909–1910, p. 132.

[30] For a good discussion of the distinction between the two, see Taylor, p. 102.

A later controversy over the mediation proposal, which had not been foreseen in 1908, arose over the question of whether the mediator should be allowed to issue an opinion justifying the terms contained in his proposal. The public representatives on the Industrial Relations Commission of 1925 argued in favor of this practice on the ground that it would provide the public with an objective account of the positions of the parties and a reasonable settlement of their differences.[31] This was never actually enacted into law, but when in 1936 the mediator nonetheless published a justification of his proposal after it had been rejected by the employers, he was taken to task by the Employers' Association in the following terms:

> The mediator has judged it his duty to determine how high wages should be, how much of a load production can bear in "good times," what part of the earnings of business should be delivered to workers with the assistance of the government. If this is the case, the press notice means not only a break with current practice in the relationship of the mediator to the government, but also with the basic principles which have hitherto guided government mediation in labor disputes. Peace alone, and not the conditions of peace, has always been the goal of the mediator's work. The mediation institution now establishes itself as a regulator of wages, using as the basis of regulation the political, social and economic views that it finds appropriate.[32]

Perhaps because of the violence of the employer reaction, subsequent mediation proposals have generally been published without comment, in line with the earlier practice.

(c) A third area of disagreement in the 1908 commission, and in subsequent industrial commissions, concerned the right of the mediator to secure economic information from the parties. In its original draft the law empowered him to issue subpoenas and take testimony under oath, but in its final form the act transferred this authority to the Labor Court. It has never proved necessary to exercise this authority.

Employers have also displayed some misgivings about the nature of the information that the mediator might want in framing his proposal, particularly in view of union demands that he have the right of access to their books. The mediator has never demanded information beyond that submitted voluntarily by the parties, however, recognizing that to do so might destroy the spirit of voluntarism that is basic to the mediation system.

[31] Arbejdskommissionen af 1925, p. 69.

[32] *Beretning om Dansk Arbejdsgiverforenings Virksomhed*, 1935–1936, pp. 36–37. The trade unions, on the other hand, defended the action of the mediator. See *Beretning om De Samvirkende Fagforbunds Virksomhed*, 1936, p. 84.

3. *Rules for voting on mediation proposals.*[33] In its original form the mediation act contained nothing on the manner in which acceptance or rejection of mediation proposals was to be demonstrated. But the emergence of the mediation proposal as the crucial stage in collective bargaining, coupled with the reluctance of workers to arm their representatives with final authority to commit the trade unions, created a need for formalizing the ratification procedure.

Employer approval has never constituted any particular problem. Mediation proposals that apply to a single industry are voted upon by the industrial association concerned; those of wider scope are submitted to the general assembly of the Employers' Association, which almost invariably accepts the recommendations of its representatives. Thus, acceptance of a mediation proposal by the employer negotiators is tantamount to final approval.

But the situation is quite different on the trade union side. Most union constitutions require ratification by referendum vote, although some permit this decision to be taken by representative assemblies.[34] Coupled with fairly low worker participation in balloting,[35] thus affording strongly organized minority groups the opportunity to attain influence out of their numerical proportion, the institution of the referendum has contributed to frequent rejection of agreements and mediation proposals which the union representatives considered reasonable.[36] There were two additional complicating factors: the insistence by each individual union on complete autonomy in reaching its decision, and equally strong employer insistence that *every* union in a combined mediation situation ratify the proposal before it became effective for *any* union. Therefore, if a small craft with special grievances were to reject a proposal, an agreement involving thousands of workers who favored its terms might be endangered.[37]

[33] In general, the ratification of collective agreements concluded without mediation follows the same rules, insofar as these rules relate to agreements covering single unions only. Such rules are found in trade union constitutions.

[34] Some unions have practiced the referendum since their formation, but in most, it was introduced during and immediately after World War I, when the radical influence in the Danish labor movement was at its height.

[35] Participation percentages of 55 per cent in 1937 and 59 per cent in 1938 were deemed "comparatively good" by the Federation of Labor. *Beretning om De Samvirkende Fagforbunds Virksomhed*, 1938, p. 127. In 1946, when worker interest in industrial relations was running high under the influence of communist agitation, a participation ratio of 55 per cent was secured. Two years later, only 43 per cent of those entitled to vote in a proposal affecting the large Laborers' Union actually cast their votes.

[36] From 1922 to 1932, some 72 mediation proposals that had received the approval of union negotiators were rejected on balloting. *Folketingets Forhandlinger*, 1933, p. 1103.

[37] This is precisely what happened in 1931, when the Shoe Workers' Union was the only craft in a wage movement involving fifteen unions to reject a mediation proposal. However, because of the poor economic conditions prevailing at the time, the Employers' Association,

The Employers' Association had long pressed the unions to reform their internal ratification procedure, but the Federation was powerless in the face of adamant craft refusal to surrender any autonomy and the strength of rank and file insistence upon the referendum. A solution was therefore sought through the medium of legislation. The first tentative efforts were contained in the following amendment to the mediation law, enacted in 1921:

If a mediation proposal is to be voted on within any organization, it shall not be submitted in any other form than that drawn up by the mediator, and the vote shall be given in the form of a simple aye or nay. [Every vote on a mediation proposal shall be taken by secret ballot and in writing.] When the result of the voting has been ascertained, the organization shall without delay notify the mediator in writing of the number of ayes and nays recorded, and also of the total number of members entitled to vote. Before the vote is taken, the organizations as far as possible shall ensure that all members entitled to vote are given the opportunity to acquaint themselves with the mediation proposal in its entirety.[38]

This provision, which was aimed primarily at the radical leadership of a few unions, did little to ameliorate the general problem. Matters were brought to a head when in 1931, for the first time, the mediator stipulated that his proposal would have to be accepted or rejected as a whole by the unions affected, thus formalizing an unwritten custom. Tactically, it enabled the Federation leaders to participate in a joint commission established to explore the problem, without having to defend themselves against charges of usurping their authority.

In the commission, the employers proposed that a minimum 75 per cent majority of workers *participating* in a referendum on a mediation proposal be required to secure its rejection. The mediator suggested the requirement of a simple majority of those *entitled to vote*, with an allowance of 10 per cent for illness and other legitimate causes of absenteeism, reducing the required vote to 40 per cent of the total electorate. For their part, the trade unions were willing to accept a sliding scale arrangement, whereby if the participation ratio were less than 55 per cent, more than simple majorities would be necessary for defeat, in inverse ratio to the degree of participation.

The discussions in the commissions laid the groundwork for amendatory legislation enacted by parliament in 1934 on the initiative of a socialist government. By handling the matter in the parliamentary

---

contrary to its usual practice, agreed to permit the proposal to become effective for the ratifying unions alone.

[38] Act No. 526, December 21, 1921. The sentence in brackets was added by subsequent amendment.

forum, and presenting it as a *fait accompli* to the next trade union congress, the Federation leadership avoided what in all probability would have been a rebuff by the congress. Their anxiety was evidenced by the unusual fact that the legislation was defended at the trade union congress by Prime Minister Stauning in a completely political speech, in which the issue was presented as a struggle between socialism and communism rather than as one involving the self-determination of national unions.[39] As good socialists, the great majority of the congress delegates had little alternative but to approve the action of their leaders, thus by indirection sanctioning a long step toward strengthening the trade union central power.

The voting rules enacted in 1934 fell into two parts: those relating to voting by a single union, and those relating to mediation proposals covering more than one union. The first category of rules, which has worked satisfactorily and remains on the statute books unaltered, stipulates that a mediation proposal may be rejected by a simple majority of those voting, provided that there is a participation ratio of at least 75 per cent. If the proviso is not satisfied, the majority necessary for rejection is increased by one-half of one per cent for every percentage by which the percentage of votes recorded falls below 75. For example, if 50 per cent of the workers eligible to vote actually cast their ballots, a $62\frac{1}{2}$ per cent majority is necessary to defeat the proposal.

The more important case, that of multiple union voting, has occasioned much greater difficulty. The mediator was empowered to determine the voting unit, that is, he could "require that the results for the various trades involved be added together, and the proposal shall then be deemed to be accepted if the grand total yields a majority for acceptance." To eliminate inequity between unions voting by referendum and those voting through representative assembly (and thereby casting 100

[39] Stauning said in part: "In every determination of a conflict situation there are several hundreds or thousands who will not vote. Their sincere wish is that the conflict shall end and work begin. But it is easier to stay home, and so they fail to express their opinions, and later complain about the unsound vote and the bad compromise. There is no reason to show craven home-sitters any consideration. Union members ought to meet and vote, if they want to preserve their impractical referendum. The most practical thing, naturally, would be to give the mandate for negotiating and concluding agreements to responsible representatives, but of course that would not provide the communists with the confusion that balloting affords. It is characteristic that the communists can never get enough freedom in this country; they cry for referendum and self-determination at every opportunity, but in Russia the workers have not even a vestige of self-determination . . . Danish trade unionists prefer their brand of self-determination, including what is in the mediation act. It is democratic majority rule that has been introduced, a legislative expression of the precept, 'All in the same boat.' Perhaps in some situations a little group will be prevented from forcing through a selfish advantage; but as a rule such advantage is paid for dearly by the great masses of those who are terrorized into taking up the struggle against sound common sense." De Samvirkende Fagforbund, *Protokol over Generalforsamlinger*, 1934, pp. 18–19.

per cent of the eligible vote), it was provided that the number of votes cast by the latter method should be reduced in proportion to the average participation ratio recorded by the referendum unions (though not below 50 per cent) before the two groups were added together.

The newly granted power of the mediator resulted in much grumbling in trade union circles. "It is wrong that bricklayers should determine working conditions for painters and painters for metal workers,"[40] was the argument frequently advanced. Moreover, the referendum unions complained that they were being deprived of their rightful voice by virtue of the fact that while their vote was always split, often quite closely, the unions voting by representative assembly usually cast a solid bloc of votes either for aye or for nay, thus augmenting their influence in the final result.[41] After several years of futile debate at Federation congresses, a compromise was finally reached in 1939, and made part of the mediation law the following year.

(a) Individual unions retain the option of voting by referendum or through representative assemblies, thus satisfying those who insisted that obligatory discontinuance of the referendum system would endanger trade union democracy.

(b) If in a referendum there is a participation ratio of less than 75 per cent, a representative assembly of the union shall cast an additional number of votes equal to the difference between the actual number of the votes cast and 75 per cent of those eligible to vote. For example, if in a union there were 1,000 eligible members and only 500 voted, a representative assembly (usually the executive committee of the national union) would cast 250 additional votes, which may be split aye and nay, although usually they are cast *en bloc*. Thus, the expression of opinion of those workers who actually voted is preserved, but at the same time the probability of ratification is increased, since the representative assembly will generally follow the recommendations of the union representatives who participated in the negotiations preceding the proposal.[42]

[40] Bundvad, p. 11.

[41] The balloting that took place in 1937 was illustrative of this situation. There were 18 crafts voting by referendum, in which 10,993 workers voted to accept and 21,161 to reject a mediation proposal. However, the Laborers' Union and a few small crafts, voting through representative assemblies, cast 51,520 votes for and 126 against the proposal. This one-sided result, even when reduced to the 55 per cent participation ratio of the referendum crafts, resulted in a favorable outcome of 39,453 to 21,231. The opponents of the innovation argued that if the Laborers' Union had also voted by referendum, enough workers would have voted against the proposal to ensure its rejection. *Beretning om De Samvirkende Fagforbunds Virksomhed*, 1937, pp. 84–85.

[42] This was well illustrated in the balloting on the 1950 mediation proposal. A majority of the workers voting by direct balloting, 139,881 to 123,875, favored rejection of the proposal, which had been approved by the leadership. In the supplementary voting by representative assemblies, however, 54,825 votes were cast in favor of the proposal to 18,217 against it. In

(c) The votes of individual unions are then combined. Suppose that two organizations, Unions A and B, are involved, each with 10,000 members, Union A voting by ballot and Union B through a representative assembly. In Union A, 6,000 workers participate in the ballot, 3,000 voting aye and 3,000 nay. The representative assembly of Union A then casts 1,500 votes, say for approval, making the tally in Union A 4,500 aye and 3,000 nay. Assume that in Union B the representative assembly casts all 10,000 votes in the affirmative; these are then reduced to the participation ratio of Union A, in this case 75 per cent, that is, to 7,500 aye votes. The final result, combining the votes of the two unions, is 12,000 ayes (4,500 plus 7,500) and 3,000 nays.

This scheme answers only in part the criticism that the referendum crafts are deprived of their correct proportional influence. Perversely, the higher the participation ratio in the referendum crafts, the more serious is this inequity likely to be. But there appears to be no way of avoiding inequity in this respect short of uniform ratification procedure by all unions, which has proved impossible of attainment. Apart from this, the voting procedure gives a decisive vote to the larger unions in a voting unit, and although this is defensible on democratic grounds, the fact remains that it represents a serious impairment of craft autonomy.[43]

This brief history of contract ratification procedure should be sufficient to demonstrate that what at first glance appears to be a hopelessly unnecessary and impossible morass of regulation actually represents a delicate adjustment of procedure to some of the fundamental conflicts in collective bargaining desiderata, democracy versus efficiency and autonomy versus centralization. The individual worker retains the right to vote upon his projected conditions of labor, but at the same time safeguards have been designed to prevent costly work stoppages occasioned by vigorous minorities and indolent majorities. A nice balance has been attained between the right of craft self-determination and the interest of the majority of trade union members in avoiding disputes that arise out of relatively unimportant craft considerations. Given the centralization of collective bargaining, some curb upon craft autonomy was inevitable; the voting rules have effected what appear to be eminently reasonable restrictions. The Danish voting rules are an integral part of the nation's labor history, and are not for export. But they illustrate how, by trial and error, a democratic society can eventually resolve deeply rooted conflicts of interest by the creation of institutions that,

addition, the unions voting directly through representative bodies cast 36,553 votes for the proposal and none in the negative, resulting in a substantial over-all majority for acceptance despite the unfavorable rank and file reaction.

[43] It is notable that the Laborers' Union has been a staunch proponent of combined voting. See *Fagbevaegelsen og De Økonomiske Problemer* (Copenhagen, 1937), pp. 48–50.

though they may be extremely complex, provide the optimum degree of satisfaction for the great majority of the individuals that are affected.

The September Agreement, the standard negotiation rules, and the mediation legislation constitute the trinity upon which collective bargaining over interests rests. Taken by themselves, however, they provide only an introduction to reality. The following chapters will treat the collective bargaining system as a functioning unit and evaluate its actual operation from the social point of view.

CHAPTER VII

THE COLLECTIVE BARGAINING SYSTEM IN OPERATION

SINCE THE ADOPTION of the standard rules for negotiation, the regular collective bargaining procedures are set in motion three months prior to the uniform March 1 contract expiration date, that is, on December 1 of the previous year. Before the latter date the employer associations and trade unions must have submitted to one another the contract changes they desire to effectuate. The employer demands are likely to be fairly uniform from trade to trade, apart from such specific matters as changes in individual piece-rate schedules, but despite efforts of the Federation of Labor to secure uniformity of approach on the part of its affiliates, there is generally considerable variation in the demands of the individual unions.

DIRECT BARGAINING — THE FIRST PHASE

The collective bargaining which lasts from December 1 to January 15, unless agreement is reached earlier, takes place directly between the national union and the industry employer association, without the intermediation of either central organization. Individual employers participate only in the event that their enterprises constitute separate bargaining units, which is the exceptional case. Under the 1945 amendments to the Mediation Act, a submediator may be called in to assist the parties; if that is done, he functions as a conciliator rather than as a mediator.

While small crafts often settle their differences during the initial stages of the first bargaining phase, a satisfactory settlement of the general wage movement cannot be hoped for until either the Laborers' Union or the Metal Workers' Union has reached agreement with its employers. The character of the rivalry between these two organizations has already been recounted; it is necessary to repeat only that while in the past the Metal Workers' Union has usually taken the initiative, the last few years have witnessed a tendency on the part of the Laborers to accept wage leadership. An agreement with one of these unions sets a pattern which other unions must ordinarily accept, and if both reach agreement, the main features of the year's collective bargaining are virtually decided.

The importance of the "key" bargain may be illustrated by the general wage movements of 1946, 1948, and 1950. In the first year, the Metal Workers' Union accepted a wage increase of 8 øre per hour early in the proceedings, creating what the Laborers' Union, which had begun with a demand for 33 øre per hour, bitterly termed "the Metal Workers' line." [1] The Laborers, a "long jump" away from their original goal, insisted that as the lowest paid workers they were entitled to a larger wage rise, but the employers were adamant in refusing, on the theory that any additional concession to the Laborers would have to be extended to the other crafts as well. Eventually, the Laborers succeeded in getting 11 øre, but only at the cost of a long strike.

In 1948, with the memory of the events of the previous wage movement still fresh in mind, the employers and the skilled trades were reluctant to conclude final agreements until it was clear what the Laborers would do, the employers because they wanted to avoid the promulgation of a wage pattern which might again create difficulties, the representatives of the skilled craftsmen because they could not afford to be outdone a second time by the Laborers. Agreement with the Laborers proved possible, however, and within a short time all outstanding disputes had been concluded on similar terms.

In 1950 it was the Metal Workers' Union which proved the stumbling block to a general settlement. After weeks of intensive negotiation, a wage agreement was reached which was approved by all negotiators with the exception of the Metal Workers' chairman. This lone holdout was sufficient to prevent the consummation of any agreements, for the Laborers' Union indicated that it could not be bound if the Metal Workers refused to participate in the settlement. Additional concessions to the Metal Workers' Union were required before any of the entire complex of agreements could be submitted to the membership for ratification.

CENTRAL ORGANIZATION BARGAINING — THE SECOND PHASE

If by January 15 an industry has not succeeded in resolving its outstanding controversies, each party is obliged to report in detail to its parent organization the area of agreement and disagreement. The two central organizations then commence the second phase of collective bargaining, with a maximum duration of one month. When general wage movements reach this stage, as they usually do, a large number of separate disputes are likely to be at issue. There are roughly 2,000 collective

[1] The Laborers' Union complained that "the employers had good support for their negative position when they offered our union the same settlement that was reached with practically all the other crafts . . . and the Employers' Association availed itself of the opportunity, when the Laborers' demands were under public debate, to point out the unreasonableness of our position with reference to the agreement with the other crafts." Axel Olsen, p. 457.

agreements between trade unions and members of the Employers' Association, the majority of which must be dealt with in central organization bargaining. This would constitute an impossible task were it not for the practice of selecting a few major issues for detailed consideration and farming out subsidiary questions to subcommittees of the central negotiating committee. Further expedition is attained by concentrating upon the major industry-wide agreements which are likely to serve as models for the many local and individual employer agreements.

This scheme amounts to national collective bargaining, and it is only feasible because of the stability and standardization of the collective agreement in Denmark. While Danish collective agreements are longer and more complicated than American agreements, on the average, the year-to-year changes in them are slight. Moreover, they are often supplemented by locally negotiated price lists, and in the "minimum" wage trades by individual worker-employer rates.

Statistics are lacking on the proportion of labor disputes settled during the first two phases of collective bargaining. It is clear, however, that controversies have tended increasingly to "go to the top," as the Danes phrase it. This has been a constant source of complaint by both parties, but particularly by the workers, who charge that minor demands which are nonetheless important to them are often shelved in the central bargaining sessions, to the detriment of sound industrial relations.[2] Many of the procedural innovations adopted since 1930 were designed to offset this tendency and to return collective bargaining to the immediate contracting parties. But protestation and formal rule changes have been of little avail against what appears to be a fundamental law of collective bargaining, namely, that the provision of a regular series of procedural steps militates against settlement at the bottom and promotes crowding at the top. Why that should be so is clear, at least in the Danish case. Apart from the two pattern setting trades, and even in those, union officials have little to lose by prolonging negotiations, since employers are hardly likely to become less conciliatory as a strike deadline approaches. Little risk is involved, since the guarantee of further procedures ensures an opportunity to effect a settlement if no additional concessions are forthcoming, while on the other hand the union leaders can then demon-

[2] For example, a former chairman of the Laborers' Union wrote: "To deprive suborganizations and individual firms of the right to negotiate meaningfully with the opposing labor organizations . . . so that sound, mutual understanding between workers and employers is wasted, and many meritorious changes that could be made are set aside, in the long run creates bitterness among workers which eventually must result in an explosion . . ." *Fagbevaegelsen og De Økonomiske Problemer* (Copenhagen, 1937), pp. 38–39. For a concurring opinion by a former chairman of the Employers' Association, see *Dansk Arbejdsgiverforenings Generalforsamlinger*, 1935, pp. 28–29.

strate the sincerity of their efforts to their constituents. The initial bargaining phases tend in fact to become preliminary, designed chiefly to winnow out the important problems that will require settlement when time grows short.

These observations are by no means intended as deprecatory of the Danish collective bargaining system. Local, direct bargaining had a successful history prior to World War I. But two wars and a major depression created economic problems that transcend the individual enterprise and industry. Extreme cyclical fluctuations render interstitial wage adjustments of secondary importance to the dominant general movements with universal repercussion. The competitive position of an export industry is affected much more profoundly by an alteration in the rates of foreign exchange than by wage movements. Localized wage bargaining was a casualty of the interwar course of economic development.

Given the inevitability of centralized wage determination, a regular series of procedures becomes necessary. That the formalization of bargaining stages reduces the possibility of agreement at the local level is regrettable, but it does not follow that formalization is unsound. Both the trade unions and the organized employers of Denmark were firm believers in the decentralization of decision making, a principle that has proved highly successful in other fields of Danish administration, yet the logic of events pushed them relentlessly in the opposite direction.

MEDIATION — THE THIRD PHASE

If no agreement is reached by February 15, either or both parties will ordinarily serve the first of the two required strike or lockout notices, making it possible for a legal stoppage of work to begin on March 1. The government mediator then enters the scene as a matter of course. When the parties accept his intervention, they empower him to delay a work stoppage for the period of one additional week, thus providing a minimum of three weeks for the mediation phase of bargaining. In practice, mediation proceedings tend to last well beyond the statutory period, since there is mutual reluctance to break off negotiations as long as the mediator retains hope of effecting a settlement.[3]

The mediator does not enter the controversy in ignorance of its subject matter. He maintains unofficial contact with the parties from the commencement of collective bargaining, and receives reports from the submediators if they have been asked to participate in the earlier bargaining

[3] Since the adoption of this collective bargaining timetable in 1936, the mediation phase of general wage movements has terminated on the following dates: March 28, 1937; March 21, 1938; April 17, 1946; February 28, 1948.

phases. Moreover, the customary lengthy tenure in office of the mediator[4] provides him with historical insight into the problems of collective bargaining, and renders unnecessary much of the orientation to which the American emergency board, the institution which most closely parallels Danish mediation, is subjected.

The intimate connection between direct negotiation and impartial fact finding constitutes a unique advantage of the Danish system of mediation. It is the task of the mediator to stimulate collective bargaining and at the same time to amass information to serve as the basis for an eventual set of recommendations. Through participation in the give-and-take of negotiations, not only in a single case, but year after year, the mediator acquires the invaluable ability to discriminate between arguments and real positions. Consequently, his findings and recommendations are not likely to contain elements that are beyond the realm of acceptance by either party as a matter of principle.

The number of the participants in mediation proceedings varies with the situation. After the preliminaries have been dispensed with, a maximum of from three to five persons from each side, always including representatives of the two central organizations, actually sit with the mediator in the bargaining conferences. During the final stages, when the issues have been narrowed down to the crucial matter of the wage level, the mediator prefers to deal with only one representative of each side, usually the chairman or vice-chairman of the Employers' Association and the Federation of Labor.

The opening sessions are generally joint, each party presenting a summary of its position for the benefit of the mediator and to delineate precisely the area of disagreement. Subsequent sessions may be either joint or separate, subject to the mediator's discretion. Questions that the mediator considers to be of lesser importance are often referred back to the parties for direct discussion. All meetings, whether joint or separate, are quite informal and are held *in camera;* the "goldfish bowl" technique is not considered conducive to realistic bargaining in this phase.

The art of mediation lies in the formulation of recommendations for dispute settlement, embodied in the so-called "mediation proposal," providing the climax of the entire bargaining process. The provisions that make up the mediation proposal are not drafted at the conclusion of

[4] The chairmen of the Danish mediation institution and their periods of service were: Michael Koefoed, 1910–1914; Adolph Jensen, 1914–1919; Axel Rasmussen, 1919–1920; K. H. Koefoed, 1920–1921; Johs. Dalhoff, 1922–1929; K. Riis-Hansen, 1929–1934; Vilhelm Topsøe, 1935–1936; Erik Dreyer, 1936-present. Most of these men served as associate mediators before becoming the chairman. The post of mediator is a part-time rather than a full-time one, because of the seasonal nature of bargaining; the present chairman, Mr. Dreyer, serves concurrently as chief of the factory inspectorate.

mediation, but rather in a piecemeal fashion as the various points of the agenda are reached. During the course of the proceedings the mediator will occasionally present to the parties draft clauses covering disputed points, both in an endeavor to reconcile them and to probe the area of possible agreement. The substance of the trial balloons may not be the same for the two parties; for example, the mediator may indicate to the employers that he is thinking in terms of a wage increase of 20 øre, and to the unions that an increase of 10 øre might be fair. Their reactions may provide him with the key to settlement at an intermediate point where the bargaining positions overlap.

When the mediator has satisfied himself that further negotiation is not likely to be fruitful, he proceeds to summarization. Before preparing the final draft of his proposal, however, the mediator informs the parties of his major findings, and secures from each one of three reactions to the proposal as a whole: rejection, acceptance, or noncommitment. There is neither a legal nor a customary obligation on the part of the mediator to issue a mediation proposal, and it has been the practice of the present mediator, Mr. Dreyer, not to do so if the negotiating committee on either side rejects it outright. On occasion, he has promulgated a proposal on which a party has refused to take a definite stand, when he was of the opinion that the chances of ratification in the required referendum were good. This contingency may arise when a negotiating committee is split along political lines and neither faction is willing for tactical reasons to take an affirmative position.

The normal case is that in which both parties have indicated informally to the mediator that they are prepared to recommend to their constituents the adoption of the proposal as he has outlined it. The mediator then prepares a final draft covering as many of the disputed issues as he deems essential to final settlement of the controversy. The mediation proposal is typically a long and complex document; that issued in the 1938 general wage movement, for example, consumed 75 printed pages, consisting entirely of draft contract provisions, without discussion of their merits. Before the proposal is printed in the form in which it will be sent out for voting, it is subjected to a final "technical revision" session, during which either party may take exception to outright errors or to the inclusion of matters that are either not germane or were not dealt with during negotiations, but not to the basic provisions to which they had given their preliminary approval.

Upon the promulgation of a mediation proposal, the parties are given a definite period of time, usually from two to four weeks, during which they must ascertain the views of their constituents through the procedures stipulated by law. It is worth repeating that it is a violation of law publicly to disclose any of the terms of the mediation proposal until the balloting is completed.[5] Every worker and employer entitled to vote has access to the full text of the proposal, and in addition the trade unions usually prepare abstracts of the major points for distribution to their membership and discussion at local meetings. The votes are tallied by each side separately, and submitted simultaneously to the mediator. The mediator then makes public the text of his proposal and announces the results of the voting; if there is an affirmative vote by both employers and workers, the relevant terms of the mediation proposal are written into collective agreements.

Now, while this is the normal course of events, it is appropriate to explore the considerations that determine whether or not a mediation proposal will be formulated in the first instance. From the point of view of the mediator, the problem is primarily one of finding a compromise which is not only satisfactory to the negotiating committees, but which also will in all probability achieve ratification. To maintain his prestige as an effective arbiter of labor disputes and to prevent the impairment of his future usefulness, the mediator strives to keep the number of rejected proposals at a minimum. If either of the negotiating committees informs him that it will recommend the rejection of a proposal, there is no chance of ratification and therefore little point in its promulgation. The mediator must be certain that at least the collective bargaining representatives, whose task it will be to sell the formula to their organizations, are favorably disposed.

To the employer representatives, the problem of a response to the mediator's initial query is mainly an economic one. As a practical matter they are armed with a mandate to commit the members of the Employers' Association, and are not faced with the difficult political task of convincing thousands of individuals of the correctness of their position. The union representatives, on the other hand, can assume that their political opponents within the organizations will seek to make capital of the fact that the terms of the proposal inevitably entail sharp departures from the original bargaining positions. Referendum rejection of a recommended proposal constitutes a serious blow to the prestige of the leadership, and must be avoided if at all possible.

On the other hand, failure to accept a mediation proposal may lead to an automatic stoppage of work, unless further government intervention of an *ad hoc* character ensues. If the gulf between the parties is wide, which is most apt to be true in the downward swing of the business cycle when employers are insisting upon reductions in money wages, the union

[5] However, the mediator may himself publish his proposal prior to the balloting if he feels that publication will enhance the chances of ratification.

representatives may have no alternative to rejection. But when the differences are not great, there are certain institutional and psychological factors in the collective bargaining process that create strong pressure for settlement:

1. The mediation proposal will rarely contain a provision that is objectionable to either party on principle or as a matter of ideology. If such an issue exists, the mediator will endeavor to skirt it; if the issue occupies a central place in the negotiations, and it cannot be resolved, no mediation proposal will be formulated.[6]

2. A work stoppage growing out of a general wage movement is likely to involve a large number of workers and to be of long duration. The centralization of collective bargaining deprives trade unions of resort to the limited work stoppage affecting one or a few employers.

3. The alternative to a work stoppage, further government intervention, also has grave disadvantages, as will be seen. For example, the appointment of a neutral board of compulsory arbitration deprives the parties of any further control over the nature of the settlement, and the final result may be less satisfactory to both parties than a mediation proposal would have been.

On the other hand, the fact that a mediation proposal will eventually be made public, and thus influence public opinion, may give trade union representatives pause in accepting it. If the odds are against ratification, it is tactically wiser for them to forestall the issuance of a mediation proposal in the first place rather than to arm employers with powerful arguments in the event of a strike. But it is also true that once a mediation proposal has been accepted by the trade union negotiating committee, the workers realize that in voting its defeat they are likely to prejudice public opinion against them.

The reader is cautioned that the foregoing description of Danish mediation is characteristic primarily of recent practice, and that historically there are exceptions to the precepts that have been set forth as guideposts for the mediator and the parties. For example, the Employers' Association complained that one mediator, K. Riis-Hansen, was partial to the trade unions, and repeatedly used his power to their advantage.[7] Mediation proposals have been promulgated with full realization that

[6] This is a significant contrast to American emergency board procedure, under which recommendations, often thinly disguised as findings of fact, are usually forthcoming on all major issues, and sometimes provide the parties with ammunition for justifying industrial warfare. A case in point was the issue of contributory versus noncontributory pensions in the 1949 dispute in the steel industry. See Steel Industry Board, *Report to the President of the United States*, September 10, 1949.

[7] Vigen, Agerholm, og Plum, pp. 34–35. Riis-Hansen was chairman of the mediation institution from 1929 to 1934, during the first years of the social democratic government in Denmark.

their ratification was highly unlikely in last ditch endeavors to avoid catastrophic work stoppages. In 1931, trade unions voted three times on the same mediation proposal, at the insistence of their leaders, before finally approving it. There have also been instances of second and even third proposals issued after the defeat of the first, sometimes with an intervening stoppage of work; in these cases, however, the subsequent proposals have differed only slightly, if at all, from the original proposal, for it is recognized that once workers gain the impression that by rejecting a mediation proposal they can secure a more favorable one at a later date, much of the present rationale of the mediation system would be destroyed.

Statistical data relating to the operation of mediation are presented in Table 13.[8] The data relate only to the number of disputes in which mediation occurred, and do not specify the number of workers involved in each, which would afford a more accurate index of the significance of mediation in the collective bargaining process. Care must be exercised in inferring trends from the data, for a year in which the number of interventions was relatively small may have actually witnessed the mediation of an important dispute involving many thousands of workers and numerous trade unions.

Nevertheless, some conclusions may be drawn from the data in the form in which they are available. It will be noted, first, that a relatively small proportion of the disputes in which the mediator intervened were settled without the issuance of a mediation proposal. From 1910 to 1919, about 30 per cent of the mediated disputes were settled by direct bargaining, while subsequently the proportion declined to about 10 per cent. These figures, however, understate the conciliatory aspects of mediation on two counts: many subsidiary issues that are included in mediation proposals have been agreed upon in direct bargaining, and even more important, the parties may prefer to have their settlement in the form of a mediation proposal even though they have reached full agreement earlier. An important consideration dictating this practice is the 1934 amendment to the mediation act which empowered the mediator to link crafts for purposes of voting upon his proposals, whereas in the alternative case of agreements concluded without his intermediation, the voting would have to be craft by craft. The mediation proposal thus carries with it the possibility of gerrymandering to augment the chances of ratification.

[8] The data for 1920 to 1949 were given to me in rough form through the courtesy of Mr. Erik Dreyer, the chairman of the mediation institution. The classifications for some years are not complete, so that total figures for the entire period do not balance. The appended notes accompanied the draft statistics.

The statistics also show, as is to be expected, that the great majority of the mediation proposals that are issued are subsequently ratified by both sides. Of the rejected proposals, more than twice as many have been defeated by workers as by employers, substantiating the observation that the ratification problem lies primarily on the trade union side. This ratio would be even higher were it not for tactical rejection by employers of proposals that are not actually displeasing to them; this may occur when the employers believe that the workers will reject a proposal, and want to avoid the establishment of a new bargaining situation in which the workers revert to their original positions but they, the employers, start from the concessions embodied in the mediation proposal.

The appearance of a figure other than zero in column (8) of Table 13 indicates that a stoppage of work occurred, unless the appended notes state to the contrary. For several of the years (1921, 1922, 1925, 1936, 1946) the work stoppages were general in character, so that the small number of entries in column (8) overstates the effectiveness of mediation in bringing about the peaceful adjustment of disputes.

The foregoing analysis of Danish mediation may be summarized in the following terms:

1. The national wage movements of the last three decades have almost without exception reached at least the mediation phase of collective bargaining.

2. A mediation proposal is issued in the great majority of mediation interventions, and with few exceptions with the concurrence of both employer and trade union representatives.

3. Most mediation proposals are ratified by employers and workers, as comparison of columns (3) and (4) of Table 13 demonstrates.

4. Even in the event of a negative initial vote on a mediation proposal, subsequent agreement is often based upon the original proposal, either after further negotiation or the application of governmental compulsion.

5. In general, employers have tended to be more critical of mediation than trade unions,[9] although expressions of dissatisfaction on the part of the latter are by no means lacking.[10] This is probably to be accounted for by the fact that for the greater part of the period in which mediation functioned, labor was the weaker of the two parties economically and

[9] The chairman of the Employers' Association once remarked to his general assembly: "I would like to note that we never wanted the mediation institution. We opposed its creation to the best of our ability, but it has never been so clear to me as it is today that we adopted the correct stand . . . When all other avenues are closed, the mediator attempts to determine whether it is possible to take a bit more from the employer and hand it over to the other side." *Beretning om Dansk Arbejdsgiverforenings Virksomhed*, 1921–1922, pp. 132–133.

[10] The Laborers' Union under Lyngsie found in mediation an unwelcome curb upon its aggressive proclivities. See Axel Olsen, pp. 171, 205, 217; Bertolt, *Lyngsie*, p. 133.

TABLE 13

STATISTICS OF OPERATION OF THE DANISH MEDIATION INSTITUTION, 1910–1949

Year	(1) Total Number of Mediation Interventions	(2) Disputes Settled by Conciliation	Mediation Proposals Issued: (3) Total	Ratified by: (4) Both Parties	Ratified by: (5) Employers Alone	Ratified by: (6) Workers Alone	(7) Rejected by Both Parties	(8) Mediation Ended without Result
1910	2							
1911	17							
1912	12							
1913	13							
1914	7	39	87	60	15	8	4	6
1915	2							
1916	30							
1917	8							
1918	9							
1919 (to July)	32							
1919 (July to Dec.)	4							
1920	24	3	21	18	1[a]	1[a]	1	0
1921	20	3	16	15	1[a]	0	0	1
1922	6	1	4	2	2	0	0	1
1923	5	3	1	1	0	0	0	1
1924	13	0	13	10	3	0	0	0
1925	18[b]	5[c]	35	26[d]	5	4	0	6
1926	3	1	2	2	0	0	0	0
1927	8[e]	0	7	6	1[e]	0	0	0
1928	4	0	4	3	1	0	0	0
1929	7	2	5	3	1[f]	0	0	1
1930	14	1	13	11	2	0	0	0

TABLE 13 (Continued)

Year	(1) Total Number of Mediation Interventions	(2) Disputes Settled by Conciliation	Mediation Proposals Issued: (3) Total	Ratified by: (4) Both Parties	Ratified by: (5) Employers Alone	Ratified by: (6) Workers Alone	(7) Rejected by Both Parties	(8) Mediation Ended without Result
1931	20[g]	1	14 + 37	13 + 2	1 + 35[h]	0	0	4
1932	5	0	5	4	0	0	1[i]	0
1933	0	0	0	0	0	0	0	0
1934	4[j]	0	21	20[k]	1	0	0	1[l]
1935	9[m]	0	87	87	0	0	0	0
1936	28[n]	—	—	—	—	—	—	—
1937	6	0	6	5	0	1[o]	0	0
1938	15	4	10	8	0	2	0	1
1939	2	0	2	0	1[o]	1[o]	0	0
1940	4	2	1	0	1[p]	0	0	1
1945	3	1	2	2	0	0	0	0
1946	13	5	8	5	2[q]	1[q]	0	0
1947	13	3	10	8	1	0	1	0
1948	16	0	16	16	2[r]	0	0	0
1949	7	0	6	6	0	0	0	1

Sources: 1910–1919, Adolph Jenson, *Forligsmands Institutionen* (Copenhagen, 1919); 1920–1949, Typewritten data prepared for the author by the Mediation Institution.
[a] Accepted subsequently. [b] One case involved 27 trades. [c] One during subsequent negotiations. [d] Rejected in one subgroup.
[e] Proposal for new vote in one case rejected by both parties. [f] Agreement reached after new negotiations. [g] One case involved 37 trades.
[h] Proposal adopted after 3 votes excepting one trade, which after a lockout concluded an agreement with the assistance of the mediator.
[i] Proposal ratified after new negotiations. [j] One case involved 19 trades. [k] One proposal ratified after strike and new negotiations.
[l] Followed by compulsory arbitration. [m] Several cases involved numerous crafts. [n] Cases not classified for this year; the majority were settled by compulsory arbitration.
[o] Mediation proposal enacted into law. [p] Subject to compulsory arbitration. [q] Two mediation proposals enacted into law. [r] Two proposals adopted after new negotiations.

had the most to gain by intervention. The redress of this balance of power, beginning with the early 1930's, has led to a notably less critical attitude toward mediation by the organized employers.[11]

GOVERNMENT COMPULSION

The failure of mediation to produce agreement leaves two alternatives, a stoppage of work or further government intervention of a compulsory character. The latter alternative was first employed in 1933, but it has been used on numerous occasions since, as Table 14 shows.[12] The practice of compulsory intervention, it is interesting to note, was inaugurated by a socialist government.

Even prior to 1933 there had been many proponents of compulsory arbitration. A socialist government that held office for a few months in 1925 had prepared a law for submission to the parliament designed to end a long strike by the Laborers' Union, but a negotiated peace made its enactment unnecessary. Representatives of the Radical Left Party (comparable to the British Liberal Party) on the industrial commission of 1925 favored permanent compulsory arbitration of major disputes, but both the trade union and employer representatives were strongly opposed on the ground that it would destroy collective bargaining.

The first actual instance of intervention came in 1933 under dramatic circumstances. The Employers' Association had been attempting to effect a general 20 per cent reduction of wages, in view of a price decline, but the trade unions refused even to discuss it. After a few brief sessions, the mediator reported that he would not be able to formulate a mediation proposal, whereupon the Stauning government immediately presented to parliament a bill forbidding work stoppages and extending all collective agreements, unaltered, for one year. The Employers' Association was assured by the leaders of the Conservative and Agrarian parties, which between them had enough votes to defeat the bill, that it would never become law. The next day, however, much to the consternation of the employers, the agrarians voted with the socialists to enact the

[11] The fiftieth anniversary history of the Employers' Association makes the following pertinent observations: "During the years preceding World War II the mediation institution again found firm ground under its feet. It had never abandoned its mandate as conciliator between employers and workers, and it always had as its purpose to further the understanding and cooperation with which their own interests and those of society as a whole could best be served. Therefore the Employers' Association, though it has not always been pleased by all mediation proceedings, looks upon the entrance of the mediation institution into its old rights, and the reassumption of its peace making activities, with sincere satisfaction." Vigen, Agerholm, og Plum, p. 360.

[12] Table 14 indicates that on three separate occasions special legislation was required in disputes involving the packing house workers. This is explicable by the fact that the meatpacking industry is a key one in Denmark, owing to the importance to the national economy of bacon exports, so that work stoppages have been regarded as emergency in character.

law, in return for a devaluation of approximately 20 per cent in the Danish crown, which was expected to promote the export of agricultural commodities.

This so-called *Kanslergade Agreement* was received with bitterness by the employers, who denounced the Agrarian Party for delivering "a brutal blow" to business interests under pressure from its semi-fascist

TABLE 14

TYPE OF GOVERNMENT INTERVENTION IN DANISH LABOR DISPUTES, 1933–1950[a]

Year	Scope of Dispute	Type of Intervention
1933	All expiring agreements	Agreements extended for one year, without change, by law. Opposed by employers.
1934	Packinghouse workers	*Ad hoc* compulsory arbitration board.
1936	National wage movement	*Ad hoc* compulsory arbitration board after a lockout lasting five weeks.
1937	National wage movement	Mediation proposal enacted into law after rejection by employers.
1938	Packinghouse workers	Mediation proposal enacted into law after rejection by employers.
1939	Typographical workers	Mediation proposal enacted into law after rejection by union.
1939	Dairy workers	Mediation proposal enacted into law after rejection by employers.
1940–1945	All workers	Compulsory arbitration of all labor disputes during the German occupation.
1946	Packinghouse workers	Mediation proposal enacted into law after rejection by workers.
1946	Laborers' Union	Mediation proposal, preceded by a strike of one month, enacted into law after rejection by employers.
1950	Agricultural laborers	Mediation proposal, in substantially altered form, enacted into law after rejection by employers.

[a] The texts of the various laws referred to in the table may be found in Knud V. Jensen, *Arbejdsretten i Danmark* (Copenhagen, 1946), pp. 224–240.

extremist wing.[13] Some doubts were also expressed in trade unions circles, but the necessity of the law from the labor point of view was clear. Unemployment stood at about 28 per cent of total trade union membership, and the employers were clearly determined to lock out their workers until the unions accepted a wage reduction. Under the circumstances, the opportunists triumphed over those who opposed compulsion in principle.

Three years later, in order to bring to an end a lockout which threatened to end in defeat for the trade unions, the socialist government again resorted to compulsion. This time, however, they were forced to act through the medium of an *ad hoc* board of compulsory arbitration, though their initial intent had been merely to enact into law a mediation proposal previously rejected. As it turned out, the arbitration board followed the mediation proposal almost literally.

Thereafter, except during the period of war and occupation,[14] enactment of the mediation proposal into law became the customary method of government intervention beyond mediation. The increasing frequency of intervention was criticized by many members of the Federation of Labor, which remained officially opposed to compulsory arbitration. Symptomatic of the difficulty that labor has had in reconciling its conflicting views on this subject is the following resolution, adopted by the 1937 congress of the Federation:

> The recent changes in the manner in which collective agreements are renewed, whereby Parliament, in the furtherance of labor peace, has intervened, have opened perspectives of great significance for the trade union movement. At the same time, the possibility of a new type of speculation in collective bargaining has been opened, for the calculating appraisal of what it is possible to achieve with or without a work stoppage is no longer the unique determinant of what stand the parties shall take. The reduced risk of work stoppages, resulting from outside intervention, may produce unfortunate irresponsibility in voting on collective agreements . . . It would therefore be regrettable if the

[13] *Dansk Arbejdsgiverforenings Generalforsamlinger*, 1933, pp. 34–39.

[14] In September 1940, on the joint recommendation of the Employers' Association and the Federation of Labor, a compulsory arbitration law was enacted, suspending the right to strike or lock out. Under the plan of this law, disputes that could not be resolved by direct bargaining were to be submitted to a Joint Committee composed of three representatives of each of the central organizations. Failure of this body to secure agreement resulted in submission of the dispute to a tripartite Labor and Conciliation Board, with power to make a binding award in final settlement.

Eighty per cent of the disputes that were brought to the Joint Committee were disposed of at that level, either unanimously or by majority vote. Of the matters that required submission to the Labor and Conciliation Board, only 40 per cent had to be decided by the neutral members. In all, prior to the abolition of compulsory arbitration in November 1945, the Joint Committee handled 1,559 disputes and the Labor and Conciliation Board, 521 disputes. *Under Samvirkets Flag*, pp. 364–367; Vigen, Agerholm og Plum, pp. 87–90.

notion became prevalent that government intervention in labor disputes is natural and normal. We warn against this idea and appeal to all positive forces instead to join together in an endeavor to build up our mediation system.[15]

The most recent instance of government intervention may mark a new phase in Danish practice. It occurred in connection with a dispute in 1950 between the Agricultural Employers' Association and the union representing agricultural workers. A mediation proposal which included a reduction of working time was rejected by the employers, who steadfastly refused to make any concession in this regard. To avoid a shutdown of the dairy industry, the socialist government introduced a bill in the parliament which would have enacted the mediation proposal into law, following customary procedure. But the farmers' party refused to agree, and the necessary parliamentary majority was not at hand. For a few days mediation sessions were held in the parliament building under the aegis of an interparty parliamentary commission, and finally the parties agreed to a settlement raising wages above the level contained in the mediation proposal, but deleting the reduction in working time. Since neither employer nor trade union representatives were willing openly to espouse the agreement, it was enacted into law by the parliament.

This dispute was notable for two facts: it represented a breach of the practice of enacting the mediation proposal into law without alteration, and it involved the parliament in the details of a labor dispute to a much greater degree than had previously been the case. If this controversy should prove a pattern for future procedure, rather than an isolated instance springing from the fact that agricultural rather than the usual industrial interests were involved, the mediation system will soon lose its meaning, and the final settlement of major labor disputes will become purely and explicitly a political matter.

The trade unions still retain an ambivalent attitude toward government intervention. In theory, they have never disclaimed their attachment to free collective bargaining. "So long as private entrepreneurs and their organizations continue to play a decisive role in the economy, it will not be advisable for the trade unions to yield any significant portion of their influence by transferring the function of wage determination to the government . . ." [16] Practice is quite another matter; the unions have not permitted general principles to stand in the way of the undoubted gains that may be achieved through political means, and admit candidly that their attitude is shaped at any given time by the character

[15] De Samvirkende Fagforbund, *Protokol over Generalforsamlingen*, 1937, pp. 20–21.
[16] *Beretning om De Samvirkende Fagforbunds Virksomhed*, 1946, p. 17.

of the government in office.[17] However, the realization is growing that under a democratic system of government, intervention cannot remain one-sided, but must be used to curb worker irresponsibility when necessary. Stauning once remarked in a prescient speech, "I have always known that major labor disputes would have to be stopped when the workers gain power in society and responsibility for its conduct." [18]

The employers, who have come out second best in most cases of intervention, remain staunch opponents of government compulsion. Recognizing, however, that the theoretical retention of their power to lock workers out is largely contingent upon their abstention from exercising it, some of the leaders of the Employers' Association have begun to think in terms of private arbitration as an extension of the mediation process.[19] The difficulty with their position, however, is that they insist that issues of *vital* interest, such as a demand for a general wage reduction during a recession, must not be subject to arbitration without the consent of both parties, and that it is precisely these intractable issues that the parties are least likely voluntarily to submit to arbitration.

It is fair to say that the necessity of government intervention to prevent general work stoppages is widely recognized in Denmark, despite the reservations that the different social groups retain. As between permanent and *ad hoc* intervention, it is the latter which has by far the greater support. Trade unions and management are united in their opposition to a permanent board of arbitration on the Norwegian or Australian model.[20] The arguments for the alternative *ad hoc* procedure, requiring parliamentary action in each separate instance, may be summarized as follows:

1. Since the machinery is not automatic, it is maintained, the parties are never certain that the government will act and must therefore be prepared to accept the full consequences of their failure to agree. If this were actually true at all times, it would constitute a telling argument, since the enervating impact of compulsory arbitration upon collective bargaining would thereby be reduced materially. In fact, however, the degree of indeterminateness is sharply reduced when labor holds political

[17] "It is natural that the position of the trade unions toward government intervention must be determined in part by their relation to the government in power . . . As long as the social democrats remain the leading political party in the parliament and in the government, the trade unions have a guarantee that the power of the state will never be used against the interests of the worker. But the same does not hold true if the government is in the hands of those with employer sympathies." *Under Samvirkets Flag*, p. 356.

[18] *Fagbevaegelsen og De Økonomiske Problemer*, p. 31.

[19] For example, the statement of Chairman Hans L. Larsen, *Arbejdsgiveren* (April 15, 1949), p. 101.

[20] For an excellent summary of the arguments against this method, see F. Zeuthen, *Arbejdsløn og Arbejdsløshed* (Copenhagen, 1939), pp. 224–234.

power. As already noted, a socialist government is unlikely to allow a general lockout of workers. Moreover, the trade union leadership is hardly likely, at the very minimum, to remain uninformed with regard to the intentions of a socialist government, and in all probability exercises considerable influence in determining its policies in this respect. The risk of an unwanted work stoppage is confined largely to unions that refuse to follow the line of the Federation leadership, particularly in the case of political opponents.[21]

2. While a particular type of government action, enactment of mediation proposals into law, has become customary, it is not certain that in a particular situation another form of intervention may not be employed. For example, the government might be reluctant to act on the basis of a mediation proposal that had been rejected by a large majority of the workers. Furthermore, should the mediator fail to issue a proposal, an alternate form of arbitration would become necessary. This uncertainty serves to place a premium upon acceptance of the mediation proposal, for neither labor nor management is disposed to welcome arbitration by a neutral board, in all probability chosen from among the judiciary, with little insight into the problems of labor relations.

3. It is the contention of the labor movement that distribution of the national income, one of the most important determinants of which is the general wage level, is essentially a political rather than an economic question, and should therefore be resolved at the highest political level. "If the state is to fix wages, it must be the parliament that does it." [22] There is considerable force in this argument, for under conditions of a controlled economy and a democratic political system there is ultimately no other forum for making this basic decision.

4. As for the specific form of *ad hoc* intervention latterly practiced in Denmark, its champions claim that it possesses a combination of flexibility and economic realism that cannot be matched by formal arbitration. The mediation proposal assures to the parties a large measure of control over the conditions which may be imposed upon them by law. In many cases failure to reach agreement results not so much from the absence of a common ground as from the unwillingness of leadership to take the responsibility for what is likely to be an unpopular settlement. By adopting a noncommittal attitude toward a mediation proposal that is subsequently enacted into law, negotiating committees are able at

[21] This is borne out by a strike of the communist-led Copenhagen printers in 1947. It was confidently expected that the government would not permit suspension of all the city's newspapers on the eve of general parliamentary elections, but when the strike deadline was reached and the government failed to act, the union was obliged to embark upon what turned out to be a long and losing work stoppage.

[22] *Under Samvirkets Flag*, p. 363.

the same time to mold an agreement and evade responsibility for its imposition.

Compulsory government intervention has had serious repercussions upon mediation. Historically, the sole concern of the mediator was to bring about a reconciliation, without regard to its impact upon the nation's economy. Although nominally a government official, he had been permitted to function in virtual independence of the regular governmental agencies, and was in fact a creature of the central bargaining organizations. But the new government policy implied the strengthening of his arbitral functions and the transformation of the mediation proposal from a private to a public document. Thenceforth the mediator was required to weigh the economic effects of his proposals as well as their dispute-settling potentialities. Moreover, for reasons of public policy it might be desirable to have him issue a mediation proposal without securing the assent of the negotiating parties, if the government desired one as the basis for parliamentary action, thus introducing a political factor into the mediation process. To the extent that government pressure is placed upon the mediator, the mediation proposal comes perilously close to being an arbitration award, and the parties will presumably adjust themselves to the new situation either by placing primary emphasis on convincing the mediator of the rectitude of their positions, or by resorting to their political power to secure a favorable mediation proposal. Thus far, however, mediation has remained remarkably free of partisan political considerations, a tribute to the present mediator.

Danish mediation is currently undergoing a functional metamorphosis, and it is not yet evident what the final result will be. Perhaps the principal lesson it carries is the inadequacy of the conceptual framework customarily employed in classifying the forms of government intervention. Elements of conciliation, mediation, fact finding, and arbitration are all present, but these categories are too discrete to describe adequately the subtle and constantly changing gradations of influence that modern government exerts upon collective bargaining. It must be realized that each of these terms covers a range of methods rather than any specific method and that the intervals frequently overlap.

Another remarkable aspect of the history of Danish industrial relations is the gradual encroachment of state intervention despite the strong ideological bent of both labor and employers toward untrammeled collective bargaining. Nostalgic references to the success of direct bargaining in Sweden continue to appear in the Danish trade press. Yet the shadow of government over the labor market continues to lengthen, suggesting the operation of underlying forces which may well be at work even beyond the borders of Denmark.

The growth of centralization in collective bargaining certainly renders it less likely that the government will refrain from intervention. Periodic work stoppages may be accepted as the price of rational wage determination as long as they are partial. But when they begin to assume the character of general industrial shutdowns, which involve serious economic loss, their repression will eventually be forced by public demand. In Sweden, where to a greater extent than in any other country of Europe the state has remained outside of labor disputes, Professor Ohlin notes the approach of "a situation in which most of the trade unions have to negotiate collective agreements at the same time every year, well knowing that whatever increases they win the white collar workers will get very soon afterwards, and the farmers as well, through an agreement with the government on farm prices." [23] There are signs that the increasing bargaining centralization is beginning to undermine traditional practice even there.

Consolidation of the wage determination function appears to be in turn a consequence of government economic intervention designed to maintain a high level of employment and output, and of more complete labor market organization. Under those circumstances, sectional wage setting becomes difficult, for the rigidity of wage structure under conditions of a high degree of union organization accentuates the repercussive effect of change at any point in the structure. Relatively minor wage adjustments may set off a chain of reactions that affect the general wage level, and therefore require reconciliation with over-all economic policy. It is not inconceivable, for example, that a small trade union could checkmate the efforts of a nation through price control to maintain the international competitive position of its products.

The great depression led in Denmark to the creation of a network of government economic controls[24] that are hardly likely to be relaxed sufficiently to permit the resumption of collective wage determination uninhibited by considerations of global economic policy. On the contrary, all signs point to the development of what Ohlin has termed the "social-liberal frame economy" [25] at the very minimum, with a further tendency in the direction of centralist socialism. In this environment atomistic collective bargaining is anachronistic, while the role of the central bargaining agencies is almost certain to be augmented.

[23] Bertil Ohlin, *The Problem of Employment Stabilization* (New York, 1949), p. 101.

[24] For an analysis of these controls, see Kjeld Philip, *Den Danske Kriselovgivning 1931–38* (Copenhagen, 1939).

[25] Ohlin, pp. 97–98.

In sum, certainly in the case of Denmark and probably elsewhere in Europe, work stoppages based upon economic disputes will be regarded with increasing intolerance. Under the circumstances, the pattern of Danish government intervention has much to commend it. It preserves some of the risks of bargaining and does not thereby completely stifle the will to agree. The instrument of government policy, the mediation proposal, is firmly rooted in the collective bargaining process but at the same time can be made to reflect public policy. Finally, the ultimate parliamentary solution provides an opportunity for functional bargaining among the broad social groups that is the only democratic alternative to a free market economy.

THE LAW OF INDUSTRIAL WARFARE

While the incidence of work stoppages has diminished in Denmark, there has by no means been a complete cessation, nor is there likely to be as long as present political institutions persist. Apart from the complex of collective agreements that expire uniformly, there are numerous smaller wage movements that occasionally give rise to open warfare. Moreover, under certain circumstances, legal work stoppages may take place even during the term of existing agreements.

Compared with the United States, the means adopted by Danish employers in their struggles with trade unions have been moderate. Denial of work opportunities, made possible by the extent of organization among employers, has been relied upon more than positive repression. While the blacklist, the "yellow dog" contract, and the use of strikebreakers are not unknown, they were largely abandoned by organized employers after the conclusion of the September Agreement in 1899.[26] The lockout, on the other hand, has been employed systematically and effectively. Through use of this weapon the Employers' Association has been able to prevent trade unions from breaking a wage line by concentrating upon the weaker employers. Union attempts to overcome employers one by one have been met with concerted employer action, occasionally having the effect of spiraling minor disputes into major stoppages by a strike–lockout–counterstrike–counterlockout process.

Perhaps the most notable difference between industrial warfare in Denmark and in the United States has been the relatively minor regulatory role of the regular courts in the former. This is attributable chiefly to the September Agreement, on the basis of which some rationale can usually be found for bringing the incidents arising out of labor disputes

[26] On the docks, however, important strikes in 1902, 1913–1914, and 1920 were defeated through the use of strikebreakers. In the latter year, the strikebreakers were provided by a group of young businessmen organized to check what they regarded as the growing lawlessness of trade unions.

between organized employers and workers to the Labor Court. Much of the law of the boycott, for example, lies within the orbit of the Labor Court, for the question is usually whether a trade union may interfere with the operations of an employer, bound by a valid agreement, who is not a party to the immediate controversy. Organized employers have endeavored whenever possible to bring their actions in the Labor Court, not least because its prestige among workers facilitates compliance. Suits in the ordinary courts have been largely brought by employers unaffiliated with the Employers' Association.

This has been a fortunate development for the labor movement, since the regular courts tended to be strict in their views on the propriety of trade union methods. The right to organize was assured by the Danish Constitution of 1849, and the right to strike in interest disputes, as a general proposition, has not been questioned since, but the means and purposes of trade union actions have been scrutinized carefully, and the allowable area of economic conflict sharply defined.

1. *Means.* Such is the degree of organization among Danish workers that overt acts of bringing pressure to bear upon employers is secondary in importance to the mere abstention from work. Picketing is rarely employed, and then never *en masse.* The customary method of announcing a strike is through a notice in the labor press, which is ordinarily sufficient to prevent any further work from being carried on at the affected establishment. Peaceful picketing for the purpose of acquainting *workers* with the existence of a strike is not unlawful, though the courts have been disposed to ban appeals to *customers* not to patronize.[27]

Nonstriking workers, in the rare instances in which they were found, were afforded a considerable degree of legal protection. Publication of the names of strikebreakers was held by the courts to be an actionable offense. The doctrine of inducing breach of contract has occasionally resulted in the outlawing of otherwise lawful means, though the "yellow dog" contract has never attained any importance, partly because the remedy is ordinarily an action for damages rather than for an injunction.

2. *Purposes.* The courts have scrutinized the purposes for which strikes were undertaken and held those to be in violation of law in which the principal aim of the union was deemed to be the inflicting of injury rather than the attainment of some legitimate union objective. The purpose of effecting changes in conditions of employment, either through a new or altered collective agreement, has generally been upheld. But there have been limitations; for example, it was considered unlawful for a union to attempt by force to seek an agreement with an employer whose operations lay outside its customary jurisdiction. Similarly, rival

[27] See the cases collected in Illum, p. 373, note 15.

union warfare has been condemned in the presence of a valid collective agreement.

It is not a necessary condition of legality that a trade union have membership among the employees of an establishment against which a strike has been declared, if its purpose is to organize the establishment. Where the September Agreement does not apply, the closed shop has been held a lawful labor objective, though the nonunion worker has been given the right by law to join the union for which his work qualifications make him eligible.[28] However, the courts have vacillated on the question of whether a union may seek to discipline a member by securing his discharge under a closed shop agreement, except where he has been guilty of strikebreaking, an offense which is regarded as proper cause for discipline.

3. *The allowable area of economic conflict.* The boycott problem never reached serious dimensions in Denmark, unlike Norway and Sweden, where it was the subject of special legislation. This is attributable to the acceptance in the September Agreement of the principle of sympathetic action. The relatively few litigated boycotts in Denmark were those imposed against unorganized agricultural employers.

An indication of the probable treatment of the labor boycott by the courts is afforded by the famous *Kolinsund* case. A dispute arose in 1923 between the Agricultural Workers' Union and a group of farmers who refused to extend collective agreements that had been in effect between the union and a corporation from which they had recently acquired their property. A strike ensued, during the course of which the union endeavored to prevent the sale of their products and the delivery of supplies. Purchasers of the boycotted goods were named in the labor press and placed on an unfair list. When the case eventually came to the Supreme Court, the employers were awarded 220,000 kroner in damages on the following basis:

> Because of the manner in which the defendant prosecuted the strike, it must be considered unlawful; weight is accorded to the fact that the defendant, in an unlawful manner, publicly accused the Owners' Association of locking out its workers; that the defendant on several occasions published the names of persons who helped plaintiffs dispose of their products; and that the defendants, by various means, including appeal to and threat of strike and boycott against plaintiff's customers, have endeavored to prevent the plaintiffs entirely from disposing of their goods.[29]

This opinion appears to take a restrictive view of the allowable area,

[28] For the evolution of this doctrine, which has its basis in general equitable rules rather than in statute, see Illum, pp. 35–45.

[29] Landarbejderforbund i Danmark, *Kolinsund* (Copenhagen, 1927); Carl Ussing, *Retsmaessige og Retsstridige Arbejdsstandsinger* (Copenhagen, 1928).

but the relatively few cases that were decided subsequently are not sufficient basis for conclusive determination of the Court's attitude. At any rate it is the Labor Court, rather than the Supreme Court, which made the significant law on this subject.

The only piece of legislation relevant to a discussion of the law of industrial warfare was an act of March 27, 1929, enacted by an Agrarian government against the vigorous opposition of both labor and industrial management. The following were its significant provisions:

1. Collective agreements that unlawfully limit the free access of an individual to commerce or employment cannot be enforced by the courts . . .
2. Any economic or personal persecution, including use of the boycott, which is intended unlawfully to limit the free access of an individual to commerce or employment or his (her) right to join or remain outside an organization, is unlawful and punishable by a maximum fine of 100,000 kroner or imprisonment.

This law merely codified previous court practice, the only new element being the addition of criminal penalties to the customary damages. Repealed in 1937, its significance was summarized in the following terms by a labor source: "The purpose of the law was clearly and distinctly to hurt the labor movement. It had no great significance in practice. In part the courts were hesitant in using it, and in part Denmark is so well organized a country, on the employer side as well, that the law was a two-edged sword which could affect others than workers." [30]

While the foregoing account of the role of the ordinary courts in labor disputes is brief, the intrinsic importance of the subject does not warrant the fuller treatment that would be mandatory in any similar account of American industrial relations. After considering some economic aspects of collective bargaining, attention will be given to the Danish Labor Court, established jointly by labor and management to provide a forum for the adjudication of collective disputes. The real corpus of Danish labor law is to be found in the many decisions of that tribunal.

[30] Christiansen, pp. 120–121.

CHAPTER VIII

WAGE MOVEMENTS

THE PREVIOUS CHAPTERS have been largely concerned with the methods of collective bargaining. The purpose of this and the following chapter is to appraise the operation of the system of labor relations through an examination of its economic results.

METHODS OF WAGE PAYMENT[1]

Except for the so-called "elastic" wage system employed in the metal trades and a few other industries, Danish methods of wage payment present little that is unfamiliar elsewhere.

Piece work

Ever since 1870, piece work has been common in Denmark, particularly in the skilled trades where equalitarianism was not strong. The socialists initially opposed payment by the piece on doctrinaire grounds, but with the growing power of trade unions and the distinct preference of many groups of workers for piece work, their policy was altered to one of neutrality. Thus, "the piece rate system at the present time has as many proponents as opponents within the labor movement." [2]

The attitude of the worker toward piece work is largely governed by the incremental wage that piece rates offer over time rates, since it is assumed that piece work entails a faster work tempo. The wage differential is influenced in part by cyclical movements, since piece-rate earnings tend to be more flexible than time-rate earnings, particularly where the piece-rate system is not based upon fixed price lists, but entails negotiation of new rates at frequent intervals. There are offsetting factors: for example, workers may attempt to maintain their earnings in the face of declining piece rates by increasing their speed. Moreover, in the absence of strict seniority there is a tendency for work tempo to rise in depression owing to the retention of the most efficient sector of the labor force. But in general, the piece-rate–time-rate differential should be

[1] An excellent discussion of this subject is to be found in Eiler Jensen, "Arbejdernes Lønformer," *Socialt Tidsskrift*, 1941, p. 225.

[2] *Under Samvirkets Flag*, p. 380.

reduced in the downswing and increased in the upswing, and trade union advocacy of piece work should fluctuate accordingly.

Table 15 shows the proportion of total labor hours performed by the piece and the percentage differential of piece- over time-rate earnings for alternate years from 1921 to 1949 (data for the years 1933 and 1935 are not available). The differential in earnings is greater in the case of the unskilled workers despite the fact that the hours worked differential is greater for the skilled workers. This may be attributed to the fact that

TABLE 15

EXTENT OF PIECE WORK AND PIECE-RATE–TIME-RATE DIFFERENTIALS IN DENMARK, 1921–1949

Year	Percentage of Total Labor Hours Performed by the Piece			Percentage Excess of Piece- over Time-Rate Earnings		
	Skilled[a]	Unskilled[a]	All Workers[b]	Skilled[a]	Unskilled[a]	All Workers[b]
1921	46.0	26.0	39.3	17.9	39.5	22.9
1923	46.7	28.7	40.7	13.8	30.6	17.1
1925	51.7	31.9	44.8	16.4	34.8	21.6
1927	48.0	31.6	43.4	14.9	33.3	19.6
1929	51.4	33.9	45.6	16.9	36.0	23.5
1931	50.2	33.9	44.5	21.0	34.4	25.2
1937	46.0	29.7	40.5	19.5	32.8	24.2
1939	47.1	31.1	41.3	20.6	31.9	24.8
1941	41.0	25.1	34.9	20.6	26.5	22.1
1943	42.8	27.1	35.1	24.5	34.1	29.1
1945	38.3	24.3	32.7	25.9	39.8	31.7
1947	46.3	29.8	38.5	22.5	44.5	32.9
1949	48.2	31.7	40.7	15.9	25.4	20.1

Sources: *1921–1925, Statistiske Meddelelser*, vol. 78, no. 1 (1927). Data for 1921 are for month of September, for 1923 and 1925, July quarter. *1927–1931, Statistiske Meddelelser*, vol. 91, no. 5 (1933). Data are for the July quarter. *1937–1943, Under Samvirkets Flag*, p. 382. Averages for the year. *1945–1949, Arbejdsgiveren*, vol. 47, no. 10, p. 142; vol. 49, no. 5, p. 69; vol. 51, no. 6, p. 78. Data are for the July quarter.

[a] Includes male workers only.

[b] Includes male and female workers.

only the better unskilled workers are afforded the opportunity of working by the piece, so that the wage differential includes a skill factor which is absent in the case of the skilled workers.

Although no precise statistical relationship between cyclical changes and piece-rate–time-rate wage differentials emerges from the data in Table 15, there does appear to have been a rough tendency for the differential to contract in times of falling wage rates, and to increase in times of rising wage rates. The inflationary period that began in 1939 constitutes the chief exception to this tendency, for particularly in the years 1939–1941 and 1947–1949 money wage rates and the differentials moved in opposite directions. It will be recalled, however, that a considerable proportion of the wage increases received by workers after 1939 was in the form of cost of living index supplements paid equally to all workers (women and youths excepted), so that at least a portion of the wage inflation exerted no direct effect upon the piece-rate–time-rate differential.

The ratio of piece-work hours to total hours worked does not appear

TABLE 16

RELATION OF WAGE CHANGES TO EXTENT OF PIECE WORK, SELECTED COPENHAGEN CRAFTS

Crafts	Percentage of Piece Work Hours to Total Hours Worked		Average Hourly Earnings (Øre)		Per Cent Increase in Earnings, 1920 to 1949
	1920	1949	1920	1949	
A. *Time work*					
Machinists	6.0	16.4	227	357	57.3
Electricians	32.9	31.6	234	367	56.8
Cabinetmakers	22.0 (1921)	44.4	235	340	44.7
Carriage makers	10.5 (1921)	24.4	254	397	56.3
Printers	5.0 (1922)	0.3	261	371	42.1
Average (unweighted)			242	366	51.2
B. *Piece work*					
Cigar makers	100.0	98.0	198	320	61.6
Ceramics workers	64.3	92.1	234	365	56.0
Upholsterers	74.4 (1921)	81.8	250	392	56.8
Painters	89.9	84.5	274	378	38.0
Tanners	70.8	81.9	279	387	38.7
Average (unweighted)			247	368	49.0

Sources: *Statistiske Meddelelser*, vol. 78, no. 1; *Arbejdsgiveren*, vol. 51, no. 6, pp. 80–81.

to have been uniquely correlated with the ratio between piece- and time-rate earnings. The former ratio displayed much greater stability than the latter, a fact to be anticipated from the institutional difficulty of shifting from one type of wage payment to another.

By 1949, as compared with 1921, the use of piece work had increased slightly for both skilled and unskilled workers. However, the differential between piece- and time-rate earnings had been compressed, particularly in the case of unskilled workers. The uniform cost of living supplement element in gross earnings undoubtedly caused part of the contraction, and the tight postwar labor market enabled many time workers to obtain special supplements to bring them nearer the piece earning level.

An interesting question is whether piece work confers a bargaining advantage upon the workers who practice it, in comparison with time work. A test is provided by comparing wage trends in the piece-rate and time-rate trades, for a relative bargaining advantage, other things being equal, should yield differentially advantageous earnings in the long run. In Table 16, average hourly earnings for ten crafts, five of them working primarily by the piece and five of them primarily on time, are compared for the years 1920 and 1949.[3] It should be noted that there has been no shift among the crafts with respect to the relative employment of piece work; a comparison of the piece-work percentages for 1920 and 1949 reveals this fact clearly.

The data in Table 16 show that the wage experience of the two groups since 1920 has been quite similar. The average wage increase of the time-work crafts was slightly higher than that for the piece-work crafts. It may be concluded, on the basis of these data, that piece work appeared to confer no advantage upon the crafts employing it for the period studied.[4]

Many different types of piece-rate systems are employed in Denmark. Group piece work is frequently found; a price is fixed for a specific job, and the total pay divided among the members of the group either equally or in proportion to their individual base rates.[5] In the absence of fixed price lists, the workers are usually protected from error in estimating jobs by guaranteed minimum hourly rates.

Piece-rate flexibility is due to the possibility of bargaining during the contract term over rates for work which is not specifically covered by agreement. If piece work is obligatory by agreement, failure to agree upon new rates may lead to work stoppages. In many trades, however, disagreement over new piece rates leads to the performance of the work on an hourly basis, with earnings intermediate between straight time

[3] The crafts were chosen so that the average earnings of the piece-rate and time-rate groups in 1920 should be approximately equal, since there has been a general tendency for the lower wage crafts to gain more percentagewise than the higher rated crafts (see below, pp. 178–180). Actually, the piece-work crafts had higher earnings than the time-work crafts in 1920, but this appears to have been due primarily to the influence of the building trades, which combined high hourly rates and high percentages of piece-work hours to total hours worked.

[4] The conclusion is restricted to the inter-craft comparison, and says nothing about relative gains of piece and time workers within the same crafts.

[5] Take, for example, a group including two journeymen with basic hourly rates of 3 kroner each, one journeyman with an hourly rate of 2.75 kroner, and a laborer with an hourly rate of 2.25 kroner. If all worked the same number of hours on a job priced at 1,100 kroner, they would receive, respectively, 300 kroner, 300 kroner, 275 kroner and 225 kroner. Wage differentials are extremely important in the case of group work, for a wage increase for one worker would actually mean a wage cut for the others.

and average piece-rate earnings. Piece-rate disputes are not generally regarded as disputes over contract interpretation, and they are therefore not within the jurisdiction of the Labor Court.

Where *ad hoc* pricing of work is the rule, the local union ordinarily maintains a rate book, in which all the relevant details of each job are entered as an aid to future pricing. Maintaining this book is one of the most important duties of the shop steward, who is also instructed to prevent any tendency toward a speed up by individual workers "by speaking to them and asking that they take into consideration the interests of their fellow workers, and if representations do no good, by bringing the matter before the competent trade union body." [6]

The "elastic" wage system

One of the most interesting features of Danish methods of wage payment is the "minimum" or "elastic" system employed in the metal trades and a few other industries. Based upon a combination of individual and collective bargaining, it is designed to afford wage flexibility within the contract term.

The 1948 collective agreement covering the metal trades, where the system is developed most fully, provided for a "minimum" wage (*minimalløn*) of 96 øre per hour, and a "least payment" (*mindstebetaling*) of 125 øre per hour. When the system was originally established, around 1900, the "minimum" wage was the actual minimum that might be paid a worker for an hour of labor. His actual earnings, then as now, were determined by individual bargaining with his employer, on the basis of the "*løfte*" paragraph, which provides that "for more skilled and responsible workers wages shall be adjusted in each case between the employer or his representative and the worker without interference by labor and employer organizations or their members."

In 1923 a new effective minimum rate, the "least payment," was introduced. The old "minimum" wage had become obsolete as a result of wartime inflation, but it was retained as the basis for calculating certain percentage supplements to wages, for example, overtime pay. Through its retention, employers were able to minimize inflation of the supplemental rates. The "minimum" wage also continues to serve as a stable base from which workers customarily measure their individual rates.

The "least payment" has itself tended to become outmoded. The 1948 "least payment" of 125 øre per hour may be contrasted with average

[6] Kaj Bundvad, Eiler Jensen, and Christian Christiansen, *Tillidsmands Kundskab* (Copenhagen, 1946), pp. 51–52.

[7] I am indebted to Mr. Holger Jensen for access to his unpublished manuscript on this subject, "Lønsystemet Indenfor Jern og Metalindustrien," 1948.

hourly earnings of 364 øre in Copenhagen and 317 øre in the provinces. Very few workers in the metal trades do not receive more than the "least payment." However, the Metal Worker's Union has been reluctant to push the rate higher lest during a business recession, as a consequence of downward wage inflexibility, unemployment be created among the less qualified workers. The union also wanted the rate low to prevent a possible invasion of the skilled jurisdiction by unskilled workers during recession. There has thus been an explicit policy of preserving wage flexibility by maintaining a wide range between going rates and the effective minimum rate.

It should not be inferred that either the "minimum" wage or the "least payment" is completely immobile. Both have moved upward slowly, and parallel. From January 1924 to March 1948, the "minimum" rose from 74 to 96 øre per hour (30 per cent), while the "least payment" rose from 95 to 125 øre per hour (32 per cent). During this same period, however, average hourly earnings increased from 169 øre to 366 øre, 117 per cent.

In addition to the two minimum rates, each worker has a base rate (the *ansat* or *grund timeløn*), which is determined by individual bargaining. For hourly rated workers, actual earnings are calculated from the base rate; for example, the effective hourly rate may be set at a specified absolute amount over the base rate. For piece workers, the base rate provides a basis for wage allocation in group piece work, common in the metal trades. Because of the many supplements to wages that have been introduced in recent years, effective rates are often much higher than base rates; in the last quarter of 1948, for example, average hourly earnings in the Copenhagen metal trades were 376 øre against an average base rate of 179 øre.

The range of effective rates in the metal trades is wide; for individual shops in Copenhagen it varied from 290 to 670 øre per hour in 1948. It must be remembered, however, that the metal trades do not comprise a homogeneous industry. The individual rates therefore reflect differences in craft as well as in skill.

Earnings, both in the case of hourly rated and piece workers, tend to move parallel to base rates in the long run, with earnings the more flexible. This is due to the fact that employers prefer to add supplements to the base rate rather than to increase the rate itself, since workers resist more strongly reductions in their base rates than in the supplements. Thus, from January 1939 to January 1946 average base rates in the metal trades rose by 19 per cent, whereas average hourly earnings (inclusive of cost of living supplements) rose by 64 per cent.

To summarize, there are four wage bands in the metal trades: the "minimum" wage, the "least payment," the base rate, and the effective rate, listed in the order reverse to their cyclical flexibility. The first two are determined by collective bargaining, the third by individual bargaining. The effective rate is fixed by the addition of collectively determined supplements to the individual base rates.

For purposes of determining the true elasticity of this system of wage payment, average hourly earnings in the metal trades are compared with all-industrial earnings for the years 1920–1948 in Table 17. During the downswing that occurred after 1920, metal trades wages moved down-

TABLE 17

AVERAGE HOURLY EARNINGS IN ALL INDUSTRY AND IN THE METAL TRADES, 1920–1948

Year	(1) Index of Average Hourly Earnings, All Industry (*1920 = 100*)	(2) Index of Average Hourly Earnings, Metal Trades (*1920 = 100*)	Year	(1) Index of Average Hourly Earnings, All Industry (*1920 = 100*)	(2) Index of Average Hourly Earnings, Metal Trades (*1920 = 100*)
1920	100	100	1935	70	66
1921	96	97	1936	70	66
1922	75	80	1937	72	69
1923	72	73	1938	76	73
1924	77	76	1939	78	75
1925	80	80	1940	87	83
1926	72	72	1941	94	89
1927	69	68	1942	98	94
1928	69	68	1943	105	100
1929	69	68	1944	112	105
1930	70	69	1945	120	113
1931	70	67	1946	130	127
1932	70	65	1947	139	137
1933	70	65	1948	151	149
1934	70	65			

Sources: *All industry*, Appendix A. *Metal trades*, 1920–1946, Holger Jensen; the 1947 and 1948 figures are for the third quarter, and were estimated from *Beretning om Dansk Arbejdsgiverforenings Virksomhed*, 1947–1948, pp. 54–55; *ibid.*, 1948–1949, pp. 58–59.

ward more slowly than wages generally, while from 1925 to 1930, the two series moved in parallel fashion. In the depression, metal trades wages displayed a greater relative downward flexibility, and in the subsequent recovery they moved upward at a slightly higher rate than the general wage level.

If the entire period is divided into three phases, 1920–1929, 1930–1936, and 1937–1948, the following conclusions emerge: during the first, the general wage level showed more movement than wages in the metal trades, while in the second and third phases, the latter were more flexible.

But the differences in the rate of change were not of sufficient magnitude to justify the common belief in Denmark that the "elastic" wage really provides a system that is very sensitive to cyclical movements.

In view of the manner in which wages are determined in the metal trades, this conclusion is somewhat surprising, for, a priori, individual wage fixing should lead to greater elasticity than collective wage determination. One explanation is that the labor market organizations are not entirely without influence on effective wage rates. For example, in the event of changes in job content, piece rates may be terminated with notice of two months, and if agreement cannot be reached on new rates by the organizations concerned, a work stoppage may ensue. The question of average time rates is not settled; the union maintains that it may intervene even to the point of a work stoppage where average rates paid in an establishment are unreasonably low, but employers insist that there is no right of intervention or of strike during the contract period. Both sides have refrained from bringing the matter before the Labor Court, since a decision either way might undermine the entire wage system, which neither employers nor workers want.

There is theoretically no right of intervention by unions or an employers' association with respect to the personal wage rate of an individual worker. In hiring a new man, the employer may inquire of the Metal Trades Employers' Association what he was paid in his last place of employment, but he is at liberty to pay more or less. On the other hand, a union may not forbid its members to work for less than a stipulated wage as long as the contractual "least payment" is exceeded, but advice may be given. In fact, the Metal Workers' Union requires of each member a quarterly statement of wage rates, earnings, and hours worked. This information, by revealing the below average shops, permits the union to proffer "advice" to the shop stewards concerned that is not far removed from a direction to see that personal rates go up.

Another stabilizing element in the system is a contractual provision stipulating that if a discharged worker is rehired by an establishment for the same job within one year of the discharge, he is entitled to the same base rate, regardless of any interim changes in the general wage level. While the principal purpose of this clause was to prevent wage cutting, through the medium of layoffs, it serves as an effective brake upon wage reductions at a time when the worker is most vulnerable.

If the "minimum" wage system does not prove to be particularly flexible from a cyclical point of view, it does permit a finer adjustment of wage rates to individual worker productivity than is true of the standard wage.[8] Moreover, it facilitates wage differentiation by enterprise, which

[8] Holger Jensen, p. 47.

is an important condition for the success of industry-wide bargaining in the metal trades, which contain a variety of small specialized shops. It is these considerations that account for the popularity of the system among employers.

There are differences of opinion among workers regarding the desirability of the system. Its chief proponents are the better paid craftsmen who perform work of high quality, while its opponents are found among those who are less skilled or who have no access to piece work. The chairman of the Federation of Labor recently expressed the view of the latter group in the following terms: "It is not surprising that there are many workers who hold to the view, all things considered, that it would be best to aim for a relatively high standard wage, so that income for the same work should be the same for all workers.[9]

What, it may be asked, is the significance of collective bargaining over minimum rates in view of ultimate individual wage determination? As already pointed out, earnings have tended to outrun the collectively determined rates, so that pressure upon union negotiators for wage increases is not as great as in the standard wage trades.[10] However, while it is true that in periods of rapid price changes earnings and the negotiated minimum rates lose contact, there is a positive long run relationship between the two sets of rates. An increase in the minimum rates tends to raise earnings, the effect being wave-like, with the workers near the minimum securing the maximum benefit, and those higher on the wage scale receiving less. The mechanism of transmission is the effort of the individual worker to maintain a fixed differential between his base rate and the minimum.

In summary, the "elastic" wage system represents a compromise between individual and collective bargaining. The general level of wages is strongly influenced by collective bargaining, while individual wage variations receive collective sanction and permit the better worker to receive a higher wage and the employer to adjust his labor costs more finely. It must be recalled, however, that behind the individual bargain stand powerful trade union and employer organizations, armed with the statistical information needed to police the system, and prepared to intervene formally or informally should an employer and his workers endeavor jointly to extend their share of the product market through "unfair" wage competition.

[9] Eiler Jensen, "Arbejdernes Lønformer."

[10] For example, in assessing the significance of an increase in the "least payment" in 1947, the employers conceded that "it meant practically nothing for either the skilled or the unskilled workers in Copenhagen." *Beretning om Dansk Arbejdsgiverforenings Virksomhed, 1947–1948*, p. 27.

Sliding scale wage adjustments[11]

Wage adjustment by reference to the cost of living index is a practice of long standing in Denmark. It was introduced in 1918 as a consequence of the wartime inflation, in the form of automatic semiannual adjustments. Until 1921 it was necessary to adjust upward only, but from 1921 to 1927 the predominant movement was downward. In 1926, for example, wage rates were reduced 12 per cent in February and 5 per cent in August. As a result, workers came to look upon the device with suspicion, and the sliding scale was removed from collective agreements in 1930, thus averting further wage cuts in the depression years.

When the cost of living began to move upward once more in 1938, the unions manifested renewed interest in the sliding scale. Collective agreements concluded in that year covered a two-year period, with reopening at the end of one year in the event of stipulated changes in the cost of living index. With the outbreak of war in Europe the trade unions, mindful of the experience of World War I, pressed for a stronger arrangement. The result was the conclusion in 1939 of an agreement between the Federation of Labor and the Employers' Association stipulating that cost of living index changes of three points or more were to be reflected semiannually in wages, to be granted in øre per index point and carried in supplemental accounts distinct from the regular wage structure.

The automatic nature of the adjustment was suspended by a wage stop law enacted in 1940, the unions conceding that workers could not hope to maintain their real wage level under the occupation. However, the wage adjustments made during the war pursuant to compulsory arbitration were based largely upon the cost of living, and with the resumption of free collective bargaining in 1945 the sliding scale was reintroduced, though with a six- rather than a three-point minimum variation, in view of the price inflation. This system remains in effect at the present writing (1951).

The purpose of calculating the cost of living supplement as a flat sum, in contrast to the Swedish practice of awarding wage increases on a percentage basis, was to bring about greater equality of earnings. Before the inception of the sliding scale system, in 1938, hourly earnings of skilled male workers exceeded those of unskilled workers by 18 per cent. By 1945, since both groups were receiving the same hourly cost of living supplement, the difference had fallen to 11 per cent. But the great scarcity of skilled labor after 1945 forced a relative rise in skilled labor rates,

[11] For a general discussion of this subject, see Henry Grünbaum, *Pristal og Lønninger* (Copenhagen, 1947).

and in the third quarter of 1949 the divergence had reached 20 per cent, despite the equal supplements.

The importance of the cost of living supplement in the Danish wage structure is indicated by the fact that in 1949 (third quarter) it constituted 28 per cent of total skilled worker remuneration and 32 per cent of unskilled worker remuneration. The unions want to incorporate the supplement into the basic wage, but employers, mindful of the greater downward flexibility of the cost of living supplement than of basic wage rates, insist that the two be kept separated. When the cost of living began to decline in 1949, for the first time since the war, trade unions began to think in terms of abolishing the sliding scale system, but the subsequent devaluation of the Danish crown, by removing the prospect of further price decline, checked this type of speculation. The problem will eventually have to be faced, however, for the cost of living supplements have acquired a rigidity of their own, as indicated in the following statement of union policy:

> Although in the short run, particularly in times of rising prices, the trade unions have accepted wage regulation based upon the cost of living index, we are opponents of automatic regulation as a permanent proposition. During normal periods, when production is rising and the amount of goods at the disposition of the population increases, sliding scale agreements mean that workers can only purchase the same amount of goods. Thus the share of the working class in real national income would constitute a steadily diminishing percentage. However, the absolute minimum demand of the working class must at all times be an unchanged share of real national income.[12]

THE MOVEMENT OF WAGES[13]

For purposes of exposition the fifty years covered by this analysis are divided into five periods, each one manifesting a consistent economic trend. After examining each of these periods in turn, the general characteristics of the half century as a whole will be summarized.

1. *The period 1899–1913*

During these years there was a gradual increase in the levels of both money and real wages (see Appendix A and Chart I). Prices rose consistently, with money wages slightly more than compensating for the price rise. The failure of money wages to increase more rapidly, in view of the growing power of the trade unions, has been attributed to two factors: popular belief in the constant value of money, and the counter-organization of employers.[14] The stability of the decade 1900 to 1910

[12] *Under Samvirkets Flag*, pp. 399–400.

[13] Unless otherwise noted, the data cited in the text of this section are from Appendix A.

[14] Jørgen Pedersen, *Arbejdslønnen i Danmark* (Copenhagen, 1930), p. 265.

contributed to money fetishism, to such an extent that most trade unions were induced to enter into five-year collective agreements in 1911, an agreement term that has never been repeated.[15]

Although the period was a relatively peaceful one from an industrial relations standpoint (except for 1899, when the general lockout caused a loss in man-days of work that exceeded total losses for the following thirteen years), labor's gains were not achieved entirely without struggle. Costly strikes occurred in 1905, 1907, and 1911, employer resistance, which might have been weak in view of favorable economic conditions, being stiffened by the policies of the young and militant Employers' Association.

Whether the income of workers as a whole rose during this period is not easy to determine. Annual income, which is the relevant criterion in considering welfare, is a function not alone of hourly earnings of employed workers, but also of losses in earnings due to unemployment, illness, and labor disputes on the one hand, and of such social benefits as unemployment insurance, workmen's compensation, and other welfare payments on the other.[16] Real annual wages adjusted for losses showed no upward trend from 1905 to 1914 (data prior to 1905 are not available). However, government assumption of part of the cost of trade union unemployment benefits in 1907, and improvement in other social legislation, undoubtedly raised indirect worker income.[17] The net result appears to be that while steadily employed workers gained both from the rise in real wages and improvement in social legislation, living standards of all workers rose only to the latter extent.

2. *The period 1914–1920*

The outbreak of World War I brought to a close the years of economic tranquillity, and ushered in an era of swift change. Prices rose rapidly, with wages lagging behind until near the close of the period, and outstripping the price level thereafter. Real hourly earnings in 1920 were 149 per cent of the 1914 level, while annual earnings adjusted for losses

[15] The 1911 agreements climaxed an increasing tendency toward long terms. In 1906, for example, the Metal Workers' Union had accepted a five-year contract, and the Printers an eight-year contract.

[16] Professor Pedersen argues that the concept of annual earnings adjusted for loss is meaningless; that it is representative neither for steadily employed workers nor for the limited group upon whom unemployment tends to be concentrated. It is his view that the two groups must be kept separate for purposes of assessing welfare. Jørgen Pedersen, *Fuld Beskaeftigelse og Økonomisk Tryghed* (Copenhagen, 1945), p. 124. Unfortunately, there is no better expression of measurement if some combined index of worker welfare as a whole is sought, provided it is corrected for supplemental transfer payments. Admittedly, the measure conceals polar variations in welfare, but it nevertheless provides a rough index of progress.

[17] It has been estimated that for the period as a whole, social benefits meant a supplement of from 5 to 8 per cent in worker income. Knud Dalgaard, p. 206.

had attained 129 per cent of the same base, and would have been even higher if not for the introduction of the eight-hour day in 1919. Except during 1918, employment remained at a high level, and not until 1919 were there significant losses due to labor disputes.

The initial economic impact of war was unfavorable to the workers. Most of the trade unions were bound by collective agreements that did not expire until 1916, and in consequence real hourly earnings fell 13 per cent from 1914 to 1916. Although there was some labor unrest, the unions were strong enough to maintain discipline, so that the decline in real wages was not accompanied by undue worker pressure.

Most collective agreements were renewed for a two-year period in 1916, but the wage increases obtained were quickly nullified by the continuing price rise. Although the wage increases in the 1916 agreements averaged 20 per cent, money wages rose by 44 per cent from 1916 to 1918 as a consequence of informal, extra-contract cost of living supplements. Real wages increased slightly, the combination of rising money and real wages contributing to the maintenance of a degree of industrial peace that was remarkable in the light of contemporary events on the Continent.

When the complex of two-year agreements expired in 1918, the leadership of the Federation of Labor was anxious to renew them peaceably in order to put a damper on revolutionary agitation inspired by the Russian Revolution. To cope with the inflation, wages were tied to the cost of living index. But through numerous wildcat strikes workers forced wage increases beyond the contractual terms, and by 1920 the real hourly wage level had reached 150 per cent of 1914. However, earnings were reduced by approximately one-ninth when the eight-hour day became effective on January 1, 1920; it proved possible for the unions to accept this reduction because of the rapid rise in money wages that was taking place at the time.

The period as a whole marked progress for industrial workers. Real adjusted annual earnings increased almost in proportion to real hourly earnings because of the low level of unemployment. Moreover, government outlays for welfare purposes increased, particularly in the form of larger subsidies to the union unemployment insurance funds.[18]

3. *The period 1921 to 1930*

The end of the year 1920 marked the high point of the postwar inflation. During the following decade prices tended to move downward, ex-

[18] It is estimated that by 1924 government welfare payments added an average 10 per cent to wages, compared with 5 to 8 per cent for the prewar period. F. Zeuthen, *Den Økonomiske Fordeling* (Copenhagen), p. 421.

cept for a brief recovery in 1923 and 1924. These years provide an interesting illustration of the difficulties experienced by a labor movement in adjusting traditional policies to take account of unfamiliar economic variables.

The return of German and English goods to the world market after 1920 created serious competitive difficulties for Danish industry. Large accumulated reserves of foreign exchange in Danish hands contributed to a rise in the value of the crown, further discouraging exports. Industry and labor were united in their demand for protection, but the fear of retaliation induced the strong farmers' bloc to oppose tariffs. The resumption of price inflation from 1922 to 1924, by reducing the value of the crown, brought some relief, unemployment falling from 20 per cent in 1922 to 10 per cent in 1924. But prices began to fall again in 1924, and the value of the crown to rise. The decision of the Danish government, taken in December 1924, to bring about a slow increase in the value of the crown until it reached its prewar dollar parity (the policy of the "honorable" crown) led to foreign speculation, with the result that in relation to dollars, the crown rose from 66 per cent of its 1914 gold par in 1925 to 92 per cent in January 1926. A year later, Denmark returned to the gold standard on its 1914 par base.

The Employers' Association, reflecting the export trades' point of view, strongly opposed restoration of the old par value, aware of the difficulty of reducing wages *pari passu* with the increase in the value of the currency.[19] Within the labor movement, however, there was much indecision. On the one hand, it was feared that an expensive crown would lead to increasing unemployment.[20] But on the other hand, many labor leaders felt that the trade unions, weakened by several years of intense industrial warfare, could best achieve higher real wages through price reduction.

The latter consideration prevailed, and the socialists threw their weight behind deflation, contrary to all precepts. The rationality of this decision must be judged against the background of labor market developments from 1921 to 1925. The abrupt halt in wartime inflation that occurred at the close of 1920 created a novel situation for Danish labor: the prospect of wage reductions. As a labor historian put it, "It had theretofore been the rule that wages should always rise, and the concept of wage reduction was entirely alien to the Danish labor mentality." [21] Ever since 1899, money wages had moved in an upward direction only, and the unions had no experience in negotiating wage cuts.

[19] *Beretning om Dansk Arbejdsgiverforenings Virksomhed*, 1925–1926, pp. 34–35.

[20] These fears were realized: unemployment rose from 8.3 per cent in July 1925 to 31.1 per cent in January 1926.

[21] Christiansen, p. 99.

Work stoppage statistics attest eloquently to the resistance of workers against reduction of their money wages. The period 1921 to 1926 contained three of the worst years, in terms of industrial disputes, in Danish labor history. The preponderance of the stoppages were lockouts rather than strikes because of the Danish bargaining system, but they represented the stubborn refusal of workers to permit any deduction from their pay envelopes. The net result of these labor struggles was a fall of almost 30 per cent in money wages. In real wage terms, the workers fared better; the decline from the postwar peak to 1926 was 6 per cent, only half the decline that occurred from 1914 to 1917.

With this experience fresh in mind, it is understandable that the labor movement should find a slow deflation preferable to inflation. Exhaustion of strike funds limited the ability of the unions to fight for higher wages. Union membership had fallen from 362,000 in 1920 to 310,000 in 1925. Although wages were tied to the cost of living index by agreement, there was an adjustment lag that redounded to the advantage of the worker, whereas rising prices would have turned this lag to the advantage of employers.

By 1930, the real wage level had approximately returned to that prevailing during the immediate postwar years. But income losses occasioned by unemployment cut more deeply than in previous decades. Whereas average annual insured unemployment from 1910 to 1919 was 10.5 per cent, the comparable figure for the period 1920 to 1929 was 16 per cent.[22] In terms of annual income adjusted for losses, the years 1920 and 1930 were the high terminal points of a deep trough; for the decade as a whole, the index of annual earnings averaged 115 (1914 = 100), compared with 129 for 1920, and 133 for 1930. While increasing social outlays compensated in part for this deficit, the decade cannot be said to have been a prosperous one for the workers.

4. *The period 1931 to 1939*

The great depression, first felt in Denmark in 1931, raised peculiar problems because of the extent to which the Danish economy was dependent upon agricultural exports of butter, bacon, and eggs to finance the importation of both feed for livestock and industrial raw materials and fuel. The most serious adverse factor was the change in the terms of trade occasioned by the increased spread between agricultural and industrial prices in world markets, the extent of which may be seen from

[22] Some portion of the increase is attributable to the extension of unemployment compensation coverage, since a greater number of marginal workers with a higher unemployment propensity were brought into the system. See K. Vedel-Petersen, pp. 416–417. There is no doubt, however, that the difference reflects a real increase in unemployment between the two decades, whatever the precise increase may have been.

Table 18. In 1929, import and export prices bore about the same relationship to one another as they had in 1913, but thereafter export prices dropped much more sharply than import prices. Denmark was thereby placed under the necessity of increasing the amount of exports per unit of import, which meant a decline in real income, other things being equal.

In order to stimulate exports and check the rising volume of unemployment that accompanied the onset of depression, the Employers' Association proposed a 20 per cent wage reduction, on that ground that it would "provide business the stimulus it requires, that reduced production costs would work themselves into the price level, and that initiative would be renewed, providing work where now there is only sluggishness and restraint.[23] To this proposal, the trade unions replied with a flat

TABLE 18

INDEXES OF WHOLESALE PRICES FOR IMPORTS AND EXPORTS, 1929–1937
(*1913 = 100*)

Year	Imports	Exports
1929	148	149
1930	127	125
1931	112	95
1932	120	84
1933	130	99
1934	138	108
1935	138	119
1936	148	126
1937	180	136

Sources: K. Vedel-Petersen, p. 248; *Fagbevaegelsen og De Økonomiske Problemer*, p. 191.

refusal: "We do not agree with the Employers' Association that a reduction in wages will stimulate employment and increase purchasing power. Foreign experience shows that wage reductions do not lead to increased employment opportunities, and that purchasing power is not augmented thereby ought to be obvious. We believe, on the contrary, that a reduction in working time and proscription of overtime will meet with general approval."[24] Unlike the situation after 1921, the trade unions possessed the power to enforce their policy of no wage cuts, and as a result money wages remained constant from 1930 to 1936.

When England abandoned the gold standard in 1931, it was necessary

[23] *Dansk Arbejdsgiverforenings Virksomhed*, 1932–1933, p. 31. The Employers' Association attributed the refusal of the trade unions to agree to a wage reduction partly "to the theory emanating from the United States, that wages should be kept up to maintain purchasing power."

[24] *Ibid.*, pp. 32–33.

for Denmark to follow suit. This did not prove sufficient to protect the crucial British market for Danish bacon, butter, and eggs, however. The problem was more than one of price, for Great Britain had embarked upon a policy of imperial preference, in pursuance of which Australia and New Zealand were accorded priorities in the British market. A measure of relief was secured through a Dano-English trade agreement, which provided, *inter alia*, for the duty free importation of Danish bacon and ham into England up to a specified quota. However, the British tariffs on butter and eggs were retained, and the British reserved the right to impose absolute quota limitations on the importation of those commodities from Denmark. As a consequence of British commercial policy, Danish bacon exports to England fell from 383.4 million kilograms in 1932 to 174.2 million in 1936, butter exports from 129 million kilograms to 109.7 million during the same period.

Coincidentally, the German market, second only to the British in importance, also shrank. Germany doubled its tariff on butter, and almost stopped the importation of cattle from Denmark. Whatever Danish exports it would accept were made contingent upon offsetting Danish imports of German manufactured goods, rather than the industrial raw materials Denmark needed to keep its industry operating, giving rise to a slogan that gained great currency among the workers: "For every ox that is shipped across the border, a textile worker becomes unemployed." [25]

The Danish labor movement was well aware of the relationship between the demand for the nation's agricultural output and industrial employment.[26] Clearly, relative prices had to be reduced so that the Danish farmer could compete with New Zealand and Eastern Europe. The mechanism chosen, by agreement between labor and the farmers, in the so-called *Kanslergade Agreement* outlined above, was further devaluation of the crown in relation to the pound, following similar action by New Zealand. The Danish crown fell from 18.18 to the pound in 1932 to 22.40 in 1934. Not only agriculture, but the export trades and shipping as well were the beneficiaries. At the same time, stringent import controls were adopted and foreign exchange made subject to rationing.

In retrospect, the policy of reducing prices through currency devaluation rather than wage reduction had much to commend it, for the following reasons:

[25] K. Vedel-Petersen, p. 253.

[26] For example, Prime Minister Stauning declared to a congress of the Federation of Labor: "Without assistance, agriculture will be faced with a crisis, and agricultural crisis is not favorable soil for industrial employment. That is because agriculture is decisive for industry in an economic sense. It is significant (1) as consumer and (2) as exporter." De Samvirkende Fagforbund, *Protokol over Generalforsamlingen*, 1934, p. 14.

1. The basic problems to be solved, in view of Denmark's great dependence upon foreign trade,[27] were the unfavorable turn in the terms of trade and the declining demand for exports. With respect to the former, Denmark could only attempt to increase the ratio of industrial to total exports, which actually did occur during the 1930's, and to diminish the volume of imports. As for the latter problem, the elasticity of demand for Danish agricultural exports during the depression was low, since the limitations on expansion lay not so much in price as in British and German restrictions on quantity. The devaluations of 1931 and 1933 were defensive rather than offensive measures.

2. For industrial wage reductions, through their indirect effect upon agricultural prices, to have effected any significant increase in agricultural exports, they would have had to be of inconceivable magnitude. Since industrial exports at the time comprised less than one-quarter of total exports, the possible gains from this sector were limited.

3. It was argued that wage reductions would stimulate domestic investment and thus afford additional employment; however, the sparkplug of the Danish economy is the export trade, and it is dubious how much new investment would have been undertaken as long as export demand remained low. Moreover, the initial income effect of wage reductions would have added to the discouraging business outlook.

From 1934 to 1936 a measure of recovery was achieved, assisted by a public works program and government financial encouragement to land reclamation and housing.[28] At the end of 1936, however, a new crisis set in, since the growing armament race in Europe reduced the demand for agricultural products and raised the prices of industrial materials. Though real wages increased slowly from 1937 to 1939, unemployment remained high. There was never a real recovery from the depression.

Danish national income statistics, which are available only beginning with 1930,[29] except for some extremely rough estimates, indicate that after a decline from 1930 to 1932, which affected investment more seriously than consumption, national income rose steadily, attaining in 1939 a level 22 per cent above that in 1930. However, the increase in per capita income was only 14 per cent. Real average hourly earnings were the same in 1939 as in 1930, while real corrected annual earnings fell by 8 per cent. Since the statistics indicate an increase in the proportion of

[27] It is estimated that about one-third the gross national product was exported in 1930, and about one-quarter in 1939. *Nationalproduktet og Nationalindkomsten 1930–1946*, Statistiske Meddelelser, vol. 129, no. 5, p. 78.

[28] The number of city flats built increased from 13,000 in 1932 to 23,000 in 1935. The high level of housebuilding during this period obviated the necessity of allocating large amounts of scarce resources to this use after World War II.

[29] *Statistiske Meddelelser*, vol. 129, no. 5.

national income consumed, then, assuming a constant ratio of the industrial labor force to total population and a constant ratio of hourly earnings to total payrolls, labor's share of the national income would appear to have declined except to the extent of the offset provided by government transfer payments. The latter, including a small item for interest on the public debt, amounted to about 7 per cent of national income in 1939. Though a comparable figure is not available for 1930, it is hardly likely that the increase in that segment of transfer payments representing a shift of income to the workers could have been of sufficient magnitude to offset the loss in the wage sector. The span of the thirties was therefore one of retrogression for labor in a relative sense, and probably one in which at best the *status quo* was maintained in terms of absolute standards.[30]

5. *The period 1940 to 1948*

The initial impact of the German occupation of Denmark was reflected in a declining national product. Consumption fell to a greater extent than national product due to German commodity requisitions; the decline in consumption amounted to 20 per cent from 1939 to 1944. Investment also remained low because of material shortages. Unemployment reached the lowest levels that had prevailed for a decade. Acute labor shortages prevailed during the summers of 1943 and 1944. The Danes were working harder for a smaller return.

For the first few years of the war, wage earner income fell more than consumption. Real average hourly earnings declined 16 per cent from 1939 to 1942, adjusted annual earnings by 18 per cent. But thereafter, thanks to increasing employment and to substantial wage increases, worker income rose, and by 1944 real average hourly earnings were only 8 per cent below the 1939 level, while adjusted annual earnings exceeded the 1939 level by 7 per cent. But this did not mean that worker living standards had improved, for the cost of living index did not reflect the serious quality deterioration consequent upon the cessation of many imports, while taxes and savings rose. A government commission of inquiry has characterized the course of events as follows:

> The decline in consumption which began in 1940 and continued subsequently had particularly adverse effects upon wage earners and *rentiers*. Farm owners have been able either to protect their living standards or to raise them. Entrepreneurs saw their real incomes somewhat lowered at the beginning of the war, but many were subsequently able to maintain consumption through disinvestment. Wage earners and *rentiers*, however, were obliged in most cases to

[30] There is evidence, however, that during the worst of the depression years, labor's share actually increased. See F. Zeuthen, *Arbejdsløn*, p. 379.

reduce consumption. The increased consumption made possible by later wage increases was difficult to realize because of increasing goods shortages. Declining unemployment did not produce the same improvement in living standards that was true in normal times.[31]

Comparisons between prewar and postwar income and consumption are difficult to make because of the effects of war and inflation upon income distribution, upon patterns of consumption and upon the quality of consumer goods. Real average hourly earnings increased 18 per cent from 1939 to 1948, and unemployment in the latter year was far lower than in the former. Yet it has been estimated that per capita consumption in 1948 compared roughly to average prewar consumption,[32] while per capita income was about the same in 1939 and 1948. The following factors may account for this apparent inconsistency, though the data necessary to make a quantitative reconciliation are not available:

1. The high level of postwar employment has undoubtedly resulted in a shift of income to the wage earner group, a fact that is concealed in the per capita average.

2. An increase in worker income is not tantamount to an increase in worker consumption. Investment as a percentage of gross national product increased from 18 per cent in 1939 to 20 per cent in 1948, the increase coming either from higher savings or taxes.

3. To the extent that quality deterioration has taken place, the cost of living index is understated and the real wage increase overstated.

4. While there have been significant changes in the patterns of consumption since 1939,[33] the effect of these changes upon living standards is not clear. The postwar availability in unlimited quantity and at low cost of cheese, eggs, potatoes, and fish has probably prevented forced uptrading in food, though the same is not true of clothing.

5. The fall in unemployment has reduced payments to workers for unemployment compensation, and to that extent offset increased wage income.[34]

All things considered, it appears warranted to conclude that worker living standards rose from 1939 to 1948, though not by as much as real hourly earnings. The aggressive wage policy of the trade unions since 1945, reflected in a high level of industrial disputes in 1946 and 1947,

[31] Finansministeriets Udvalg af 30 Januar 1943, *Økonomiske Efterkrigstidsproblemer* (1945), p. 10.

[32] *Economic Survey of Denmark, National Budget for 1949*, p. 68.

[33] *Ibid.*, p. 69.

[34] Social expenditures declined from 8.4 per cent of national income during the fiscal year 1938–1939 to 6.1 per cent during 1948–1949. While expenditures for old age and invalidity pensions rose, there was more than a compensating offset in unemployment compensation expenditures. See "Socialpolitikken i Danmark," *Socialt Tidsskrift*, 1949.

undoubtedly contributed to the achievement of this advance. Underlying the gains, however, have been foreign trade developments to the advantage of Denmark. The worldwide shortage of foodstuffs resulted in a favorable turn in the terms of trade. Reliance upon Great Britain as a customer declined (30.4 per cent of total exports went to Great Britain in 1948 against 56.1 per cent in 1938), thus permitting purchases of imports to be placed in the most advantageous markets. Finally, and of greatest significance in the long run, industrial exports increased from 25 per cent of total exports in 1938 to 33 per cent in 1948.

Summary

A recapitulation of the separate periods into which the half century 1899 to 1948 has been divided and an examination of Chart 1 and the underlying statistical data in Appendix A yield the conclusion that the living standards of Danish workers have improved substantially over the entire period. Though neither hourly nor annual earnings are meaningful statistics in making comparisons over so long a time span, in view of the rapidity of technological change and the alteration of consumption habits, few would dispute that life has become easier for the average worker.

Improvement has not been a matter of uniform growth, however, but has come in waves. Workers achieved their greatest gains immediately after the two world wars, under conditions of wage-price inflation and high levels of employment. Whether as cause or effect, both these periods were marked by a considerable radicalization of the trade union movement and aggressive union wage policy. There was a third wave of progress between the termination of deflation in 1927 and the onset of depression in 1931, due to a drop in living costs rather than to a money wage rise, but the net effect of this phase was little more than recapture of the losses sustained in the postwar deflation. This throws some doubt upon the common assumption that workers are never the beneficiaries of inflation, though the existence of a strong labor movement in Denmark must be remembered in this connection.

Though the two major deflationary cycles, 1921–1927 and 1930–1937, were both marked by retrogression in labor welfare, they differed substantially in the relative depth and form of the decline. In the first of these periods, the trade unions were unable to resist employer determination to reduce money wages by a greater percentage than living costs. The result was a reduction of almost 10 per cent in real hourly earnings and of almost twice as much in adjusted annual earnings within the space of a few years, for employment did not react to the wage reduction in the manner often postulated in economic theory.

During the second cycle, 1930–1937, the trade unions possessed sufficient economic and political power to maintain their money wages intact. The decline in real earnings, both hourly and adjusted annual, was about of the same magnitude as in the previous period, but considering the relative adversity of international trade factors, this must be considered a significant achievement. It is small wonder that in the light of these contrasting developments the Danish labor movement should be wedded firmly to a policy of downward-inflexible money wages.

LABOR'S SHARE IN THE NATIONAL INCOME

A rise in living standards carries no implication as to its source. Labor may share equally in the growth of national product attendant upon increased productivity; or its gains may be achieved at the expense of the income shares falling to other social groups; or there may be combinations of both elements. The published national income statistics for Denmark do not permit the formulation of definitive conclusions on this subject. For the years prior to 1930, the only data available are based upon income tax returns, and are very incomplete. For the years beginning with 1930, national product and national income statistics have been calculated, but not in sufficient detail to segregate wage earner income.[35]

However, the director of the Danish Statistical Department, Mr. Einar Cohn, has published some estimates designed to indicate the share of wage earners in national income from 1870 to 1947.[36] These data, which are reproduced in Table 19, yield the conclusion that the wage share of the national income has been remarkably stable for the past eighty years. But since increased expenditures on social services have redounded mainly to the advantage of the wage earner, labor's share of the national income would have increased accordingly. Assuming that the calculations, however rough, provide valid approximations, rising worker living standards have come about (a) through increasing productivity and (b) through the enlargement of welfare services by the state.[37]

It is not correct, as is sometimes done, to conclude from estimates of this character that neither labor organization nor collective bargaining can have any fundamental influence on labor's share in the national

[35] Statistiske Meddelelser, vol. 129, no. 5, *Nationalproduktet og Nationalindkomsten 1930–1946*.

[36] These estimates have been criticized on conceptual grounds. See Henry Stjernqvist, "Nogle Bemaerkninger . . . ," *Nationaløkonomisk Tidsskrift*, 1950, p. 79.

[37] In 1948, social security payments accounted for 5.2 per cent of net national income. From this would have to be subtracted (a) welfare payments in 1870 and (b) transfers to other than wage earners, in order to find the increased share of labor in national income, from this source, since 1870. Neither of these figures is available, but they are not likely to be of a large order of magnitude.

TABLE 19

SHARE OF WAGES IN NATIONAL INCOME, 1870–1947

Year	National Income (*Mill. of kroner*)	Number of Wage Earners (Including Agriculture)	Average Annual Wage (*Kroner*)	Total Wage Earner Income (*Mill. of kroner*)	Wage Earner Share of National Income (*Per Cent*)
1870	500	350,000	500	175	35
1905	1,400	600,000	900	540	38
1930	5,000	810,000	2,200	1,740	35
1947	15,000	1,050,000	5,000	5,250	35

Source: Einar Cohn, "Nationalindkomstens Fordeling Mellem Samfundsgrupper," *Nationaløkonomisk Tidsskrift* 1949, p. 369.

income. There is in the first place no assurance that without a strong labor movement the wage share would not have been lower. Moreover, it must not be forgotten that during the last fifty years the power of labor was curbed by an organized employer movement of at least equal strength. It may very well be that the growing preponderance of labor power will change distributive shares of the national income in the future.

RELATIVE WAGE MOVEMENTS IN DENMARK, NORWAY, AND SWEDEN

Further insight into the causes and significance of Danish wage movements can be secured by international comparisons. The Norwegian and Swedish experience is most suitable for this purpose, not only because of the institutional similarities among the three Scandinavian countries, but also because they are all small nations greatly dependent upon foreign trade and thus subject to similar exogenous influences.

Table 20 shows the real wage indices of Norway and Sweden expressed as percentages of the Danish real wage index for selected years between 1900 and 1948 (1914 = 100).[38] These figures, the data in Appendix A from

[38] The data in Table 20 relate to relative wage movements based upon the level in each country in 1914, and do not purport to compare absolute wage standards. The latter is a much more difficult task. For many years the Danish Employers' Association claimed that absolute labor standards were higher in Denmark than in Sweden. An estimate for the year 1919 purported to demonstrate that on the average Danish wages exceeded Swedish wages by 15 per cent, though closer examination reveals that a portion of the difference is attributable to the varying urban-rural distribution of the labor force in the two countries. The difference between the wages of male workers in Copenhagen and Stockholm was only 8 per cent. *Beretning om Dansk Arbejdsgiverforenings Virksomhed*, 1919–1920, pp. 74–76. It was asserted that in 1927 Danish metal trades wages exceeded the Swedish by 10 per cent, and

which they were computed, and Chart 2, which shows the relative movement of real average hourly earnings and the cost of living in the Scandinavian countries from 1899 to 1948, indicate that up to 1932 the movement of real wages in the three countries was roughly parallel. There were some divergences: during the first world war, Swedish real wages did not fall to the same extent as Danish and Norwegian, though the subsequent relatively greater rise in the latter two restored the 1914 relationship by 1920. From 1920 to 1930 the Swedish real wage index remained at a moderately higher level than the others, a consequence of

TABLE 20

INDEXES OF REAL AVERAGE HOURLY EARNINGS IN NORWAY AND SWEDEN, EXPRESSED AS PERCENTAGES OF REAL AVERAGE HOURLY EARNINGS IN DENMARK[a]

(1914 = 100)

Year	Norway	Sweden
1900	102	101
1905	95	97
1910	91	99
1914	100	100
1915	102	114
1920	99	97
1925	101	103
1930	103	107
1932	103	101
1935	110	111
1940	120	122
1945	109	118
1948	112	114

Source: Computed from Appendix A.

[a] The Danish wage index covers all workers, while the Norwegian and Swedish indices cover male workers only. Although the trend toward reduction of the male-female wage differential, particularly after 1939, affects the comparability of the series, the total effect is not so great as to impair the validity of the conclusions that may be drawn from the data.

the more drastic price deflation that occurred in Sweden. But by 1932, the Danish, Norwegian, and Swedish real wage (as well as money wage and cost of living) indices had returned to the relationship prevailing among them in 1914. After 1932, however, the Danish real wage index fell markedly below the Norwegian and Swedish indices, and except for

by even greater amounts in other export trades, though it was conceded that building trades wages were the same in the two countries. *Ibid.*, 1926–1927, p. 120. In 1932, it was claimed that the Danish wage level exceeded the Swedish by 17 per cent. *Ibid.*, 1932–1933, p. 26. The present contention, however, is that Danish and Swedish real wages are approximately equal, with Norwegian real wages about 10 per cent lower. *Arbejdsgiveren*, 1946, p. 165. A recent informal wage conference among trade union economists tentatively ranked absolute wage levels in Sweden, Denmark, and Norway in that order, though the difference between the Swedish and Danish level is probably small.

a brief period during the war, it has remained consistently lower. The cause of this divergence was the greater increase in Danish living costs, rather than a lag of money wages in Denmark.

Why did the Danish real wage level fail to keep pace with Norwegian and Swedish wages after 1932? Such simple institutional explanations as differences in trade union strength, for example, do not provide an answer. The Danish trade unions are as strong and embrace as large a proportion of the eligible workers as their Scandinavian counterparts. Moreover, in my judgment, they have mastered the techniques and the art of collective bargaining to a higher degree than the Norwegian and Swedish unions. The answer must be sought in the basic economic forces that mold and limit wage development.

TABLE 21

INDEXES OF OUTPUT PER WORKER IN MANUFACTURING INDUSTRY IN DENMARK, NORWAY, AND SWEDEN, 1931–1948[a]

(1931 = 100)

Year	Denmark	Norway	Sweden
1931	100.0	100.0	100.0
1932	99.2	102.3	98.5
1933	102.0	102.1	101.9
1934	100.9	101.1	114.3
1935	99.4	103.5	120.7
1936	98.9	104.0	125.8
1937	98.5	105.9	130.0
1938	98.3	104.4	129.1
1939	95.3	110.8	136.0
1940	83.4	99.8	126.5
1941	77.8	92.2	124.1
1942	76.3	84.8	124.6
1943	75.0	80.6	126.5
1944	73.2	67.9	132.0
1945	67.3	63.2	122.6
1946	81.6	88.4	142.8
1947	93.1	93.7	145.6
1948	96.6	97.2	n.a.

Sources: Denmark: *Production* — International Labor Office, *Year Book of Labor Statistics*, 1937, p. 217; *ibid.*, 1941, p. 196; *ibid.*, 1947–1948, p. 290; *Danmarks Statistiske Årbog*, 1949, p. 331. *Employment* — International Labor Office, *Year Book of Labor Statistics*, 1941, p. 32; *ibid.*, 1947–1948, p. 40; *Danmarks Statistisk Årbog*, 1949, p. 92. Norway: *Production and Employment* — Letter from the Norwegian Central Statistical Office, March 1950. Sweden: *Production and Employment* — International Labor Office, *Year Book of Labor Statistics*, 1941, pp. 33, 196; *ibid.*, 1947–1948, pp. 41, 290.

[a] The indices were calculated simply as the ratio of production to employment. The data necessary to convert the indices to output per man-hour are not available for all countries. However, the general equality of working hours in the three countries during the period under consideration renders it unlikely that refinement to a man-hour basis would significantly alter the relationships shown above.

1. *Productivity*. Table 21 contains estimates of output per worker in manufacturing industry for Denmark, Norway, and Sweden for the

years 1931 to 1948. It must be emphasized that the data carry no imputation of absolute productivity; for example, absolute output per worker in the base year might be higher in one country than in another, yet the relationship shown is one of equality, and the discrepancy is carried forward into subsequent years.[39] The reader is also cautioned that the data provide rough estimates at best;[40] that they are subject to considerable margins of error; and that therefore they should be taken as indicative only of general trends.

With these qualifications in mind, it is seen from Table 21 that from 1931 to 1939, Danish and Norwegian labor productivity remained fairly constant (except for 1939, when the Norwegian figure showed a significant increase), whereas there was an average increase of 4.5 per cent per annum in Swedish productivity. Denmark and Norway experienced a severe decline during the war, but by 1948 each had almost regained the 1931 level. Swedish productivity continued to rise after the war at even more than the prewar rate, after a wartime decline in productivity.

There does not appear to be a unique relationship between productivity and real wages. While it is true that in Denmark, a 5 per cent productivity decline between 1931 and 1939 was accompanied by a 7 per cent fall in real hourly earnings, and that Norwegian real hourly earnings increased by 10 per cent to the accompaniment of a 12 per cent productivity increase, the two indices for Sweden show wide variance: a 36 per cent productivity increase against a 4 per cent real wage increase. However, the data do suggest that the failure of Danish labor productivity to keep pace with productivity in Norway and Sweden may be among the causes of the Danish wage lag.

2. *The terms of trade.* The effect of adversity in trade terms upon the Danish wage level has already been remarked. It remains now to consider whether this factor can help account for the contrasting wage developments in Scandinavia.

The dependence of the three countries upon foreign trade is not identical, so that changes in the terms of trade do not affect all alike. Denmark's exports as a percentage of national product were about 33 per

[39] An exhaustive study of comparative labor productivity in Denmark and other countries of Europe yielded the conclusion that while the Danish wage level is relatively high, costs are low because of high labor productivity. Particularly pertinent was the comment of the management of the European Ford plants that "in Denmark, where we pay the highest wage in Europe, we find the lowest cost." See Finn T. B. Friis, "Arbejdseffektiviteten i Danmark," *Socialt Tidsskrift*, 1946, p. 285.

This high level of labor productivity, to which a Danish engineer who has performed construction work in many countries testified to me in personal conversation, may be attributed, among other things, to the rigid training of the Danish worker and to the lack of anti-employer feeling among workers to the extent prevailing elsewhere.

[40] For example, no adjustment is made for changes in hours and days worked per annum.

cent in 1930 and 25 per cent in 1939.[41] Norwegian exports may be estimated roughly at 35 per cent of national product in 1939,[42] while Swedish exports fell from 19 per cent to 15 per cent of national product during the thirties.[43]

Table 22 shows the ratio of import prices to export prices for Denmark, Norway, and Sweden for the years 1929 to 1948 (omitting the war years), expressed as relatives on a 1929 base. These data provide the most important clue to the divergence of Danish from Norwegian and Swedish real wage levels in the thirties. Beginning with 1931, the terms of trade

TABLE 22

INDEXES OF RATIOS OF IMPORT TO EXPORT PRICES, DENMARK, NORWAY, AND SWEDEN, 1929–1948
(*1929 = 100*)

Year	Denmark	Norway	Sweden
1929	100	100	100
1930	102	99	86
1931	119	101	83
1932	145	97	99
1933	133	96	97
1934	129	97	92
1935	116	95	98
1936	118	96	94
1937	134	97	85
1938	119	100	87
1939	119	106	100
1945	137	104	129
1946	138	96	112
1947	125	100	98
1948	114	101	92

Sources: Denmark: 1929–1937, *Fagbevaegelsen og De Økonomiske Problemer* (Copenhagen, 1937), p. 191; 1939–1943, *Økonomiske Efterkrigstidsproblemer* (Copenhagen, 1945), Appendix, p. 6; 1944–1948, *Danmarks Statistiske Årbog*, 1947, 1949. Norway: Data supplied by the Norwegian Central Statistical Office. Sweden: 1929–1936, data supplied by the Swedish Central Statistical Office; 1937–1948, *Statistisk Årsbok for Sverige*, 1941, p. 224; 1949, p. 216.

turned very sharply against Denmark, whereas Norway and Sweden either maintained substantial equality between import and export prices, or improved their positions (the lower the ratio, the more favorable the situation for the country concerned).

To emphasize the effect of changes in terms of trade upon the economies of the Scandinavian countries, year-to-year variations in the ratios

[41] *Supra*, p. 159.

[42] Handelsdepartementet, *Nasjonalbudsjettet 1948*, p. 5.

[43] The Swedish Institute for Industrial Research, *Sweden's Trade Policy After the War* (Stockholm, 1945).

of the terms of trade, as computed in Table 22, were applied to the foreign trade sectors of the economies. The results appear in Table 23. A plus sign denotes a favorable development, that is, a relative increase in export prices, a minus sign an unfavorable development. To illustrate, from 1930 to 1931 the adjusted Danish terms of trade moved adversely by 4.3 per cent. This means that Denmark could have imported 4.3 per cent less goods in 1931 than in 1930 with the same volume of exports. Other things being equal, there would be a proportionate effect upon the combined total of consumption and investment. Table 23 emphasizes what was already apparent from Table 22, the relative adversity of

TABLE 23

LINK RELATIVES OF CHANGES IN THE TERMS OF TRADE, APPLIED TO PERCENTAGE OF NATIONAL PRODUCT EXPORTED, 1930–1939

(*In percentages*)[a]

Year	Denmark	Norway	Sweden
1930	−0.6	+0.4	+2.8
1931	−4.3	−0.7	+0.6
1932	−5.4	+1.4	−2.8
1933	+2.4	+0.4	+0.3
1934	+0.9	−0.4	+0.9
1935	+3.0	+0.7	−1.0
1936	−0.5	−0.4	+0.7
1937	−3.6	−0.4	+1.7
1938	+3.3	−1.1	−0.4
1939	0.0	−2.0	−2.2

Source: Table 22.

[a] For the purposes of this computation, it was assumed that the average ratio of exports to gross national product for the period was: Denmark, 30 per cent; Norway, 35 per cent; Sweden, 17 per cent.

Danish trade terms for most of the period. Only toward the close of the decade did Denmark begin to recoup some of the ground lost earlier.

The foregoing brief review of Scandinavian real wage movements may be summarized as follows:

1. The real wage level in Denmark, after moving roughly parallel to that in Norway and Sweden from 1899 to 1932, suffered a relative decline thereafter.

2. Among the causes contributing to the lag in the Danish real wage level was the failure of Danish labor productivity to increase with that of the other countries.

3. Perhaps the most important single contrast between Denmark on the one hand and Norway and Sweden on the other lay in the relative adversity of terms of foreign trade that affected the Danish economy

after 1930. This may be attributed to differences in the composition of exports, Denmark having the largest percentage of agricultural exports and Sweden of industrial exports, with Norway occupying an intermediate position.

CHAPTER IX

OTHER ECONOMIC ASPECTS OF LABOR RELATIONS

THE STRUCTURE OF WAGES

SEVERAL FACETS of Danish wage structure have already been touched upon, for example, wage differentials between skilled and unskilled workers and between Copenhagen and the provinces. It is proposed in this section to consider in greater detail the principal changes that have taken place in the structure of wages over the past thirty years. For this purpose, Table 24 has been constructed; it shows average hourly earnings for 43 skilled male trades, 22 unskilled male trades, and 14 unskilled female trades, for the city of Copenhagen, for stated quarters of the years 1920 and 1949 (columns 1 and 2).[1] Both the percentage and absolute wage increases from 1920 to 1949 were calculated for each craft (columns 3 and 4), and the individual craft percentage increase expressed as a relative based upon the average increase for the relevant major group, that is, skilled males, unskilled males, and females (column 5). Finally, employment by craft in 1949 is shown in column 6.[2]

The crafts have been subdivided into rough industry classifications; some of these consist of closely related crafts, but others group crafts that are actually in separate industries, for example, textiles and clothing. The division into skilled male, unskilled male, and female crafts follows Danish statistical practice.

The trades listed in Table 24 represent all those for which 1920 wage data are available. However, they do not comprise the entire list of trades for which wage data are currently reported. Wage statistics for 1949 show separately 67 skilled male crafts, 71 unskilled male trades, and 54 female trades. The skilled trades are thus most completely represented in the tabulation.

There is available an analysis of wage changes between 1914 and 1945,

[1] The form and availability of the statistical material dictated the choice of Copenhagen alone, rather than the entire county, and of selected quarters rather than entire years; however, neither of these factors introduces any bias, for the purpose for which the data are employed.

[2] Industry and major group wage averages were secured by weighting the individual craft rates by 1949 employment. The use of fixed weights was dictated by the unavailability of employment data for 1920.

TABLE 24

WAGES IN COPENHAGEN, 1920 AND 1949

Craft or Occupation	(1) Average Hourly Earnings, Fourth Quarter 1920 (*Øre*)	(2) Average Hourly Earnings, Third Quarter 1949 (*Øre*)	(3) Earnings in 1949 as a Percentage of Earnings in 1920 (*Col. 2 ÷ Col. 1*)	(4) Absolute Increase in Hourly Earnings, 1920–1949 (Øre) (*Col. 2 − Col. 1*)	(5) Relative Percentage Increase in Wages of Each Craft or Occupation	(6) Employment in Craft or Occupation, September 30, 1949
I. *Skilled males*						
A. *Food and beverage*						
Cigar makers	198	320	162	122	113	836
Bakers	220	313	142	93	99	752
Chocolate makers	248	342	138	94	96	52
Average[a]	210	318	151	108	105	Sum 1,640
B. *Textiles, clothing*						
Rope makers	178	359	202	181	140	5
Tailors (order)	223	328	147	105	102	57
Tailors (ready-made)	223	354	159	131	110	319
Glovemakers	233	431	185	198	128	97
Shoe workers	247	381	154	134	107	1,256
Hat makers	266	458	172	192	119	31
Tanners	279	387	139	108	97	126
Average[a]	244	379	155	135	108	Sum 1,891
C. *Building trades*						
Glaziers	219	335	153	116	106	155
Linoleum layers	239	351	147	112	102	56
Plumbers	269	396	147	127	102	847
Painters	274	378	138	104	96	1,969
Stucco workers	278	406	146	128	101	26
Carpenters	284	413	145	129	101	1,018
Timberers	371	431	116	60	81	1,214
Masons	376	472	126	96	88	1,763
Average[a]	316	417	132	101	92	Sum 7,048
D. *Woodworking*						
Brush makers	209	363	174	154	121	52
Woodworkers	227	357	157	130	109	590
Turners	228	343	150	115	104	30
Carvers	230	338	147	108	102	9
Cabinetmakers	235	362	154	127	107	851
Coopers	249	380	153	131	106	99
Upholsterers	250	392	157	142	109	316
Piano workers	252	339	135	87	94	103
Carriage makers	254	397	156	143	108	105
Gilders	256	318	124	62	86	29
Average[a]	237	365	154	128	107	Sum 2,184

TABLE 24 (Continued)

WAGES IN COPENHAGEN, 1920 AND 1949

Craft or Occupation	(1) Average Hourly Earnings, Fourth Quarter 1920 (*Øre*)	(2) Average Hourly Earnings, Third Quarter 1949 (*Øre*)	(3) Earnings in 1949 as a Percentage of Earnings in 1920 (*Col. 2 ÷ Col. 1*)	(4) Absolute Increase in Hourly Earnings, 1920–1949 (Øre) (*Col. 2 — Col. 1*)	(5) Relative Percentage Increase in Wages of Each Craft or Occupation	(6) Employment in Craft or Occupation, September 30, 1949
E. *Stone, glass*						
Ceramics workers	234	365	156	131	108	303
Stonecutters	272	377	139	105	97	79
Pavers	322	506	157	184	109	68
Average[a]	254	388	153	134	106	Sum 450
F. *Metal trades*						
Gold and silversmiths	236	425	180	189	125	404
Grinders	251	425	169	174	117	384
Braziers	252	397	158	145	110	250
Metal workers	268	386	144	118	100	13,732
Coppersmiths	270	403	149	133	103	88
Pressers	289	531	184	242	128	51
Molders	300	407	136	107	94	406
Ship timberers	320	388	121	68	84	236
Average[a]	268	389	145	121	101	Sum 15,551
G. *Graphic trades*						
Etchers	230	379	165	149	115	402
Lithographers	250	395	158	145	110	338
Bookbinders	258	378	147	120	102	569
Printers	261	371	142	110	99	2,996
Average[a]	257	375	146	118	101	Sum 4,305
Average,[a] skilled males	270	388	144	118	100	33,069
II. *Unskilled males*						
A. *Food and beverage*						
Cigar makers	177	292	165	115	115	64
Conserves workers	182	291	160	109	112	82
Packinghouse workers	194	298	154	104	108	280
Chocolate makers	205	276	135	71	94	233
Sugar workers	207	297	143	90	100	320
Average[a]	199	291	146	92	102	Sum 979

TABLE 24 (Continued)

WAGES IN COPENHAGEN, 1920 AND 1949

Craft or Occupation	(1) Average Hourly Earnings, Fourth Quarter 1920 (*Øre*)	(2) Average Hourly Earnings, Third Quarter 1949 (*Øre*)	(3) Earnings in 1949 as a Percentage of Earnings in 1920 (*Col. 2 ÷ Col. 1*)	(4) Absolute Increase in Hourly Earnings, 1920–1949 (Øre) (*Col. 2 — Col. 1*)	(5) Relative Percentage Increase in Wages of Each Craft or Occupation		(6) Employment in Craft or Occupation, September 30, 1949
B. *Textile and clothing*							
Rope makers......	175	332	195	157	136		229
Textile operatives..	189	304	161	115	113		1,712
Tanners...........	223	365	164	142	115		397
Average[a]........	193	317	164	124	115	Sum	2,329
C. *Building trades*							
Terrazzo workers...	231	385	167	154	117		109
Mason helpers.....	284	415	146	131	102		1,201
Heavy construction.	291	376	129	85	90		4,117
Average[a]........	288	385	134	97	94	Sum	5,427
D. *Woodworkers*.......	181	283	156	102	109	Sum	367
E. *Stone, glass*							
Ceramics workers...	192	329	171	137	120		712
Quarry workers....	203	328	162	125	113		96
Average[a]........	193	329	170	136	119	Sum	808
F. *Metal workers*......	212	308	145	96	101	Sum	11,049
G. *Graphic trades*							
Paper workers.....	189	276	146	87	102		325
Lithographers......	201	311	155	110	108		131
Printers' helpers....	202	298	148	96	103		588
Average[a]........	198	293	148	95	103	Sum	1,044
H. *Other*							
Warehousemen.....	181	269	149	88	104		1,791
Firemen (heating)..	191	287	150	96	105		357
Sulphuric acid plants	201	306	152	105	106		52
Longshoremen.....	290	354	122	64	85		1,399
Average[a]........	225	304	135	79	94	Sum	3,599
Average,[a] unskilled males.........	226	324	143	98	100	Sum	25,602

TABLE 24 (Continued)

WAGES IN COPENHAGEN, 1920 AND 1949

Craft or Occupation	(1) Average Hourly Earnings, Fourth Quarter 1920 (Øre)	(2) Average Hourly Earnings, Third Quarter 1949 (Øre)	(3) Earnings in 1949 as a Percentage of Earnings in 1920 (*Col. 2 ÷ Col. 1*)	(4) Absolute Increase in Hourly Earnings, 1920–1949 (Øre) (*Col. 2 − Col. 1*)	(5) Relative Percentage Increase in Wages of Each Craft or Occupation	(6) Employment in Craft or Occupation, September 30, 1949
III. *Females*						
A. *Food and beverage*						
Packinghouse workers	113	194	172	81	103	1,383
Chocolate makers	129	185	143	56	86	749
Sugar workers	129	188	146	59	87	144
Cigar makers	145	257	177	112	106	1,242
Average[a]	128	214	167	86	100	Sum 3,518
B. *Textile and clothing*						
Rope makers	120	228	190	108	114	218
Seamstresses	128	235	184	107	110	4,041
Textile operatives	142	215	151	73	90	4,463
Shoe workers	148	235	159	87	95	1,486
Average[a]	137	226	165	89	99	Sum 10,208
E. *Ceramics workers*	146	238	163	92	98	781
F. *Metal workers*	127	222	175	95	105	4,713
G. *Graphic trades*						
Paper workers	125	191	153	66	92	1,128
Bookbinders	139	227	163	88	98	879
Printers	139	217	156	78	93	368
Lithographers	140	216	154	76	92	75
Average[a]	133	209	157	76	94	Sum 2,450
Average,[a] all females	133	222	167	89	100	Sum 21,670

Sources: Danmarks Statistik, "Arbejdsl nnen i Industrien," *Statistiske Meddelelser*, vol. 78, no. 1 (1927); *Beretning om Dansk Arbejdsgiverforenings Virksomhed*, 1921–1922, pp. 70–73; *Arbejdsgiveren*, LI (March 1950). 80–83.

[a] Weighted by employment.

covering a somewhat different group of trades.[3] While these data are not reproduced, appropriate reference will be made to the conclusions derived from them.

The range of wages

The following data show the ratio of wages in the highest to the lowest craft for each of the major groups of workers:

	1920	*1949*
Skilled males	211	170
Unskilled males	166	154
Females	131	139

As the figures indicate, there has been a significant compression in the range of rates for male workers, but a tendency toward a greater spread in female wage rates.

The ranges conceal the true concentration of rates about the group averages. Twenty-eight out of 43 skilled crafts were within a range of ±10 per cent of 388 øre per hour, while 35 out of 43 were within a range of ±15 per cent of 388 øre. The 8 crafts outside the latter range comprised but 10 per cent of the total number of skilled workers covered in Table 24. For unskilled male workers, a range of ±15 per cent about the group average of 324 øre includes 18 out of 22 crafts, but excludes 28 per cent of the covered workers, indicating that within a narrower range the wages of unskilled workers are less concentrated about the group average.

While there is little information available on intra-craft wage variation, some of the major crafts appear to have ranges approaching or even exceeding 15 per cent about the craft average. For the Copenhagen metal trades in the fourth quarter of 1948, the range of the subcraft wage averages about the trade average was −7 to +20 per cent; the range of individual earnings was much greater.[4] Thus, older and more experienced workers in the lower paid trades are likely to earn as much or more than younger workers in the high wage crafts.

Inter-industry differentials

As noted above, not all the industry groups in Table 24 are homogeneous. Comparisons must therefore be limited to those which include closely related trades, the building, metal, and graphic trades falling into this category. The following data are abstracted from Table 24:

[3] P. E. Milhøj, "Nogle Traek af Forholdet Mellem De Industrielle Lønninger i Danmark Siden 1914," *Nationaløkonomisk Tidsskrift*, 1948, p. 111.

[4] Dansk Smede og Maskinarbejderforbund, *Lønoversigt for København*, 1948.

	Average hourly earnings 1920 (øre)			*Average hourly earnings 1949 (øre)*			*Per cent increase 1920–1949*		
Industry	*Skilled*	*Un-skilled*	*Female*	*Skilled*	*Un-skilled*	*Female*	*Skilled*	*Un-skilled*	*Female*
Graphic	257	198	133	375	293	209	46	48	57
Metal	268	212	127	389	308	222	45	45	75
Building	316	288	—	417	385	—	32	34	—

Considering the fact that the graphic trades produce for the domestic market and the metal trades largely for export, the stability of the wage relationship between the two over a thirty-year period is remarkable. The smaller percentage wage increase for the building trades is attributable to the general compression of the wage structure when measured in percentage terms, a phenomenon which is considered below. The figures thus suggest that market forces were a less important factor in wage change since 1920 than the position of the industry in the wage scale in 1920.

Intra-industry differentials

The comparisons shown above indicate another interesting fact, that the percentage wage increases received by unskilled male workers in an industry closely paralleled the increases of the skilled male workers in the same industry so that absolute differentials between the two groups widened. To test this relationship further, the skilled crafts in Table 24 with counterparts among the unskilled and female workers were segregated and arranged in Table 25 in the order of descending percentage increase magnitude for the skilled crafts.

For seven of the ten unskilled male crafts shown in Table 25, the percentage wage increases for 1920 to 1949 were very close to the increases for skilled workers in the corresponding crafts. In one case, ceramics workers, the money wage increase received by the two was similar in magnitude. Unskilled masons and tanners gained in relation to their skilled counterparts. In general, there was a tendency toward the maintenance of a constant percentage relationship between the wages of the skilled and unskilled workers within each trade, or put differently, a percentage wage increase among the skilled workers in a trade tended to be associated with an equal percentage increase for the unskilled workers in the same trade, confirming the observation drawn from comparing the graphic, metal, and building trades.

The female workers in most of the trades secured percentage wage gains in excess of those achieved by the male workers. However, there was a tendency for the percentage wage increases among the female

TABLE 25

COMPARATIVE WAGE INCREASES FOR SKILLED, UNSKILLED, AND FEMALE WORKERS, 1920–1949

	Skilled		Unskilled		Female	
Craft	(1) Per Cent	(2) Øre per Hour	(3) Per Cent	(4) Øre per Hour	(5) Per Cent	(6) Øre per Hour
Rope makers..........	102	181	95	157	90	108
Cigar makers.........	62	122	65	115	77	112
Lithographers.........	58	145	55	110	54	76
Woodworkers.........	57	130	56	102	—	—
Ceramics workers......	56	131	71	137	63	92
Shoe workers.........	54	134	—	—	59	87
Bookbinders..........	47	120	—	—	63	88
Printers..............	42	110	48	96	56	78
Metal workers........	44	118	45	96	75	95
Tanners..............	39	108	64	142	—	—
Chocolate workers.....	38	94	35	71	43	56
Masons..............	26	96	46	131	—	—

Source: Table 24.

trades to vary with the percentage wage increases among the corresponding male trades (the deviation may be measured by the extent to which the numbers in column 5 fail to read in descending order).

Differentials between skilled and unskilled male workers

The observations made immediately above suggest that the percentage wage relationship between skilled and unskilled workers was the same in 1920 and 1949, but that the differential between male and female wages has narrowed. For the workers represented in Table 24, the skilled wage increase for 1920 to 1949 was 44 per cent, the unskilled increase 43 per cent, and the female wage increase 67 per cent, tending to substantiate these conclusions.

The terminal years, however, conceal a considerable degree of variation in the ratio of unskilled to skilled wages. This emerges clearly from Table 26, where the ratio of unskilled to skilled hourly earnings (all Denmark) is shown for alternate years from 1914 to 1949. The absolute difference in earnings is also shown for the same years.

For the 35-year period as a whole, wage differentials between the two groups of workers have been reduced. The movement toward equality was most pronounced during the inflation of the two war periods, but in both cases there was subsequent retrogression to wider differentials.

During the years 1920 and 1949 the wage difference between the groups was almost identical.

The changes in absolute money differentials help to explain the cyclical nature of the percentage relationships. Workers and unions are much more conscious of absolute than of percentage wage differentials; while they are apt to offer strenuous resistance to any narrowing of the former, they are less likely to object to narrowing of the latter, provided

TABLE 26

RATIOS OF UNSKILLED AND FEMALE TO SKILLED HOURLY EARNINGS, DENMARK, 1914–1949

Year	(1) Ratio of Unskilled to Skilled Male (*Per Cent*)	(2) Absolute Difference (*Øre*)	(3) Ratio of Female to Skilled Male (*Per Cent*)	(4) Absolute Difference (*Øre*)
1914	75	15	49	31
1916	78	16	49	37
1918	77	24	51	51
1920	82	42	54	106
1922	81	33	53	82
1924	81	34	52	84
1926	79	35	54	77
1928	80	31	54	72
1930	80	32	54	74
1932	83	27	55	71
1934	83	27	55	71
1936	84	26	56	71
1938	85	26	56	75
1940	84	31	56	85
1942	86	31	56	94
1944	88	29	57	104
1946	86	41	60	117
1948	83	56	59	137
1949 (third quarter)	83	59	60	143

Source: *Arbeidsgiverforeningens Håndbog*, 1949–50, p. 3.

he money differences either remain unchanged or increase. Inflation us provides an opportunity for the lower paid workers to secure relave percentage gains, which are difficult to maintain when money wages egin to fall.

An apparent exception to this rule is provided by the behavior of wage differentials from 1944 to 1949, a period of rising wage levels. The explanation lies in the degree of equalitarianism that had been achieved in 1944 as a consequence of Federation of Labor wage policy. It was widely felt after the war that 12 per cent was too small a wage difference between skilled and unskilled labor. As a trade union publication has stated, "In many unions there was a general belief that a limit had been reached, at least temporarily, for the possibilities inherent in an equalitarian wage policy — the higher paid workers refused to relinquish their claims any longer . . ." [5] The results of the policy reversal emerge clearly from Table 26.

Differentials between male and female workers

There is also shown in Table 26 the ratio of female wages to those of skilled male workers. This differential has diminished steadily from 1914 to 1949 in percentage terms, although the absolute wage differential between the two groups has increased.

Inter-craft differentials

In Table 24, the crafts in each industry were arranged in ascending order of their absolute wage levels in 1920. Inspection of the skilled craft group reveals a consistent inverse relationship between the level of wages in 1920 and the percentage wage increase from 1920 to 1949. While there are exceptional cases, they are to be found among the small handicrafts whose members are able to exact monopoly profits for their work.[6]

The same equalitarian trend is manifest among the unskilled workers.[7] Here the most interesting item is the relatively small increase recorded for longshoremen. This can be explained by the fact that the longshoremen, among whom the revolutionary spirit reached its apogee in the years following the end of the first world war, had already attained in 1920 a level of wages higher than the average skilled wage. As long as foreign trade was maintained at a high level, the longshoremen were able to exact high wages, but most of these gains evaporated with the collapse after 1921. Their average hourly earnings in 1925 were only 66 per cent of the 1920 level, whereas the warehousemen, who were at a lower level in 1920, fell to only 73 per cent of that level by 1925.

The relationship between 1920 wages and subsequent increases does not hold true for the female workers. This corresponds to the observation made above that the range of wage rates in female occupations has not narrowed since 1920.

[5] *Under Samvirkets Flag*, p. 287.

[6] The rope, glove, hat, and carriage makers fall into this category. Among them, they had 238 workers employed in 1949 in Copenhagen.

[7] The sugar workers owe their relatively favored position to special legislation in support of the domestic sugar industry. See Philip, pp. 80–86.

TABLE 27

RELATIVE WAGE INCREASES OF MAJOR COPENHAGEN TRADES, 1920–1949

Trade	Average Hourly Earnings, 1920 (*Øre*)	Percentage Wage Increase, 1920–1949	Index of Percentage Wage Increase (*Group average = 100*)	Rank in 1920	Rank in 1949
A. *Skilled males*					
Cigar makers	198	62	113	10	9
Bakers	220	42	99	9	10
Cabinetmakers	235	54	107	8	8
Shoe workers	247	54	107	7	5
Printers	261	42	99	6	7
Metal workers	268	44	100	5	4
Painters	274	38	96	4	6
Carpenters	284	45	101	3	3
Timberers	371	16	81	2	2
Masons	376	26	88	1	1
B. *Unskilled males*					
Warehousemen	181	49	104	5	5
Textile workers	189	61	113	4	4
Mason helpers	284	46	102	3	1
Longshoremen	290	22	85	2	3
Heavy construction workers	291	29	90	1	2
C. *Females*					
Packinghouse workers	113	72	103	9	7
Paper workers	125	53	92	8	8
Metal workers	127	75	105	7	5
Seamstresses	128	84	110	6	3
Chocolate workers	129	43	86	5	9
Bookbinders	139	63	98	4	4
Textile workers	142	51	90	3	6
Cigar makers	145	77	106	2	1
Shoe workers	148	59	95	1	2

Source: Table 24.

To illustrate these tendencies more clearly, the major trades in Table 24 (those with employment exceeding 750 in 1949) have been segregated and ranked in the order of their 1920 levels of wages, in Table 27. A coefficient of rank correlation comparing relative wage standing in 1920 and 1949 was computed for each major group, with the following result:

	Coefficient of rank correlation
Skilled males	.93
Unskilled males	.70
Females	.63

These figures emphasize the high degree of relative wage stability among the male trades,[8] and the lesser degree of stability among the female trades.[9]

Inter-craft differentials, employment, and unemployment

While the inverse relationship between the absolute level of wages in 1920 and subsequent wage increases is good, it is not perfect. In an effort to ascertain the causes of aberration, the skilled trades shown in Table 27 were arranged in the order of the magnitude of their percentage wage increases from 1920 to 1949, and information relating to changes in employment and average unemployment in each trade appended. The results appear in Table 28. If there were a positive correlation between wage increases and expansion of employment, the figures in column 2 would appear in descending order of magnitude, while if there were an inverse correlation between wage increases and the degree of unemployment, the figures in columns 3 to 5 would appear in increasing order of magnitude.

Though no unique relationship emerges, the data do suggest the influence of expanding employment opportunities and unemployment upon wages. The baking trade, for example, should have secured an above-average wage increase on the basis of its relatively low wage scale in 1920. Its failure to do so may be attributed to excessive supply in relation to reduced demand for labor; the excess of young entrants to the trade was promoted by the customary provision of board and lodging by master bakers, thus relieving the parents of much of the economic burden of support. The possibilities of achieving independent entrepreneurship have been another element tending to attract an unduly large number of baker apprentices. Unemployment undoubtedly exercised a dampening effect upon wages, though it may be noted that the masons, whose wage level exceeded that of the timberers in 1920, enjoyed a larger wage increase for 1920 to 1949, notwithstanding a smaller expansion in employment opportunities.

Some of the other trades, however, do not fit into the anticipated pattern, for example, the shoe workers. While studies of individual industries might clarify some of the observed divergences in wage movements,

[8] Because of the small number of unskilled male trades the coefficient of rank correlation is not an entirely suitable measure of correlation. It will be noted that only one of the trades in question was displaced in rank.

[9] Milhøj's conclusions on the basis of his 1914–1945 comparisons were: "If one analyzes the changes that have occurred, there is a striking feature in addition to invariance, namely, that the crafts have moved closer to one another in wage terms through reduced differentials. This equalization has not resulted in any great displacement, but was characterized largely by tighter bunching of the crafts about the class average." Milhøj, pp. 117–118.

TABLE 28

EMPLOYMENT, UNEMPLOYMENT, AND WAGE CHANGES IN TEN MAJOR COPENHAGEN SKILLED TRADES

Trade	(1) Relative Percentage Increase in Wages, 1920–1949[a]	(2) Percentage Increase in Employment, 1930–1949[a]	(3) Percentage of Unemployment Prevailing in 1927[b]	(4) Percentage of Unemployment Prevailing in 1937[c]	(5) Percentage of Unemployment Prevailing in 1947[d]
Cigar makers	113	33	23.7	20.3	2.5
Shoe workers	107	39	24.5	29.0	1.1
Cabinetmakers	107	91	n.a.	n.a.	n.a.
Carpenters	101	53	36.0	22.0	1.8
Metal workers	100	126	36.1	12.1	0.1
Bakers	99	−22	28.4	29.0	2.9
Printers	99	n.a.	14.1	9.6	0.3
Painters	96	146	29.0	25.2	8.4
Masons	88	86	26.6	32.4	13.3
Timberers	81	135	35.3	31.1	5.7

Sources: [a] Table 24.
[b] *Statistisk Aarbog*, 1928, p. 119.
[c] *Statistiske Meddelelser*, vol. 115, no. 4, p. 36.
[d] *Statistiske Meddelelser*, vol. 133, no. 1, pp. 50–51.

it may be concluded on the basis of the data in Table 28 that the general trend toward inter-craft wage equality was of greater significance in determining the course of wages than the two economic factors of unemployment and expansion of the trade.

Agricultural wages

The wages of agricultural workers have displayed a much greater elasticity over the business cycle than industrial wages, lack of organization among the farm workers undoubtedly being the major cause. This appears from the following data:

Year	*Ratio of average hourly earnings of heavy construction workers to earnings of agricultural workers*
1923	184
1926	192
1929	204
1932	268
1935	232
1938	219
1942	186

Source: Jørgen Pedersen, *Fuld Beskaeftigelse* (Copenhagen, 1945), p. 50.

During the great depression, wages of heavy construction workers (chosen as a yardstick because such workers are often employed in rural areas) remained virtually unchanged, the increasing differential thus being due entirely to declining agricultural wages. By 1942, however, agricultural wages had again risen to a level sufficient to restore the 1923 wage relationship.

The differential between industrial and agricultural wages and its underlying *raison d'être* have been crucial factors in determining the pattern of internal labor migration. Professor Pedersen expressed this when he wrote:

> The higher the percentage of unemployment, the greater the differential between the wages of unskilled industrial labor and agricultural labor . . . When there is considerable unemployment, rural youth is less apt to depart from the country, since it is difficult to secure work outside agriculture, and the risk of unemployment is very great. They will compete for the available farm jobs, and wages of agricultural helpers will fall. Since trade unionism has thus far played an insignificant role among these workers, the lower limit of wages is set by work opportunities outside agriculture, and by the amount of assistance that can be secured during unemployment.[10]

This relationship raises serious problems for Danish full employment policy. If a high level of industrial employment is maintained through government intervention, rural wages will tend to approach industrial wages, thus causing an agricultural price rise and adding to the pressure of inflation. Moreover, since export prices will also rise, the competitive position of Danish agriculture will be threatened. This constitutes one of the principal difficulties of effectuating full employment in a country in which agricultural employment plays an important role, and ultimately some form of manpower control to preserve the agricultural labor force without virtual elimination of the industrial-agricultural wage differential may prove essential.

Summary of findings

Before considering the causes of the observed changes in wage structure, it may be well to summarize the principal findings to this point:

1. The range of wages for male workers has undergone compression from 1920 to 1949, while the female wage range expanded slightly.

2. Among the major industrial groups, relative wages have risen to the greatest extent where absolute wage levels were lowest in 1920.

3. Although there has been a long run trend in the direction of wage equality between skilled and unskilled workers, this differential varied

[10] Jørgen Pedersen, *Fuld Beskaeftigelse*, p. 52. See also Kjeld Philip, pp. 65–68.

over the business cycle, tending to narrow in inflation and widen in deflation.

4. Wage differences between male and female workers diminished slowly but steadily over the period studied.

5. While there has been an inverse relationship between the wage increases attained by individual crafts since 1920 and 1920 craft wage ranking, the movement has not been sufficient to disturb the traditional ranking of crafts in the wage spectrum.

6. Neither the effect of relative expansion in employment nor unemployment appears to have had sufficient influence to offset the tendencies noted above.

Some factors affecting wage structure

The first thing to be noted in endeavoring to account for the great stability of the Danish wage structure from 1920 to 1949 is the small absolute change in money wage levels between these years. Average hourly earnings of nonagricultural workers were 188 øre in 1920 and 295 øre in 1949, an increase of 57 per cent. It is true that the increase is 130 per cent if 1928 rather than 1920 is employed as the base from which to measure the change. But in the United States, by comparison, average hourly earnings in manufacturing rose 194 per cent from 1920 to 1949, and 217 per cent from the 1933 low point to 1949. Structural stability is undoubtedly furthered by the minimization of variation in the general wage level.

Centralized collective bargaining has been of paramount significance in preventing inter-craft wage change. The evolution of pattern bargaining, on the basis of the metal trades agreement, has led and is likely increasingly to result in the maintenance of prevailing wage relationships, in their immunity from the play of other economic forces.[11] Dynamic technological change, which altered the structure of industry, might have broken through the barriers of bargaining uniformity, but the Danish economy of the twenties and thirties was characterized rather by a slow growth of production and the gradual rationalization of what continued to be predominantly small-scale industry.

The factors responsible for the principal change that did occur in the wage structure, a compression of rates about the average, were as follows:

1. The power of the Laborers' Union undoubtedly contributed to the

[11] "Bargaining situations in which individual crafts, by independent action, have secured special wage advances for themselves, have not occurred, apart from the years immediately following the first world war . . . there has scarcely been room for the influence upon craft wage relationships of factors other than the efforts of the collective bargaining organizations and the government to obtain uniformity and a socially beneficial line in wage development." Milhøj, pp. 122–123.

reduction of wage differentials between skilled and unskilled labor. However, the domination of the Federation of Labor by the skilled crafts and the importance of the Metal Workers' Union in the collective bargaining system placed definite limits upon what the Laborers could achieve through their economic strength.[12]

2. Since 1939, wage regulation by the cost of living index has provided an important equalizing factor. The index adjustments of the twenties were in percentage terms, thus preserving percentage differentials. But the recent practice of awarding identical flat sums to all adult male workers has had an opposite effect. The same is true of the male-female wage ratio, since female cost of living supplements have been at about two-thirds the male amount, that is, in excess of the basic wage relationship.

3. Early in the 1930's, the Federation of Labor initiated the so-called "solidaristic" wage policy, whereby lower paid workers were to receive extra wage concessions. The precise effect of this somewhat vague policy is difficult to evaluate, though it did contribute to the maintenance of unskilled wages during periods of high unemployment.

4. Last, but by no means least, the same forces that are everywhere tending to reduce wage differentials — mechanization, work simplification, and the breakdown of skills — were also operative in Denmark.

Conclusion

In previous sections dealing with movements of the wage level, the effects of such economic factors as the demand for Danish exports, changes in the terms of trade, and productivity of labor were stressed as the principal causative elements. Labor market institutions appeared to play a secondary role, at least in respect to real wages.

But given the level of wages, the distribution of the wage bill among the several claimants is influenced primarily by collective bargaining and the organization of the labor market. It is difficult to escape the conclusion that despite the slow tempo of economic change in Denmark since 1920, the absence of centralized collective bargaining would have resulted in greater scrambling of craft wage differentials, and in less equalitarianism. Nationwide bargaining on the Danish model creates a propensity toward rigidity in wage structure. It also affords the possibility of systematic wage reforms that are deemed to be "socially desirable," but would be difficult to realize under atomistic bargaining.

[12] Philip (p. 264) exaggerates "the great significance and weight of the Laborers' Union under the new voting rules [of 1934] regarding the linking of crafts."

QUANTITATIVE ASPECTS OF LABOR DISPUTES

The concentration of work stoppages

A remarkable aspect of Danish labor history is the concentration of work stoppages in a few "bad" years, leaving the remaining years relatively free of work interruption from this source. Some 73 per cent of the total man-days lost due to labor disputes within the period 1899 to 1948 occurred in seven particular years. Comparative data for Norway and Sweden (covering the years 1903 to 1948) show 67 and 60 per cent.[13] These figures lend support to a generalization made earlier, that the centralization of collective bargaining tends to concentrate the incidence of labor disputes, for of the three Scandinavian countries, Denmark has had the most extensive bargaining unit.

Strikes versus lockouts

Statistics are available on the number of workers affected each year by strikes and lockouts. Since there is no reason to assume that there is any consistent difference in the average duration of strikes and lockouts, the data may be taken as indicative of the relative incidence of these two forms of labor disputes. From Appendix A it appears that during the fifty years 1899 to 1948, 359,000 workers have been on strike and 329,000 locked out. Since 1936, lockouts have almost disappeared as causes of labor disputes.

The figures must be interpreted with caution; if Danish bargaining procedure were similar to that practiced in the United States, for example, the ratio of lockouts to strikes would be much smaller. When a Danish employer desires to reduce wages at the expiration of a contract, and the union refuses to accept the reduction, the ensuing stoppage of work would ordinarily be classified as a lockout since the employer took the initiative in serving notice of intention to terminate contractual relationships, even though the union had ordered its members to stop working.

It is clear, nevertheless, that the organized employers of Denmark have followed an aggressive collective bargaining policy. Almost half the volume of labor disputes (measured by workers affected)[14] have occurred

[13] Man-days lost due to labor disputes in the United States are available only since 1927. Taking the worst 7 out of the 22 years from 1927 to 1948, about 65 per cent of the total man-days lost occurred during these years. This compares with 73 per cent in 7 out of 50 years in Denmark.

[14] Since the largest work stoppages have been lockouts, the actual number of separate strikes is undoubtedly far in excess of the number of lockouts.

as a consequence of their initiative in seeking to change terms of employment. One may assume that an affirmative policy leading to this result is a concomitant of employer organization for collective bargaining purposes.

Work stoppages, money wages, and real wages

We turn next to an aspect of industrial relations that has been a source of controversy, the relationship of work stoppages to wage movements. Lord Keynes asserted that "workers, though unconsciously, are instinctively more reasonable economists than the classical school, in as much as they resist reductions of money wages, which are seldom or never of an all-round character, even though the existing real equivalent of these wages exceeds the marginal disutility of the existing employment; whereas they do not resist reductions of real wages, which are associated with increases in aggregate employment and leave relative money-wages unchanged, unless the reduction proceeds so far as to threaten a reduction of the real wage below the marginal disutility of the existing volume of employment. Every trade union will put up some resistance to a cut in money-wages, however small. But . . . no trade union would dream of striking on every occasion of a rise in the cost of living . . ." [15] On the other hand, Professor Dunlop, on the basis of an analysis of British strike statistics, observes that "trade unions have been as willing to strike for advances in wage rates when the cost of living has risen by more than a 'small' amount as to strike for the maintenance of a wage rate when threatened with a reduction," the term "small" being defined as an increase of less than 5 per cent.[16]

What light do Danish statistics throw on this problem? The relevant variables are compared in Chart 3, based upon the data in Appendix A. The bars show strike losses, the lines, respectively, the movement of real and money wages. It appears that in Denmark, during the past fifty years, money wages fell during one period only, 1920 to 1926 (interrupted by a temporary rise in 1924). Real wages, on the other hand, were reduced on four occasions: by 20 per cent from 1911 to 1917; by 15 per cent from 1921 to 1923; by 11 per cent from 1932 to 1937; and by 17 per cent from 1939 to 1942. Except for the period 1921 to 1923, the decline in real wages was accompanied by stable or rising money wages.

The effect of money wage reductions upon industrial relations is im-

[15] J. M. Keynes, *The General Theory of Employment, Interest and Money* (New York, 1935), pp. 14–15. Some support for these dicta may be found in John I. Griffin, *Strikes* (New York, 1939), pp. 49–50, and Alvin Hansen, "Cycles of Strikes," *American Economic Review*, XI (1921), 616.

[16] John T. Dunlop, "The Movement of Real and Money Wage Rates," *The Economic Journal*, September 1938, p. 426.

mediately apparent. Thirty-six per cent of total labor dispute losses during the entire fifty years occurred in the deflation period 1921–1927, about 2.5 times greater than "expected" losses if the incidence of stoppages had been evenly distributed over the entire fifty years 1899–1948. If the lockout of 1899, which was not primarily a wage dispute, is excluded, the percentage rises to 41. Had it not been for the temporary wage upturn in 1923 and 1924, when work stoppage losses were negligible, the period would probably have shown even greater proportional losses.

The relationship between real wage reductions and industrial disputes is not so clear. The decline in real wages from 1911 to 1917 provoked little disturbance; the cost of living rose 16 per cent from 1914 to 1915, 16 per cent from 1915 to 1916, and 15 per cent from 1916 to 1917. Only in 1919 and 1920 did the trend of strike losses rise, and though the preceding cumulative decline may have been a causal factor, the revolutionary spirit then sweeping over Europe was probably of greater significance.

The real wage decline of 1921–1923 was coincidental with a decline in money wages, so that the effects cannot be separated. The next real wage decline, 1932–1937, was due entirely to rising living costs, since money wages remained unchanged. However, the upward movement in living costs was gradual, every annual change falling into Dunlop's "small" category. Moreover, a high level of unemployment prevailed, acting as a deterrent to strikes. Up to 1936, work stoppages were negligible, but in that year, perhaps as a consequence of the real wage losses during the preceding four years, union insistence upon a wage increase led to the second most severe work stoppage in Danish labor history.

The wartime period need not concern us, for work stoppages were prohibited. The only other important strike year was 1946, when prices were stable and real wages displayed an upward trend. This strike had political overtones, however, and was in many ways a consequence of the abnormal period following the abolition of wartime restrictions.

The following conclusions can be drawn from the preceding observations:

1. There is little doubt that an attempt by employers to reduce money wages will provoke sharp worker reaction. There are those in Denmark who maintain flatly that money wage cuts are impossible in the existing political climate.

2. In two periods when money wages were fairly stable, real wages were reduced without undue union resistance. In one case, the cost of living rose by "large" annual increments, in the other by "small" annual increments.

3. However, both these periods were concluded by severe work stoppages, suggesting that there may be limits which vary with the level of unemployment and the political situation beyond which real wages cannot be reduced through rising prices, even gradually, without creating industrial strife.

4. Although the Danish experience is by no means conclusive, it does suggest that workers have been much more sensitive to money wage cuts than to reduction in real wages through the medium of price increases. But fifteen years of wage regulation by the cost of living index, during which publication of the index has been front page news, may have altered the psychology of the Danish worker. Paradoxically, the institution of cost of living supplements held separate from basic wages may result in greater downward flexibility in money wages and more downward rigidity in real wages.

Labor disputes in Denmark, Norway, and Sweden

The Danish statistics of labor disputes shown in Appendix A do not of themselves provide a yardstick against which to measure the effectiveness of the collective bargaining system in averting industrial warfare. Fortunately, the basic similarities in labor relations among the Scandinavian countries allow comparisons with some degree of confidence in the meaningfulness of the results. To this end, Tables 29 and 30 have been constructed; Table 29 relates man-day labor dispute losses to total industrial employment, while Table 30 relates man-day losses to the number of workers organized in trade unions. In each case, the Danish ratio is expressed as a percentage of the corresponding Norwegian and Swedish ratios.

Before examining the data, a few remarks about the concepts employed are in order. The use of gross employment data as the basis for measuring work stoppage losses, while appropriate if what is sought is a measure of the relative impact of labor disputes upon two economies, may give a very misleading picture of the effectiveness of collective bargaining if the two differ in the degree to which their workers are organized. Characteristically, the incidence of work stoppages is much higher among organized than among unorganized workers.[17] A country with little labor organization might have strike losses that are slight compared with total employment, and yet have a poor record of industrial peace in the organized sector. Conversely, an excellent record of industrial relations might appear relatively bad in a highly organized country. A better index of industrial peace is secured if work stoppage losses are related to the *organized* labor force.

[17] Griffin, p. 100; Paul H. Douglas, "An Analysis of Strike Statistics 1881–1922," *Journal of the American Statistical Association*, XVIII (1923), 866.

This is apparent from a comparison of Tables 29 and 30. In the comparison between Denmark and Norway, the figures in Table 29 are consistently higher than those in Table 30, highlighting the greater degree of trade union organization in the former country.[18] The same is true for the Danish-Swedish comparison, although the numerical difference — and the degree of organization — is not so great here.[19]

TABLE 29

RATE OF MAN-DAYS LOST BECAUSE OF LABOR DISPUTES PER 1,000 PERSONS EMPLOYED, 1927–1947

Year	Danish Losses as a Percentage of (1) Norwegian	(2) Swedish
1927	8.8	82.2
1928	3.1	0.6
1929	21.0	16.8
1930	61.7	34.1
1931	2.4	20.5
1932	23.0	6.2
1933	4.4	2.1
1934	55.3	37.3
1935	7.5	10.4
1936	721.5	1,354.7
1937	1.9	4.6
1938	n.a.	25.3
1939	n.a.	18.5
1945	n.a.	1.0
1946	n.a.	8,815.4
1947	n.a.	1,659.6

Source: Robert Morse Woodbury, "The Incidence of Industrial Disputes," *International Labor Review*, November, 1949, pp. 452–453.

Although the industrial coverage of the three countries is approximately the same, the Swedish statistics are unique in their inclusion of indirect losses, that is, days lost by workers thrown out of employment by labor disputes but not themselves directly involved. How important indirect losses are in relation to total losses cannot be determined from

[18] The Norwegian data include only members of the Federation of Labor, while the Danish data include all organized workers. For some of the earlier years this introduces a significant error, but after World War I there were very few organized workers, probably not exceeding 2 per cent, outside the ranks of the Norwegian Federation of Labor.

[19] The Swedish data exclude the large independent union of white-collar workers and civil servants. This seems appropriate in view of the limitations upon the ability of the civil servants to strike and the general disclaimer of the strike weapon by white-collar workers. The number of such employees organized by the Danish and Norwegian Federations of Labor is relatively small.

TABLE 30

RATIO OF MAN-DAYS LOST BECAUSE OF LABOR DISPUTES TO NUMBER OF ORGANIZED WORKERS, 1903–1948

Year	Danish Losses as a Percentage of (1) Norwegian	(2) Swedish
1903	1.3	2.6
1904	15.6	19.8
1905	295.3	24.7
1906	18.4	22.1
1907	26.1	102.7
1908	9.0	8.3
1909	11.2	0.6
1910	13.1	1,700.0
1911	25.2	101.2
1912	4.9	15.0
1913	129.7	112.2
1914	14.3	7.6
1915	4.4	300.0
1916	13.8	51.2
1917	82.1	21.9
1918	36.2	13.4
1919	59.0	40.7
1920	42.9	16.1
1921	10.9	60.7
1922	688.9	95.8
1923	0.6	0.3
1924	1.0	19.8
1925	191.8	231.8
1926	0.3	0.3
1927	2.7	48.1
1928	0.1	0.3
1929	7.7	10.3
1930	24.6	25.5
1931	1.3	17.0
1932	9.3	5.1
1933	1.3	0.6
1934	26.7	31.6
1935	3.8	2.7
1936	434.7	1,121.1
1937	0.9	3.0
1938	10.7	12.8
1939	1.2	20.0
1945	50.0	0.9
1946	1,042.9	7,300.0
1947	833.3	833.3
1948	14.3	25.0

Source: Appendix A.

the published Swedish data. However, a study of international strike statistics yielded the general conclusion that "the number of days lost indirectly is small in proportion to those lost by workers directly involved, averaging in most countries less than 10 per cent." [20] The Danish Statistical Department estimated that for the years 1926 to 1930, the inclusion of indirect strike losses would have added about 6 per cent to the reported direct losses.[21] Even assuming that the Swedish work stoppage losses are subject to overstatement, in comparison with the Danish, on the order of from 5 to 10 per cent, for only a few of the years under consideration would this be sufficient to reduce the Swedish losses below the Danish where the opposite relationship is now shown.

One final note of caution is essential. Percentage comparisons are subject to distortion where one of the variables under comparison takes on very low values. For example, in Table 30, the Danish 1946 stoppage losses were approximately 10 times the Norwegian and 73 times the Swedish (all on a relative basis) though 1946 was not Denmark's worst year; both Norwegian and Swedish losses that year were very small. Extreme values, both high and low, should be discounted.

From an examination of the data, it is apparent that by whatever criterion strike losses are measured, the Danish record is better than the Norwegian or Swedish. This is made clearer in Table 31, in which the figures in Tables 29 and 30 are summarized. For the great preponderance of the years, the man-day losses due to labor disputes were significantly higher in Norway and Sweden than in Denmark.

Why this should have been so is a difficult matter to determine. Among the hypotheses which may be advanced are the following:

1. The different character and timing of industrial development in the three countries were contributing factors. The modern Danish economy, as contrasted with the Norwegian and Swedish, grew slowly out of a medieval handicraft economy. The unit size of enterprise is smallest in Denmark, and there was not the same rapid growth of large-scale enterprise that gave rise to so much labor unrest in Norway and Sweden.

2. The corporate spirit was much stronger in Denmark than in the other countries, leading to earlier and closer collaboration between trade unions and employers.

3. The institutional devices for avoiding work stoppages developed earliest and received their greatest elaboration in Denmark. Agreements comparable to the Danish September Agreement were not reached until 1935 in Norway and 1938 in Sweden.

[20] "Days Lost Through Industrial Disputes in Different Countries," *International Labour Review*, XXXVII (1939), 674.

[21] *Statistiske Meddelelser*, vol. 88, no. 5 (1931), p. 12.

TABLE 31

COMPARISON OF DANISH, NORWEGIAN, AND SWEDISH WORK STOPPAGE LOSSES

	Based upon Total Employment (Table 29)		Based upon the Number of Organized Workers (Table 30)	
	Norway	Sweden	Norway	Sweden
1. Number of years in which Danish work stoppage losses were significantly[a] less than comparable losses in	10	12	33	31
2. Number of years in which Danish work stoppage losses were significantly[a] greater than comparable losses in	1	3	7	6
3. Number of years in which work stoppage losses were approximately equal in Denmark and in	0	1	1	4
Total years compared	11	16	41	41

[a] The nature of the data renders the calculation of precise estimates of error in collection a formidable task. A band of 25 per cent above and below equality is here adopted as a rough benchmark to test significance. This should be sufficient to allow both for errors in collecting data and for such bias as that noted in the text for the conceptual difference in the Swedish data. An increase of the ratio to ±50 per cent would have little effect upon the conclusions.

4. Danish workers enjoyed higher living standards than Norwegian and Swedish workers during most of the period.

Significance of work stoppage losses

At least brief consideration should be given to an aspect of industrial relations that has received too little attention: the economic losses entailed in work stoppages. It is usually assumed that the economic effect of labor disputes can be measured by the ratio of man-days lost to potential working time. While this may be valid on the assumption of full employment, it is misleading in a situation in which unemployment exists.

Professor Winding Pedersen has undertaken a study of the major Danish disputes from this point of view, and from them drawn the following observations:[22]

1. In general, the temporary reduction in employment resulting from a major conflict will be made good unless a business recession follows

[22] H. Winding Pedersen, "Arbejdsstandsningernes Økonomiske Virkninger," *Nationaløkonomiske Tidsskrift*, LXXV (1937), 290.

closely upon its termination. There is a distinct tendency for the lost days of labor to be regained.

2. Workers may even gain on balance from a stoppage (aside from wage increases), if it proves necessary to work overtime in order to recoup work stoppage losses.

3. A long drawn out conflict can strengthen a tendency toward recession. However, a strike itself does not result in any serious reduction in orders, since it is regarded as temporary. Nor can it be said that a stoppage of work is in itself apt to cause a depression.

While these results are hardly conclusive, they do raise an issue of paramount significance from the point of view of public policy. There is much to be said for the strike or the lockout as a method of settling disputes that prove intractable in direct bargaining. The principal argument in favor of limiting conflict through government intervention has been the magnitude of the economic loss entailed. If in fact economic loss turns out to be negligible for most stoppages, much contemporary thinking on the subject will have to be revised.

OCCUPATIONAL MOBILITY

The persistence of the gild tradition in Denmark is nowhere more manifest than in the structure of the labor market. Out of 179,000 male workers employed by members of the Employers' Association on June 30, 1949, 75,000, or 42 per cent, were skilled craftsmen who had undergone formal apprenticeships. By collective agreement, reinforced by law, the craftsmen enjoyed exclusive hegemony over some 90 different work jurisdictions. Unskilled workers are barred from these occupations, and there is little movement among them. The result is a closed system in which the adaptation of labor supply to demand takes place very slowly, if at all.

When the gilds were abolished, the formerly closed trades were opened to anyone, one of the results of which was a serious deterioration of training standards. Many of the early trade unions displayed keen interest in the restoration of the old employment monopolies,[23] and though they were not able to advocate such measures *per se*, they succeeded, in cooperation with their employers, in reinstituting a closed occupational system in the skilled trades through the medium of the apprenticeship. A series of laws was enacted to regulate this relationship, culminating in the Apprenticeship Act of 1937.[24]

[23] Bruun, p. 433.

[24] A detailed analysis of this law, still on the statute books, may be found in K. Bülow, K. A. Hansen, and K. G. Rønn, *Laerlingeloven i Praksis* (Copenhagen, 1942).

This law, applying generally to industry and commerce, requires that all young workers entering a trade in which apprenticeship is customary must enter into a written contractual relation of apprenticeship, administrative determination of appropriate trade coverage being left jointly to the Ministries of Labor and Commerce. The minimum age for inception of apprenticeship is fixed at 14 years, the maximum at 18 years, although in practice it is difficult for a young man to enter into an apprenticeship after his fifteenth year.[25] The apprenticeship term is limited to a maximum of four years, but the Ministries may increase the term up to five years upon application by the joint labor-management committees established in each trade to assist in the administration of the Act. Such extensions of term have been granted freely, and in 1939 one-third of the trades covering two-thirds of the new entrants had secured dispensation from the four-year rule and were requiring up to five years of training.[26]

The Act of 1937 sets forth the mutual obligations of master and apprentice in general terms, leaving the specific conditions relating to training, wages and hours, and the qualifying examination to joint labor-management committees and to collective bargaining. Collective agreements ordinarily contain separate wage scales for apprentices, with age gradations. Remuneration of apprentices is usually entirely in money, but in rural areas payment in kind is often provided as well.

While the cornerstone of craft monopoly lies in the legal requirement of apprenticeship, provisions in trade union constitutions and collective agreements provide the operational sinews. The skilled unions customarily require successful completion of apprenticeship as a condition of membership. The collective agreement in the metal trades, typical in this respect, commits the unions "not to accept a worker as a skilled member, unless he has produced his journeyman credentials . . . The union will provide each member with a membership book, which shall include his full name, the name of his former master, the apprenticeship term and the date of the journeyman's certificate . . ."[27] The employers in turn agree to accept the union membership book as proof of the worker's qualifications,[28] and by implication, agree to exclude from skilled employment workers not in possession of the stated documents.

Collective agreements further place quantitative restrictions upon entrance to the trade by specifying maximum ratios of apprentices to

[25] K. Vedel-Petersen, *Ungdommen og Arbejdsmarkedet i Dag* (Copenhagen, 1947), p. 15.
[26] Henning Friis, "Laerlingetilgangen 1935–1944," *Socialt Tiddskrift*, 1945, p. 24.
[27] *Overenskomst Indenfor Jern og Metalindustrien*, March, 1948, Sections 14, 15.
[28] *Ibid.*, Section 16.

journeymen.[29] There is no guarantee that the maximum permissible number of apprentices will be taken on; it has been found that the actual number of new entrants varies closely with employment conditions in the trade.[30] But since entrance to the trade is exclusively through apprenticeship, there have been distortions in the age composition of individual trades, for a deficiency once incurred can never be made good. For example, a study of the Copenhagen building timberers revealed a gap for the age group that would have been apprenticed during the severe building depression of 1909–1911.[31] A decline in apprenticeships during the thirties, because of high unemployment, has already been reflected in a serious lack of some types of skilled labor. There is no possibility of rapid adjustment to meet short run fluctuations in the demand for skilled labor.

The arguments that have been advanced in favor of maintaining the present labor market structure may be summarized as follows:

1. Denmark's international competitive position is dependent upon the production of quality goods. Exports of machine tools, for example, can only be maintained if Danish producers are able to deliver precision tools of a widely diversified character. This calls for highly skilled labor, an adequate supply of which can be assured only through stringent training.[32]

2. Conceding that skill requirements can be reduced by breaking down existing job classifications, proponents of the present system nevertheless maintain that the small scale of Danish industrial enterprise renders further labor specialization difficult and dangerous. All-round mechanics are needed, rather than narrow specialists, to afford a maximum of intra-plant mobility. Moreover, because of limited job opportunities, the narrow specialist faces a greater unemployment risk than the mechanic with multiple skills.

The validity of this position depends upon the accuracy of the factual premises. Unfortunately, Danish industrial structure has never been examined from this point of view. There are competent observers, however, who find that a good deal of the work currently performed by skilled labor could just as readily be performed by semiskilled labor,

[29] These contractual provisions are collected in *Beretning om De Samvirkende Fagforbunds Virksomhed*, 1940, pp. 89–96.

[30] Henning Friis, p. 19.

[31] K. Vedel-Petersen, pp. 85–87.

[32] *Social Denmark*, p. 374. It has been asserted, however, that adequate training could be accomplished without formal apprenticeship through a combination of vocational schools and practical job experience. Moreover, many types of export commodities do not require a high degree of labor skill in their manufacture.

and that increased mechanization has made greater specialization a reality.[33]

3. An argument of somewhat dubious ethical justification, but one of great practical importance, is typified by the following extract from a statement by the head of the Metal Workers' Union:

> That we act with a certain degree of care to protect work for our members does not mean that we want to maintain a monopoly position; but our point of view is that skilled, trained labor cannot let work slip out of its hands so that one fine day the skilled worker will find himself at the employment office, while unskilled labor carries on with production.[34]

It is the vested interest of the skilled worker, his desire to protect an investment in training, that is at the bottom of inertia in labor market organization. Moreover, by carving out a segment of job opportunities as its exclusive domain, a group of workers can maintain wage levels impossible in a free market for long periods of time, and depending upon the size and importance of the trade, reduce the risk of unemployment.

A number of weighty arguments can be marshaled against the perpetuation of a closed labor market:

1. The multiplicity of exclusive jurisdictions prevents rational allocation of the available labor resources, increases costs, and impedes technological advance. For instance, an entrepreneur, in planning a new factory, cannot determine freely the optimum combination of men and machines, for if his industry is within the jurisdiction of a skilled union, he will be limited to the use of skilled labor and the payment of corresponding wage rates. Tradition rather than productivity determines the composition of his labor force.

2. Through its barriers to inter-occupational mobility, craft monopoly accentuates inequality of employment levels within the labor force. As Table 32 shows, unemployment has been consistently higher in the unskilled than in the skilled trades, indicating a maldistribution of work opportunities between the two. There were periods after 1945 in which acute shortages of skilled labor prevailed side by side with serious unemployment among unskilled workers.[35]

3. As a consequence of trade monopoly, unemployed skilled workers are reluctant to move out of their trades, because often the only feasible move is downward to the ranks of the semiskilled. Employers are aware of this, and though some employer groups (for example, the metal trades)

[33] K. Vedel-Petersen, pp. 85–87; Ove Ravnemose, *Faglaert Kontra Ufaglaert Arbejdskraft?* (Copenhagen, 1949).

[34] Hans Rasmussen, *Faglaert Kontra Ufaglaert Arbejdskraft?* (Copenhagen, 1949).

[35] The 1950 national budget for Denmark noted that "the unemployment problem for unskilled workers is highly structural in character." *Economic Survey of Denmark*, 1950, p. 30.

have pressed for loosening the system, other groups favor its retention as guaranteeing an oversupply of labor.[36]

4. Wages have lost much of their significance as factors in the allocation of the labor supply. Increased wages in a particular trade could operate to augment the labor supply only very slowly, through the attraction of apprentices up to the limits imposed by collective agreement. Similarly, a relative wage fall in a trade would affect a shrinkage of the labor supply primarily through the discouragement of new recruits, for those currently employed have little alternative but to remain in the trade at reduced wages.

5. Finally, there is the problem of justifying, in a democratic society, a system which requires occupational choice at a youthful age and thereafter debars workers from seeking admission to the most attractive and lucrative portion of the labor market. Moreover, there is no allowance

TABLE 32

PERCENTAGE OF UNEMPLOYMENT AMONG UNSKILLED WORKERS AND SELECTED SKILLED CRAFTS

Year	Unskilled Workers	Metal Workers	Building Carpenters	Woodworkers
1936	26.4	12.9	19.4	17.1
1938	27.0	12.3	27.0	24.5
1940	29.2	16.8	26.8	23.3
1946	7.9	1.2	1.2	3.4
1948	7.4	0.2	2.6	4.3

Sources: *Statistiske Meddelelser*, vol. 115, no. 4, pp. 36–37; vol. 130, no. 1, pp. 86–87.

for the correction of error by individuals who find upon serving part of their apprenticeships that they lack the aptitudes for their chosen vocations. This line of argument has been well summed up by Mr. Vedel-Petersen:

> For the youth who has reached the age of 18 years and is only an unskilled laborer, there is nothing in principle to prevent him from becoming an engineer or an architect — but he could never become a mason or a timberer unless he started when he was 15 years old. And I believe that there are many more who do not become skilled workers because of economic barriers than those who do not go to the university for the same reason. I believe that we must consider the democratization of vocational education.[37]

[36] Unemployment insurance is not financed, as in the United States, by a payroll tax levied on employers. Thus, the employer has no immediate financial incentive to reduce unemployment *in his own trade,* as he does under experience rating, though unemployment in general imposes a financial burden on him through higher income taxation.

[37] K. Vedel-Petersen, p. 25.

A parliamentary resolution introduced in 1950 by the Radical Party called for the establishment of a commission to consider "to what extent the present customary and contractual division of the labor market leads to limitation upon the ability of the unskilled to obtain work which does not require skilled labor. The commission shall also investigate the extent to which it is expedient and possible to permit work hitherto performed by skilled labor to be performed by workers who have had a shorter training than is presently required, or by unskilled workers suitably trained." [38] The resolution manifests mounting public concern over the adequacy of an institution of dubious economic and moral justification.

WELFARE SERVICES

An account of Danish labor would scarcely be complete without some reference to the nonpecuniary benefits available to workers through law and collective agreement. No western nation, with the possible exception of Sweden, merits the appellation "welfare society" more than Denmark. Were it not for the availability in English of adequate material describing the Danish social services,[39] the present section would have had to be greatly amplified.

Table 33 compares, for Scandinavia and Great Britain, the percentage of national income devoted to social security payments during the fiscal year 1945–1946 (1947 for Norway). While for this year the Danish figure is the highest, subsequent reform of the Swedish social insurance has probably raised it above Denmark. The British percentage has also risen as a consequence of the augmentation of social service under the Labor government.

There is also shown in Table 33 the manner in which social security payments were financed. Denmark showed the highest percentage of government contribution and the lowest contribution by employers and by the insured themselves. However, this does not necessarily signify a greater degree of income redistribution in Denmark, since it tells nothing of the origin of the government funds. Professor Zeuthen has estimated that in the years immediately preceding the war, there was less redistribution in Denmark on this account than in Sweden or England.[40]

[38] *Arbejdsgiveren,* February 15, 1950, p. 54. As of 1951, this commission had secured some improvement in labor mobility in the metal trades. The continuing level of high employment has rendered workers more favorably disposed toward the commission's objectives.

[39] Orla Jensen, *Social Services in Denmark* (Copenhagen, 1948); *Social Denmark* (Copenhagen, 1945); Sigurd Wechselmann, *The Danish National Insurance Act* (Copenhagen, 1936); H. H. Koch, *The Danish Public Assistance Act* (Copenhagen, 1936); Henning Friis, *Scandinavia between East and West* (Ithaca, 1950).

[40] Frederick Zeuthen, *Social Sikring* (Copenhagen, 1948), pp. 264–270.

TABLE 33

SOCIAL SECURITY PAYMENTS IN RELATION TO NATIONAL INCOME, SCANDINAVIA AND GREAT BRITAIN

	Denmark 1945–46	Sweden 1945–46	Norway 1947	Great Britain 1945–46
1. Social security payments as a percentage of national income	7.6	4.1	5.3	3.6
2. Percentage of payments financed by national and local governments	81.2	76.1	48.9	57.3
3. Percentage of payments financed by the insured	16.0	19.1	36.8	17.7
4. Percentage of payments financed by employers	2.8	4.5	14.3	21.2
5. Interest on funds	—	0.3	—	3.8

Source: F. Zeuthen, *Social Sikring* (Copenhagen, 1948), pp. 250–251.

Unemployment insurance

The Danish unemployment insurance system is based upon separate trade union insurance funds, though union membership is not a condition of eligibility to insurance. Coverage of nonagricultural employees is virtually complete. Benefit payments vary with the liberality of the individual funds. While the benefit maximum may not exceed two-thirds of average daily wages in the trade (four-fifths including child and rental allowances), the actual payments have amounted to approximately 50 per cent of normal earnings.

After a waiting period (usually a week), the unemployed worker may receive "ordinary" benefits for a maximum period that varies with the separate fund from 90 to 160 days. If still unemployed when this series is exhausted, he draws "continuation" benefits, which generally duplicate the "ordinary" benefits with respect to both amount and duration. The *average maximum* duration of total benefits in 1945 was found to be 208 days, compared with 26 weeks under the most liberal United States laws.

To be initially eligible for benefits, a worker must have been a member of a fund for at least 12 months, and have worked 39 weeks, 26 of them in the preceding 18 months. Once he has qualified, it is the general rule that the worker may draw maximum benefits for four successive years without further work experience; but he is thereafter disqualified unless he returns to work at the trade and pays contributions to the fund as a beneficiary member for a year. There is a further disqualification, testing continued attachment to the labor market: a worker receiving benefits may lose the right to further payments if he was not employed for 26 weeks during the previous three years, though benefits again become payable when he has once more secured employment for 26 weeks in 12 consecutive months. These provisions are sufficiently liberal so that except for the chronic unemployed, Danish workers are insured for a large percentage of their lost time.[41]

The significance of the distinction between "ordinary" and "continuation" benefits lies in the way they are financed. Ordinary benefits are financed in large part by the insured themselves,[42] although the government grants subsidies that vary inversely with earnings in the trade. Continuation benefits are financed to a greater extent by the government, though with some help from a national unemployment fund to which employers pay small annual contributions.[43] The theory of this distinction is that while it is fair to require the workers themselves to finance short-run employment, chronic unemployment is a social cost that no one group should be required to carry alone.

Since the contribution tax upon the worker depends upon the experience of the individual fund to which he belongs, every insured worker has a direct and immediate interest in the prevention of fraud. Attached to each fund is an employment exchange, which does most of the placement work within the trade. The manager of the fund, who is ordinarily a trade union official as well, has at his disposal an inventory of employment conditions in his trade; therefore, there are both the incentive and the means to apply the tests of availability for work in suitable employment as conditions of eligibility. Were it not for decentralization of administration, the high degree of protection against unemployment might constitute a greater problem in reducing the incentive to work.[44]

Sickness and disability insurance

About 90 per cent of the Danish population is insured against sickness and disability through 1,600 sick benefit societies, each one of which is

[41] It was estimated that during 1942–1943, for example, 81 per cent of all days of unemployment were compensated.

[42] The practice of worker contributions was inherited from the years prior to government insurance, when the cost of benefits was borne entirely by trade unions.

[43] During the fiscal year 1943–1944, the government financed half the ordinary benefit payments, while the combined government and employer contributions were equal to two-thirds of the cost of continuation benefits.

[44] The following advice given by the Federation of Labor to fund administrators is of interest in illustrating the interplay between unemployment insurance and industrial relations under the Danish scheme: "The employment exchanges must be administered wisely. They can be used as a part of trade union policy, and should so be used against employers who place obstacles in the way of sound and natural cooperation with workers, all with due consideration to legal obligations. On the other hand, the good employer should be rewarded. Yes, to speak frankly, cultivated. A well treated 'customer' returns." *Tillidsmands Kundskab* (Copenhagen, 1946), p. 78.

confined to a local area, with little overlapping. Individuals whose income exceeds the skilled worker level are not eligible to membership in a society, though they are required to pay a small annual tax for "passive" membership which gives them the right to enter a society whenever their incomes fall below the maximum level, regardless of their current health status.

Membership fees are subject to considerable variation, depending upon the scale and extent of benefits offered by a society, with the average fee tending to equal one per cent of wages. About 70 per cent of society expenditures come from membership fees, government subsidies providing the remainder. Benefit payments are of two categories: obligatory benefits, which every society must pay in order to qualify for government subsidies, and optional benefits which may or may not be adopted. Included within the first category are free medical care by a general practitioner; free hospital treatment, including surgical care; a small daily cash allowance in disability; vital medical supplies, up to three-fourths the total cost; maternity benefits; and funeral assistance.[45] The optional benefits may include specialist treatment (which is now almost universal), dental care up to half the cost, home nursing, and treatment in rest and convalescent homes.

Cash benefits are limited in duration to 26 weeks during any 12 successive months. There is a further limitation of benefits to 60 weeks within three consecutive calendar years. Persons exhausting disability benefits, and still in need of assistance, may apply for "continuation" benefits, which are entirely financed by the government and represent welfare rather than insurance payments.

While a large proportion of the cost of sickness insurance is borne by the insured, the government grants sizable subsidies to the societies, and in addition provides the societies with what almost amounts to free hospital service for its members.

Old age pensions

The Danish old age pension system is noncontributory, the entire cost being borne by national and municipal governments. The general pensionable age is 65 years, though single women become eligible at the age of 60 years. Individuals may elect to defer their pensions until they reach either 67 or 70 years of age, in which event the benefit amounts are raised by stated percentages.

[45] In most societies, each member selects from a panel a physician who will treat him for the minimum period of a year; the physician may be changed at the expiration of a year. The physician receives from the society a fixed annual fee per patient, with extra payment for night visits and certain other services. Some societies permit their members to select any physician in the area for each separate illness, and reimburse the physician for each call.

The benefit amount is a uniform basic sum plus supplements designed to correct for differences in local living costs, both amounts being adjusted periodically in accord with changes in the cost of living index. The pension is reduced if the pensioner is in receipt of income exceeding 50 per cent the basic pension by an amount equal to 60 per cent of the excess income except that income from the pensioner's own work up to 60 per cent of the pension amount is disregarded. The possession of capital resources exceeding certain fixed limits also results in reduction of the pension. In 1948 a married pensioner in Copenhagen, retiring at the age of 65 years, was entitled to a pension of 8.22 kroner per day (without any income deductions). Since average daily male wages at the time were 26.24 kroner, the pension provided slightly more than 30 per cent of average full-time earnings, a ratio that appears to be quite general.[46]

In addition to pensions, a great deal has been done in constructing homes for the aged and state-subsidized apartments specially designed for occupancy by pensioners. The latter are particularly impressive; the rental is well within the means of the pensioner, there are communal eating facilities, and the layout takes into consideration the physical limitations of old people. The great popularity of these institutions will undoubtedly result in their expansion.

Invalidity insurance

This system is financed primarily by the government, with small contributions by the insured and employers. Coverage is compulsory for all members of sick benefit societies. The system is administered, however, by a Court of Invalidity Insurance, which decides whether claimants are sufficiently disabled to warrant payment of pensions, and upon the advisability of payments for curative measures and retraining. The basic eligibility requirement is reduction of working capacity to one-third of the normal, measured on both a medical and a social basis. Mental diseases and tuberculosis have constituted the greatest claim load.

Invalidity pensions are calculated in much the same manner as old age pensions. The average daily invalidity pension in Copenhagen in 1948 was 7.19 kroner, about 28 per cent of average wages. However, invalids who require the assistance of others are given specified supplements; for example, the blind are given extra payments amounting to 35 per cent of the pension.

[46] *Social Denmark,* p. 66.

Vacations

On the basis of legislation enacted in 1938, every employee is entitled to an annual vacation with pay of one day for each month of employment during the "vacation base year" April 1 to March 31. Service need not have been for one employer during the entire period, but to be counted, a spell of employment with an individual employer must have lasted at least six days. A regular work week of three days or more constitutes a qualifying week.

The vacation must be given, at the request of the employee, between May 2 and September 30, though it is the prerogative of the employer to fix the actual date. Unless there are industry funds to guarantee payment of vacation wages, such as have been set up by many of the affiliates of the Employers' Association, the employer is required to affix an appropriate number of stamps in his workers' vacation books each week. When the vacation is to begin, the employer certifies that fact in the book, and it may then be cashed at any post office.

One of the most successful welfare ventures of the Danish labor movement is the People's Vacation Society, which provides cheap vacation facilities for workers. In addition to rental arrangements with private hotels, the Society has built a number of "holiday towns," each consisting of about 50 single family bungalows. The Society has also exploited successfully the facilities available in private farmhouses, where owners want to take in summer boarders — a vacation arrangement with political overtones.

While these constitute the major welfare programs available to Danish citizens, there are a number of additional schemes on more or less familiar lines. It is not the uniqueness of the Danish system, but its comprehensiveness that constitutes its distinctive characteristic. For this reason, evaluation of the change in worker welfare with reference only to real wage trends results in serious understatement of labor's progress during the past fifty years.

PART THREE

THE MAINTENANCE OF INDUSTRIAL PEACE UNDER THE COLLECTIVE AGREEMENT

CHAPTER X

THE SETTLEMENT OF CONTRACT DISPUTES

THERE ARE TWO MAJOR AGENCIES in Denmark for the adjudication of disputes arising over the interpretation of collective agreements: the Labor Court (*Den faste Voldgiftsret*), and a network of industrial arbitration boards. The arbitration boards handle the greater volume of disputes, but the Labor Court is the more important in that its decisions constitute the basic labor law of Denmark, and set the tone not only for arbitral awards, but also for the many informal settlements that inevitably accompany the administration of collective agreements.

THE LABOR COURT

Origins of the Labor Court

The idea of arbitrating contract disputes is an old one in Denmark. Beginning in 1875 with the printing trades, a number of trade unions agreed with their employers to establish private arbitration boards, and by 1900 this was the rule, rather than the exception, in the skilled trades. A parliamentary commission set up in 1875 to investigate labor conditions recommended the creation of a labor court, but the time was not yet ripe for such a step.

As with most other Danish labor institutions, the Labor Court arose out of the collaboration of organized employers and workers. One of the stipulations of the September Agreement was that a permanent arbitration board be established to settle disputes with respect to the meaning of that agreement. This board (*Den permanente Voldgiftsret*) consisted of seven members: three elected by the organized employers, three by the trade unions, and an impartial chairman elected by the parties jointly. At the bidding of the parties, the parliament enacted a law permitting the board to take testimony under oath. The Permanent Arbitration Board remained in existence from 1900 to 1910, deciding 32 cases during this period. Though its competence was limited to alleged violations of the September Agreement, it nevertheless rendered decisions of major importance. It refused, for example, to find the Federation of Labor liable for a strike called by an affiliated union in violation of the strike notice provisions of the September Agreement, holding that the responsibility of the Federation was limited to strikes decreed, approved, or supported by it. The board also made it clear that included in the contractual obligation of employers was the duty to refrain from interfering in internal union affairs, and to remain completely neutral with respect to the organizational efforts of their employees.

It soon became obvious that the jurisdiction of the Permanent Board of Arbitration was too limited to serve the function of maintaining industrial peace under the collective agreement. There were numerous work stoppages in violation of collective agreements with which the board was not competent to deal. Consequently, one of the important items on the agenda of the Industrial Commission of 1908, established by the government at the behest of the collective bargaining parties, and composed of representatives of the parties with an impartial chairman appointed by the government, was the expansion of the authority vested in the board. Although there was disagreement on two points, namely, the pecuniary consequences of breach of contract and the collective responsibility of organizations for contract violations committed by their members,[1] the Commission was able to report out a draft bill which was enacted into law on April 12, 1910. With some relatively minor amendments in 1919, 1934, and 1939, this law constitutes the present basis for settling contract interpretation disputes in Denmark.[2]

Jurisdiction of the Labor Court

Unlike its predecessor, the Permanent Board of Arbitration, the Labor Court has jurisdiction not only over alleged breaches of the September Agreement, but over all violations of collective agreements,[3] and questions regarding the legality of strikes and lockouts. Any additional matter of dispute may be brought before the Court provided that a majority of five members agrees, and provided that a collective agreement covering the subject matter of the dispute exists.

The line of demarcation between the jurisdictions of the Labor Court and the industrial arbitration boards, while it can be stated theoretically, is often difficult to draw in practice. In theory, the Court is limited to disputes over contract *breaches*, while disputes over *interpretation* fall

[1] For a discussion of these points, see *Beretning fra Faellesudvalget af 17 August 1908*, pp. 10–19.

[2] For the present text of the law, see Appendix E.

[3] The only exempted category is contract violation by an individual worker, without the assistance of his union or fellow workers. This exemption was insisted upon by the trade union representatives on the 1908 Commission in order to limit union responsibility for the individual acts of members.

within the province of industrial arbitration. The purpose of thus limiting the jurisdiction of the Court was to prevent its involvement in a myriad of detailed problems, for example, interpretation of a piece-rate schedule. But often, disputes involve elements of both contract breach and interpretation. The problem has been solved in practice by the development of customary rules for the guidance of the parties, in case of doubt. For example, cases involving allegedly illegal discharges of shop stewards generally go to industrial arbitration, while those involving the rights of foremen go to the Labor Court. If the application of a wage schedule is in dispute, or a question of fact rather than one of principle, the matter usually belongs in industrial arbitration. The law permits the Labor Court to dismiss a case which in its opinion belongs to the industrial arbitration boards, or to postpone its judgment until factual points are clarified by arbitration, procedures which are often followed unless the facts are clear and no special technical competence is necessary to interpret them.

The close relationship between the Labor Court, which represents the interests of the state as well as of the parties, and private industrial arbitration is the cornerstone of Danish labor arbitration. Unless private arbitration had been so well developed, and the Labor Court empowered to slough off to the arbitration boards the many factual disputes that arise, the Court would not have been able to keep its dockets free to decide major questions of principle.

Several important categories of disputes, however, belong exclusively to the Labor Court. These include cases in which a fine, as well as damages, is sought, since the arbitration boards can only award damages; unlawful strikes provide the most frequent example of such cases. The refusal of either party to abide by a decision of an arbitration board obviously belongs to the Labor Court, which here performs the important function of reinforcing the arbitration system.

The Labor Court is a statutory body, with exclusive jurisdiction over an entire range of breaches of collective agreements. Its decisions are final, have full legal effect, and cannot be appealed to the ordinary courts. Moreover, the Labor Court is finally responsible for determining whether or not a case falls within its jurisdiction. The strength of this rule has its origin in the desire of both labor and management to avoid recourse to the ordinary courts, which in Denmark, as in other countries, lack the flexibility, the speed, and the expertness necessary in dealing with industrial disputes. Isolated individuals have occasionally attempted, unsuccessfully, to question the extraordinary powers of the Labor Court in this respect, but the Federation of Labor and the Employers' Association have never been disposed to make this an issue.

Composition of the Labor Court

The quasi-public status accorded to the Federation of Labor and the Employers' Association in Danish law is nowhere better illustrated than in their power to select the partisan members of the Labor Court, notwithstanding that the jurisdiction of the Court extends to organized and unorganized employers and employees alike. The Court consists of seven members, three chosen by each of the above-named organizations, and a presiding judge chosen jointly by the partisan members.[4] The partisan members are appointed for two-year terms, and they elect the presiding judge annually. If they cannot agree within a stipulated period of time upon the presiding judge, he is elected by the presiding justice of the Danish Supreme Court and the several Copenhagen courts, in joint session.

Ordinarily, the presiding judge is selected from among the members of the regular judiciary. Although his term is for one year at a time only, there is little turnover in office. Only once in the forty years the Court has existed has there been any difficulty in connection with personnel. This incident occurred in 1937, when the labor members of the Court, dissatisfied with a decision rendered by one of the alternate presiding judges, refused to vote for his reappointment, whereupon the employer members, in retaliation, refused to reëlect the presiding judge of the Court, who had occupied that position for twelve years, making it necessary for the chief justice of the Supreme Court and his Copenhagen colleagues to select the impartial judge.[5] Ordinarily, however, adverse decisions are regarded as the fortunes of war, and with this one exception neither side has followed the practice of placing pressure on impartial judges, realizing that it would soon mean the end of the Court.

Election of the presiding judge for a one-year term is in sharp distinction to the practice in other Danish courts, where judges are usually accorded life tenure. The purpose of the short term is to make certain that the presiding judge retains the confidence of both parties. This is undoubtedly a sound rule, and to judge by the attitudes of the interested parties and the history of the Court, it has resulted in the selection of judges with insight into the peculiar problems of industrial relations and an ability to get along with their colleagues from the organized employer and labor movements.

[4] In addition, each party selects eight deputy members, and three alternate presiding judges are elected. One partisan judge from each side is required to be a lawyer.

[5] The relevant documents on this incident are contained in *Beretning om De Samvirkende Fagforbunds Virksomhed*, 1937, pp. 62–65, and *Arbejdsgiveren*, 1937, p. 406.

There is general agreement that the tripartite character of the Court has been an important element in its success. While the majority of cases that require formal judgment are decided by the vote of the impartial judge, he has the advantage of consulting with his colleagues with respect to the evidence. There are no minority opinions, all members of the Court signing the decision without indicating how they voted, which serves to strengthen the effect of the decision.

The parties before the Court

The Labor Court is concerned only with breaches of collective agreements between a labor organization on the one hand and an employer association or a single firm on the other. Cases are brought and defended by the most extensive organizations of which the plaintiff and defendant are members — that is, the Federation of Labor and the Employers' Association handle all cases on behalf of their members. An individual worker has no standing before the Court; he must prosecute his case through his trade union.[6] This attitude toward the collective agreement as an instrument conferring rights upon an organization rather than upon the individual is consonant with the corporate spirit that permeates the Danish employment relationship. The limitation upon the right to bring actions before the Labor Court serves the useful function of preventing a multiplicity of inconsequential cases from cluttering up its docket. In effect, it is the central bargaining organizations, the Federation of Labor and the Employers' Association, which usually determine whether a dispute is of sufficient importance to be prosecuted, and if so, whether it belongs before the Labor Court or an industrial arbitration board. The central organizations endeavor to prevent weak cases, or those which might result in the setting of undesirable precedents, from reaching the Court. In this respect, however, their powers are limited by two factors: their internal political situations, and the ability of unassociated employers and nonmember unions to appear before the Court.

The first of these factors is of particular importance on the trade union side, since the Employers' Association is less sensitive to pressure by an individual employer than is the Federation of Labor vis-à-vis its national unions. The Federation representative before the Court must often present cases for political reasons, even though he knows that there is little chance of winning them. The result is that not only are the majority of cases brought in by the unions, but that the union plaintiff cases tend,

[6] An unorganized worker cannot bring a case to the Labor Court, but if he has a claim based upon an individual as contrasted with a collective agreement, he may prosecute it in the ordinary courts.

on the average, to be weaker than those brought by employers. The disparity in number between union-plaintiff and employer-plaintiff cases would be even greater were it not for the fact that so important a part of the Court's work consists of unlawful strike cases brought in by employers.

The second limitation upon the authority of the central organizations is more important on the employer side, since the great majority of organized workers are in the Federation of Labor, and individual workers have no standing before the Court. During the years 1938 to 1948, employers were party to 1,552 Labor Court cases, but the Employers' Association was involved in only 48 per cent of the total number. However, this does not measure accurately the degree of control exercised by the Employers' Association in deciding which cases are to be brought before the Court; a better index is provided by the role of associated and unassociated employers as party plaintiff. Of the 1,552 cases, employers were the plaintiffs in 551, the Employers' Association in 447, and unassociated employers in 104. Thus, unassociated employers were responsible for bringing in only 19 per cent of the cases in which the initiative was taken by employers.[7]

Labor Court work is regarded as one of the most important functions of the central organizations, and is carried on by high-ranking officials: in the case of the Federation of Labor, by its vice-chairman, and in the case of the Employers' Association, by one of its directors. It is symptomatic of the significance of the Labor Court that a book analyzing Danish labor law, which consists mainly of the work of the Labor Court, prepared for the use of worker study groups, should have been written initially by a former chairman of the Federation of Labor and revised in later editions by the present chairman. Though the current employer representative before the Court is a lawyer by training, the Federation representative is not, there being no general rule in this respect. Like many European labor movements, the Danish Federation of Labor has displayed an aversion toward the use of lawyers except where absolutely essential, as in cases before the ordinary courts, and it has generally been represented before the Labor Court by an elected trade union official. Whether this has proved a handicap cannot be determined from the outcome of cases, since other factors presently to be considered play a more important role. To judge by the knowledge of Labor Court work displayed by the incumbent union representative, however, lack of formal legal training is not a consideration of importance in determining union success or failure before the Court.

[7] The data are from *Beretning om Dansk Arbejdsgiverforenings Virksomhed*, 1947–1948, p. 61.

Statistics of Labor Court operation

During the 39-year period from 1910 to 1948, a total of 4,117 cases was brought before the Danish Labor Court, as Table 34 shows. The average number was 105 per year, though there was considerable variation from year to year. The peak was reached during the war years 1941 to 1945, when the trade unions had frequent resort to the Court to force unassociated employers to honor agreements.[8] The number of cases declined sharply after 1945, and in 1948 reached the lowest level since 1930. These data show that the work load of the Danish Labor Court has never become unmanageable, particularly in view of the fact that a sizable proportion of the cases initiated never go to final judgment.[9] That there has not been more litigation may be ascribed primarily to the sifting function performed by the central bargaining organizations. The fact that the Court follows the rule of *stare decisis* also contributes to the relatively low case load, though this principle, applied too rigidly, is not without its dangers to labor tribunals.

Table 34 also indicates that the majority of cases has been brought by trade unions, although the ratio is not too far from one of equality between labor and management. The proportions have shifted somewhat over the years; up to the early 1930's, it was the employers who filed the majority of cases, reflecting the fact that unlawful strikes have constituted one of the major categories of Labor Court work. From 1935 to 1945, the cases brought by trade unions exceeded the employer-plaintiff cases in every year, in some years by very substantial margins. As already pointed out, however, most of these cases were against unassociated employers, in a union drive to secure better compliance with collective agreements entered into individually with unassociated employers. Thus, in the years 1938 to 1945, members of the Employers' Association were named as defendants in 247 cases, while unassociated employers were defendants in 578 cases. If only the organized employers are considered, the disparity between employer and union plaintiff cases increases. Nevertheless, the fact that the average annual number of complaints brought by trade unions has only been 59, with a maximum of 167 in 1942, indicates that the Federation of Labor has been able to exercise considerable discretion with respect to the union initiated cases brought

[8] *Dansk Arbejdsgiverforenings Virksomhed*, 1943–1944, p. 74.

[9] By comparison, the National Labor Relations Board, operating under the Wagner Act, rendered annually 260 final decisions in unfair labor practice cases and 950 decisions in representation cases. See Walter Galenson, *Staff Report on the National Labor Relations Board*, Hoover Commission, 1948 (mimeographed). While many of the NLRB representation cases were a matter of routine, the average NLRB unfair labor practice case had a much larger record and involved far more work than the average Danish Labor Court case.

TABLE 34

WORK LOAD OF AND CASE DISPOSITION BY THE DANISH LABOR COURT, 1910–1948

Year	Total Number of Cases Filed	Number of Cases Filed by: Employers	Unions	Cases Disposed of by: Final Judgment	Settlement at Preliminary Hearing	Withdrawal
1910......	31[a]	16	14	27	2	2
1911......	29	14	15	23	2	4
1912......	27	15	12	22	3	2
1913......	24	16	8	17	4	3
1914......	26[a]	16	9	21	4	1
1915......	27	14	13	13	10	4
1916......	23	14	9	11	6	6
1917......	34	21	13	20	11	3
1918......	44	34	10	27	8	9
1919......	57	42	15	36	10	11
1920......	97[b]	61	35	51	14	32
1921......	117	40	77	59	40	18
1922......	104	40	64	44	42	18
1923......	89[a]	60	28	29	50	10
1924......	81	50	31	25	23	33
1925......	119[a]	64	54	44	51	24
1926......	108	54	54	65	28	15
1927......	91	50	41	43	37	11
1928......	87	39	48	34	28	25
1929......	86	45	41	45	25	16
1930......	103	50	53	53	29	21
1931......	121[a]	60	60	50	45	26
1932......	160	69	91	62	80	18
1933......	159	68	91	57	83	19
1934......	159	90	69	62	74	23
1935......	159	74	85	60	72	27
1936......	142	44	98	36	80	26
1937......	144	44	100	35	75	34
1938......	126	44	82	21	95	10
1939......	151	44	107	34	86	31
1940......	151	21	130	23	77	51
1941......	159	26	133	32	81	46
1942......	207	40	167	41	120	46
1943......	164	60	104	38	94	32
1944......	166	81	85	40	87	39
1945......	186	82	104	35	92	59
1946......	125	77	48	18	76	31
1947......	130	74	56	21	83	26
1948......	104	51	53	12	62	30
Total...	4,117	1,804	2,307	1,386	1,889	842

Sources: Annual Reports of the Danish Employers' Association and the Danish Federation of Labor.
[a] One case filed jointly by employer and union.
[b] One case filed by the Unemployment Insurance Inspectorate.

before the Labor Court, when the potential dispute load arising out of Denmark's large and intricate collective agreement system is taken into account.

Statistics of case disposal are also contained in Table 34. For the period 1910 to 1948 as a whole, only one-third of the cases before the Labor Court progressed as far as final judgment. An additional 20 per cent of the complaints filed were withdrawn without formal action, while the remaining cases, slightly less than half, were disposed of in preliminary proceedings that resemble mediation. There have been significant shifts over the years in the method by which cases were disposed of, with mediation steadily growing and formal judgment diminishing in importance. In the first five years of the Court's existence, 1910 to 1914, 80 per cent of all cases required final judgment, while only 11 per cent were settled by mediation. From 1944 to 1948, however, only 18 per cent of the cases required final judgment, whereas 56 per cent were settled by mediation. The number of formal decisions rendered in 1948, twelve, was less than in any year of the Court's existence with the exception of 1916.

Court procedure

A case is initiated when a central organization, on behalf of an affiliate, submits a complaint alleging breach of the September Agreement or of a collective contract. The secretary of the Court sends copies of the complaint to the other party and to all the judges. Within a short time the matter is set down for preliminary hearing. Such hearings are held on Friday afternoon of each week; their function is to acquaint the Court with the facts of the case and to narrow factual differences as much as possible. Each side has ordinarily submitted a brief, and there is oral discussion of the briefs, as well as of new matters. The preliminary meeting is one of the crucial points in Labor Court procedure. Counsel for the parties may agree to have the presiding judge "explain" the relevant law for the benefit of the local participants present, and such exposition often makes it clear to them that nothing is to be gained by pursuing the matter further.[10] This is particularly true in cases in which unions are the complaining parties, for the Federation of Labor is often obliged to bring weak cases to the Court; under such circumstances, the constituent national or local unions are generally satisfied with the Federation's assiduity if the matter is carried as far as the preliminary hearing.

The effectiveness of preliminary "explanation" in reducing litigation is clear from the statistics. From 1938 to 1948 the Labor Court dealt

[10] Theoretically, the presiding justice is not permitted to offer any suggestions for a settlement. Actually, by adroit questioning, he may indicate quite clearly what the proper solution is.

with 2,119 cases in all. Of these, 1,455, or 69 per cent, got as far as the preliminary hearing, and only a little over 30 per cent required further action by the Court. Were it not for this device, the purpose of which is partly to remove from the central organizations the onus of refusing to prosecute cases that have little chance of success, the Labor Court might have found itself with a very heavy case load.

The cases that are not settled at the Friday session are put down for trial on Saturday morning. Trial procedure before the Court is formal, but contrary to usual judicial procedure, the sessions are not open to the public and may not be discussed in the press, a practice that is regarded as sound by both labor and management. Each side states its case, following which there may be rebuttal and questions by the judges. The Court votes immediately after the hearing is closed, without any preliminary caucuses by the partisan judges, each one being polled in turn, the presiding justice casting the last vote. The latter then prepares a draft decision which is discussed and voted upon at a subsequent meeting of the Court.

Danish Labor Court procedure provides a good balance between flexibility and formality. The device of the preliminary hearing permits informal sifting of cases; those that survive, presumably involving novel questions of principle, are treated in much the same manner as ordinary cases at law. There is always opportunity for a case to be withdrawn, so that neither party must finally commit itself to a potentially bad precedent until final judgment is voted upon. The judgment usually levies costs upon the losing party. However, the amount thus collected is not turned over to the winning side, but helps defray the cost of the Court's operation. The Court may divide the costs between the parties if, for example, the case has been a close one. At the present time, the usual amount of costs levied per case is 300 kroner.

Three to four months is the maximum period of time that ordinarily elapses from the filing of a charge to the issuance of judgment. In particularly important cases where time is of the essence, as in unlawful strikes, hearings and judgment may be completed within a very short time. There have been cases in which unlawful strikes were condemned by the Court the day following their inception.

Penalties levied by the Court

The losing party in a Labor Court suit may be obliged to pay a fine, at the discretion of the Court, which is partly in the nature of damages, and partly in the nature of penal restitution. The significance of this distinction is that the amount of the fine does not necessarily depend upon the extent of the loss occasioned by the breach of contract; it may exceed the loss if there are aggravating circumstances, while on the other hand it may be less than the loss suffered, or be waived altogether. The fine constitutes a judgment which may be executed by the winning party in the same manner as any judgment at law.[11]

The purpose of substituting the fine for damages was to provide greater flexibility in dealing with the peculiar relationship created by the collective agreement. As the Joint Commission of 1908 noted, many breaches of collective agreement may be of great importance although no pecuniary loss is involved, for example, the performance of overtime work in violation of an agreement. On the other hand, even where there is pecuniary loss, the psychological circumstances surrounding a breach of contract may be such as to render inequitable full or even partial reparation. For example, a strike in violation of contract, while clearly unlawful, might be mitigated by the conduct of the employer. Moreover, it is often very difficult to assess the true measure of damages in a labor dispute.[12] While the discretionary fine as contrasted with damages was originally adopted at the insistence of the trade unions, experience has shown that it is a practicable method of enforcing collective agreements.

In fixing the amount of the fine, the Court is guided by the following provisions of the Labor Court Act:

> Where damage is sustained, the fines shall be assessed with due regard to the extent of the damage and to the extent to which the breach of agreement is deemed excusable. In particularly extenuating circumstances the fines may be completely waived. The fine for an unlawful stoppage shall be waived if the party against whom the stoppage is directed, by acting in violation of an agreement, is considered to have given reasonable cause for the stoppage.
>
> It shall be regarded as a particularly aggravating circumstance, if the party breaking the agreement has refused to allow the dispute to go to arbitration, although bound by agreement to do so, or has acted contrary to a decision reached by lawful process of arbitration or to an existing decision of the Labor Court on the same issue.[13]

The Court, as a general rule, is guided by the extent of the damage inflicted in fixing the amount of the fine. The problem is ordinarily not difficult in union plaintiff cases, for the employer will generally be required to pay some disputed amount to his workers. Illegal strike cases constitute a much more difficult category, particularly when the fine is levied against individual workers. The Court under such circumstances

[11] In no other branch of Danish law is a fine awarded to a plaintiff. In this case, it is true, the fine is partly in the nature of damages, but even where no damage has actually been suffered, the plaintiff may nonetheless receive the fine.

[12] *Beretning fra Faellesudvalget af 17 August 1908*, pp. 10–13.

[13] Sections 5(2) and 5(3).

"will not fix a greater amount than that required to ensure the maintenance of a collective agreement, with regard to the individual's ability to pay; the highest amount which has been levied against an individual worker in any one case is 100 kroner per month, and even this amount was only levied, as a rule, when a smaller fine proved futile, or when a preliminary judgment of the Court regarding the resumption of work was not obeyed."[14] Provocative action or lack of understanding of workers' problems on the part of the employer may lead the court to reduce the fine to a minimal amount, or to waive it entirely, even in the event of a strike in violation of contract. For this reason, even cases of obviously illegal strikes must be tried carefully, and all the facts brought out.

If a strike takes place despite the conciliatory efforts of the employer, or when the legality of the required strike notice is being litigated before the Labor Court, an "aggravating circumstance" may be found to exist which can result in large fines. The greatest amounts have been levied against unions and workers for refusing to honor arbitration awards or judgments of the Labor Court. For example, in 1918 a strike called by the local of Copenhagen bricklayers without legal notice resulted in the imposition of a fine of 1,000 kroner against the local; when the workers refused to resume work, an additional fine of 10,000 kroner was imposed, and further defiance was met by fining the local 60,000 kroner. When the union was declared bankrupt and the men persisted in their refusal to work, each striker was fined 100 kroner. The maximum amount levied in a single case has been 800,000 kroner in an illegal dock strike in 1919, resulting in the bankruptcy of the union after confiscation of all its property.

An unusual feature of Danish Labor Court practice lies not so much in the manner in which fines are determined, but in the fact that once an amount is fixed, it is collected, barring the bankruptcy of the defendant. The law provides that where damage has been suffered, the fine shall be paid to the injured party, and in other cases, to the plaintiff. Lest its members be tempted to waive fines in an effort to conciliate workers, the Employers' Association requires its members to remit the full amount of all fines to the Association itself, whereupon the employer may receive the money back in partial reimbursement of his loss. It is common for an employer to check off amounts of from five to ten kroner per week from wages in payment of a fine. If a worker has shifted employment, the new employer is requested to check the money off, while if the worker is no longer employed, the sheriff may be asked to levy upon any

[14] Illum, p. 305. Since this statement was written (1939), the Court has on a few occasions set higher amounts, because of wage inflation. See Labor Court, Cases No. 3305, 3356, 3370, and 3705.

property he has. The Employers' Association often spends more money in executing a judgment than the amount finally collected, but the expenditure is deemed a good investment in upholding the sanctity of collective agreements. That judgment can be levied against individual workers, as well as against unions, attests to the status which the Labor Court occupies in Denmark; there are few parallels to be found anywhere in the world.

The fact that fines are routinely executed and levied makes the precise responsibility of trade unions in strike situations a matter of paramount importance. The law provides that in the absence of an agreement to the contrary,[15] "an organization can be required to assume legal responsibility only if it has contributed toward the institution of the stoppage, or to its continuance, or if the dispute concerns the interpretation of an existing price list (with general provisions) or of a general agreement between the organizations." Despite the seeming generality of this language, the Labor Court has been reluctant to hold unions responsible for the acts of individual members. It must be shown first that the union has acted in bad faith, either in doing something positive or in failing to take appropriate remedial action. For example, a resolution by a competent union body in support of a strike or the active complicity of high union officials has been held to establish the union's liability.[16]

A more difficult situation arises when the leadership of the union endeavors to prevent a strike which has the clear support of a majority of the union's members. When the position of the membership has been made clear through a formal vote, the Labor Court will hold the union responsible. Other circumstances may attest to the sentiment of the membership majority: for example, the failure of other workers in the trade to fill places left vacant by a strike, despite appeal by the leadership.

Despite the fact that the Court has gone behind organizational formalities on occasion, it should not be inferred that a doctrine which regards the union and its membership as identical prevails. The Court has developed rules for unions to follow if they desire to avoid responsibility. As soon as an illegal strike has developed, the local union, and in important cases the national union, must take whatever steps are necessary

[15] Until recently, there was a clause in the textile industry agreement making the union absolutely responsible for illegal strikes. Because of the many wildcat strikes that took place after the war, the agreement was amended to provide that the employer could proceed against the union only after failure to collect from the individual. However, there are still agreements, for example, those in the lithographic and photoengraving trades, which contain unqualified provisions for collective responsibility.

[16] The cases on union responsibility are collected in Knud V. Jensen, pp. 62–65, and Illum, pp. 313–319.

to bring the conflict to an end. If necessary, the union must seek to replace strikers with workers from other areas by advertising. A general membership meeting of the local union must be called to vote either support or rejection of the strike, failure to take such action being considered an important datum in fixing union responsibility.[17] The union must withhold all economic support from the strikers. However, the Labor Court has refused to require unions to expel members who engage in an unlawful strike, on the theory that such action, by depriving the union of all further control over the workers, is likely to prolong rather than to shorten the conflict.

From the nature of the problem, it is usually the local union rather than the national union which bears the major responsibility for preventing strikes in violation of contract and for terminating strikes that have occurred. Even though a number of local unions possess property, the financial danger to the trade union movement arising out of illegal strikes is not as serious as it would be were the Labor Court more disposed to hold the national union responsible.[18] The importance of this issue is illustrated by the incident, arising in 1937, which resulted for the first time in the displacement of a neutral judge of the Labor Court through an adverse vote of the partisan judges. The dispute involved an unlawful stoppage by dock workers in a single port; the Labor Court held the Laborers' Union, the parent organization, responsible for the stoppage, on the ground that it had failed to act with sufficient energy in endeavoring to bring the stoppage to a close.[19] The Federation of Labor took the unprecedented step of protesting the decision formally in a letter to the Labor Court, arguing that the complicity of the national union had not been proved, and inquiring whether "any new precedent has been shaped in this sphere, which could result in a completely unforeseen and impracticable change in the relation of the national union to the local and its membership." [20] Although assured by the presiding justice of the Court that the case set no new precedent, the Federation, as already noted, prevented the reappointment of the judge responsible for this decision.

The importance attached by the trade unions to this issue has not

[17] This requirement makes it difficult for the leadership or the members of a trade union to assist illegal strikers without being held responsible. Even if the leaders of a union are opposed to an illegal strike, they may find themselves outvoted at a general meeting if the strike has aroused sympathy among the rank and file.

[18] A local union may be thrown into bankruptcy and declared nonexistent for failure to pay a fine levied against it. Workers may not thus escape their obligations, however; in several cases, a new local union formed by the same workers was held responsible for the debts of the old.

[19] Labor Court, Case No. 2415.

[20] *Beretning om De Samvirkende Fagforbunds Virksomhed*, 1937, p. 63.

been lost upon the Labor Court. While the Court on appropriate occasion will merge a local union and its membership pursuant to a doctrine of collective responsibility, the same is not true of the national union. It is generally necessary to prove the direct complicity of the national officers, or of a national representative body, if the national union is to be implicated.[21]

A former presiding justice of the Labor Court noted that "limited collective responsibility is the weak side of the arbitration law. One can always expect a fine to be paid by the employer. But if only individual workers, and not trade unions, are found guilty, the fine will not always be paid." [22] Nonetheless, the Danish Labor Court has succeeded in enforcing its decisions to a degree that would be unthinkable in other countries with as powerful a labor movement.[23] Danish workers have accepted the onerous side of the Labor Court in return for a quick and cheap forum in which to obtain redress against contract breaches by employers.

The outcome of Labor Court cases

Tables 35 and 36 contain statistics that indicate the outcome of cases decided by the Labor Court from 1910 to 1948. In Table 35, the number of cases won and lost by employers is compared with the number won and lost by unions, classified separately into employer-plaintiff and union-plaintiff cases. The employer record is considerably better than that of the unions, in this respect. Of 745 employer-plaintiff cases in which the judgment of the Court represented a victory for either side, almost 80 per cent were won by the employer, and only 20 per cent by the union. While a preponderance of employer victories is to be expected in this category, the union margin in union-plaintiff cases is not nearly as great: of 624 decisive judgments in the latter category, only 64 per cent were won by the union, and 36 per cent by the employers.

It may also be noted from Table 35 that there were more Court judgments in employer-plaintiff than in union-plaintiff cases, despite the fact that a majority of the total actions brought to the Labor Court were initiated by unions (see Table 34). Union-plaintiff cases are thus less likely to proceed to final judgment than employer-plaintiff cases, while those that do reach final judgment are less apt to result in victory for the union than employer-plaintiff judgments for the employer. This cannot be ascribed to any difference in ability between employer and union

[21] The Federation of Labor itself is responsible only in the case of breach of agreements to which it is itself a party.

[22] V. Topsøe-Jensen, *Den faste Voldgiftsret gennem 25 Aar*, p. 13.

[23] On occasion, judgments against unions have been executed by attaching and selling their real and other property. This was done in 1931 in the case of a 20,000 kroner judgment against the Copenhagen longshoremen's local.

TABLE 35

Outcome of Danish Labor Court Cases, 1910–1948

Year	Judgments in Employer-Plaintiff Cases			Judgments in Union-Plaintiff Cases		
	Total Number	Won by Employer	Won by Union	Total Number	Won by Employer	Won by Union
1910	15	11	4	11	5	6
1911	9	8	1	14	7	7
1912	12	7	5	10	3	7
1913	12	10	2	5	2	3
1914	13[a]	9	3	7	2	5
1915	9	7	2	4	1	3
1916	6	5	1	5	2	3
1917	11	10	1	9	3	6
1918	22[a]	18	2	5	1	4
1919	25[a]	19	5	10	6	4
1920	28	21	7	23	11	12
1921	22	18	4	37[a]	10	26
1922	19	12	7	25	11	14
1923	18	10	8	10	4	6
1924	20	15	5	5	4	1
1925	27[a]	19	7	16	6	10
1926	32	24	8	33	15	18
1927	24	22	2	19	9	10
1928	16	13	3	18	7	11
1929	24	18	6	21	8	13
1930	26	18	8	27[a]	8	18
1931	27	21	6	22	9	13
1932	31	20	11	31	10	21
1933	25	23	2	32	18	14
1934	45	34	11	17	7	10
1935	34	24	10	26	9	17
1936	17	12	5	19	5	14
1937	18	16	2	17	5	12
1938	15	12	3	5	2	3
1939	15	10	5	19	4	15
1940	5[a]	4	0	18	6	12
1941	10[a]	8	0	21	4	17
1942	14	13	1	27	4	23
1943	22	22	0	17	7	10
1944	27	26	1	13	4	9
1945	20	19	1	15	5	10
1946	15	13	2	3	0	3
1947	16	14	2	5	1	4
1948	7	6	1	5	1	4
Total	753	591	154	626	226	398

Sources: Annual Reports of the Danish Employers' Association and the Danish Federation of Labor.
[a] Discrepancy due to cases in which there was no clear-cut decision.

TABLE 36

Costs and Fines Levied by the Danish Labor Court, 1910–1948

(In kroner)

Year	Costs		Fines	
	Against Employers	Against Unions and Workers	Against Employers	Against Unions and Workers
1910	1,475	1,550	200	1,500
1911	975	1,975	580	100
1912	1,225	1,675	1,764	2,800
1913	500	1,650	450	1,920
1914	1,075	1,575	700	1,700
1915	545	1,355	0	3,700
1916	650	900	300	1,000
1917	1,175	2,425	400	40,800
1918	1,225	4,055	1,498	99,880
1919	1,875	5,975	600	893,145[a]
1920	5,900	9,700	6,996	1,060,600[b]
1921	8,300	9,650	4,886	5,300
1922	6,550	6,950	6,200	18,400
1923	3,950	4,950	490	6,669
1924	2,650	5,250	500	12,000
1925	4,400	8,900	10,425	10,500
1926	6,450	11,550	6,400	17,823
1927	4,000	8,500	6,817	13,930
1928	4,000	6,100	6,195	6,176
1929	5,100	8,000	12,475	23,470
1930	7,200	7,800	6,412	12,632
1931	5,700	9,600	9,759	37,000
1932	8,600	9,000	13,854	16,057
1933	4,950	12,150	8,222	26,693
1934	6,302	12,450	16,405	142,805
1935	8,658	9,034	36,253	14,722
1936	4,700	5,400	19,836	8,317
1937	3,715	6,100	13,189	59,023
1938	1,975	3,650	10,219	26,715
1939	4,800	4,900	22,798	21,229
1940	3,525	2,625	19,954	10,075
1941	5,050	3,150	27,855	7,259
1942	6,500	4,800	35,258	38,002
1943	3,075	7,275	29,986	157,713
1944	3,000	9,150	21,408	571,694
1945	3,050	8,250	19,587	263,499
1946	525	4,875	11,460	171,105
1947	2,400	4,350	21,586	108,725
1948	1,725	2,025	11,293	45,789
Total	147,470	229,269	423,210	3,960,467

Sources: Annual Reports of the Danish Employers' Association and the Danish Federation of Labor.
[a] Includes 800,000 kroner for an illegal dock strike.
[b] Includes one million kroner for illegal dock strikes.

representatives before the Labor Court, but undoubtedly has its origin in the relative inability of the trade unions to resist pressure to process cases which have little chance of success.

Another barometer of the outcome of cases is provided by the costs charged against the parties. As indicated above, the Labor Court is prone to divide the costs between the parties if the case is a close one, notwithstanding the formal outcome.[24] Table 36 shows that from 1910 to 1948, 60 per cent of all costs were levied against trade unions, and 40 per cent against employers, indicating clearly the greater success achieved by employers before the Labor Court.

The amounts of the fines levied against employers and unions from 1910 to 1948 are also shown in Table 36. The figures show that union fines exceeded employer fines more than ninefold. This fact is subject to several qualifications, however. In the first place, 45 per cent of the amount assessed against unions arose out of two strike situations, in 1919 and 1920. Moreover, while it may be assumed that the amounts assessed against employers were collected in large measure, the same assumption cannot be made with respect to fines levied against unions and individual workers, particularly in the case of the large fines arising out of worker recalcitrance in illegal strikes. Though there are no statistics on the collection of fines, it may be presumed that while there would still be a disproportion between the employer and union amounts, the degree of inequality would be far less than that indicated in Table 36.

Against this background, it is not difficult to appreciate the popularity of the Labor Court among employers. The official history of the Employers' Association contains this encomium: "The Labor Court is the cornerstone of our industrial relations, and only the authority of the Court in the final analysis and in the long run can ensure cooperation between conflicting interests . . . For no greeting will the Employers' Association give warmer support than that accorded to the Labor Court." [25]

While there is less enthusiasm for the Court on the part of labor, no responsible trade union leader has even suggested that the abolition of the Court would constitute a gain for the workers. From the point of view of the union leadership, the Court is of great assistance in policing the observance of collective agreements, and for the individual worker it represents a legal guarantee that his contract rights will be respected.

INDUSTRIAL ARBITRATION

Supplementing the Labor Court in the adjudication of contract disputes is a system of voluntary industrial arbitration, the origins of which

[24] For a supporting statement, see *Dansk Arbejdsgiverforenings Virksomhed*, 1945–1946' p. 74.

[25] Vigen, Agerholm, og Plum, p. 361.

go back 75 years. In 1875, arbitration boards were established in the printing, cigar, and building carpentry trades, arousing considerable public discussion.[26] While these boards were swept away during the depression of 1877, they provided a model for other industries during the following decades. A Scandinavian labor congress held in Gothenberg in 1886 adopted a resolution urging "the establishment of industry arbitration boards appointed jointly by the organizations of workers and employers." Thereafter, collective agreements contained arbitration provisions with increasing frequency. By 1900, most of the important crafts in Copenhagen had established arbitration boards. Instrumental in spreading the idea to the remainder of the country were national collective agreements, which increased in number after the turn of the century.[27]

It was in the metal trades that the modern system of industrial arbitration first developed. Although arbitration had been practiced in this industry only since 1895, a milestone was reached with an agreement in 1902 specifying in considerable detail the rules for settling contract disputes.[28] These rules provided the basis for the so-called "standard rules" which the Industrial Commission of 1908 urged the trades to adopt and which thereafter found their way into most collective agreements. The standard rules were made mandatory by law in 1934 for all trades which did not have other adequate provision for industrial arbitration, thus making the system universal.

Preliminary mediation

The standard rules for settling contract disputes provide that disputes must first be submitted to mediation if either party so requests. Although there is no rule as to the size of the mediation commission, it ordinarily consists of one person from each side. In the metal trades, both the union and the employers' association employ traveling mediators, and ordinarily the commission consists of organization officials rather than of local personnel. In fact, the standard rules provide that no one may be a member of a mediation commission (or of an arbitration board) if the matter at issue involves a question in which he is personally interested. As a rule, the mediation commission meets at the factory in which the dispute has occurred, and it must assemble within five days (three days in Copenhagen) of the demand for mediation by one of the parties.

There are no national statistics on the results of mediation. In the textile industry, about 100 mediation meetings are held each year, most of

[26] Bruun, pp. 388–389.

[27] Nørregaard, pp. 422–426.

[28] The original agreement is contained in J. A. Hansen, *Dansk Smede og Maskinarbejder Forbunds 25 Aars Jubilaeum* (Copenhagen, 1913), pp. 237–242.

them resulting in settlement of the dispute. Only four or five a year, on the average, require further action.[29] More comprehensive data are available[30] covering disputes between the Metal Workers' Union and the Metal Trades Employers' Association. From 1905 to 1948 inclusive, 7,274 mediation meetings were held, in which 10,987 separate disputes were involved. Although the average annual number of meetings was 170, there was considerable variation from year to year. The number of disputes tended to rise in years of rapid wage and price change, and to fall when economic conditions were stable; thus, the greatest annual number of disputes requiring mediation was in 1919, when there were 924, whereas by 1926 the number had fallen to 177. Since 1945, the annual average number has been about 560 disputes. It is probable that the number of disputes in the metal trades is more sensitive to cyclical change than is true generally, because of the great potential for disputes inherent in the wage system practiced in the industry.

The figures on the results of mediation reveal the similar influence of economic conditions. Of the 10,987 disputes requiring mediation from 1905 to 1948, 58 per cent proved amenable to settlement by mediation, the remainder requiring further action. During the years 1921 to 1935, which were characterized either by falling or stable money wage rates, there was relatively little success in mediating disputes, only 39 per cent of the matters handled in these years having been settled by mediation. When wages began to rise, the mediation system worked more satisfactorily; from 1936 to 1948, 65 per cent of the disputes were disposed of in mediation, and in the postwar years alone, 80 per cent. Of course, many of the disputes that require mediation do not involve wages, but there is no doubt that the feasibility of adjusting wages upward facilitates the settlement of disputes.

The lesser success of mediation in the metal trades than in the textile industry may be due to the existence of a step between mediation and arbitration peculiar to the metal trades, the "ten-man committee." This is an *ad hoc* body consisting of five union and five employer representatives, essentially mediatory in character. Disputes that cannot be settled by a mediation commission are referred to a ten-man committee, which hears them and endeavors to reach a settlement. There is no voting, nor any provision for an impartial umpire. From 1905 to 1948 there were 716 ten-man committee meetings in the metal trades, at which 3,256 separate disputes were taken up. Some 58 per cent of the disputes were settled, while 42 per cent went beyond this stage. As in the case of the mediation

[29] Interview with Mr. Erling Larsen, Textile Employers' Association.

[30] Centralorganisationen af Metalarbejdere i Danmark, *Beretning om Virksomhed*, 1947–1948, pp. 238, 254.

commission, the ten-man committee has proved most successful in periods of rising prices and wages. From 1921 to 1935, only 47 per cent of the disputes handled by the ten-man committees were settled by them, compared with 64 per cent from 1936 to 1948, and 81 per cent from 1945 to 1948.

The following figures for the year April 1, 1947, to March 31, 1948, illustrate the manner in which grievances are settled in the metal trades:

Number of disputes arising during year		583
Settled by mediation	460	
Sent to ten-man committee	99	
Other disposition	17	
Withdrawn	7	
Number of disputes sent to a ten-man committee		99
Settled by committee	74	
Remanded for further negotiation	4	
Arbitrated	1	
Sent to Labor Court	5	
Other disposition	2	
Remaining on docket	13	

During this period, only three cases required arbitration, two of them involving issues not necessarily subject to submission to a ten-man committee. Twelve metal trades cases were brought before the Labor Court, the five indicated in the tabulation and seven additional cases, involving illegal strikes and discrimination against shop stewards, which may be taken directly to the Court. It is thus apparent that the pre-arbitration grievance machinery in the metal trades is highly effective, and that only a very small percentage of the initial disputes require formal arbitration. The successful operation of both industrial arbitration and the Labor Court is due in large measure to this preliminary procedure, which leaves for formal adjudication, as a rule, only those disputes which involve important matters of principle.

Arbitration boards

The final stage in the grievance procedure is submission of the dispute to arbitration. Under the standard rules, if a dispute "concerns the interpretation of an existing price-list with general conditions or a general agreement existing between the organizations," submission to arbitration is mandatory upon the demand of *either* party. In all other cases, the dispute need go to arbitration only upon joint agreement of the parties.[31] The quoted language is construed broadly in practice, and as a rule arbitration cannot be by-passed and a work stoppage instituted

[31] In the metal trades, joint agreement upon arbitration is required in all disputes.

unless one of the following circumstances is involved: (a) failure of the employer to pay workers on the appointed pay day; (b) regard for life, welfare, or honor; (c) lack of a collective agreement upon which the dispute is grounded. However, there may be additional circumstances in which a party is justified in refusing to submit to arbitration;[32] and a dispute over the arbitrability of an issue may be submitted to the Labor Court for adjudication.

As indicated above, the boundary line between the jurisdiction of the Labor Court and of arbitration boards is not a sharp one. A perusal of the subject matter of recent arbitrations indicates that they tend to involve detailed questions which require specialized knowledge of the trade. In one case, for example, the issue was whether a changeover of electric current from 220 to 440 volts in a chemical plant, involving a stoppage of work, constituted *force majeure* under the terms of an agreement, in which event the workers would not have been entitled to receive pay for the period of the interruption. In another, the question was whether men performing excavation work were entitled to extra pay because there was so steep an incline that the workers had to assist in pushing the trucks. Labor Court cases, on the other hand, are largely concerned with actual and threatened strikes. The Labor Court may, and often does, remand a case to arbitration on the ground that the latter is the proper forum for hearing the dispute in question.

The usual arbitration board consists of two representatives of each of the parties, who jointly choose an impartial chairman. Customarily, the representatives of the parties are organization officials, and not lawyers. Though a few trades have permanent arbitration boards, *ad hoc* selection of the arbitrators is the more common practice. The impartial chairman is chosen from a panel which is largely limited to judges of the regular courts; in the event that the parties cannot agree upon a chairman, the choice is usually left to the chairman of the Labor Court. Normally, the chairman's fee is divided equally between the parties.

Arbitration procedure is informal and, in general, is similar to that followed in the United States. Few cases are settled by agreement, unlike Labor Court practice, probably because arbitration cases involve a certain admixture of interest conflict elements, whereas the Labor Court cases tend to be purely disputes over rights that are more amenable to conciliation once factual discrepancies are cleared up. At the close of the proceedings, the arbitrators retire to debate the case, and in the majority of instances arrive at their decision within an hour. In

[32] For example, a dispute over piece rates applicable to entirely new work would involve conflicting interests rather than contract rights, and neither party could oblige the other to accept arbitration.

the event of the usual disagreement between the partisan arbitrators, the chairman casts the deciding vote; and it is well established that he may adopt any position between those argued by the parties, even though he is not supported by any other arbitrator.

The standard rules provide that the award must be given not later than fourteen days after the submission to arbitration. The decision must be in writing, and it is usually supported by an opinion. The judgment cannot be appealed except on the allegation that the board has exceeded its competence. However, an arbitration award does not have the force of a legal judgment, and in the event of failure of the losing party to abide by it, a very rare occurrence, the winning party may bring the matter before the Labor Court on the theory of breach of contract to arbitrate, and execute thereafter upon the basis of a Labor Court judgment. It must be emphasized, however, that the Labor Court is not an appeals tribunal for the arbitration boards; it merely acts as an enforcement agency, without power of substantive review.

Because of the *ad hoc* nature of most arbitration boards, as well as the peculiarly complicated factual situations involved in most cases, a strict rule of *stare decisis* is impracticable. However, as Illum points out, the boards "show the same tendency as the ordinary courts to follow earlier decisions, where there is no decisive basis for altering existing practice." [33] In some fields a coherent body of common law has been built up by the arbitration boards which serves as a point of departure for argument in new cases.

THE CONTRACT BOARD OF 1939

A new development in the settlement of contract disputes came in connection with an agreement in 1939 between the Federation of Labor and the Employers' Association tying wages to the cost of living index. The agreement established a board, consisting of three representatives of each of the parties, with the principal government mediator as chairman, to resolve disputes over its interpretation. The board rendered a number of decisions in connection with cost of living supplements payable to seamen, women, and youthful workers, and also resolved some controversy over the applicability of the cost of living supplements to overtime rates.

The wage stop law enacted in 1940 gave the Contract Board authority to adjudicate problems arising out of its application. The Board was also empowered to interpret decisions of the wartime board of compulsory arbitration. The Contract Board rendered important decisions in connection with pay for work interruptions due to air raid alarms and

[33] Illum, p. 292.

the rationing of electric power. The Board also continued to supervise the operation of the cost of living wage supplement system. Since 1945, the Contract Board has been continued as an arbitration tribunal by agreement of the parties. In principle, it now decides the same type of case as the industrial arbitration boards. Practically, however, the Contract Board confines its activities to matters of general interest that transcend industry lines, whereas the industrial boards are concerned with more parochial issues. Occasionally one of the parties will endeavor to bring before the Contract Board a matter which belongs in industrial arbitration, but the present Board chairman, who has served in that capacity since its creation, has firmly resisted such attempts.

The *raison d'être* of the Contract Board, which continues to operate on the basis of contract and has no statutory authority, is the opportunity it affords for settling disputes over the interpretation of broad agreements between the two central organizations with a minimum of formality. Like most Danish labor market institutions, it was created by the bargaining parties to fill a real need, in this case to arbitrate in the newly developed field of wage agreements directly between the central organizations. It will probably remain in existence, and may eventually attain the position of a statutory body.

Denmark has developed the most complete and best integrated system of settling contract disputes in all Europe, if not the world. Its strength lies in the fact that it grew slowly, to meet the demands of specific situations, rather than having been jerry-built in the heat of crisis. It is entirely the work of the Federation of Labor and the Employers' Association and their affiliates, the state serving the function of formalizing what had already been agreed upon. Thus, the system is endowed with the essential ingredient for success: the confidence and assent of employer and worker alike.

CHAPTER XI

THE LAW OF INDUSTRIAL RELATIONS[1]

THERE HAVE BEEN two main tendencies in Danish labor law: to concentrate authority and responsibility in the organization rather than the individual, and to deprive the ordinary courts of jurisdiction over labor cases in favor of tribunals established by the central collective bargaining organizations themselves. The previous chapter dealt with the history and organization of the special labor tribunals; it is now proposed to consider the substantive rules developed by the Labor Court and the arbitration boards.[2]

THE COLLECTIVE AGREEMENT

Danish legal theory looks upon the collective agreement as a document that is binding both upon the contracting organizations and upon the individuals covered by it.[3] In this, it adopts a middle ground between the tendency that was marked in pre-Nazi German law to consider that the collective agreement conferred rights and obligations upon the organization alone, and a pure agency theory in which all rights and obligations flow ultimately to individual trade union members.[4]

The consummation of agreements

Unlike Norwegian and Swedish practice, an oral collective agreement is as binding as a written one in Denmark. However, agreements with associated employers are almost universally reduced to writing, oral agreements being confined to those with unassociated employers.[5]

The competence of organizations of employers and workers to act on

[1] In this chapter, I have drawn heavily upon two volumes by Professor Knud Illum: *Den Kollektive Arbejdsret* (Copenhagen, 1939), and *Dansk Tillidsmandsret* (Copenhagen, 1949). These are cited as Illum I and Illum II respectively.

[2] Danish labor legislation, in contrast to that in Norway and Sweden, contains few substantive rules, being largely confined to procedure. The principal explanation lies in the existence of the September Agreement, which provides the basic legal framework.

[3] See Hj. V. Elmquist, *Den Kollektive Arbejdsoverenskomst* (Copenhagen, 1918), pp. 83–98.

[4] Norwegian theory is closely akin to that of Denmark, while in Sweden the organizational interest in the collective agreement is given greater emphasis.

[5] The ordinary case of an unwritten agreement is that of the unassociated employer who agrees to meet the organized wage scale prevailing in the trade. See Knud V. Jensen, pp. 178–181, for the relevant cases on this subject.

behalf of their members is contingent upon the subject matter of the agreement and upon their constitutional authority. It will be recalled that the Federation of Labor is empowered to bind its affiliates only on matters of general interest, for example, cost of living bonuses. In most trade unions, the national union may enter into collective agreements on behalf of its locals, while the power of the local to contract is severely circumscribed. The national union must be vigilant, however, for in the absence of actual or constructive notice to an employer that a local union is acting *ultra vires*, an agreement contracted by the local may be binding upon it.

Interpreting collective agreements

The intent of the parties at the time an agreement is signed provides the point of departure for its interpretation. Minutes of collective bargaining and mediation meetings may be adduced as evidence of intent. If it appears that there was no mutually clear intent, the literal language of the agreement is decisive, unless the consequences are patently impossible.

The fact that a particular issue is not explicitly covered by an agreement does not necessarily deprive the Labor Court of jurisdiction over it. The collective agreement presumes that there shall be no interruptions in work during its term, and a dispute that threatens this basic objective falls within the aegis of the Labor Court. Custom and practice are of paramount importance in such cases, since it is presumed that if an important issue was not considered during collective bargaining the parties must have intended to follow previous practice. Whether a definite custom exists is a matter of proof; length of time is not necessarily conclusive in this respect. For example, it has been held that the employment of piece work for a long period of time did not shape a binding custom, but merely reflected the method of wage payment which the employer found expedient at a particular time.[6]

Even in the absence of a definite custom, however, the parties are not usually free to resort to economic force. It is basic to the whole concept of the collective agreement in Denmark that strikes and lockouts shall not take place over differences in interpretation. In many cases, the Labor Court and the arbitration boards have supplied regulations in consonance with the general intent of the agreement.

Invalidity of agreements

A collective agreement concluded through force is not binding upon the party against whom the force was directed, in accordance with cus-

[6] Labor Court, Case No. 482.

tomary contract rules. Force does not encompass the threat or effectuation of a strike or lockout, but implies the use of violence or other methods in violation of law. However, a strike in violation of contract is regarded as the application of unlawful force, and the employer may escape the obligations entered into for the purpose of avoiding or terminating such a stoppage, unless there is evidence of his acquiescence in the new terms after the conclusion of the incident. Thus if workers, by threatening to strike in violation of contract, are able to raise their wage rates above those stipulated in the agreement, the employer may later seek repayment of the gains secured in this manner.[7]

An agreement entered into in violation of the contractual rights of third parties is invalid in the event of full knowledge on the part of both contracting parties. Lack of knowledge by one party does not validate the agreement, but merely gives that party the right to seek damages. These rules are of importance in the event of conflicting union jurisdiction. In the absence of an express stipulation, a collective agreement does not confer upon a trade union the exclusive right to all work covered by the agreement over which it claims jurisdiction; but it has been held that the contract confers a measure of right to the work which cannot arbitrarily be destroyed by the employer through a new agreement with another union. While the Employers' Association has successfully opposed the closed shop in its agreements on the basis of the September Agreement, the Labor Court has held that closed shop clauses in agreements with employers not subject to the September Agreement operate as a bar to collective agreements with rival unions.

A contract otherwise valid, or portions of it, may be renounced before the stated expiration date under certain circumstances. A drastic change in economic or technical conditions may justify one of the parties in seeking an interim alteration in an agreement. For example, a reduction in working hours necessitated by the rationing of electricity was held not to constitute a breach of contract,[8] the same conclusion being reached in the case of unilateral changes in working conditions due to the order of the German occupation authorities during the war.[9] However, the Labor Court has refused to permit unilateral contract renunciation in the face of changing prices, even when the changes were very marked.

The scope of agreements

A collective agreement is binding upon all affiliates and members of the contracting organizations who it is intended shall be covered, as

[7] Labor Court, Cases No. 368, 644, 719, 1485, 2097, 2599.
[8] Labor Court, Case No. 3384.
[9] Labor Court, Case No. 3386.

well as upon those who join the organizations subsequent to the consummation of the agreement, except to the extent that the latter have existing inconsistent contractual obligations. However, if an unassociated employer is engaged in a dispute with a trade union and during the course of the dispute joins an employers' association, it does not necessarily follow that he automatically falls under the master agreement with the association. The Labor Court has held that the employer may not thus escape the consequences of the dispute. The crucial question is whether a dispute actually prevailed at the time he joined; a strike or a threat of strike constitutes a dispute, but mere negotiations are not necessarily evidence of a dispute.

On the other hand, an employer who withdraws from an employers' association is not thereby freed of the contractual obligations undertaken in his behalf by the association. And while an individual worker who leaves a trade union cannot be held to the collective agreement, workers who dissolve their organization for the purpose of escaping an agreement remain subject to its terms, and liable for any breach thereof.

In the event that a firm changes ownership during the term of an agreement, the tendency is to regard the contract as a continuing one if the connection between the old and the new firm is close, for example, if a partnership is transformed into a corporation. Moreover, if a new firm is operated with substantially the same employees as its predecessor and under the same general conditions, the collective agreement remains in effect. However, if a firm merely purchases the physical property of another and does not continue to operate it as an entity, it does not inherit the collective agreement. The strictness with which these rules are applied renders impossible the evasion of contractual obligations through fictitious changes in ownership.

A closely related problem is that of work contracted out by the primary employer. If the contract-out arrangement is merely a disguised employment relationship, a breach of contract will lie if the primary collective agreement terms are not honored. But if the subcontract is genuine, and particularly when it conforms with customary practice in the trade, as in the building trades, the subcontractor is not bound by an agreement with the general contractor. Similarly, where an entrepreneur accepts an employee into partnership, if the arrangement is genuine the collective agreement no longer applies to the new partner; but if it is fictitious, he must be paid according to the agreement.[10]

[10] The collective agreement in the barber trade requires prior approval of a partnership by both the Employers' Association and the trade union to prevent evasion of the agreement terms.

One of the most important rules established by the Labor Court is that the provisions of a collective agreement apply to all employees of the class covered by the agreement, whether or not they are members of the contracting union, unless the contract explicitly states to the contrary. The premise for this rule is that if an employer were permitted to pay below-contract wages to his nonunion workers, it would be advantageous for him to discriminate against union members, in contravention of the intent of the September Agreement. But the logical analogue, namely, that organized workers should not be permitted to accept employment with independent employers on terms less favorable than those prevailing at associated establishments was rejected by the Court in the following terms:

> . . . Trade unions will always seek to secure for their members the best possible conditions, and therefore they will not be prone to sign with an unassociated employer for less favorable terms than those contained in collective agreements. If a trade union is persuaded to accept less favorable conditions from an unassociated employer, it will not be for the purpose of promoting unfair competition for the members of the employers' association, which would be in violation of the conditions of the collective agreement, but must be attributable to other factors, *e.g.*, local or customary conditions, or particular circumstances prevailing in the individual case.[11]

A national collective agreement is applicable to work done by the contracting organizations anywhere in the country. If one of the contracting parties operates only within a certain geographical area, the contract is limited to that area. A building contractor who belongs to an employers' association confined to a single city need not conform to the terms of an agreement entered into by the association in the case of work performed outside the city, nor is he obliged to adopt the conditions prevailing at the site of the work unless a custom can be shown to that effect. However, an employer must pay the contract wages covering a locality for work performed in that locality, notwithstanding the fact that the workers were hired from an area in which lower wage rates prevail.

Wage enforcement

The payment of below-contract wages, whether in the form of lower time or piece rates or kickbacks by the employee, is clearly a breach of contract, regardless of the acquiescence of the individual employee. If an appropriate case is made, the Labor Court will not only order the

[11] Labor Court, Cases No. 2051 and 2053.

employer to honor the agreement in the future, but it may also impose a fine upon him at least equal to the amount of the underpayment. If organized workers are involved, they are generally reimbursed out of the fine, since the fine is paid to the contracting union, but if unorganized workers are involved, the fine remains with the union. The theory of this distinction is that unorganized workers enjoy no contractual rights, but that the trade union may suffer injury in the event of payment of below-contract wages to unorganized workers.

An employer may offer his workers more favorable conditions than those contained in the collective agreement, but whether or not the conditions are actually more favorable must be judged from the point of view of the trade union. An individual worker cannot on his own initiative make wage concessions in return for other benefits, since what he regards as a favorable bargain may conflict with the collective interest. In one extreme case, an employer was deemed to have violated his agreement by giving his workers the right to a longer period of dismissal notice than that required by contract, on the ground that the worker's loyalty to the employer might be strengthened, and his loyalty to the union weakened thereby.[12]

Terminating agreements

Ordinarily, a collective agreement is limited in duration, with the stipulation that if notice of termination is not given by either party within a certain period, the contract continues in force. The September Agreement provides that there must be at least three months' notice of termination, but this period was shortened to 14 days by subsequent agreement between the central bargaining organizations.

When an agreement has expired after proper notice of termination, the general rule is that the conditions of labor contained in the agreement remain in effect, and neither party may alter them unilaterally. For example, if an employer were to reduce wages after the expiration of an agreement without a new agreement having been reached, his action is considered tantamount to a lockout effected without proper notice. A party can free itself from an agreement only by giving the requisite notice and *actually* establishing a stoppage of work. The rationale of this important rule is as follows:

> Point 2 of the September Agreement includes only the right to effect a work stoppage, and to this concept the notice rule is added. Two possibilities are envisioned: either that work continues, or that work stops after proper notice. No alternative possibilities are assumed, and there is no provision giving an organization, through notice, the right to establish conditions of labor to which

[12] Labor Court, Case No. 621.

the opposite party has not agreed, and which it may be interested in preventing from coming into force.[13]

This concept of the collective agreement permits collective bargaining to continue after the expiration of agreements without danger of a work stoppage caused by precipitate action on the part of one of the parties. It constitutes recognition of the fact that labor conditions are vested with social significance, in limiting the power of the employer to determine conditions even in the absence of agreement. While the rule is ostensibly grounded in the September Agreement, it provides a good example of judicial legislation by the Labor Court.

If there is any doubt as to the continued effectiveness of an agreement, the party seeking to free itself may take direct action only at its own risk. The proper procedure is to test the agreement in the Labor Court, a feasible procedure in view of the speed with which an adjudication can be obtained.

THE REPRESENTATION OF WORKERS

One of the paramount features of American labor law, that centering about the determination of the appropriate collective bargaining agency and the specification of its rights, is largely without a counterpart in Denmark. The explanation lies in the virtual absence of rival unionism in Denmark, combined with the relatively clear cut delineation of craft lines. The trade unions that have remained independent of the Federation of Labor are confined to a few trades into which the Federation has not attempted to enter, and occasional attempts at poaching within the Federation, as well as genuine jurisdictional disputes arising out of technological change, have been dealt with by the disputes machinery of the Federation. Only rarely has inter-union controversy raised questions for the Labor Court.

In the normal course of events, a Danish employer signs a separate agreement with each trade union having members within his establishment. The situation is analogous to that prevailing in the United States printing trades, where there is a contract for each craft and a representation question rarely arises. Strictly speaking, a trade union represents only its own members, but in effect it is the exclusive representative of all the employees in its craft, by virtue of the Labor Court doctrine of quasi-extension of collective agreements. The nonunion and the union workers jointly select a shop steward, and since the latter is almost always a union man (in some industries he must be, by contract), the grievance machinery is a monopoly of the union. No provision exists for holding representation elections, nor is it necessary.

[13] Labor Court, Case No. 564.

Similarly, the collective bargaining unit offers no problems; it is determined largely by the jurisdictional lines of the craft unions. In large factories, where difficulty might be anticipated, the division of the unit among the crafts, each with a few members, and the Laborers' Union, representing all but the skilled workers, is generally amicable. The structure of the labor movement is horizontal, which is reflected in a horizontal bargaining unit.

The role of the Labor Court in representation has been limited to cases in which the apportionment of work between two unions was involved, which is to be distinguished from competition between two unions for the control of the same group of workers. The Court has held that an agreement specifically recognizing the right of one union to a particular type of work bars agreement with another union for the same work during the contract period. But

> even where there is no exclusive agreement, the same rule prevails, to a certain extent. When an agreement is concluded with an organization in a certain branch of industry or trade, it does not give the members of the union any exclusive right to the work encompassed; but it does confer upon them a right which cannot arbitrarily be set aside by the employer. A new agreement with an organization of workers outside the group to which the work is secured cannot normally be concluded . . .
>
> When a collective agreement is concluded covering specific work, it will be in conflict with the purposes of the agreement if the employer, during the contract period, permits the work to be done by an entirely different category of workers than those for whom the agreement determines labor conditions. A mason contractor belonging to the Masons' Association and bound by the collective agreement in the trade, will normally not be entitled to allow work belonging to the masons to be performed by timberers, even if the work could be regarded as timbering. The various crafts make certain that their members are not deprived of work which they have hitherto performed, and the customary craft boundaries, for skilled and unskilled workers respectively, must to a certain extent be respected by the employer.[14]

At the expiration of an agreement, the employer has the legal right to choose freely among unions with respect to future work. This is largely an academic right, however, owing to the strength of customary craft lines. Fifty years of collective bargaining between organizations of employers and workers, together with a unified labor movement, have resulted in a satisfactory solution of the representation problem.

[14] Illum I, pp. 117, 184. However, where there is any doubt as to jurisdiction, or in the event of technological change, the employer may freely select from among the competing trades.

THE PREROGATIVES OF MANAGEMENT

Reference has already been made to Paragraph 4 of the September Agreement, whereby the trade unions acknowledged "the employer's right to direct and distribute the work and to use what labor may in his judgment be suitable at any time . . ." Although it is this section of the Agreement that initially met with the greatest opposition within the labor movement, it is precisely the one that the Labor Court has employed in preventing employers from interfering with the organization of workers.

It was decided in 1911 that by this clause, the trade unions had renounced the right to demand the exclusive employment of union labor, that is, the closed or union shop.[15] The employer may hire workers without regard to their union status, any intervention on the part of a trade union constituting a breach of contract. Although employers may waive this right, the Employers' Association has consistently forbidden its members to do so. In one case, the Carpenters' Union in Copenhagen attempted to apportion the available work by requiring all union members to obtain jobs through the union's employment exchange. The Court held even this to be unlawful, on the ground that "the union was not within its rights in forbidding its members to come in contact with employers who addressed themselves to the workers in regard to employment." [16] The employer's right to hire and retain foremen who were unpopular with the workers was also protected.

But while the employer may choose his employees with regard to their efficiency,[17] deliberate discrimination against union members with the purpose of interfering with their organizational rights has been held to constitute a misuse of Section 4 and a violation of the mutual grant of the right to organize implied in the September Agreement as a whole. Employers may neither seek to prevent workers from joining trade unions, nor encourage them to drop their membership, whether by threat, promise, or discrimination. This interpretation of the September Agreement by the Labor Court conferred upon the Danish labor movement the protection afforded American trade unions by Section 7 of the National Labor Relations Act.

An employer may discharge a worker for any reason except for the

[15] Labor Court, Case No. 58.

[16] Labor Court, Case No. 956.

[17] Employers' associations may maintain employment records for all workers in a trade for the purpose of advising employers with respect to the efficiency of individuals. Use of these records to discriminate against workers because of their union status or their militancy in representing fellow workers is unlawful.

purpose of interfering with organization. However, it has been held that the union has a right to receive a statement of the reasons for discharge, so that it may determine whether in its estimation there has been a breach of the employer's contractual obligations. If it feels that there has been discrimination, the burden of proof is entirely upon the union to establish that fact.

In general, it is the right of the employer to establish such working rules as he considers necessary for the efficient operation of his business. However, the Labor Court has placed numerous restrictions upon the seemingly sweeping language of the September Agreement to this effect. For example, while the employer may unilaterally establish "control measures which obviously have no other purpose than ensuring that work proceeds in its normal course, which have no offensive implications for workers, and which do not cause workers any loss or serious inconvenience," he must negotiate with the union before adopting measures "with regard to which there is reasonable doubt whether they fall within the enumerated limits." [18] Among the specific measures which the Court has permitted the employer without prior negotiation are the installation of time clocks, search of workers upon leaving the plant, the requirement of detailed time sheets for work performed, and the introduction of time study as an aid to piece-rate setting. The employer may also establish rules governing the conduct of workers within the establishment, though a rule forbidding the drinking of beer during the lunch hour was held to go beyond the prerogatives of management.

In a leading case, the Labor Court summarized its conception of Paragraph 4 in the following terms:

> The right of employers to direct work is not a one-sided right, but a right that obligates employers to cooperate with their workers . . . it is the duty of management to seek to direct the workers and negotiate with their representatives in such a manner as not to give the workers reasonable grounds for complaint.[19]

THE EMPLOYMENT OF ECONOMIC FORCE

A strike exists within the meaning of the Labor Court Act when "a group of workers in unison, with a common aim in view, refuses to bargain or continue an employment relationship." [20] The crucial determination in many cases is whether a work stoppage is a strike as thus defined, or merely the result of individual refusal to work. The Court ordinarily examines the motives of the workers; if they are based primarily

[18] Labor Court, Case No. 106.
[19] Labor Court, Case No. 2058.
[20] Illum I, p. 211.

on individual grievances, and there has been no preliminary consultation among the workers, no strike exists despite the fact that more than one employee may have left work, whereas the quitting of work in connection with a collective demand or purpose constitutes a strike. This distinction is not an easy one, and acquires meaning only within the context of individual circumstances. If, for example, a trade union has forbidden its members to accept certain work, or even if there is some oblique indication by union officials that a job is to be boycotted, a strike exists. Inability of an employer to secure labor despite the existence of unemployment provides strong evidence of collusion.

A lockout is a situation in which "one or more employers undertake the discharge of a group of workers or refuse to accept the services of workers, without cause based upon business necessity." [21] The relevant inquiry in determining whether a lockout prevails is into the existence or nonexistence of genuine economic motives for discharge.

Except in a few sharply circumscribed instances, work stoppages, to be lawful, must be preceded by prescribed notice. This requirement often leads to the determination of the legality of a strike or lockout *in advance* of its effectuation, since the receiving party may test the validity of the notice of work stoppage in the Labor Court. Many of the details of the requisite notice have been made specific by Labor Court decision: the proper party to give and receive notice, the organizational instance competent to make the decision to strike or lockout, the meaning of the requirement of "at least three-quarters of the votes cast at a competent meeting" to validate the notice, and the work area covered by a strike notice.

Upon the institution of a lawful strike, all workers, whether or not members of the initiating union, may remain away from the affected establishment without further notice, while workers who have been locked out may be barred from employment by all associated employers. Moreover, "all organized workers may refuse to perform the work that should have been done for the employer against whom a strike has been declared, including, for example, work on material transferred to another employer whose employees are not on strike." [22] So-called "struck work" does not include transportation to and from the struck plant, nor work transferred to another employer for reasons not connected with the strike. But these limitations do not mean that the secondary boycott is illegal. In fact, the sympathetic strike, discussed below, constitutes a legal and regularized form of coercing a primary employer through secondary employers. The point is that with the exception of "struck

[21] *Ibid.*, p. 214.
[22] *Ibid.*, p. 229.

work," a secondary boycott may be invoked only after due and proper notice to the secondary employer.

1. Limitations upon work stoppages imposed by the September Agreement. Some inhibitions upon the right to strike or lockout stem directly from the September Agreement. Strikes and lockouts below the level of the central organizations for the purpose of effecting changes in the September Agreement are banned. Work stoppages called for the purpose of destroying an opposing organization are in violation of the mutual recognition of the right to organize, while those called for purposes other than the determination of future conditions of labor may conflict with the mutual pledge to coöperate. Jurisdictional strikes have been placed in the latter category by the Labor Court.

2. Stoppages to alter valid agreements. As a rule, there may be no work stoppages for the purpose of forcing changes in an unexpired, valid collective agreement.

3. Conditions not covered by collective agreement. A prolific source of controversy has arisen from demands for employment conditions not covered by collective agreement, particularly in the case of new work not included in contractual rate schedules. Whether the right to strike or lockout exists under such circumstances depends upon the collective agreement, which in most cases preserves such right on the theory that the dispute is actually one over interests rather than over interpretation. When the right to strike exists, notice is unnecessary, since a notice requirement would oblige workers to perform work for which no rate of pay has been established. If there is any doubt over whether the disputed work is actually covered by agreement, a stoppage is improper until an appropriate ruling has been obtained from the Labor Court or a board of arbitration. If a party chooses to act rather than to litigate under doubtful circumstances, it does so at its own risk, the law favoring industrial peace.

General demands, as contrasted with specific demands over the application of a wage scale — for example, for the closed shop or increased vacation periods — do not ordinarily justify a strike during the contract period, particularly if such demands had been rejected in previous collective bargaining. Demands of this character can be justified only on the ground that a fundamental change in conditions has taken place, which could not have been foreseen when the agreement was concluded.

4. Sympathetic stoppages. The sympathetic work stoppage, so important in Denmark because of the strength of organization among workers and employers, is roughly akin to what is termed the secondary boycott (excluding consumer boycotts) in the United States. The legality of such stoppages, even in the face of existing collective agreements, is expressly guaranteed by the September Agreement. There is an important limitation, however, in that a sympathetic stoppage must have the prior approval of the appropriate central organization — that is, any union desiring to call its members out in support of another union must first secure the permission of the Federation of Labor, except where the action is limited to the members of a single national union involved in the primary dispute. Thus a local union may come to the aid of a sister local without prior sanction of the Federation.

The Danish equivalent of the product boycott is the *conditional* sympathetic strike, that is, a sympathetic strike conditioned upon the failure of the secondary employer to interrupt commercial intercourse with the primary employer. This is a logical variant of the sympathetic strike itself, and it is lawful provided permission is obtained of the central organization. Legality is premised upon the theory that if a union may lawfully strike against a secondary employer, it should have the right to adopt the less drastic measure of threatening to strike unless the employer complies with its demands. It will be recalled that these rules are based upon the September Agreement and were originally confined to employers bound by that agreement, the ordinary courts having tended to adopt a more restrictive view.[23] But this exception has become without practical significance in the case of all employers whose workers are organized, since the Standard Negotiation Rules establishing that it "shall be without prejudice to the right of the two organizations or their members to take part without previous mediation and arbitration in a stoppage of work, ordered by the Danish Employers' Association or the Federation of Labor," were incorporated by law into all collective agreements without comparable rules for the settlement of disputes.

The associative philosophy upon which the sympathetic work stoppage rests is further exemplified by a provision in the September Agreement making it a breach of contract for either of the signatories to support a nonmember employer or trade union engaged in a dispute with an affiliated trade union or employer. Therefore, a union affiliated with the Federation of Labor may not boycott a member of the Employers' Association in support of an unaffiliated union. However, an affiliated union engaged in a dispute with an unaffiliated employer may threaten to boycott an affiliated employer who continues to deal with the primary employer; but in this case the Employers' Association may retaliate by declaring a counterlockout against the union.

The close relationship prevailing among the Scandinavian labor movements has given rise to the question of the legality of strikes called for the purpose of assisting foreign labor movements. In 1921, the Dan-

[23] See above, p. 139.

ish transport unions attempted to prevent the loading of ships destined for Norway, and a boycott of Finnish ships was undertaken in 1928. The strikes were declared unlawful in both instances on the ground that there was no dispute between Danish workers and employers within the intent of the September Agreement. In a later case, however, the Labor Court upheld the right of Danish printers to refuse to perform work that had been let to a Danish firm owing to a strike of printers in Norway.

Finally, it should be noted that the legality of a sympathetic strike, lockout, or boycott is contingent upon the existence of a legal primary stoppage. It is not necessary that the primary stoppage be effective, but merely that it shall have been called properly.

5. *Stoppages to enforce collective agreements.* It is generally unlawful to effect a strike or lockout for the purpose of enforcing a collective agreement or a particular interpretation thereof. The Labor Court and the boards of arbitration were established precisely to adjudicate these matters. Nor does the breach of a collective agreement by one party justify the employment of economic force by the other, since the Labor Court provides a swift means of redress.

There are several exceptions to the general rule, however. An employers' association may be justified in resorting to lockout if a trade union refuses to terminate a strike held illegal by the Labor Court. More important are the instances in which workers may refuse to continue in employment until a disputed issue is settled. Workers may leave their jobs in the event of the failure of the employer to pay them for work already performed, owing to his insolvency. Failure of the employer to meet his payroll for other reasons does not constitute justification for a collective work stoppage, since redress can be secured through the Labor Court. It is customary in the building trades that when a contractor has gone into bankruptcy on a particular job, his successor is liable for unpaid wages. In such cases, the job may be struck without notice until the new contractor meets his obligations. Mere apprehension on the part of the workers that an employer may not meet his payroll is not good cause for a strike, although the workers in doubtful cases may require the employer to put up a bond as a guarantee of payment.

A stoppage of work without preliminary notice is also permitted if "regard for life, welfare or honor affords compelling reasons." With respect to fear for life, good faith on the part of the workers is required; if, for example, workers are willing to continue a dangerous job at a higher rate of pay, the Court will not find good faith. There is rarely sufficient threat to "welfare or honor" to justify a strike. Only in the event that an employer has grossly defamed workers is there sufficient cause for a stoppage, and then only the workers so defamed may leave.[24]

6. Political strikes and demonstrations. Stoppages of work that do not arise out of the labor conditions in an establishment are in violation of contract, and a union and workers engaging in them are financially liable.

THE SHOP STEWARD

A considerable body of law has grown up about the status of the shop steward, an office that is more important in Denmark than is ordinarily true in the United States. In almost every establishment, workers designate one of their number to represent them in the myriad of individual problems that arise in the course of administering a collective agreement. The right of the workers to choose a local representative and the protection accorded the representative so that he may perform his duties without fear for his own employment are stipulated by contract and custom. The regulations governing the relationship between the employer and the shop steward have been developed through arbitration awards. Though the Labor Court has formal jurisdiction over many types of shop steward disputes, it has refrained from exercising it in all but a few cases, maintaining that disputes of this character are better handled through private industrial arbitration.

The modern form of the shop steward institution may be traced back to an agreement of 1900 in the metal trades. While the shop steward is to be found in almost every industry, it is in the metal trades that the institution has received its most complete development. Unless otherwise specified, the term "agreement" as used in this section refers to the national agreement in the metal trades, the shop steward provisions of which constitute a model for other industries.

It is the right and duty of the shop steward "to conduct the initial negotiations when disputes arise between workers and employers, and through negotiation to seek a satisfactory solution." [25] Refusal of the employer to deal with the shop steward constitutes a breach of contract. In the metal trades, although not in other industries, the shop steward must be a member of the union. Actually, he will almost invariably be a union man, and in effect the local representative of the union.

The precise functions performed by the shop steward vary in each industry and establishment. Sometimes he may be consulted on the order in which layoffs should take place, although there is a strong

[24] "A charge of untruthfulness can only impinge upon the honor of the person against whom it is directed, and moreover, if redress is desired, that is best secured through negotiation and investigation, and as a first step, through mediation . . . while a stoppage of work would tend only to hinder this purpose." Labor Court, Case No. 113.

[25] Kaj Bundvad, Eiler Jensen, Chr. Christiansen, *Tillidsmands-Kundskab* (Copenhagen, 1946), p. 31.

feeling in the labor movement that in the absence of a regular layoff procedure, the performance of this function may embroil him with the workers and reduce his effectiveness. In some industries the shop steward is intimately involved in the application of piece-rate schedules, and he is always enjoined to keep watch on rate setting to prevent the undermining of union standards. But the shop steward may not conclude any agreement interpreting or in contravention of a collective agreement, all such matters requiring action by the local union.

Election of shop stewards

The metal trades agreement contains the following provisions with respect to the election of shop stewards:

The shop steward shall be elected from among the recognized competent workers (members of the union), who have been employed for at least 1½ of the preceding 2 years in the shop concerned. Where there are not at least five eligible workers, the group shall be supplemented up to that number from among the members who have worked the longest. In shops employing five or fewer workers, no shop steward shall be elected unless both parties desire it, and a shop steward who is elected at a time when a larger number of workers is employed, ceases to be such if the number of workers during a period of three months has been reduced to five or fewer, unless both parties desire the position retained.

These provisions relate only to the workers, union and nonunion, who are covered by the particular collective agreement. Therefore, if an establishment has agreements with several craft unions, there will ordinarily be a separate shop steward for each craft, provided there is the minimum necessary employment in each. As the agreement states, the reduction of employment below the specified number for a certain period of time automatically terminates the stewardship, and it is well established that a new election is required to reinstate it in the event that employment once more rises to the necessary minimum.

The requirement that a worker be "competent" in his trade to hold the office of shop steward arises from the belief that "workers demand that the man who represents them shall not only be a good organization man, but also of recognized competence in his trade. This ensures the election of a shop steward who can judge a piece of work quickly and surely, and who because of his skill has a certain 'goodwill' with the employer which may be helpful during negotiations." [26]

As for the election itself, the agreement provides that it shall be conducted "among the workers who are employed in the establishment at the time the election takes place, and it shall be deemed valid only when

[26] Kaj Bundvad, *et al.*, p. 45.

more than half of the employed workers have voted for the shop steward." A further condition for validity of an election is approval by the executive committee of the employers' association of the individual elected. If the association takes exception to an election, an unusual occurrence, it must raise the question with the executive committee of the union, and if agreement cannot be reached, the matter must be submitted to arbitration. Until the employers' association gives its approval (it must act within a reasonable period of time), the individual elected is not formally a shop steward, though he is protected against any attempt by the employer to get rid of him before his election is finally validated. If the employers' association decides to contest the election, the shop steward nevertheless may act in that capacity until there is an adverse decision of the arbitration board.

There is a further provision in the agreement that in "larger" establishments a shop steward shall be elected in each department, and that one of the shop stewards may be designated as the chief shop steward. The meaning of the term "larger" has led to some litigation, though the employment of over 100 workers appears to place an establishment in this category. With respect to departments, the views and practices of management are not necessarily determining; arbitrators have tended rather to inquire into the degree of common interest among workers within the establishment, and to delineate separate interest groups, for example, men versus women, piece-rate versus time-rate workers.

Duties of the shop steward

The metal trades agreement specifies the following as the function of the shop steward:

> When one or more of his fellow workers, either because they consider themselves injured or for other reasons, desire it, he is obligated to bring their complaints or proposals to the employer if the matter cannot be adjusted satisfactorily with the representative of the latter (the foreman).
>
> The shop steward may also raise complaints and direct proposals to the employer with respect to hygienic conditions and measures to prevent accidents and injuries.
>
> If no satisfactory adjustment is obtained, the shop steward is free to request his organization to take the matter up, but work must continue uninterruptedly until a contrary determination is made by the leadership of the organization.

The shop steward is not limited to the presentation of grievances at the behest of a worker, but may himself take the initiative. Moreover, he is not obligated to present all grievances, having the right to exercise discretion. The redress of an individual worker who feels himself aggrieved by the failure of a shop steward to process his complaint is through the local trade union.

It is the contractual duty of the shop steward to work for good industrial relations. This does not mean that he should reject justifiable grievances merely for the sake of peace, nor that he must be diffident in his relations with the employer. But he is bound to follow all procedural rules carefully, and above all, to prevent work stoppages over contract disputes. "His activities must not assume such character that his work for harmonious cooperation deprives him of the confidence of fellow workers. Tact and goodwill are required of him, but not to such an extent as to constitute a drag upon his activities in the interests of the workers." [27]

It is the general rule that the functions of the shop steward should be performed with the least possible interruption to his ordinary work. Matters that are not of urgent character may not be presented during working hours, and the shop steward may in no event confer with his fellow workers during working hours without the consent of the employer. In the case of negotiations undertaken at the request of the employer, the shop steward must be compensated by the employer for the time spent, and it is the custom in most establishments to pay the shop steward for all time away from his job in pursuit of his official duties.

Discharge of shop stewards

It has been remarked that "the legal essence of all shop steward law is protection against improper discharge of the shop steward." [28] The metal trades agreement provides that "the discharge of a shop steward shall be based upon compelling reasons (*tvingende aarsager*), and the employer is obligated to give him two months' notice. If the discharge can be attributed to lack of work, there is no obligation of notice." [29] The majority of shop steward arbitrations involve the application of this language to specific circumstances.

It is unquestionably more difficult to discharge a shop steward than an ordinary worker. The employer must have "compelling reasons," in the absence of a general layoff, and the burden of proof is upon him to

[27] Illum II, p. 63.

[28] Allan Rise, "Tillidsmandsinstitutionen belyst ved Retspraksis," *Ugeskrift for Retsvaesen*, January 1945.

[29] The notice requirement was introduced into the metal trades agreement in 1926, and it is not common elsewhere. It has been interpreted as meaning that the shop steward must be kept on the job for the period of the notice, that is, that he may not be dismissed immediately with two months' pay. This is important in that the two-month period of notice provides an opportunity to litigate the discharge, particularly in view of the great reluctance of arbitrators and the Labor Court to order reinstatement of a shop steward whose employment has been severed physically.

demonstrate the legitimacy of the discharge. But it is not true, as often believed, that the shop steward is the last fired and the first rehired. There are many circumstances under which a shop steward may be discharged before other workers; his protection, while considerable, is by no means absolute.

Among the individual grounds for discharge that have been the subject of litigation are the following:

1. Unsatisfactory work. Failure to perform his ordinary duties in a manner satisfactory to the employer may provide a "compelling reason" for his discharge. However, minor lapses are not sufficient cause, the practice being to require proof of serious deficiency.

2. Breach of discipline. Because of his privileged position, the shop steward owes a particular duty to observe the disciplinary rules of the establishment. Such actions as the repeated use of improper language toward management representatives, the violation of safety regulations, and improper loitering in washrooms after prior warning have been held to constitute valid grounds for discharge.

3. Dishonesty. The discharge of a shop steward on the ground that he had falsified his piece work records was upheld.

4. Refusal to perform work. The shop steward must perform the work to which he is directed by the management. However, the work must be within the normal compass of his duties; for example, when a shop steward was ordered to remove from the wall of the company rest room a socialist campaign placard that he had affixed, an arbitrator held that this "did not involve the performance of work falling within the activities of the establishment, but rather a disciplinary demand that George Larsen should make reparation for an act considered by management to constitute a breach of discipline . . . Larsen's refusal to accede to the demand cannot be regarded as a refusal to work, under the circumstances . . . and his conduct must be viewed in the light of the fact that he felt himself called upon to protect the interests of the workers in the dispute over whether the workers or management should determine what posters were to be affixed in the rest room." [30]

5. The duty to work for good industrial relations. The shop steward may not with impunity foment or engage in a strike action in violation of contract. Even mere passivity may be dangerous, since the shop steward has the positive obligation of preventing unlawful strikes. There are also other categories of conduct, in addition to strike action, that may manifest a lack of will to coöperate. A threat against a foreman that the steward would force his discharge was held to be in violation of the duty to work for good relations. Advice to fellow workers to act in disregard

[30] Illum II, p. 109.

of contract terms, refusal to negotiate in accord with stipulated procedure, and insistence upon dealing with the owner of a firm in disregard of a duly authorized representative were all held to justify the discharge of shop stewards.

The best known discharge case arose out of a threatened strike in violation of contract at the Burmeister and Wain shipyard in Copenhagen, in 1934. The threat had been made against a long-standing background of friction between the management and the workers. In an effort to avert the strike, the chief shop steward requested the permission of management to meet with the other shop stewards during working hours. He held the meeting despite the refusal of management to grant permission, whereupon he was discharged. On appeal to an arbitrator, it was held that the shop steward was acting in conformance with his contractual obligations and that his discharge was unjustified.

6. Lack of work. If the discharge of a shop steward is motivated purely by business conditions, there is no right to receive notice. However, even in this case, the shop steward has acquired some degree of protection, for he is "the last to be discharged among the workers with whom he is on a par with respect to qualifications and seniority." [31]

In the event of a complete shutdown, there can of course be no question of the validity of a discharge. The same is true of the closing of a department in which the shop steward is employed. The fact that he represents workers in departments which are not closed down is not relevant, since there is generally no right of transfer if it means the displacement of other workers. A more difficult situation is a reduction in force within the department in which the shop steward is employed. If it is clear that the shop steward is less qualified than other workers, he may be discharged before them. While it is up to the employer to judge the relative qualifications of workers, his judgment may be challenged by the union if it considers that there has been discrimination against the shop steward, and in this event the employer must document his action. Only if he is able to do so will "compelling reasons" for the discharge be found to exist.

A shop steward may not demand that he be transferred to other work, even if he is fully qualified to perform it, if the transfer would lead to the displacement of another worker. However, if work within a department is more or less interchangeable, the employer may be required to retain the shop steward where no skill differences are involved.

There are two cases in which the discharge of shop stewards was upheld although they could have continued at their work, because their

[31] Illum II, p. 142.

retention would have necessitated the discharge of other workers whom the management considered more necessary to the establishment. But these are borderline circumstances, and the employer must present a very convincing case. As an arbitrator declared, "the firm cannot provide proof of its right to discharge a shop steward merely by alleging the necessity of reducing its staff . . . It must show that on specific grounds it is reasonable to discharge the shop steward, *e.g.*, out of regard for older workers, or because it might be necessary to place the shop steward on other work if he were retained." [32]

If it is customary for an establishment to lay off workers by seniority (contractual seniority is rarely found in Denmark), a shop steward may be discharged when his place on the roster is reached. But where seniority is not customarily taken into consideration, it may not be utilized *de novo* as the basis for discharging a shop steward:

The collective agreement contains no warrant to discharge the shop steward merely because he has less seniority than other workers in the employ of the firm. There may be occasions when partly out of regard for the workers themselves, and partly out of regard for the interests of the firm, it may be reasonable to retain an older, deserving and experienced worker in preference to a younger shop steward. In the present case, however, the shop steward was elected by the very older workers who are threatened with discharge. If, in such event, the management were permitted to discharge the shop steward as the youngest, he would not have the protection which it is the clear purpose of the contract to provide him.[33]

Rehiring of shop stewards

Upon lawful severance of his employment, the shop steward ceases to have any privileges attaching to his former office. There is no preferential right to be rehired, provided that his severance was final. Arbitrators have refused to distinguish between discharge and layoff, on the theory that even in the latter event, there is no legal right of rehire. However, there must always be good faith on the part of the employer, for a layoff designed to secure the dismissal of a particular shop steward constitutes an attack upon the very foundation of the institution.

There may be circumstances in which the shop steward retains a preferential employment right in the event of an interruption of work. This is the case when a plant closes down temporarily during vacation or for repairs and where there is an intention to resume work at the end of a stated period with the same staff. The case of a strike or lockout is more

[32] Illum II, p. 168.
[33] Illum II, p. 172.

doubtful, the weight of opinion leaning to the view that the shop steward status survives an interruption in work from this cause.

Remedies for unlawful discharge

Arbitration awards fall into three categories with respect to the remedies for unlawful discharge of shop stewards:

1. In the majority of cases, the shop steward is awarded damages, the amount usually falling between 100 and 1,000 kroner, and rarely exceeding two months' pay.

2. Where the shop steward has received notice, but is still on the job, the employer will be ordered to continue him in employment.

3. In only one case was an employer ordered to reinstate the shop steward.

The unwillingness of arbitrators, otherwise so solicitous of the rights of shop stewards, to utilize the remedy of reinstatement, is remarkable. The theoretical basis of this position was summarized by the Labor Court in the following terms: "It is well established in Danish law that no one, with respect to a contract for labor, whether for physical or mental work, can claim to enter upon or remain in employment against the will of the employer, the remedy for unlawful discharge being damages . . .[34]

The actual explanation must be sought elsewhere, however, for in other respects Danish labor law has displayed great flexibility and independence of formal legal maxims. Fundamentally, the reluctance to order reinstatement may be attributed to a desire to maintain harmony in the plant. That a shop steward has been singled out for discharge is evidence of a lack of good industrial relations, and his reinstatement would hardly be conducive to improvement. The acquiescence of the trade unions in this rule is a sign of strength rather than of weakness, for it indicates an absence of fear that the displacement of a shop steward may undermine the position of the union in the establishment.

The usual remedy for unlawful discharge is the award of damages, and even this may be minimal if, shortly after his discharge, the shop steward obtains other appropriate work. Arbitrators have no power to impose fines, but in a few cases involving gross contract breaches the Labor Court, contrary to its customary practice, accepted jurisdiction and imposed fines. In the Burmeister and Wain case, cited above, the company was fined 10,000 kroner for the unlawful discharge of shop stewards.

[34] Illum II, p. 199.

THE STATUS OF FOREMEN AND OFFICE WORKERS

History of organization

With industrial workers and employers well along the road to organization by 1900, the remaining nonagricultural employee groups began to feel the necessity of similar organization for the advancement of their economic interests. Even before 1900 several small associations of foremen had been formed, but the movement toward the organization of this group, most of whom had been recruited from the ranks of the industrial workers, first gained real impetus during the decade 1900 to 1910. At first, the purpose of the foremen's associations was primarily defensive in character, to preserve the neutrality of the foremen during labor disputes, and it was only later that collective bargaining became the major goal.

In 1910, four foremen's associations united in the formation of the Joint Council of Danish Foremen's Unions, which was joined subsequently by three other associations. The Joint Council now has a membership of 19,000 and includes the large majority of foremen in the industries it covers: building construction, shipping, the metal trades, textiles, and other manufacturing. During the first decade of the Council's existence, the Employers' Association adamantly refused to recognize it as the collective representative of its members, and it was not until 1920 that the first agreement, specifying general terms of employment and recognizing the neutrality of foremen in labor disputes was reached.[35] Because of Section 5 of the September Agreement, affording salaried foremen full liberty to remain outside trade unions, the unions have never attempted to force foremen to join them.[36]

Collective agreements are now concluded between the affiliates of the Joint Council and the corresponding affiliates of the Employers' Association. Normally for one- or two-year terms, the agreements usually specify merely that rates of pay must bear a proper relationship to wages of ordinary workers, with the actual rates being determined through individual bargaining. Machinery for processing grievances is also provided in the agreements. Strikes have been rare; there have been a few among the seagoing members, and an occasional building job has been declared unfair, but in most cases differences are adjusted amicably.

[35] For the details of the negotiations leading to the agreement, see *Dansk Arbejdsgiverforenings Virksomhed*, 1919, pp. 87–88.

[36] The neutral status of foremen has been strengthened by decisions of the Labor Court to the effect that the protection given foremen by the September Agreement is contingent upon their refraining from acting as strikebreakers.

The Joint Council is nonpolitical despite the fact that many of its members, as ex-workers, are socialists.

In recent years price inflation has led to dissatisfaction among foremen with respect to wages. Before 1940 there had been a customary differential of approximately 30 per cent between the wages of foremen and workers. Because of the practice of paying foremen and workers the same absolute cost of living supplements, this differential has fallen to between 20 and 25 per cent. Foremen have another grievance in that the higher paid among them are excluded from membership in the state supported unemployment insurance funds.

White-collar employees lagged behind the foremen in their organizational efforts, and it was not until the inflation following the first World War that associations of any consequence were formed among this group. Until 1932 the principal white-collar organization, the Commercial and Office Employees' Union, refused any connection with the labor movement, but in that year the Union voted to affiliate with the Federation of Labor. At present, with a membership of almost 60,000, it is one of the largest national unions in the country.

The Employers' Association long refused to enter into any negotiations with the Commercial Union, although contracts were obtained with an independent association of commercial employers, the *Principalforening*. Affiliation with the Federation of Labor broke down employer resistance, however, and the Association of Employers of Commercial and Office Workers was formed, membership in which is obligatory for all members of the Employers' Association contracting with the Commercial Union. Since the September Agreement does not apply to white-collar workers, the organizations, in 1939, concluded a master agreement modeled upon the September Agreement. This was supplemented in 1945 with a standard collective agreement for small employers, obviating the necessity of negotiating separate contracts for each separate establishment.

There are in addition to the Commercial Union a number of smaller independent organizations catering to narrow occupational groups. There is a Bank Employees' Union with 5,000 members; an Insurance Employees' Secretariat, with 2,000; an Association of Savings Banks Employees, with 1,000. Together with similar groups, these organizations federated in 1945 in the Central Association of Danish Employee Organizations, which has attained a membership of 13,000. The Central Association and the Joint Council work closely together, and have entered into a jurisdictional agreement to prevent competition.

The extent of organization among Danish foremen and white-collar workers has been estimated as follows for the year 1947:[37]

Total number (excluding civil servants)		180,000
Total organized employees		92,000
Commercial and Office Workers' Union	57,000	
Joint Council of Foremen's Unions	17,000	
Central Association of Employee Organizations	13,000	
Independent associations	5,000	
Total unorganized employees		88,000

This is the only area, apart from agriculture, in which the Danish labor movement has an opportunity for expansion. And even here, the degree of organization already attained compares favorably with that in any other nation in which organization is voluntary.

The Employee Act[38]

A unique aspect of Danish labor law is the Employee Act, a statute regulating the employment of nonmanual employees. Enacted in 1938 and amplified by amendment in 1948, the legislation codified the more advanced practices of previous collective agreements. Neither the trade unions nor employers favored the legislation, the former because they preferred to work through collective bargaining and feared that special protective legislation would weaken the interest of nonmanual employees in organization; the latter because they preferred working within the context of the private employment contract. But neither could afford politically to antagonize this growing sector of the population, and they were forced to accede to the enactment of the legislation.

1. Coverage of the statute. The legislation applies to all commercial and office employees, persons engaged in technical and clinical work, and foremen and other supervisors, but specifically excludes civil servants. It is a necessary condition for coverage that an individual occupy a position of service and that he be subject to the instructions of an employer. Doubtful cases are resolved by the ordinary courts, which have jurisdiction over disputes arising under the statute, to the exclusion of the Labor Court.

2. Discharge notice. The framework about which the statute is built is mandatory advance notice of discharge. Persons employed in an establishment for six months or less are entitled to discharge notice of one month; persons employed in an establishment for more than six months are entitled to three months' notice, plus one additional month for each three years of employment, up to a maximum of six months' notice. No notice is necessary, however, in the case of employment of less than three months' duration for temporary or trial work. On the

[37] O. Bouet, *Privatfunktionaerstanden* (Copenhagen, 1948), p. 18.

[38] For the details of this legislation and its interpretation by the courts, see O. Bendik Elmer, *Funktionaerloven* (Copenhagen, 1948).

other side, an employee is required to inform the employer one month in advance of his intention to quit, and even longer notice may be provided by written contract if the employer correspondingly augments the mandatory minimum term of notice. No notice is necessary in the event of a labor dispute, apart from the customary strike notice.

The remedies available to an employee if the employer fails to give the prescribed notice fall into two categories: (a) if at the time of the discharge the employee has a right to a maximum of three months' notice, he is entitled to compensation equal to his full salary up to the day on which his employment could lawfully have been terminated; (b) if at the time of the discharge the employee has a right to more than three months' notice, compensation is determined according to the ordinary rules of torts, with the minimum equal to full pay corresponding to three months' notice. Similar rules apply where an employee is forced to leave his employment as a consequence of gross violation of contract by the employer. The significance of the distinction between the two methods of compensating employees lies in the employment experience of the discharged employee subsequent to the discharge. If he secures new and equivalent employment immediately, he is entitled to three months' severance pay, but no more, despite the length of notice to which he has a formal right. To secure in excess of three months' pay, the employee must have suffered economic loss beyond three months of unemployment. The law thus compromises between the protection of the employee and the avoidance of encouragement to idleness.

If it is the employee who fails to give the specified notice, or if he is discharged for gross violation of his contract, the employer is entitled to compensation for any loss suffered therefrom, with a minimum equal to half a month's wages of the offending employee, unless "special circumstances" militate to the contrary. For example, if an adequate replacement can be secured with no difficulty, or where failure to conform with the notice requirement is merely a formal lapse, the employer may not receive any compensation at all. As a practical matter, it is difficult for the employer to collect more than the minimum.

3. Illness, military service, maternity, death. As a general rule, an employee who is absent from work as a consequence of illness can be discharged only after the ordinary period of notice. However, in order to prevent obstacles to the hiring of older workers, the law provides that the employer and the employee may enter into a written agreement limiting the period of notice of discharge to one month when an employee has received at least 120 days of pay while ill during a period of 12 consecutive months. No notice is required when the employee fraudulently conceals the fact of a chronic illness at the time he is hired, or when the illness is due to his own gross negligence, for example, injuries sustained as a result of drunken driving.

To enable the employer to decide whether or not to retain a sick employee, it is provided that in an illness exceeding 14 days in duration, the employer has the right to seek information regarding the employee's condition from the latter's physician and also to have the employee examined by a specialist, at the expense of the employer. Refusal of the employee to accede to these requirements may justify immediate discharge without notice.

When an employee is called up for his first period of compulsory military service, he may be discharged, but only after the standard notice period. However, the employee is under an obligation to notify the employer of the call-up date as soon as he receives definite word, failure to do so justifying the termination of employment on the call-up date without notice. If the employer does not exercise his option of terminating the employment relationship, the employee may resume his former employment at the end of the period of service, though he may be discharged at any time thereafter, with notice. There is no claim for wages during the initial period of military service. For subsequent tours of duty, however, the employer is required to pay full salary for the month in which the call-up occurs and the following month.

Regardless of contractual provisions to the contrary, the marriage of a female employee does not give an employer the right to discharge her without notice. During pregnancy, the employee is required to inform the employer, at least three months before the anticipated birth, of that fact; if she does not do so, she may be discharged on the date of incapacity to work, without notice. When due notice is given, there must be the standard discharge notice, and if the employer elects to retain the employee, he must pay one-half the salary during the period of incapacity, which has a maximum limit of three months before and one month after the birth of a child.

The death of an employee entitles the widow or dependent children to one, two, or three months' wages, depending upon the length of service of the employee in the same establishment. Dependent children of female employees have the same rights. Thus, termination notice is regarded as a property right rather than as a mere personal privilege.

4. The right to organize. While the Commercial Employees' Union, as a matter of principle, opposed enactment into law of the foregoing provisions, it favored the following section on account of the resistance of many employers to the organization of their white-collar employees:

Employees have the right to organize to protect their interests and to give information to organizations concerning their own wages and working conditions.

Every work force, regardless of size, has the right through its organization to demand negotiations with management on wages and other conditions of labor.

The law further provides, through an amendment adopted in 1948, that in the event of failure to agree in direct negotiations, either side may demand further negotiation with the assistance of a mediator, appointed in Copenhagen by the Labor Court and elsewhere by the county prefect. The mediator may presumably submit mediation proposals, though his precise functions are not codified and have not yet developed through actual experience.

There are a number of additional features of the Employee Act, but those outlined above constitute the major items of general import. It should be emphasized that there is no attempt anywhere in the statute to require an employer, against his will, to retain an employee. Discharge is always lawful provided that appropriate notice has been given. The principal purpose of the statute is to afford to all white-collar employees protection against discharge without prior warning.

GOVERNMENT EMPLOYEES

It should come as no surprise that Danish government employees, in common with the other economic groups in the population, are well organized. The government employees are divided into two distinct categories from the point of view of their employment status: ordinary workers in such enterprises as state-owned railways and navy yards, and civil servants proper. The former are organized within the regular trade unions, though often in separate departments, and their terms of employment are regulated by collective agreement between the unions and the employing enterprises. The agreements follow closely the wage provisions contained in private industry agreements for comparable work, though they are usually more liberal with respect to such fringe items as pensions and sick pay. This group enjoys a full right to strike and falls under the general mediation law.

The working conditions of civil servants, however, are determined by statute.[39] The civil servants are organized into separate trade unions, most of them affiliated with the Federation of Labor. The so-called Central Organization I caters to the lower echelons — postmen, laborers — while Central Organization II includes the middle bureaucracy. The

[39] See Ulrik Andersen og Hugo Engmann, *Tjenestemands Loven* (Copenhagen, 1948).

highest stratum, judges, engineers, and lawyers, have their own associations which are not in the Federation of Labor.

The Civil Service Act applies the principle of exclusive representation to each department within a ministry that is specified as a bargaining unit. To qualify as the exclusive agent, a local union must be open to all employees within the department and to no others, and it must represent a majority of the constituents. Local unions are permitted to federate, the Central Organizations constituting the major federations; federations receive recognition from the Ministry of Finance, which supervises the Act, to represent larger groups of employees.

The representative agencies of the employees are entitled as a matter of legal right to receive in advance of their effectuation proposed alterations in the law or regulations which will change wages and other working conditions. The organizations may negotiate with government representatives on these questions, as well as upon any other matters relating to employment conditions, with the exception of the employment and discharge of individuals. If satisfaction is not obtained during negotiations, the matter may be taken up to the responsible minister. A tripartite arbitration board has been established to determine procedural controversies, but it has no authority over substantive issues.

The wages of civil servants are fixed by law, so that basic changes must be sought through political means. Since 1919, civil service wages have been subject to regulation on the basis of a cost of living index. At present, the adjustment is made semiannually in the form of a complicated system of supplements to legally specified wage brackets.

To resign from a civil service position, an employee is required to give three months' notice. Theoretically, civil servants may not participate in collective work stoppages, though there is nothing to prevent individuals from giving notice of resignation at the same time. The effect of resignation is to terminate completely the civil service status, with loss of accumulated pension and other rights. Consequently, it is virtually impossible to secure collective action by the civil servants. However, the negotiation rules, the cost of living adjustments, and the fact that for the past few decades a socialist administration generally sympathetic to the claims of civil servants has been in office, have obviated the necessity of direct action to protect the economic standards of the civil servants.

PART FOUR

CONCLUSION

CHAPTER XII

THE FUTURE OF THE LABOR RELATIONS SYSTEM

For the past fifty years, the Danish system of industrial relations has provided the country a degree of freedom from labor conflict that is impressive when the strength of the trade union movement and contemporary events elsewhere in Europe are taken into consideration. The major elements of the system and the economic and political background which conditioned it have been described. It remains now to consider whether, with modification, present-day Danish labor relations can survive the changes that are slowly but surely affecting western democratic society.

This appraisal falls into two major categories. First, it is germane to inquire whether contemporary political and economic forces are of such a character as to threaten the very foundations of the system, or whether, on the contrary, these forces will permit continuation of the gradual evolution that has hitherto characterized the development of labor relations in Denmark. Second, if it is concluded that the outlook is for retention of the existing system in substantially its present form, the focus of the inquiry shifts to the internal points of stress and the remedial action that has been suggested to overcome the deficiencies.

ECONOMIC DEVELOPMENTS

While Denmark was by no means the first of the continental European countries to become industrialized, the industrialization process did take place at an early enough period to afford the country some of the advantages that accrue from an early start.[1] But there are indications that the

[1] Denmark preceded Norway and Sweden in the transformation of its economy from an agricultural to an industrial status, for example. Professor Montgomery has noted, in commenting on Swedish developments, that "it was first at the end of the nineteenth and the beginning of the twentieth centuries that industrial techniques had developed so far that the natural resources of Norway and Sweden could be utilized. Through the pulp and paper industry, the forests could be used in a considerably more effective manner than previously. Through the growth of the technology of electricity, it became possible to exploit our great reserves of water power, while at the same time the expansion of the metallurgical industries abroad increased the demand for our iron ore. Denmark's principal natural resource was its fertile soil, and this could be exploited at an earlier stage in economic development." Arthur Montgomery, *Industrialismens Gennombrott i Sverige* (Stockholm, 1947), p. 185.

advance of Danish industry has failed to keep pace with corresponding developments in other countries and that, for example, the Norwegian and Swedish industrial economies have drawn ahead of the Danish, in terms of magnitude and productivity. Thus in 1949, net output of industry (manufacturing, mining, handicrafts, and building) as a percentage of the national income was only 32 per cent in Denmark compared with 46 per cent for Norway and 56 per cent for Sweden.[2] The Danish factory is the smallest in Scandinavia,[3] and its energy consumption relatively low. Moreover, to judge by recent investment[4] and productivity data,[5] the Danish industrial economy is the least dynamic of the three.

The causes of the Danish industrial lag are complex, involving such diverse factors as the nature of the country's natural resources and the importance and character of agriculture. A serious obstacle to efficient production in Denmark has been the wide assortment of products that are customarily manufactured for a small domestic market, unlike Norway and Sweden, where the major manufacturing industries produce for an international market. Swedish industrial development and to a somewhat lesser extent that of Norway have been sparked by favorable demand and price conditions for exports, whereas Denmark, since 1930, has been faced with an unfavorable gap between import and export prices.

Part of the Danish problem is certainly the entrepreneurial and trade union psychology that I have elsewhere termed "the spirit of corporatism." The favorable aspect of this phenomenon is that it has contributed greatly to the growth of an excellent industrial relations system. But the lack of strong competition among businessmen for control of markets,

[2] United Nations, *Economic Survey of Europe in 1949*, p. 21.

[3] In 1948, the number of workers per factory in Danish establishments employing more than five workers was 30.0. The comparable figure for Norway was 32.3 (1947), and for Sweden, 36.7 (1946). These figures are not to be confused with average employment in *all* factories, cited above, p. 9.

[4] The relative investment levels of the Scandinavian countries are shown by the following figures:

Net Investment in Fixed Capital, Per Head of Population
(1938 dollars)

	1938	*1947*	*1948*	*1949*
Denmark	27	29	27	32
Norway	41	52	50	59
Sweden	33	52	44	36

Percentage of Net National Income, at Factor Cost, Devoted to Domestic Capital Formation (Net)

	1938	*1947*	*1948*	*1949*
Denmark	9	9	10	12
Norway	15	23	23	26
Sweden	12	16	13	10

Source: United Nations, *Economic Survey of Europe in 1949*, pp. 23, 39.

[5] See above, p. 166.

and the substitution for it of price and market agreements, are not conducive to industrial efficiency and expansion. Norwegian and Swedish industrialists were forced, as were the Danish farmers, to keep abreast of technical and productive developments in competing countries, but the Danish entrepreneurs could divide up the sheltered domestic market and continue to produce as they had in the past. The acceptance by Danish employers of nationwide collective bargaining reflects a desire to stabilize prices by the removal of wages as a competitive cost factor.

For their part, the trade unions have abetted restriction and contributed to the failure of industrial productivity to rise more sharply by insisting upon the maintenance of an archaic labor market structure. The compartmentalization of the labor market into small, exclusive units augmented the monopoly power of the unions, but it also led to the underutilization of manpower resources.

The contemporary economic crisis in Denmark, which is reflected in a continuing deficit in the balance of payments, has led many to question the restrictions that prevail in the nation's economic organization. Antitrust legislation has been enacted, and labor market organization is under study by the parliament. But it seems likely that if any radical changes take place, they will do so as a result of government regulation rather than through free enterprise initiative. The danger to continuance of the centralized labor relations system lies not in heightened doses of competition among entrepreneurs, but rather in the possibility of economic planning.

At the present time, the Danish economy more closely conforms to the ideals of *laissez faire* than those of Norway and Sweden. The principal restriction is that on imports. Though the free list has been gradually widened since the war to include such important investment goods as animal feed, iron and steel, fuel, and chemicals, the government possesses considerable regulatory power through its control of a long list of other producer and consumer goods. But this authority is not sufficient to provide the government with the means to direct the economy of the country in any fundamental fashion. In issuing a so-called national budget for 1950, the government noted that the document was "even more than its two predecessors, a prognosis of coming developments. This is connected with the fact that the government's possibilities of taking direct regulatory action are much less now that not only a major part of the foreign trade has been liberalized, but the scope of domestic restrictions — rationing schemes, allocation systems and price regulation — has been reduced very considerably."[6]

The outlook for a greater degree of direct economic planning is con-

[6] *Economic Survey of Denmark*, 1950, p. 48.

tingent mainly on developments outside Denmark. If the foreign exchange position of the country should continue to be critical, it is not unlikely that the government will have to interfere more positively in the allocation of resources. The Social Democratic Party would have liked to move in this direction before, but it has been held in check by a lack of parliamentary strength combined with seemingly favorable foreign trade developments. To judge by the experience of other countries, the introduction of genuine economic planning would operate with devastating effect upon the substance of collective bargaining, even though it might prove expedient to retain its formalities.

POLITICAL DEVELOPMENTS

The political history of twentieth century Denmark has been characterized chiefly by the rise of social democracy to power. The appended figures[7] show the expansion of the industrial and the decline of the nonindustrial sectors of the population, the major factor in the growth of socialist political power. The relevant question is whether continuation of this trend is to be anticipated.

There is no simple or certain answer. The important variables are the extent to which there is continued augmentation of the industrial sector of the population and the extent to which the socialists can make headway among farmers and white-collar workers. In the latter connection, the socialist parties of Norway and Sweden owe their critical margins of parliamentary strength to the support they have gained among small farmers, by playing upon the divergent economic interests of the subsistence and capitalist farm producers. In Denmark, where practically all farmers produce for export, regardless of size, the socialists have been unable to win over any appreciable number of farm votes. The Danish farmers' party is far stronger than the Norwegian and Swedish, even though the gainfully employed agricultural population of Norway is relatively greater than that of Denmark and the Swedish agricultural percentage not much smaller than the Danish.[8]

[7] The percentage division of the population by occupational groups, for the major categories, was as follows:

	1901	*1921*	*1930*	*1940*
Agriculture	38.1	33.3	30.0	27.7
Manufacturing, building, transportation	34.8	36.0	36.1	39.9
Trade and commerce	8.8	10.0	10.8	12.6

Source: K. Vedel-Petersen, *op. cit.*

[8] The Danish farmers' party (*Venstre*) won 21 per cent of the total popular vote in the 1950 general elections. The comparable figures for Norway and Sweden are 5 per cent and 12 per cent, respectively, in the most recent general elections.

The prospects for splitting the Danish farm vote are not bright. Unless the Danish socialists are able to win over the nonmanual employees who now support the Radical (Liberal) and Conservative parties, the most plausible hypothesis is that their share of the total electorate will stabilize at about the present level of 40 per cent, with some slow growth as the industrial working class increases in relation to the population. This percentage is sufficient to give the socialists by far the largest parliamentary representation of all the parties, and to make it difficult, if not impossible, to govern Denmark without their consent. But because of the proportional representation system employed in Danish elections, the socialists cannot hope for an independent parliamentary majority without a very considerable increase in their popular vote;[9] they must continue to cooperate with the parliamentary political groups with whom they are in sharp disagreement on the major issue of economic planning and control.

Danish trade unions must therefore continue to formulate their policy upon the assumption that they will operate for the indefinite future under an economic system in which collective bargaining will play its traditional role in determining the wage level. The fact that the political party with which they are allied, the socialist party, will probably constitute the parliamentary opposition to the government in power, or at best succeed in forming an unstable minority government, is of the utmost significance. Unlike their confreres in the other Scandinavian countries, the Danish trade unions cannot utilize other economic variables, such as taxation and price control, in the pursuit of their goals, but are largely limited to wage policy in their efforts to alter the distribution of income in favor of the workers. By the same token, collective bargaining over wages retains its focal interest for employers, whose profits are directly contingent upon the outcome.

The Danish labor unions have not yet had to face, as have the Norwegian and Swedish unions, the impact upon their traditional functions of a new type of economy characterized by rigid price stabilization, the equalization of real incomes through price subsidies and heavily progressive taxation, and the maintenance of full employment through a combination of direct government investment and low interest rates.[10] They have not had to attempt the task of reconciling rank-and-file pressure for higher money wages with the requirement that the total wage bill conform to the amount allocated to consumption in a national plan. Nevertheless, the rise of political socialism has had an inevitable effect

[9] The 1950 general elections gave the Social Democratic Party 59 out of 149 seats in the lower house. Even if they had captured all 7 seats won by the Communist Party, they would have fallen short of the requisite majority of 75 seats.

[10] The effective interest rate on government obligations at the end of 1949 was 4.4 per cent in Denmark compared with 2.5 per cent in Norway and 3 per cent in Sweden.

upon habits of thought and actual policy. The changing outlook was forecast in 1937 by Prime Minister Stauning when he wrote:

> The activities of the trade unions shall continue, but adjustment to the new times is necessary. It is another society that we live in than that which existed when the labor movement was in its infancy. The working class has moved forward to power and responsibility, but just for that reason it is essential that the leaders of the trade unions take a broad view of the economic and industrial situation, that they understand how to exploit all available opportunities, including political activity, to further the interests of the workers.[11]

The necessity for heightened trade union responsibility has been echoed by union leaders on many subsequent occasions. The chairman of the Federation of Labor declared recently, for example: "The trade unions have taken a broad social point of view. We know very well that one should not saw off the branch on which he is sitting, and we have therefore made ourselves the spokesmen for increasing output, strengthening industry, and increasing export possibilities and therefore imports and production for the home market."[12]

The fact that there have been labor governments in Denmark, though only minority ones, in which trade union leaders occupied ministerial posts, is of great psychological importance in affording the unions a sense of security and in lessening tensions between workers and employers. There are few events that have done more to break down the undeniable class antipathies and distinctions that prevailed in Denmark, as in most of Europe. A labor government affords the trade union leadership the possibility of escaping from a narrow wage functionalism and of experimenting with other means of improving labor standards, experiments which might otherwise not be tolerated by a rank and file impatient for immediate money wage gains. New vistas are opened for the labor leader whose prestige and political life were theretofore dependent upon the outcome of the year's collective bargaining results.

There are signs that the Danish trade unions are undergoing a process of "socialization." The Federation of Labor has been drawn increasingly into a number of joint ventures with employers and the government, the objects of which are to further the general welfare rather than merely the parochial interests of the wage earner. In 1947, for example, the Federation of Labor and the Employers' Association concluded an agreement providing for the establishment of labor-management production committees, which have been taken more seriously by the Danish trade unions than is true of most of the other European countries in which similar

[11] *Fagbevaegelsen og De Økonomiske Problemer*, p. 32.
[12] *Arbejderen*, June 1, 1950, p. 131.

bodies have been set up. The Danish unions have been active in spreading information relating to rationalization and more effective production among their members. The Federation is participating in a Labor Market Commission, the purpose of which is to consider means of improving the utilization of manpower with special reference to the closed jurisdictions of the skilled crafts, and in a Productivity Commission, which has the task of weighing measures suggested for increasing industrial productivity. Similar joint or tripartite commissions have dealt with such problems as the length and seasonality of vacations, hours of work, and the validity of the cost of living index.

These ventures into a wider sphere of social activity do not represent for the Danish unions as much of a break with the past as would be true, for example, in the United States. From their earliest days, they displayed great interest in various membership benefit schemes, including the establishment of a union unemployment insurance system. But the Danish unions are moving into new areas, notably that of increasing production, which were previously considered antithetical, or at best, peripheral, to their interests. Even without the subordination of wage determination to national economic planning, the Danish labor movement has moved a considerable way toward welfare unionism.

THE COLLECTIVE BARGAINING SYSTEM

Though there are corrosive forces at work, the collective bargaining system of Denmark is quite stable, and a consideration of its future far from academic. Both labor and management agreed, as part of the 1950 general wage settlement, to the establishment of a joint committee looking toward revision of the bargaining procedure in the light of recognized defects:

> Negotiations between local organizations with regard to contract demands begin too late, and
>
> The time that is left to the central organizations for negotiating is therefore too short, with the result that they cannot conclude their negotiations within the time stipulated in the procedural rules, the middle of February; this year, for example, they first ended their work after March 1, so that mediation proceedings were delayed . . .[13]

The trade unions have expressed interest in eliminating the requirement that all contract demands be specified in full by December 1, for reasons already set forth.[14] The Employers' Association has suggested, as a means of sloughing off the tremendous amount of detail with which

[13] *Maeglingsforslag fra Forligsmanden*, March 21, 1950, p. 46.

[14] See above, p. 107.

the central negotiating committee presently has to deal, the compulsory arbitration of an agreed range of subject matter in the event that direct bargaining proves futile. Presumably there would be a joint board to determine whether specific items in dispute were of the category that the parties had agreed to arbitrate. Major wage questions would *not* be included among the arbitrable issues under this plan.

Both proposals attest to the necessity of somehow making local bargaining more effective on matters of purely local import, of reversing the continuing trend toward the centralization of bargaining. But whether it proves possible to do so without at the same time decentralizing collective bargaining on major wage issues remains to be seen. Theoretically, the parties already have ample opportunity to settle the narrower issues at the local level; that they have not done so in an effective manner attests to the interdependence of all aspects of the collective agreement. The Danish system, as it is presently constructed, presupposes that minor and local issues will be settled in advance of the major wage questions, whereas in actual practice the former category of issues has proved stubborn in the absence of agreement upon the latter.

There has been growing annoyance among the stronger national unions at the limitations placed upon their individual bargaining power by the necessity of carrying along weaker unions. It will be recalled that centralized bargaining was never the free choice of trade unions, but rather was forced upon them by the Employers' Association's bargaining tactics. The 1950 congress of the Laborers' Union adopted the following resolutions, attesting to restiveness in this regard:

> Since the recent negotiations have demonstrated that the steadily increasing mass of disputed issues cannot satisfactorily be handled under the auspices of the mediation institution, particularly when price lists and local issues are involved, it is essential that the mediation law be subjected to thoroughgoing revision. In the same connection, there is reason to protest against the current voting rules which deprive the individual union of the right and possibility independently to determine the wage and working conditions of its members.

Even stronger was a resolution passed by the 1950 congress of the Metal Workers' Union, the other powerful affiliate of the Federation of Labor:

> The Congress instructs the executive committee to seek to secure the adoption of measures which will make it possible for the metal trades contracts not to be involved in the general settlement. The Congress suggests that the negotiating rules of 1936 and the September Agreement be amended to pave the way for separate contract renewal in the metal trades. Since all workers in the metal trades are now affiliated with the Metal Trades Department, with which

the Metal Trades Employers' Association concludes a master agreement, it should be possible to bargain without interference from the outside.

This suggestion from the Metal Workers' Union, long a proponent of greater centralization, must be read against the background of the "elastic" wage system prevailing in the metal trades. In the 1950 wage negotiations, for example, the union made no request for a general wage increase, but concentrated rather upon hours of work and vacation pay. The remaining unions, with no opportunity to receive intra-contract period wage changes, favored a general wage increase, with the result that the Metal Workers' Union was forced to accept a wage settlement which meant less to its members than an adjustment in hours and vacation pay. The employers opposed concessions to the Metal Workers along the lines of their special interests lest such concessions subsequently be demanded by other unions as well.

Separate settlements of the nature envisioned by the Metal Workers' Union could be rendered feasible only if both central organizations forbore from the use of the sympathetic strike or lockout as a means of policing the general wage settlement. The chairman of the Metal Workers' Union asserted recently that the trade union movement "has not kept up with the times in its organizational structure, and it is perhaps correct to try to abolish the right to declare sympathetic strikes and lockouts, a contributing cause to the inability of the Metal Trades Department to conclude its agreements separately."[15] But he evoked little sympathy among the other unions. The chairman of the Laborers' Union, despite his critical attitude toward some of the details of the bargaining procedure, stated that "the smaller and weaker organizations could not get anything if the right to declare sympathetic strikes were abolished, and they were forced to bear the full burden of their disputes alone . . ."[16] while the chairman of the Federation of Labor declared flatly: "We will not give up the right to the sympathetic strike. That is too dangerous."[17]

But even if additional support for the idea could be obtained within the labor movement — and it is likely that other of the stronger crafts, because of their monopolistic positions, would welcome independent bargaining — it is highly unlikely that the Employers' Association would consent to waive its right to the sympathetic lockout. To do so would constitute an open invitation to the unions to institute "leapfrog" bargaining tactics, whereby agreements obtained first from weak employers or employer associations would be used as levers to obtain similar terms from other employers subsequently. The sympathetic lockout has always

[15] *Arbejderen,* June 1, 1950, p. 135.
[16] *Ibid.,* p. 136.
[17] *Ibid.,* p. 137.

been the ultimate weapon against a powerful labor movement, backing up employer refusal finally to conclude any agreements until all were in order. It is therefore improbable that there will be any fundamental change in the bargaining system in the direction of decentralization.

The stability of the collective bargaining system is threatened from another, and perhaps more serious source, government intervention. Despite the numerous past occasions on which government compulsion was employed to prevent work stoppages (and it may be remarked parenthetically that on some of these occasions the government was acting on behalf of negotiators who had reached agreement but were unable publicly to espouse it for tactical reasons), the heart of the collective bargaining system lies in the possibility that there may be an ultimate resort to economic force. With the exception of the Radical Party, no political group in Denmark favors compulsory arbitration of all labor disputes. Employers and trade unions are equally fervent in their disavowal of such means of resolving their differences.

Government labor market intervention was initially a product of Denmark's critical balance of payments problem in the early 1930's, and it may be wondered whether continuation of this problem will not result in the regularization of what hitherto has been an *ad hoc* procedure. Every separate instance of government intervention has been premised, with considerable justification, on the grave danger to the Danish economy that would flow from a stoppage of work. For the forseeable future, the same considerations are likely to prevail.

But it is highly improbable that there will be any attempt to formalize government intervention into an explicit system of compulsory arbitration. As long as workers and employers retain the conviction that they are living under voluntary bargaining and that government intervention is an emergency measure invoked only after careful consideration of each case, there is no reason why present bargaining procedures should not continue to function successfully. Only if the repeated use of government power gives rise to an expectation of its inevitable application will the voluntary system begin to crumble. Future governments may have to weigh carefully the considerable social cost of this contingency against the alternative cost of an occasional strike or lockout.

CONCLUSION

The problems discussed in the foregoing pages are not unique to Denmark. They are shared more or less by the entire Western world. Though the expression of the problems varies from country to country, they have a common origin — the growth of an industrial labor force, its increasing political power, and the inability of economic systems which have been disrupted by two wars to produce sufficient goods to satisfy the material aspirations of the workers. The specific Danish approach to a solution of these problems is unique. But this cannot be attributed simply, as is often done, to the peculiarities of the Danish (or French or British or German) character and mentality. It should be abundantly clear by now that the peaceful labor relations of Denmark have been rooted in the economic and political history of the country. Only a favorable conjuncture of factors permitted Denmark to escape much of the widespread industrial strife that has proved so costly to other nations.

It is therefore neither practicable nor desirable to attempt the literal transplantation of Danish labor institutions to an alien soil. Yet there is much to be learned from the Danish experience. Our own history and practices acquire new meaning when compared with those of a people who, like ourselves, have retained as an ideal the concept of individual freedom, and have not resorted to ruthless suppression of the rights of the individual as a means of solving economic problems. We can gain new ideas and insights into our own society.

Danish labor relations are not static, despite the remarkable stability they have shown during fifty years. There is at work the disruptive force of a labor movement which is still augmenting its power and seeking for its members a larger share of the national product and a higher social status. To judge by the past, however, achievement of these ends will be sought only through means that are consonant with political democracy. If there is any nation that can peacefully adjust the social conflict arising from industrialization, with equal regard to the welfare of the individual citizen, whether he be worker, farmer, or businessman, it is Denmark.

APPENDIXES

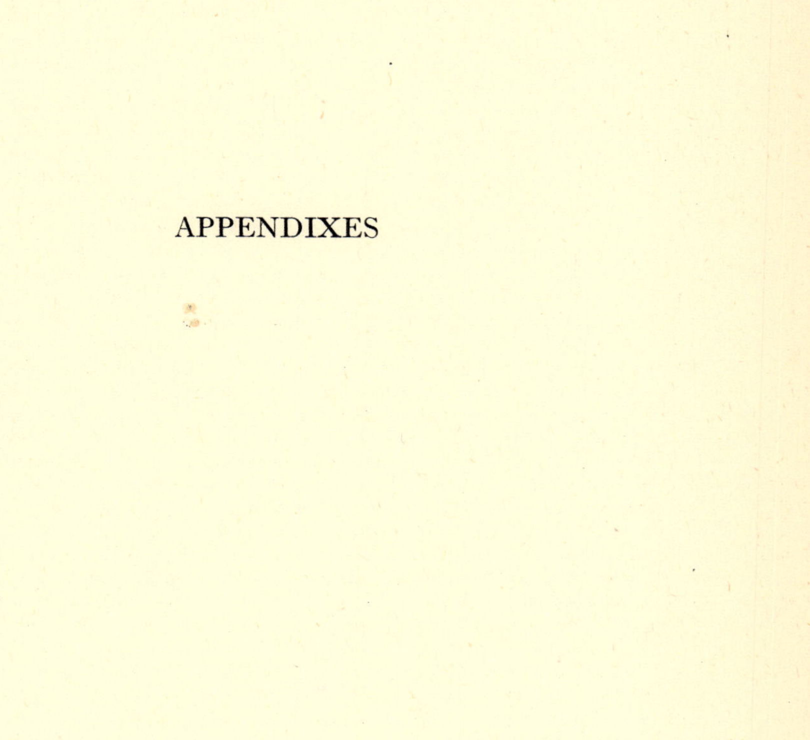

APPENDIX A

TABLE A1

Wages and Prices in Denmark, 1899–1949

(1) Year	(2) Average Hourly Earnings[a] (Øre)	(3) Index of Average Hourly Earnings (1914 = 100)	(4) Cost of Living Index[b] (1914 = 100)	(5) Index of Real Average Hourly Earnings (1914 = 100)	(6) Index of Wholesale Prices[c] (1913 = 100)
1899	30	62	77	81	81
1900	31	64	79	81	85
1901	32	66	79	84	82
1902	33	68	80	85	84
1903	34	70	80	88	81
1904	35	72	81	89	83
1905	36	75	81	93	85
1906	37	77	82	94	88
1907	39	81	85	95	91
1908	41	85	87	98	88
1909	43	89	88	101	89
1910	45	93	89	104	93
1911	47	97	90	108	95
1912	48	100	94	105	102
1913	49	101	97	104	100
1914	48.3	100	100	100	112
1915	49	101	116	87	141
1916	57	118	135	87	189
1917	64	133	155	86	252
1918	82	170	179	95	304
1919	143	296	215	138	326
1920	188	389	261	149	390
1921	181	375	232	162	224
1922	141	292	200	146	171
1923	136	282	206	137	186
1924	144	298	216	138	226
1925	150	311	211	147	210
1926	135	280	184	152	163
1927	129	267	177	151	153
1928	128	265	175	151	153
1929	128	265	173	153	150
1930	131	271	165	164	130
1931	131	271	155	175	114
1932	131	271	155	175	117

TABLE A1 (Continued)

(1) Year	(2) Average Hourly Earnings[a] (Øre)	(3) Index of Average Hourly Earnings (1914 = 100)	(4) Cost of Living Index[b] (1914 = 100)	(5) Index of Real Average Hourly Earnings (1914 = 100)	(6) Index of Wholesale Prices[c] (1913 = 100)
1933	131	271	159	170	125
1934	132	273	166	164	132
1935	133	275	171	161	135
1936	132	273	174	157	143
1937	135	280	180	156	161
1938	142	294	183	161	152
1939	147	304	187	163	159
1940	163	337	234	144	232
1941	176	364	271	134	274
1942	184	381	281	136	288
1943	198	410	286	143	289
1944	210	435	288	151	293
1945	225	466	291	160	288
1946	245	507	289	175	284
1947	262	542	298	182	313
1948	283	586	305	192	343
1949	295	611	309	198	351

[a] Sources: 1899–1913, *Arbejdsgiverforening Gennem 50 Aar*, p. 363; 1914–1925, *Statistiske Meddelelser*, vol. 78, no. 1, p. 28; 1926–1931, *Statistiske Meddelelser*, vol. 91, no. 5, p. 19; 1932–1946, *Under Samvirkets Flag*, p. 376; 1947–1949, *Statistisk Årbog*, 1950.

This series is based upon quarterly reports submitted by members of the Danish Employers' Association. It has the following deficiencies: (1) It does not include workers not employed by members of the Employers' Association. However, several studies have indicated that wage movements (though not absolute wage levels) of the non-member group follow closely wage movements of the member firms. (2) Since it is based upon wages of employed workers, the craft weights are shifted depending upon relative employment in the craft. However, except for the years 1899 to 1913, the data in the table were corrected by the Statistical Department through the use of constant weights.

[b] Sources: 1899–1913, Knud Dalgaard, "Arbejderklassens Økonomiske Kaar i Danmark," *Nationaløkonomisk Tidsskrift*, 1926, p. 158; 1914–1949, publications of the Statistical Department.

The data prior to 1914 are not official, but the result of a private investigation. However, they are approximated by another careful examination of worker family budget changes for the period: Jørgen Pedersen, *Arbejdslønnen i Danmark* (1930), pp. 314–315.

[c] Sources: 1899–1912, Jens Warming, *Danmark's Erhvervs-og Samfundsliv* (Copenhagen, 1930), p. 104; 1913–1949, publications of the Statistical Department.

TABLE A2

UNEMPLOYMENT AND ANNUAL EARNINGS (CORRECTED) IN DENMARK, 1903–1949

(1) Year	(2) Per Cent of Unemployment among Trade Union Members[a]	(3) Average Annual Earnings of Fully Employed Workers ($303\frac{1}{2}$ Days)[b] (*Kroner*)	(4) Index of Real Annual Earnings of Fully Employed Workers[b] (*1914 = 100*)	(5) Average Annual Earnings Corrected for Loss Because of Unemployment, Sickness, and Labor Disputes[b] (*Kroner*)	(6) Index of Real Annual Earnings Adjusted for Losses[b] (*1914 = 100*)
1903	13	—	—	—	—
1904	12	—	—	—	—
1905	13	1,128	101	965	97
1906	6.12	1,141	101	1,015	100
1907	6.79	1,183	101	1,013	98
1908	10.95	1,205	100	1,026	96
1909	13.31	1,208	100	1,004	93
1910	11.40	1,238	101	1,053	96
1911	9.2	1,213	98	1,073	97
1912	7.5	1,259	97	1,138	98
1913	7.3	1,300	97	1,177	98
1914	9.9	1,378	100	1,232	100
1915	7.7	1,406	88	1,275	90
1916	4.9	1,526	87	1,511	91
1917	9.2	1,827	86	1,633	86
1918	17.4	2,339	95	1,866	85
1919	10.7	3,689	125	3,183	120
1920	6.1	4,565	127	4,138	129
1921	19.7	4,395	138	3,334	117
1922	19.3	3,423	124	2,544	104
1923	12.7	3,302	117	2,771	109
1924	10.7	3,496	118	3,042	114
1925	14.8	3,642	125	2,846	110
1926	20.7	3,278	129	2,521	111
1927	22.5	3,132	128	2,348	108
1928	18.5	3,108	129	2,466	114
1929	15.5	3,108	130	2,564	120
1930	13.7	3,181	140	2,686	133
1931	17.9	3,181	149	2,541	134
1932	31.7	3,181	149	2,102	110
1933	28.8	3,181	144	2,196	111
1934	22.1	3,205	140	2,435	119
1935	19.7	3,229	137	2,534	120
1936	19.3	3,205	134	2,435	113
1937	21.9	3,278	132	2,483	112
1938	21.3	3,448	137	2,601	115
1939	18.4	3,569	139	2,813	122
1940	23.9	3,958	123	2,900	101
1941	18.4	4,273	114	3,334	100

TABLE A2 (Continued)

(1) Year	(2) Per Cent of Unemployment among Trade Union Members[a]	(3) Average Annual Earnings of Fully Employed Workers ($303\frac{1}{2}$ Days)[b] (*Kroner*)	(4) Index of Real Annual Earnings of Fully Employed Workers[b] (*1914 = 100*)	(5) Average Annual Earnings Corrected for Loss Because of Unemployment, Sickness, and Labor Disputes[b] (*Kroner*)	(6) Index of Real Annual Earnings Adjusted for Losses[b] (*1914 = 100*)
1942	15.1	4,466	115	3,669	106
1943	10.7	4,807	122	4,246	120
1944	8.3	5,099	129	4,578	131
1945	13.4	5,463	136	4,615	129
1946	8.9	6,046	151	5,355	150
1947	8.9	6,361	155	n.a.	n.a.
1948	8.6	6,871	163	n.a.	n.a.
1949	9.6	7,115	167	n.a.	n.a.

[a] Source: *Under Samvirkets Flag*, pp. 412–413; *Statistiske Efterretninger*, *passim*. For the conceptual problems involved in this series, see K. Vedel-Petersen, *Danmarks Statistik*, pp. 415–417.

[b] Sources: 1905–1913, P. Andersen, *50 Aars Jubilaet Festskrift, Dansk Smede og Maskinarbejderforbund* (Copenhagen, 1938), p. 431; 1914–1946, *Under Samvirkets Flag*, pp. 376–377; 1947–1949, estimated from average hourly earnings on the basis of an eight-hour day. The data prior to 1914 are based upon the experience of the Metal Workers' Union, since data for all workers are not available. Actual earnings in the metal trades have been linked to the 1914 base for all workers.

TABLE A3

MEMBERSHIP IN DANISH TRADE UNIONS AND EMPLOYER ASSOCIATIONS, 1899–1949

(1) Year	(2) Membership in the Federation of Labor[a] (*Thousands*)	(3) Total Number of Trade Union Members[a] (*Thousands*)	(4) Number of Employers in the Employers' Association[b]	(5) Workers Employed by Members of the Employers' Association[b] (*Thousands*)
1899	75	89	5,272	48
1900	77	96	6,970	61
1901	73	95	7,191	57
1902	64	88	7,034	55
1903	63	86	6,829	55
1904	65	88	6,203	55
1905	69	88	6,277	61
1906	78	99	6,339	65
1907	91	112	6,703	66
1908	97	117	6,865	67
1909	99	120	7,434	67
1910	102	123	7,813	66
1911	105	128	8,304	69
1912	107	139	8,348	74
1913	115	153	8,480	83
1914	121	159	8,620	83
1915	132	173	8,845	93
1916	151	192	9,663	105
1917	179	224	11,279	105
1918	255	302	12,300	110
1919	277	359	15,910	128
1920	279	362	17,509	154
1921	244	323	18,177	116
1922	233	305	15,521	114
1923	233	303	14,539	129
1924	237	306	14,351	135
1925	240	310	13,019	119
1926	156	313	12,548	124
1927	156	310	12,339	115
1928	156	311	12,272	124
1929	250	328	12,198	143
1930	259	339	12,157	151
1931	270	354	12,163	144
1932	300	369	12,305	127
1933	302	404	12,413	143
1934	355	422	12,743	160
1935	381	438	13,252	171
1936	407	462	13,612	184
1937	452	491	14,246	190
1938	470	509	14,957	193
1939	500	538	15,540	215
1940	516	544	15,990	199

TABLE A3 (Continued)

(1) Year	(2) Membership in the Federation of Labor[a] (*Thousands*)	(3) Total Number of Trade Union Members[a] (*Thousands*)	(4) Number of Employers in the Employers' Association[b]	(5) Workers Employed by Members of the Employers' Association[b] (*Thousands*)
1941	527	551	16,250	211
1942	545	569	17,074	228
1943	564	588	17,735	247
1944	579	604	18,632	244
1945	604	630	19,362	222
1946	605	631	20,633	245
1947	614	640	21,849	265
1948	623	650	22,852	274
1949	636	664	23,675	285

[a] Source: *Under Samvirkets Flag*, pp. 558–559; *Statistisk Årbog*, 1950.
[b] Source: *Arbejdsgiverforeningen Gennem 50 Aar*, p. 363; *Statistisk Årbog*, 1950.

TABLE A4

STRIKES AND LOCKOUTS IN DENMARK, 1899–1949

(1) Year	(2) Number of Workers Affected by Strikes[a]	(3) Number of Workers Affected by Lockouts[a]	(4) Man-Days Lost Because of Labor Disputes[b] (*Thousands*)	(5) Ratio of Man-Days Lost to Potential Maximum Working Time of Trade Union Members[c]
1899	8,295	29,730	2,828	.1059
1900	7,126	480	218	.0076
1901	3,574	487	52	.0018
1902	3,745	97	133	.0050
1903	958	190	19	.0007
1904	1,855	698	69	.0026
1905	5,677	64	499	.0189
1906	3,787	654	68	.0023
1907	5,700	2,457	255	.0076
1908	3,481	4,119	85	.0024
1909	769	1,591	58	.0016
1910	1,681	797	61	.0017
1911	5,964	22,792	648	.0169
1912	2,048	2,067	50	.0012
1913	9,721	0	382	.0083
1914	3,349	19	56	.0011
1915	1,666	252	32	.0006
1916	14,318	8	241	.0042
1917	9,785	318	214	.0032
1918	9,385	381	194	.0021
1919	34,718	857	916	.0085
1920	19,129	2,836	1,306	.0120
1921	13,356	34,791	1,321	.0136
1922	640	48,219	2,272	.0248
1923	1,941	0	20	.0002
1924	8,993	765	175	.0019
1925	35,477	66,854	4,139	.0445
1926	975	75	23	.0002
1927	537	2,314	119	.0013
1928	469	0	11	.0001
1929	1,040	0	41	.0004
1930	5,349	0	144	.0014
1931	997	2,695	246	.0023
1932	516	5,240	87	.0008
1933	448	44	18	.0001
1934	10,816	730	146	.0012
1935	827	0	14	.0001
1936	403	96,459	2,946	.0213
1937	1,367	5	21	.0001
1938	3,645	5	90	.0006
1939	523	0	16	.0001
1940	257	0	5	.0000

TABLE A4 (Continued)

(1) Year	(2) Number of Workers Affected by Strikes[a]	(3) Number of Workers Affected by Lockouts[a]	(4) Man-Days Lost Because of Labor Disputes[b] (*Thousands*)	(5) Ratio of Man-Days Lost to Potential Maximum Working Time of Trade Union Members[c]
1941	65	0	3	.0000
1942	3,155	0	11	.0001
1943	14,627	168	31	.0002
1944	8,885	0	89	.0005
1945	9,656	0	66	.0003
1946	56,304	0	1,386	.0073
1947	16,174	0	473	.0025
1948	4,448	0	10	.0001
1949	n.a.	0	10	.0001

[a] Source: *Under Samvirkets Flag*, p. 560.

[b] Sources: 1899–1930, *Statistiske Meddelelser*, vol. 19, no. 6; *ibid.*, vol. 38, no. 3; *ibid.*, vol. 54, no. 2; *ibid.*, vol. 66, no. 2; *ibid.*, vol. 75, no. 5; *ibid.*, vol. 88, no. 5; 1931–1947, *Under Samvirkets Flag*, p. 560; 1948, *Statistisk Årbog*, 1950. For the years 1945 and thereafter, the data include only stoppages affecting members of the Employers' Association. The error resulting therefrom is small, however.

[c] Calculated as the ratio of total man-days lost because of labor disputes to the total number of trade union members multiplied by 300.

TABLE A5

WAGES, PRICES, AND LABOR DISPUTES IN NORWAY, 1899–1949

(1) Year	(2) Cost of Living Index[a] (*July 1914 = 100*)	(3) Index of Real Average Hourly Earnings, Male Workers[b] (*1914 = 100*)	(4) Membership in the Federation of Labor[b] (*Thousands*)	(5) Man-Days Lost Because of Labor Disputes[b] (*Thousands*)	(6) Ratio of Man-Days Lost to Potential Maximum Working Time of Trade Union Members[c]
1899	n.a.	91	1.6	n.a.	n.a.
1900	n.a.	83	4.8	n.a.	n.a.
1901	n.a.	88	7.6	n.a.	n.a.
1902	n.a.	92	7.5	n.a.	n.a.
1903	n.a.	92	7.9	130	.0549
1904	n.a.	91	9.0	45	.0167
1905	n.a.	88	15.6	30	.0064
1906	n.a.	85	25.3	95	.0125
1907	n.a.	84	39.0	340	.0291
1908	n.a.	88	47.2	380	.0268
1909	n.a.	95	43.2	185	.0143
1910	n.a.	95	45.9	179	.0130
1911	n.a.	97	53.1	1,115	.0700
1912	n.a.	93	60.8	446	.0245
1913	n.a.	98	63.8	122	.0064
1914	100	100	67.6	156	.0077
1915	115	90	78.0	315	.0135
1916	138	82	78.9	720	.0304
1917	171	77	93.9	109	.0039
1918	240	90	107.5	187	.0058
1919	257	n.a.	143.9	623	.0144
1920	300	147	142.6	1,199	.0280
1921	277	158	96.0	3,584	.1244
1922	232	144	83.6	91	.0036
1923	218	142	85.6	796	.0310
1924	239	139	92.8	5,152	.1851
1925	243	148	95.9	667	.0232
1926	206	162	93.1	2,205	.0789
1927	186	154	94.2	1,374	.0486
1928	173	157	106.9	364	.0114
1929	166	165	127.0	197	.0052
1930	161	169	139.6	240	.0057
1931	153	174	144.6	7,586	.1749
1932	149	181	153.4	394	.0086
1933	147	181	157.5	364	.0077
1934	147	181	172.5	235	.0045
1935	150	177	214.6	168	.0026
1936	155	178	268.3	396	.0049
1937	166	179	316.0	1,014	.0107
1938	171	190	340.0	567	.0056
1939	173	191	352.5	860	.0081
1940	202	177	306.5	n.a.	n.a.

TABLE A5 (Continued)

(1) Year	(2) Cost of Living Index[a] (*July 1914 = 100*)	(3) Index of Real Average Hourly Earnings, Male Workers[b] (*1914 = 100*)	(4) Membership in the Federation of Labor[b] (*Thousands*)	(5) Man-Days Lost Because of Labor Disputes[b] (*Thousands*)	(6) Ratio of Man-Days Lost to Potential Maximum Working Time of Trade Union Members[c]
1941	237	156	293.8	n.a.	n.a.
1942	251	149	289.0	n.a.	n.a.
1943	258	148	280.5	n.a.	n.a.
1944	261	148	n.a.	n.a.	n.a.
1945	265	174	338.6	65	.0006
1946	272	184	398.0	79	.0007
1947	273	204	442.0	41	.0003
1948	272	215	456.0	92	.0007
1949	272	226	473.6	105	.0007

[a] Source: Mimeographed release of the Norwegian Central Statistical Bureau.

[b] Source: Walter Galenson, *Labor in Norway*, pp. 18–19. The data prior to 1914 were deflated by an index of wholesale prices. Since the original data are in terms of daily earnings, the index was calculated on the assumption of a nine-hour day to 1919 and an eight-hour day thereafter.

[c] Calculated as the ratio of total man-days lost because of labor disputes to membership in the Federation of Labor multiplied by 300.

TABLE A6

WAGES, PRICES, AND LABOR DISPUTES IN SWEDEN, 1899–1949

(1) Year	(2) Cost of Living Index[a] (*1914 = 100*)	(3) Index of Real Average Hourly Earnings, Male Workers[a] (*1914 = 100*)	(4) Number of Trade Union Members[b] (*Thousands*)	(5) Man-Days Lost Because of Labor Disputes[c] (*Thousands*)	(6) Ratio of Man-Days Lost to Potential Maximum Working Time of Trade Union Members[d]
1899	85	79	64	n.a.	n.a.
1900	86	82	66	n.a.	n.a.
1901	84	84	67	n.a.	n.a.
1902	84	86	66	n.a.	n.a.
1903	86	84	78	642	.0274
1904	85	88	98	386	.0131
1905	87	90	104	2,390	.0766
1906	89	92	180	479	.0089
1907	92	94	231	514	.0074
1908	94	94	213	1,842	.0288
1909	93	98	148	11,800	.2658
1910	93	103	118	39	.0011
1911	91	107	114	570	.0167
1912	98	102	122	292	.0080
1913	98	105	136	303	.0074
1914	100	100	144	621	.0144
1915	114	100	158	83	.0018
1916	130	96	194	475	.0082
1917	163	94	253	1,109	.0146
1918	227	97	305	1,436	.0157
1919	263	110	367	2,296	.0209
1920	264	145	399	8,943	.0747
1921	227	161	396	2,663	.0224
1922	184	143	344	2,675	.0259
1923	170	147	365	6,907	.0631
1924	170	150	417	1,205	.0096
1925	173	151	444	2,560	.0192
1926	167	161	472	1,711	.0121
1927	166	162	494	400	.0027
1928	166	164	527	4,835	.0306
1929	165	168	568	667	.0039
1930	160	175	614	1,021	.0055
1931	154	179	648	2,627	.0135
1932	152	176	656	3,095	.0157
1933	149	179	648	3,434	.0177
1934	150	177	668	760	.0038
1935	152	178	713	788	.0037
1936	153	178	773	438	.0019
1937	158	181	857	861	.0033
1938	162	188	911	1,284	.0047
1939	167	186	972	159	.0005
1940	188	180	980	78	.0003

TABLE A6 (Continued)

(1) Year	(2) Cost of Living Index[a] (*1914 = 100*)	(3) Index of Real Average Hourly Earnings, Male Workers[a] (*1914 = 100*)	(4) Number of Trade Union Members[b] (*Thousands*)	(5) Man-Days Lost Because of Labor Disputes[c] (*Thousands*)	(6) Ratio of Man-Days Lost to Potential Maximum Working Time of Trade Union Members[d]
1941	212	172	994	94	.0003
1942	230	172	1,026	53	.0002
1943	233	178	1,042	94	.0003
1944	235	180	1,072	228	.0007
1945	235	189	1,110	11,321	.0340
1946	237	201	1,150	27	.0001
1947	252	217	1,197	125	.0003
1948	262	219	1,241	151	.0004
1949	262	226	1,256	21	.0001

[a] Source: Ragnar Casparsson, *L O Under Fem Årtionden* (Stockholm, 1948), vol. II, p. 713.

[b] Source: Jörgen Westerstahl, *Svensk Fackförenings Rörelse* (Stockholm, 1945), p. 31. Membership in the Swedish syndicalist center, constituting a few per cent of total trade union membership, is excluded. Membership in the Tjänstemännens Centralorganisation is also excluded.

Trade union membership was estimated for the years 1945–1949 by assuming continuance of the relationship between Federation of Labor membership and total membership prevailing in 1944.

[c] *Statistisk Årsbok for Sverige*, various years.

[d] Calculated as the ratio of total man-days lost because of labor disputes to trade union membership multiplied by 300.

APPENDIX B

THE SEPTEMBER AGREEMENT

Agreement between The Danish Employers' Association
and The Danish Federation of Labor
September 5, 1899

1. All agreements concerning hours of work, wage conditions, price lists, and rules of arbitration which were in force when the stoppage of work began continue in force, subject to modifications contained in the following conditions. [This clause is now only of historical interest.]

2. The Danish Employers' Association and the Danish Federation of Labor hereby acknowledge each other's right to decree and approve stoppages of work, but no lockout or strike of any kind may be decreed or approved by either side before it has been approved by at least three-quarters of the votes cast at a competent meeting. The intention to bring a proposal of stoppage of work before such a meeting shall be notified to the Executive Committee of the other side in writing and by registered post at least fourteen days before the proposed stoppage is to take effect, and the decision of the meeting shall be made known to the other side at least seven days before the stoppage takes effect. Both sides bind themselves not to approve or support a strike or lockout which conflicts with this condition. A strike or lockout is considered to exist if the factory or workshop is systematically evacuated or is gradually closed down through the action of the central organization of either side (or of one of its affiliated organizations) or with its express or tacit approval after due notification from the other side. It is hereby agreed that it shall be regarded as a breach of this agreement if either of the central organizations supports an unaffiliated workers' or employers' organization in a dispute with either of the central organizations or their affiliated organizations.

3. The central organizations shall be responsible for ensuring that the agreements concluded between them are respected and carried out by all affiliated organizations.

4. The employer's right to direct and distribute the work and to use what labor may in his judgment be suitable at any time is acknowledged by and, if necessary, must be supported by the workers' central organization. As regards a worker or workers to whom a definite job has been allotted with an agreed piece work rate without any reservations, and who is carrying out the job properly, the employer is not justified in altering the conditions to the detriment of the worker without making good any economic loss sustained by the

worker in consequence. A dispute arising in this particular respect is to be decided by mediation, or if necessary by arbitration, to which all complaints by employers and workers of a breach of this agreement or abuse of it shall be referred.

5. Salaried foremen, as such, shall have full liberty not to become members of a trade union. By salaried foremen is understood persons who are the employers' chosen representatives in relation to the workers, who do not undertake piece work, and who are not interested in piece work earnings.

6. Agreements concerning price lists and other working conditions can be denounced only after at least three months' notice, while the *terminus ad quem* (term of expiration) must be stated in every agreement. Existing agreements remain unaffected by this condition until they run out.

7. After a dispute is settled, there must be no boycotting of any kind by either side.

8. After the termination of the dispute all workers shall return to the jobs on which they were employed when the dispute began. It is taken for granted that all workshops will be opened at the same time and as far as possible to the same extent as when the stoppage began. Similarly all the workers shall as far as conditions permit resume work in the same workshops where they were employed before the lockout.

9. It is taken for granted that the Federation of Labor will be willing to work together with the Danish Employers' Association for peaceful, stable, and good relations, and first and foremost that under no circumstances will any organization try to prevent any worker from exercising his natural right to do as good work and as much work as his abilities and training permit. It is also considered important that the central organizations shall coöperate in discouraging overindulgence in alcohol wherever it may occur. A term of notice between employers and workers in various professions is regarded as being in the interest of both parties. Of equal importance are arrangements for payment of overtime, rates of apprentices on piece work, and the establishment of fairly uniform rules for arbitration for the settlement of industrial disputes in all trades. The central organizations therefore agree to work together for a satisfactory solution of these problems.

10. In the case of a breach of agreement by an affiliated organization or by an industrial worker or employer, the question shall first be dealt with by the Executive Committee of the central organizations, unless existing agreements provide other arrangements for dealing with the matter or if such arrangements have been tried without success. If this does not bring about a solution, either of the central organizations, through its Executive Committee, can institute proceedings in the Copenhagen Courts.

11. If either of the central organizations is thought to have violated this agreement, the Executive Committee of the other may bring the question before the same courts.

12. The foregoing agreement is signed by the Executive Committee of the Danish Federation of Labor on behalf of all its affiliated organizations and certain unaffiliated workers' organizations and is binding on all these; and by

the Executive Committee of the Danish Employers' Association on behalf of all its affiliated organizations and is binding on all these.

13. Trade unions or employers cannot, by resigning from the central organization, escape the obligations entered into by this agreement. They continue to apply until the central organization concerned terminates the agreement in regard to that particular employer or union.

APPENDIX C

RULES FOR NEGOTIATION OF AGREEMENTS

Agreement between The Danish Employers' Association
and The Danish Federation of Labor
October 5, 1936

§ 1.

All agreements shall have the same date of expiration, *viz.* March 1.

§ 2.

In order that the period of notice of three months may be used to the best advantage in the interest of negotiations between the parties, the following rules are laid down:

a. The length of notice of three months provided for in agreements shall be shortened to fourteen days.

b. The party wanting amendments to an existing agreement shall not later than three months before the date of expiration of the agreement submit proposals for such amendments. If proposals are not submitted in due time, the agreement shall remain in force for another year.

c. The negotiations between the suborganizations shall be commenced immediately on receipt of the proposal, and shall be concluded not later than six weeks afterwards.

d. As soon as the negotiations have been declared finished in the suborganizations, they must be commenced in the central organizations.

§ 3.

In the course of the negotiations in the suborganizations the parties may decide that one or several of the matters at issue concerning wages and conditions of work within the field covered by the agreement in question shall be subject to direct consideration and decision by a special court of arbitration set up for each trade under the arbitration rules in force for the particular trade.

The court of arbitration shall not be competent to decide on questions of a general nature within the particular field of agreement, such as a general change of the hours of work, or a general demand for a change of the wage level, or any question which is not submitted with the consent of both parties. Such questions shall be subject to negotiation between the organizations in the ordinary way, and may be decided through a strike or lockout.

In the course of its deliberations for determining the fair price for the work in question, the court of arbitration may for its orientation require all information regarding conditions of work, prices, wages, and piece work earnings within the trade. Where local price lists are concerned, reasonable regard must be had to the local conditions prevailing.

§ 4.

Immediately on the conclusion of negotiations in the suborganizations both parties shall be obliged to submit a detailed and precise report to their respective central organizations containing information about:

1. The agreements hitherto in force.
2. The questions which have been decided by negotiation or arbitration in the suborganizations.
3. The questions which are still outstanding with a statement of the proposals and other documents exchanged between the parties.

§ 5.

As soon as the negotiations in the suborganizations have been brought to a conclusion, and there are questions which have not been decided, the central organizations, as stated in § 2 d, shall commence negotiations to reach agreement on the matters at issue.

If by negotiations between the central organizations agreement is reached between the suborganizations about referring more questions for consideration by the arbitration mentioned in § 3, it shall be possible to do so, provided that the questions are such as may be referred to arbitration in pursuance of § 3.

The central organizations agree that this court of arbitration shall not be competent to consider and decide upon questions other than those which the parties during previous negotiations, partly in the suborganizations and partly in the central organizations, have agreed to submit to it.

The negotiations in the central organizations, to which representatives of the suborganizations are summoned, must be brought to a conclusion before the extended period of notice takes effect.

§ 6.

This agreement shall remain in force until it is denounced by the serving of six months' notice terminating on the first day of July, but not before July 1, 1940.

APPENDIX D

THE MEDIATION ACT

Act No. 82, 12 April 1910 Concerning Mediation in Labor Disputes
As Amended by Act No. 526, 21 December 1921, Act No. 34, 28 February 1927,
Act No. 5, 18 January 1934 Concerning Inervention in Labor Disputes,
As Amended by Act No. 96, 20 March 1940 and Act No. 602,
21 December 1945

I

MEDIATORS

1. (1) The Minister of Labor and Social Affairs on the recommendation of the Labor Court shall appoint three mediators for the whole Kingdom, to assist in the settlement of disputes between employers and workers in the manner prescribed in this Act. The appointments shall be made for three years at a time, provided that one mediator shall retire at the end of each year and that in December of each year a mediator shall be appointed in place of the mediator who is retiring. Reappointment shall be permissible.

(2) In addition, the Minister of Labor and Social Affairs, also on the recommendation of the Labor Court, shall appoint a substitute for the mediators for a period of three years at a time. Reappointment shall be permissible.

(3) The recommendation made by the Labor Court must have the support of at least one of the members of the Court elected by the employers and the workers respectively. In case of failure to make such a recommendation on or before December 15 in each year, the Minister of Labor and Social Affairs shall make the appointment independently of any recommendation.

(4) In the event of a mediator's death or of his placing his resignation in the hands of the Minister of Labor and Social Affairs and its being approved by the latter, the Labor Court shall make a recommendation in accordance with the foregoing rules within one month of the despatch by the Minister of Labor and Social Affairs of a request for the recommendation. In default of a recommendation within the said period, the Minister of Labor and Social Affairs shall appoint a new mediator independently of any recommendation, and the said mediator shall retire on the date on which the person whom he replaces would have retired.

2. (1) The mediators shall elect a chairman from their number for a year at a time, who shall act as administrative director of the Mediation Board.

(2) The mediators shall at all times keep in touch with the general situation as regards conditions of employment, especially wages, and shall meet as often as may be considered necessary, at the invitation of the chairman, to discuss the existing situation under his direction.

(3) The Mediation Board shall be entitled to require every employers' organization or undertaking and every workers' organization to send it copies of every collective agreement to which it is a party.

(4) Further, every independent employer and every employers' or workers' organization shall be bound to transmit to the Mediation Board a copy of every notice of a stoppage of work sent out, where the question at issue is not by the nature of the case within the jurisdiction of the Labor Court. However, in the case of organizations which are subject to the provisions of the September Agreement with respect to such notices, it shall be sufficient to transmit to the Mediation Board a copy of the second notice sent out.

(5) The mediators shall specify, by means of standing orders drawn up for each calendar year or for each special case, the labor questions in which each of the three mediators shall intervene as cases arise. Each mediator shall carry out the task of intervention which he undertakes without the assistance of the other mediators, except as provided in section 5, and shall complete it even if the period for which he was appointed has expired in the meantime.

(6) The Mediation Board shall make an annual report to the Minister of Labor and Social Affairs on its activities.

3. (1) If there is reason to fear a stoppage of work, or if a stoppage of work has occurred, and the mediator within whose competence the case lies [*cf.* section 2, subsection (5)] deems the effects and scope of the dispute to be of public importance, he may on his own initiative or at the request of either of the parties convene the parties to the dispute for negotiations, where negotiations have already been carried on by the parties in accordance with the rules agreed upon between them and have been declared by either party to be closed without arrival at a settlement. The parties themselves shall designate the persons whom they wish to represent them, provided that these shall not be persons from outside the organizations, central confederations, or undertakings concerned.

(2) The parties shall be bound to appear when summoned by the mediator.

(3) When the mediator has decided to intervene or actually intervenes to prevent an impending stoppage of work, he may at any time before or during the negotiations require the parties as a condition of his intervention to refrain from giving effect to the stoppage until the negotiations have been declared by the mediator to be closed. Nevertheless, this requirement shall not apply to a period exceeding one week, and shall not be imposed more than once in the course of the same labor dispute.

4. (1) In the course of the negotiations with the parties the mediator shall have the right to submit proposals for concessions which seem likely to lead to an amicable settlement of the dispute.

(2) If the mediator in the course of the proceedings becomes convinced

that some or all of the questions at issue between the parties either have not been the subject of actual negotiations on their merits between the parties or on account of their special occupational character should be settled by direct negotiation between the parties, he may require such negotiations to be opened and refuse to continue his intervention until these negotiations have taken place. With the consent of both parties, or one of them, the mediator may decide that the resumed negotiations shall be carried on under the chairmanship of a submediator (see below under Part II). In such cases section 8, subsection (5), likewise applies. The mediator shall fix the time limit within which the negotiations must be completed.

(3) If the mediator considers it advisable, he may submit a mediation proposal, provided that this shall not be published without his consent so long as the replies of the two parties concerning the said proposal are pending. Before the mediator submits his proposal, he shall discuss the formal wording of the draft with representatives of each of the parties, and also with one representative of each of the central organizations, if the parties belong to a central organization.

(4) The mediator in agreement with the parties shall fix the time limit for the communication of the reply accepting or rejecting the mediation proposal.

5. If a dispute actually in progress is in the mediators' opinion of considerable public importance, they may decide that all three mediators in concert shall intervene in the dispute in question. Any such decision shall be communicated to the organizations (central organizations) or undertakings concerned, and all three mediators shall take part in the subsequent negotiations. The chairman shall preside over the negotiations.

6. (1) If a difference of opinion arises respecting wages, hours of work, overtime, etc., in any dispute which has given rise to the intervention of a mediator under section 3, and precise knowledge of the actual conditions which have subsisted in this connection is considered of importance for the settlement of the dispute, the mediator shall have the right to require the parties to give information thereon.

(2) If the information so given appears to the mediator to be unreliable or inadequate, he shall have the right to require the Labor Court to take evidence.

(3) The mediator shall have the right to be present during the taking of such evidence before the Labor Court and may require that any further questions to which the statements of the witnesses may give rise be put to them respecting the matters specified in subsection (1).

II

SUBMEDIATORS

7. (1) The Minister of Labor and Social Affairs on the recommendation of the Labor Court shall further appoint up to twelve submediators for the whole Kingdom to assist the mediators in the settlement of disputes between em-

ployers and workers as regards wages and other conditions of work in the manner prescribed below. The appointments shall be made for three years at a time, provided that one-third of the submediators shall retire at the end of each year, on the first two occasions by the drawing of lots, and that in December of each year the requisite number of submediators shall be appointed in the place of those retiring. Reappointment shall be permissible. The remuneration of the submediators shall be fixed by the Minister of Labor and Social Affairs after consultation with the Minister of Finance.

(2) The Minister of Labor and Social Affairs on the recommendation of the Labor Court shall also appoint three alternates for the submediators for a period of three years at a time. Reappointment shall be permissible.

(3) The provisions of section 1, subsections (3) and (4), shall likewise apply to the appointment of submediators and their alternates.

(4) The mediators may also act as submediators.

8. (1) Where the negotiations carried on between the suborganizations and the central organizations in a trade concerning the demands put forward at the renewal of agreements have failed, the Mediation Board, at the request of the central organizations or one of them, may decide that the negotiations be resumed either in the suborganizations or in the central organizations with a submediator as chairman.

(2) Similar rules shall apply as regards individual undertakings or organizations not members of the central organizations.

(3) As regards large trades of great importance, it may be decided by the Mediation Board at the request of the parties (the central organizations) or one of them that the submediator shall step in as chairman while the negotiations in the suborganizations are in progress.

(4) The Mediation Board shall decide which submediator shall act in each case, and shall at the same time decide whether any of the demands put forward shall be omitted from the negotiations between the parties for discussion at a later date. It may fix a time limit within which the negotiations must be completed.

(5) It shall be the submediator's duty to try to obtain agreement between the parties during the negotiations carried on under his chairmanship. If he does not succeed, the submediator shall submit a report to the Mediation Board of the demands originally put forward, the demands which have been dropped later, the questions agreed upon, and the concessions otherwise made by the parties during negotiations. A copy of the report shall be communicated to the parties. The Mediation Board may decide that the negotiations between the parties under the chairmanship of the submediator be resumed.

9. In arranging their work, mediators and submediators should aim at a final conclusion of the negotiations by the time at which the parties may denounce the agreements in pursuance of the notices of stoppage of work given.

III

RULES OF VOTING

10. (1) If a mediation proposal is to be voted upon within any organization, it shall not be submitted in any other form than that drawn up by the mediator, and the vote shall be given in the form of a simple yes or no. Every vote on a mediation proposal shall be taken by secret ballot and in writing. When the result of the voting has been ascertained, the organizations shall without delay notify the mediator in writing of the number of yes and no votes recorded, and also of the total number of members entitled to vote. Before the vote is taken, the organization shall as far as possible ensure that all members entitled to vote are given the opportunity to acquaint themselves with the mediation proposal in its entirety.

(2) The results of a general ballot shall be ascertained in conformance with the following rules:

A mediation proposal shall be deemed to be rejected if more than 50 per cent of the persons who voted cast their votes against the mediation proposal and not less than 75 per cent of the members entitled to vote took part in the ballot. The percentage of the recorded votes necessary for rejection shall be increased by $^1/_2$ per cent for every unit by which the percentage of votes recorded is below 75.

If the number of persons who voted is less than 25 per cent of the number entitled to vote, the mediation proposal shall be deemed to be accepted.

Ballots which are blank or otherwise invalid shall not be included for the purpose of ascertaining the result.

(3) Nothing shall be published or made known regarding the results of the voting in sections, unions, or central organizations until the mediator has published the general result.

11. (1) If disputes occur in various trades at the same time, and the mediator considers that they can only be settled in conjunction with one another, he may direct in the mediation proposal proposed by him to deal generally with the said disputes that they shall be considered wholly or in part as forming a whole, irrespective of the question whether the trades concerned in the disputes are organized (as independent trade unions, federations, or employers' organizations, or as members of a federation of trade unions, federations, or employers' organizations). Organizations consisting of foremen etc. who are covered by paragraph 5 of the September Agreement or who are of the same standing as the persons covered by the Agreement cannot be included in such a composite proposal covering several trades.

(2) In order to ascertain whether such a mediation proposal is accepted or rejected by the workers' organizations, the mediator may require that the results for the various trades involved be added together, and the proposal submitted shall then be deemed to be accepted if the grand total gives a majority in favor of acceptance. Within each federation (union, section of union) the

decision is arrived at either by general ballot or by a competent meeting. If the number of persons who voted by general ballot within a federation (union, section of union) does not amount to 75 per cent of the persons entitled to vote, the competent meeting shall adopt a decision as regards the remaining votes up to 75 per cent.

In calculating the total result for the various trades concerned, the ballots, where the decision has been adopted in this way, shall be taken as the basis, in conjunction with the votes recorded by the competent meeting, if any, whereas, where the decision is adopted by competent meetings only, the voting of the latter shall be taken as a basis for the assessment. In cases where a ballot has been taken and also a decision adopted by a competent meeting in the same body of voters, the result of the voting shall be calculated as follows: the percentage of votes recorded for the whole body of voters covered by the ballot shall be calculated, so that in federations, where the number of persons voting amounts to less than 75 per cent, and where consequently the competent meeting has adopted a decision as regards the remaining members up to 75 per cent, a percentage of 75 of the votes recorded shall be taken into account. The total membership within the field for which the decision has been adopted by a competent meeting only shall then be reduced in proportion to the ascertained percentage of votes recorded within the field covered by the general ballot. The membership thus reduced shall be divided between the yeses and noes in the same proportion as the votes recorded at the competent meeting, and the number of votes thus obtained shall then be added to the number of votes from the field covered by the general ballot.

(3) In organizations belonging to the Employers' Association the weighting of the votes shall be calculated according to the rules hitherto in force. If both organizations belonging to the Employers' Association and organizations not belonging to it are involved in the same mediation proposal, the weighting of the votes shall be calculated according to the wages paid by the members of the organization in question during the last complete calendar year.

IV

VARIOUS PROVISIONS

12. Declarations shall not be drawn up or witnesses produced respecting statements or proposals made by the parties during negotiations presided over by a mediator or a submediator, unless both parties agree thereon and parts of the mediation proposals are involved or the submediator's declaration is made in pursuance of section 8, subsection (5).

13. (1) Contraventions of the provisions of this Act shall be punished by a fine or imprisonment for not more than three months, unless a heavier penalty is incurred under other legislation.

(2) In adjudication of cases relating to contraventions of the prohibition of publication or communication laid down in subsection (3) of section 4 and subsection (3) of section 10, it shall be deemed to be an exceptionally aggravat-

ing circumstance if the matter has been communicated to the public, even if this has been done through the press in the form of a "report."

(3) Fines imposed under this Act shall accrue to the Treasury.

14. (1) Expenditure for salaries, office supplies, etc., shall be defrayed by the State out of a grant under the annual Finance Act or a special Act.

(2) Any question regarding the competence of the mediators may be referred to the Labor Court for decision.

APPENDIX E

THE LABOR COURT ACT

Act No. 81, April 12, 1910, amended by Act No. 536, October 4, 1919, concerning the Labor Court as amended by Act No. 135, May 2, 1934 and Act No. 88, March 15, 1939.

§ 1.

The Labor Court shall consist of 6 regular members and 16 deputy members, a president, two vice-presidents (or if the Court deems it necessary three vice-presidents), and a secretary.

So long as the Danish Employers' Association and the Danish Federation of Labor predominantly represent the employers and workers engaged in agriculture, forestry, industry, handicraft, transport, and civil engineering, these associations shall each elect 3 of the members and 8 of the deputy members. Should these associations cease to be predominantly representative a proposal to alter the method of election shall be forwarded after negotiations between the associations to the Minister of Labor and Social Affairs who shall take steps to have the act amended.

Members are elected for 2 years, and the election shall take place every second year in October, the secretary of the Court being informed immediately of the result of the election. Every year the secretary shall summon the elected regular members — including, where necessary, deputy members — for the election of the president and vice-presidents for the following calendar year, the election to be determined by a majority vote and to take place before December 1.

Should the election of the president — or vice-presidents — fail to take place by the appointed date, the secretary shall report the matter to the president of the Supreme Court, who together with the presidents of the other Copenhagen Courts where several judges sit together shall elect them from among the judges of those courts.

Should the election of the other members (or deputies) fail to take place by the appointed date, the secretary shall report the matter to the Minister of Labor and Social Affairs, who with due regard to the principle of equal representation within the Court of employers' and workers' interests shall himself appoint members as required.

The secretary of the Court is nominated by the Minister of Labor and Social Affairs in accordance with the Court's recommendation. In the absence of the secretary the president shall appoint a deputy pro tem. Should the absence exceed one month, the appointment shall be made by the Minister of Labor and Social Affairs on the recommendation of the Court.

The secretary shall summon the ordinary members to the court meetings, or their deputies in accordance with a roster previously agreed with them.

§ 2.

(As amended by Act No. 88, March 15, 1939.)

Ordinary members and deputy members must be Danish citizens, of age, of good repute, and solvent. The president, vice-presidents, and one ordinary member on each side, and a corresponding number of deputy members on each side must fulfill the legal conditions for appointment as regular judges in an ordinary court.

Judges in the Copenhagen Courts — except the presidents — are bound to accept election as president or vice-presidents. This rule will not apply, however, to anyone who has filled such a post for 3 years.

Should it appear that the duties of president or vice-presidents in the Labor Court are so onerous as to prevent anyone elected to these posts from carrying out his official duties in the ordinary courts, the necessary assistance for these Courts must be procured.

Should the work of the Labor Court prove to be beyond the capacity of a single court, the Minister of Labor and Social Affairs on the recommendation of the Court shall set up one or more similar courts with a limited sphere of activity. Detailed arrangements shall be drawn up in a royal decree after prior consultations with the Danish Employers' Association and the Danish Federation of Labor.

§ 3.

The fees of the president, vice-presidents, and secretary and subsistence allowances for the members of the Court, together with the general expenses of the Court, are to be paid by the State by an appropriation voted under the Finance Law, in so far as they are not covered by costs.

§ 4.

A. Questions concerning breach of the agreement concluded between the Danish Employers' Association and the Danish Federation of Labor on September 5, 1899 shall be brought before the Court.

B. Breaches of agreements between a workers' organization on the one hand and either an employers' organization or an industrial undertaking (single employer, firm, or limited company) on the other hand may, in the absence of any express conditions in the parties' agreement to the contrary, be brought before the Court in accordance with the undermentioned rules and with the legal effects mentioned in § 5.

1. When an employers' organization is guilty of an action whereby an agreement with a workers' organization is infringed,

2. When one or more members of an employers' organization takes action in conflict with an agreement which it has entered into, with the result that

the rights of the workers' organization concerned or the rights under the agreement of individual members of the said organization are infringed,

3. Or, conversely, when a workers' organization is guilty of an action, or its members take concerted action, whereby an agreement with an employers' organization is infringed, the organization whose rights or whose members' rights are infringed can lodge a complaint with the Court against the organization concerned.

4. When an individual undertaking has concluded an agreement with a workers' organization, the organization and the undertaking may bring each other before the Court for breaches of agreement as are mentioned in 1–3 above.

5. When an employers' organization or members of an employers' organization give a workers' organization or members of a workers' organization notice of lockout, and the workers' organization against whose members the lockout is directed maintains that the lockout, or the rejected demand of which the lockout is the result, is in conflict with an existing agreement and within 5 days makes a formal protest as to the legality of the lockout by sending a registered letter to the organization which has given notice of stoppage of work or whose members have given such notice — or as the case may be the individual undertaking which has declared the lockout — either party may bring the question as to the legality of the lockout before the Labor Court.

Conversely, the question of the legality of a strike notice issued by a workers' organization or by members thereof to an employers' organization or to members thereof or to an individual undertaking may be brought before the Labor Court.

6. When an employers' organization, or members thereof, or an individual undertaking effect a lockout or persist in a lockout of a workers' organization or members thereof, the latter organization may, if it is of the opinion that the lockout itself or the rejected demand of which the lockout is the result is in conflict with existing agreements, or with lawfully promulgated awards of a Board of Arbitration, or with a judgment of the Court, bring the employers' organization or the individual undertaking before the Labor Court.

7. Similarly when a workers' organization or members thereof in conflict with existing agreements, Board of Arbitration awards, or a judgment of the Court, call a strike or persist in a strike against the employers' organization or members thereof or an individual undertaking, the employers' organization or the individual undertaking may bring the workers' organization before the Labor Court.

C. Other matters of dispute between employers and workers may be brought before the Court, provided a majority of at least 5 of the Court members agrees, and provided also that a general or special agreement covering the matter has been concluded between an employers' and a workers' organization or between an individual undertaking and a workers' organization.

D. Where one of the above-mentioned organizations or individual undertakings is a member of a larger organization, proceedings shall be instituted by or against the larger organization, which accepts judgment on behalf of the plaintiff or defendant.

§ 5.

A. 1. As regards items § 4 B 1–4 the Labor Court shall decide to what extent the alleged offense is in conflict with existing agreements and whether the decision complained of as being contrary to agreement is invalid, and can fine the party responsible for the alleged offense. Where damage has been suffered, the fines shall be paid to the injured party, in other cases to the plaintiff.

Should the breach of agreement consist of a failure to pay monies due, the Court may order the payment of the due amount instead of imposing fines.

In the absence of an agreement to the contrary, an organization can only be required to assume legal liability when it has been party to the alleged offense.

2. Where damage is sustained, the fines shall be assessed with due regard to the extent of the damage and to the extent to which the breach of agreement is deemed excusable. In especially extenuating circumstances the fines may be completely waived. The fine for an unlawful stoppage shall be waived if the party, against whom the stoppage is directed, by acting in violation of an agreement, is considered to have given reasonable cause for the stoppage.

3. It shall be regarded as a particularly aggravating circumstance, if the party breaking the agreement has refused to allow the dispute to go to arbitration, although bound by agreement to do so, or has acted contrary to a decision reached by lawful process of arbitration or to an existing decision of the Labor Court on the same issue.

4. In the circumstances mentioned in § 4 B, subparagraphs 6 and 7, fines may be imposed on the responsible parties in accordance with the rules stated in paragraphs 1 to 3. Where there are two issues before the Court, viz. the question of the legality of a stoppage and the question of imposing fines, the Court may decide the first question preliminarily, should the second question require more time for examination.

In the absence of any agreement to the contrary, an organization can only be required to assume legal responsibility, if it has contributed toward the institution of the stoppage, or to its continuance, or if the dispute concerns the interpretation of an existing price list (with general provisions) or of a general agreement between the organizations.

5. In accordance with the rules laid down in this paragraph fines may also be imposed in cases coming before the Court under § 4 A and 4 C.

B. 1. Where there exists a right to take proceedings before the Labor Court, proceedings before an ordinary court of law are prohibited, but an individual worker is not thereby prohibited from applying through the ordinary court for an award for outstanding wages due to him, unless the organization in taking proceedings before the Labor Court has waived this claim on behalf of the worker.

2. If a strike or lockout is not contrary to law, the mere public announcement of a strike or lockout notice or of the actual institution of a strike or lockout is not illegal.

§ 6.

The usual seat of the Court shall be Copenhagen, but the Court may sit in another place at its discretion. The president of the Court shall determine the time of meeting. The records of the Court shall be kept in accordance with the rules set out in Chapter 3 of the Procedure Act. The secretary of the Court shall act as clerk to the Court. The vice-presidents shall act in the absence of the president.

§ 7.

In bringing an action, the plaintiff shall provide the Court with at least two copies of the charge. The president shall convene a meeting of the Court as quickly as possible, summoning the two parties and at the same time furnishing the defendant with a copy of the charge-sheet. The president may also permit a respite in the course of which the defendant shall furnish the Court with a written reply to the charge. Exceptionally a further exchange of written communications may be permitted and the convening of the Court accordingly postponed.

Before the actual hearing of the case, the president may, with the authority of the Court, in order to facilitate mediation between the two parties or in order to obtain further information from the two parties by way of preparation for the hearing summon them to a preliminary meeting of the Court, to which the rest of the Court's members need not be summoned.[1]

§ 8.

As concerns the rules of procedure, the regulations applicable to civil processes (as set out in Book 2 and Chapters 27–30 of the Procedure Act) apply, subject to necessary modifications. The special procedure mentioned in Chapter 39 of the Act is applicable.

The right of both parties to be represented by counsel before the Labor Court is unrestricted. The Court shall decide to what extent one party may be justified in being represented before the Court by several counsel; the Court shall likewise decide what other persons, apart from the parties to the dispute and their counsel, shall be admitted to the Court.

Where an organization is acting on behalf of a subordinate organization, whether as plaintiff or defendant, the rules laid down in § 282 and Chapter 29 of the aforementioned Act concerning the examination and the taking of oath by parties apply to him or them on whose behalf the case is being conducted.

§ 9.

The president may, if he finds it necessary, serve a writ on the defendant in accordance with § 155 of the Procedure Act, and unless this has been done the provisions of § 341, cfr. §§ 363, and 434 of the Procedure Act concerning the nonappearance of the defendant, will not apply.

[1] In practice this course is nearly always followed.

The defendant is bound to appear before the Labor Court, even if the court is outside the jurisdiction to which he belongs.

§ 10.

The Court should ensure that industrial arbitration agreements between the two parties are observed. If the case as a whole is appropriate for industrial arbitration, the Court may dismiss it; if, however, the Court considers that to obtain an industrial arbitration decision would be impossible or would be attended by disproportionate difficulties or delays, or if both parties wish it, the Court may itself decide the case.

If certain aspects of the case can appropriately be dealt with by industrial arbitration, the Court may postpone passing sentence until the award of the industrial arbitration board is available. Where information is required concerning technical points, the Court may establish direct communication with the appropriate industrial arbitration board, and if it considers it necessary, may seek the assistance of experts who have the right to express their views during the negotiations, and as far as possible each side shall be represented by equal numbers. By decision of the Court, the experts may be present when voting takes place.

§ 11.

The rule laid down in Chapter 29 of the Procedure Act requiring the parties to appear personally before the Labor Court to answer questions applies regardless of distance. Exceptionally, however, the Court may rule that the hearing may take place before a county court in the district in which they reside.

§ 12.

Any person is bound to appear as a witness regardless of distance, if the Court so rules. Moreover, any person may be required to give evidence in a case which lies before the Court as a witness before a subordinate court in the district in which he resides when summoned in accordance with the current rules concerning writs and summonses.

§ 13.

With regard to the Court's authority for appointing men to make inspections and estimates (surveyors and appraisers) the limits of the Court's jurisdiction shall be taken to be the distance from the Court's place of meeting prescribed in § 171, subparagraph 2 (2), in the Procedure Act.

As regards the obligation of these men to appear before the Court to answer questions and certify their inspection, the existing rules laid down in § 12 of this Act apply.

§ 14.

The president of the Court shall decide by decree disputes which may arise before the Court while evidence is taken or inspection and estimate made.

Appeals shall be made to the High Court within the jurisdiction of which the award is given.

§ 15.

As regards subsistence and loss of earnings allowances for witnesses, surveyors, and appraisers §§ 192 and 211 of the Procedure Act apply.

§ 16.

Decisions of the Labor Court shall be observed as final and legally binding decisions. Where the sentence of the Court provides for payment of costs, such payment shall be paid into the exchequer of the Court.

§ 17.

(As amended by Act No. 135, May 2, 1934.)

The term "organization" as used in this Act shall signify *either* a group of employers who employ workers in industry, handicraft, trade or commerce, agriculture, horticulture, civil engineering, or transport and who combine together to enter into an agreement with a group of workers and who on condition that the workers observe certain obligations, pledge themselves to offer certain conditions of work to workers in their employ, *or* a group of workers who by means of an agreement with an employers' organization or an individual undertaking, on condition that they fulfill certain obligations, are assured of certain conditions of work when they are employed by the employers concerned.

By royal decree, promulgated by the Minister of Labor and Social Affairs, the jurisdiction of the Labor Court may be extended to cover industrial relations in undertakings outside industry etc. if the Court unanimously recommends such extension.

If an organization which brings an action or is the subject of an action before the Court is of such small extent and importance that the value to be derived from the Court's hearing the case is considered to be disproportionate to the expense of time and money involved, the Court is empowered to dismiss the case.

Where a collective agreement between two undertakings or two organizations does not contain other adequate provisions for the settlement of disagreements of an industrial character (trade disputes), the conditions prescribed by the Joint Committee of August 17, 1908 in the Standard Rules for dealing with trade disputes shall be deemed to apply. The conciliation committee mentioned in paragraph 2 of the Standard Rules shall consist of 2 members, one of whom shall be elected by each of the parties to the agreement. The industrial arbitration board mentioned in paragraph 6 of the Standard Rules shall consist of 4 members of whom 2 shall be elected by each of the parties. Where the board is not unanimous in the choice of the umpire, the president of the Labor Court shall appoint him.

§ 18.

Five years after the date of the Act's coming into force, the Minister of Labor and Social Affairs shall appoint a committee of similar constitution to the committee which prepared the present Act in order to review the Act and, if necessary, to propose amendments thereto.

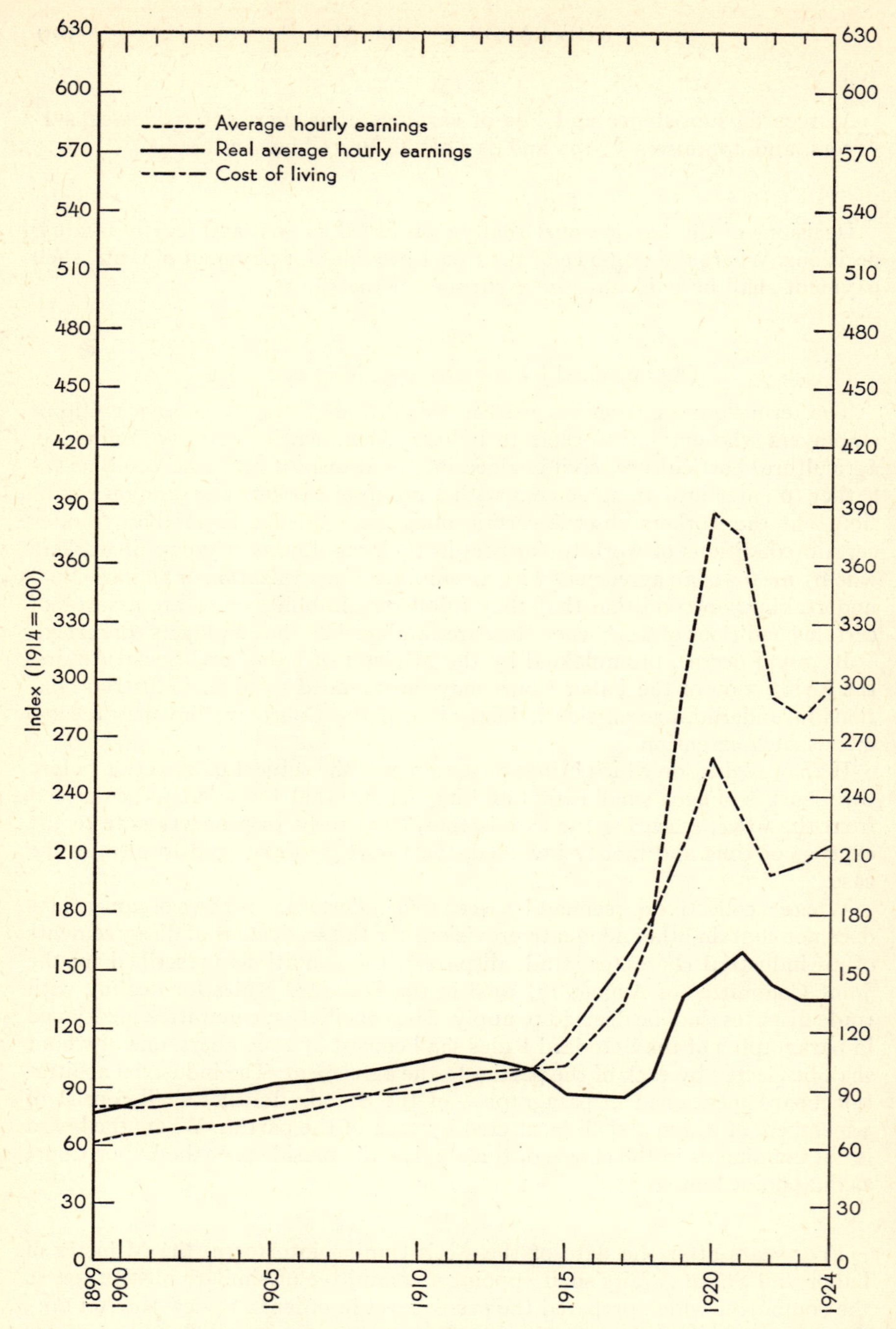

Chart 1. (A) Indexes of Average Hourly Earnings, Real Average Hourly Earnings, and the Cost of Living in Denmark, 1899–1924

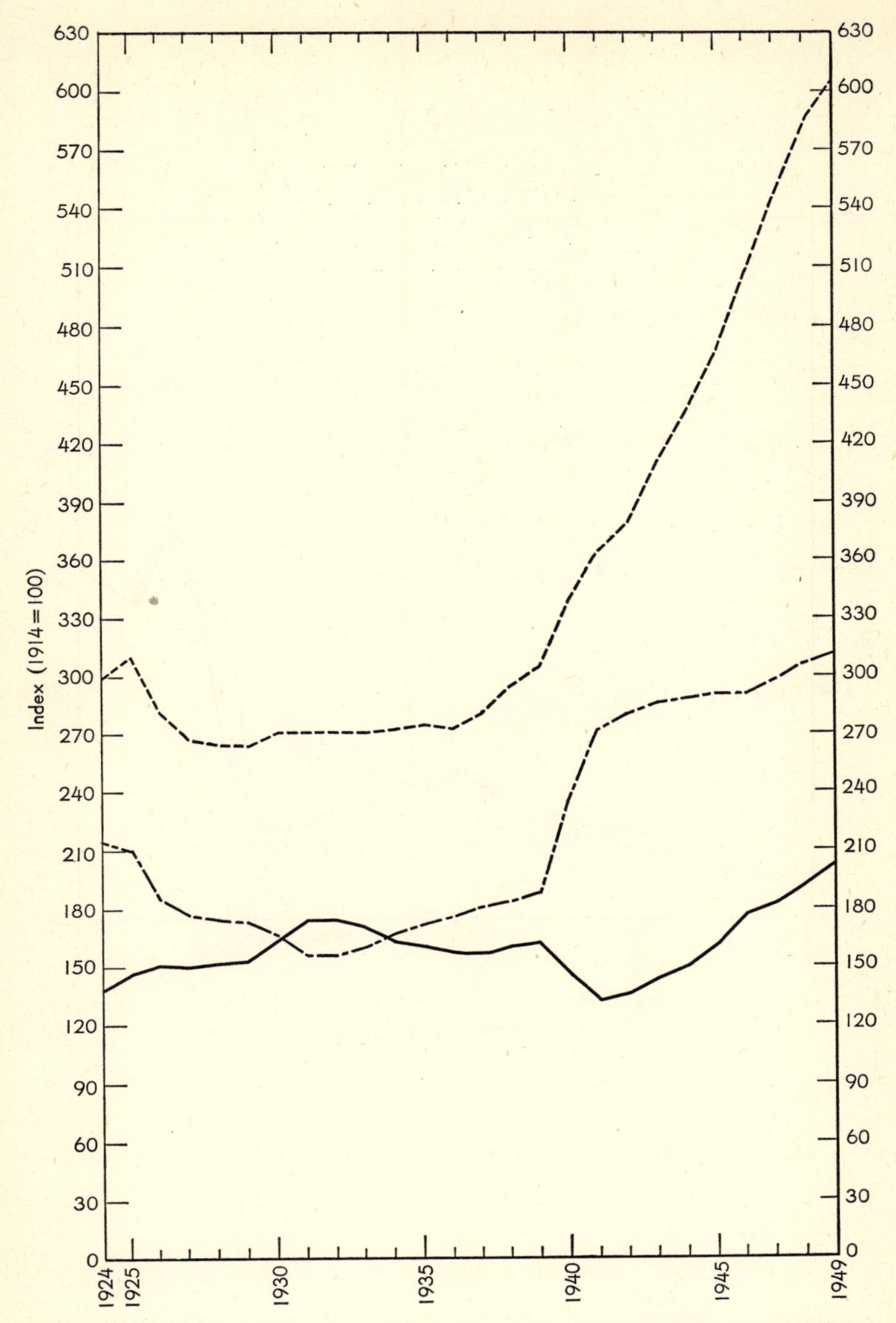

(B) Indexes of Average Hourly Earnings, Real Average Hourly Earnings, and the Cost of Living in Denmark, 1924–1949

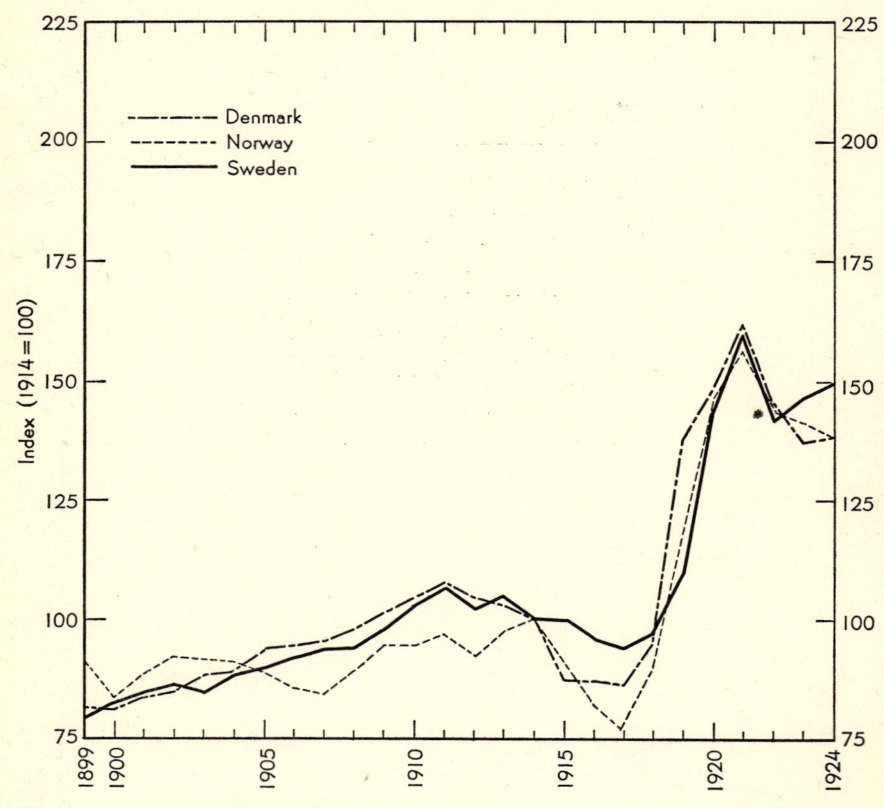

Chart 2. (A) Indexes of Real Average Hourly Earnings, Denmark, Norway, and Sweden, 1899–1924

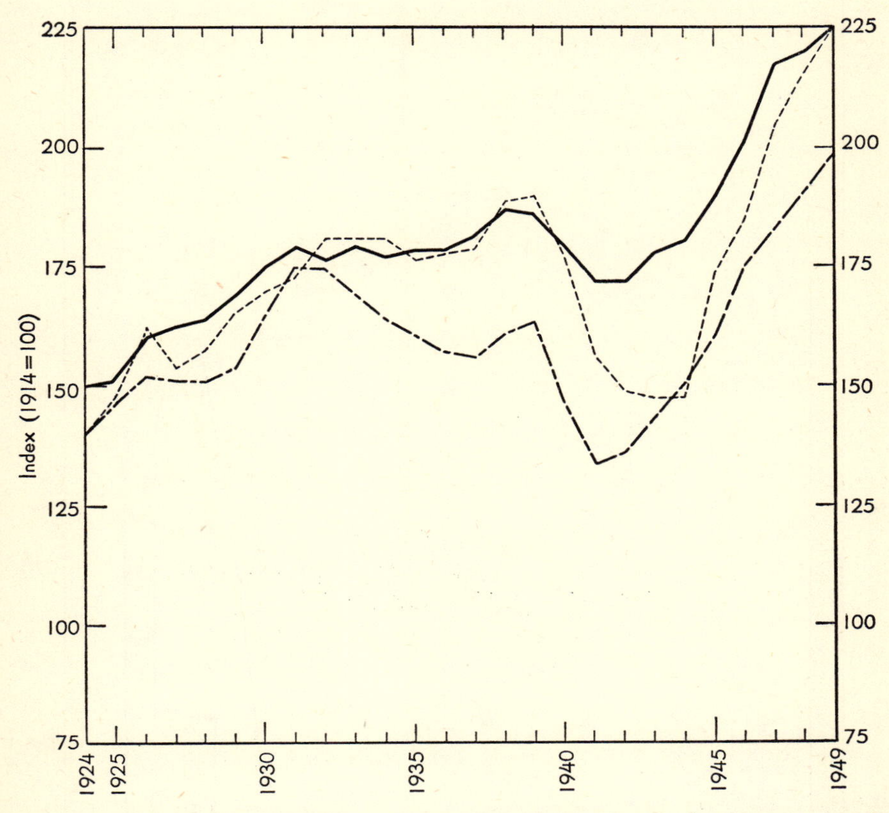

(B) Indexes of Real Average Hourly Earnings, Denmark, Norway, and Sweden, 1924–1949

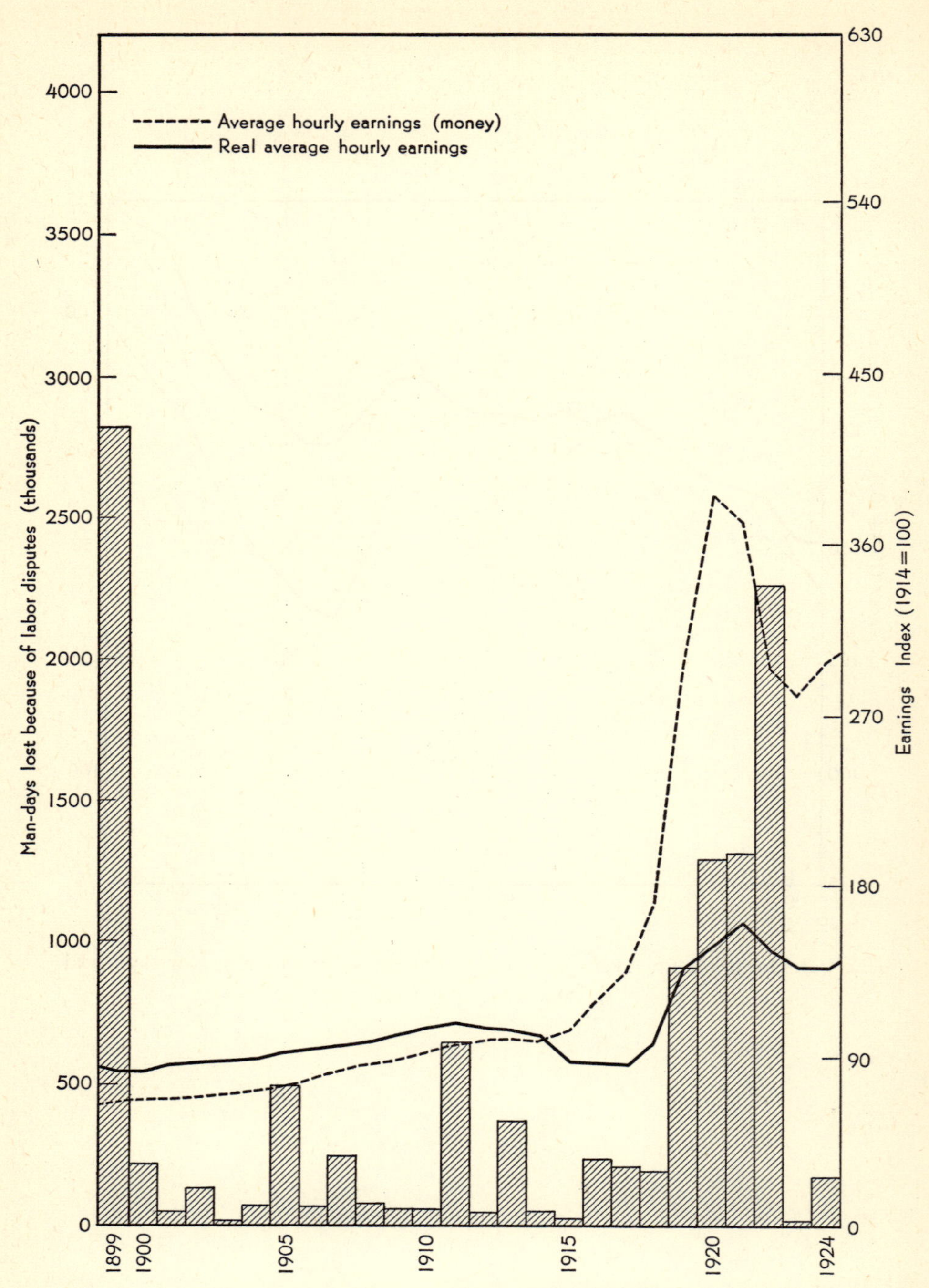

Chart 3. (A) Labor Disputes and Indexes of Money and Real Average Hourly Earnings in Denmark, 1899–1924

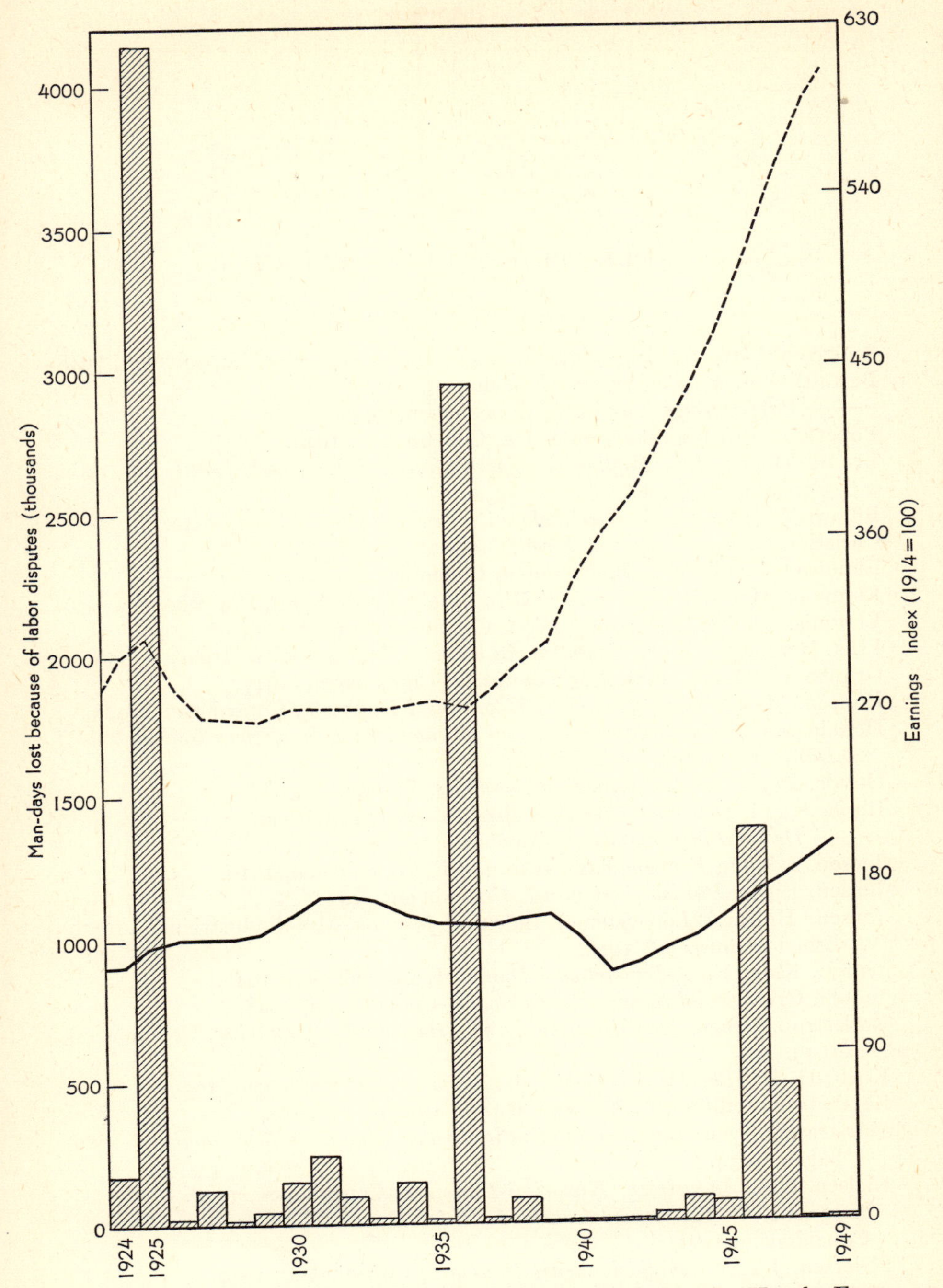

(B) Labor Disputes and Indexes of Money and Real Average Hourly Earnings in Denmark, 1924–1949

SELECTED BIBLIOGRAPHY

BOOKS AND PAMPHLETS

Andersen, Ulrik, og Hugo Engmann, *Tjenestemands Loven*, Copenhagen, 1948.

Bertolt, Oluf, *M. C. Lyngsie*, Copenhagen, 1944.

——— *Fagforenings Kundskab*, Copenhagen, 1946.

Bouet, O., *Privatfunktionaerstanden*, Copenhagen, 1948.

Bruun, Henry, *Den Faglige Arbejderbevaegelse i Danmark Indtil Aar 1900*, Copenhagen, 1938.

Bülow, K., and others, *Laerlingloven i Praksis*, Copenhagen, 1942.

Christiansen, Ernst, *Danske Smede*, Copenhagen, 1948.

Elmer, O. Bendik, *Funktionaerloven*, Copenhagen, 1948.

Elmquist, Hjalmar V., *Den Kollektive Arbejdsoverenskomst*, Copenhagen, 1930.

Elmquist, Walter, *Septemberforliget*, Copenhagen, 1930.

Friis, Henning (editor), *Scandinavia between East and West*, Ithaca, 1950.

Grünbaum, Henry, *Pristal og Lønninger*, Copenhagen, 1947.

Hansen, Max Kjaer, *Industriens Udvikling i Danmark*, Copenhagen, 1925.

Henningsen, Sven, *Studier Over Den Økonomiske Liberalismes Gennembrud i Danmark*, Göteborg, 1944.

Hovde, Bryn, *The Scandinavian Countries*, Boston, 1943.

Illum, Knud, *Den Kollektive Arbejdsret*, Copenhagen, 1939.

——— *Dansk Tillidsmandsret*, Copenhagen, 1949.

Jensen, Adolph, *Forligmands Institutionen*, Copenhagen, 1919.

Jensen, Einar, *Danish Agriculture*, Copenhagen, 1937.

Jensen, Holger, "Lønsystemet Indenfor Jern og Metalindustrien," unpublished manuscript, 1948.

Jensen, Knud V., *Arbejdsretten i Danmark*, Copenhagen, 1946.

Jensen, Orla, *Social Services in Denmark*, Copenhagen, 1948.

Kallestrup, Lauge, *Arbejdsanvisning og Arbejdsløshedsforsikring*, Copenhagen, 1946.

Koch, H. H., *The Danish Public Assistance Act*, Copenhagen, 1936.

Lund, Hans (editor), *Folkestyrets Maend*, Copenhagen, 1949.

Marstrand, Even, *Arbejderorganisation og Arbejderkaar i Danmark*, Copenhagen, 1934.

Nielsen, Axel, *Industriens Historie i Danmark*, Copenhagen, 1944.

Nørregaard, Georg, *Arbejdsforhold Indenfor Dansk Haandvaerk og Industri*, Copenhagen, 1943.

Pedersen, Jørgen, *Arbejdslønnen i Danmark*, Copenhagen, 1930.

——— *Fuld Beskaeftigelse og Økonomisk Tryghed*, Copenhagen, 1945.

Philip, Kjeld, *Den Danske Kriselovgivning 1931–38*, Copenhagen, 1939.
Ravnholt, Henning, *The Danish Cooperative Movement*, Copenhagen, 1947.
Social Denmark, Copenhagen, 1945.
Topsøe-Jensen, V., *Den Faste Voldgiftsret gennem 25 Aar*, Copenhagen.
Ussing, Carl, *Retsmaessige og Retsstridige Arbejdsstandsinger*, Copenhagen, 1928.
Vedel-Petersen, K., *Danmarks Statistik*, Copenhagen, 1946.
——— *Ungdommen og Arbejdsmarkedet i Dag*, Copenhagen, 1947.
Wechselman, Sigurd, *The Danish National Insurance Act*, Copenhagen, 1936.
Wiinblad, E., og Alsing Andersen, *Det Danske Socialdemokratis Historie 1871–1921*, Copenhagen, 1921.
Winding, Kjeld, *Den Danske Arbejderbevaegelse*, Copenhagen, 1943.
Zeuthen, F., *Arbejdsløn og Arbejdsløshed*, Copenhagen, 1939.
——— *Social Sikring*, Copenhagen, 1948.

ARTICLES IN PERIODICALS AND BOOKS

Bisgaard, H. L., "Den Store Lockout," *Nationaløkonomisk Tidsskrift*, 1899.
Bruun, Henry, "Arbejdsgiverforeningen i Danmark i Aarene 1862–1898," *Skrifter Udgivet af Institutet for Historie og Samfundsøkonomi*, Copenhagen, 1931.
Cohn, Einar, "Nationalindkomstens Fordeling Mellem Samfundsgrupper," *Nationaløkonomisk Tidsskrift*, 1949.
Dalgaard, Knud, "Arbejderklassens Økonomiske Kaar i Danmark," *Nationaløkonomisk Tidsskrift*, 1926.
Friis, Finn T. B., "Arbejdseffektiviteten i Danmark," *Socialt Tidsskrift*, 1946.
Friis, Henning, "Laerlingetilgangen 1935–1944," *Socialt Tidsskrift*, 1945.
Jacoby, H., "Fagforenings Beskaeftigelsespolitik," *Nationaløkonomisk Tidsskrift*, 1937.
Jensen, Eiler, "Arbejdernes Lønformer," *Socialt Tidsskrift*, 1941.
Milhøi, P. E., "Nogle Traek af Forholdet Mellem De Industrielle Lønninger i Danmark Siden 1914," *Nationaløkonomisk Tidsskrift*, 1948.
Pedersen, H. Winding, "Arbejdsstandsningernes Økonomiske Virkninger," *Nationaløkonomisk Tidsskrift*, 1937.

GOVERNMENT PUBLICATIONS

Arbejdskommission af 1925, *Betaenkning Vedrørende Maegling og Voldgift*, Copenhagen, 1926.
Beretning Fra Faellesudvalget af 17 August 1908, Copenhagen, 1910.
Danmarks Statistisk Aarbog (annual).
Handelsdepartementet, *Nationalbudsjettet 1948*.
——— *National Budget for 1949*.
Statistiske Meddelelser, *Arbejdsoverenskomster i Danmark*, vol. 81, no. 1 (1928).
——— *Arbejdslønnen i Industrien*, vol. 78, no. 1 (1927); vol. 91, no. 5 (1933).
——— *Nationalproduktet og Nationalindkomsten*, vol. 129, no. 5 (1950).
——— *Strejker og Lockouts*, vol. 19, no. 6 (1906); vol. 38, no. 3 (1912); vol. 54,

no. 2 (1917); vol. 66, no. 2 (1922); vol. 75, no. 5 (1926); vol. 88, no. 5 (1931).

TRADE UNION PUBLICATIONS

Arbejderen (journal of the Danish Federation of Labor).
Bundvad, Kaj, and others, *Tillidsmands Kundskab*, Copenhagen, 1946.
——— *Afstemnings, Samarbejds og Forhandlingsregler*, Roskilde, 1940.
Dansk Smede og Maskinarbejderforbunds 25 Aar Jubilaeum, Copenhagen, 1913.
Dansk Smede og Maskinarbejderforbund, *Festskrift i Anledning af 50 Aars Jubilaet*, Copenhagen, 1938.
De Samvirkende Fagforbund i Danmark 1898–1923, Copenhagen, 1923.
De Samvirkende Fagforbund, *Graensesager*, 1943.
——— Annual Reports, 1900–1950.
——— Proceedings of Congresses, 1899–1950.
Fagbevaegelsen og De Økonomiske Problemer, Copenhagen, 1937.
Jensen, J., og C. M. Olson, *Oversigt over Fagforenings-bevaegelsen i Danmark 1871–1900*, Copenhagen, 1901.
Olsen, Axel, *Dansk Arbejdsmands Forbund Gennem 50 Aar*, Copenhagen, 1947.
Under Samvirkets Flag, Copenhagen, 1948.

EMPLOYER ASSOCIATION PUBLICATIONS

Arbejdsgiveren (journal of the Danish Employers' Association).
Arbejdsgiverforening Gennem 25 Aar, Copenhagen, 1921.
Arbejdsgiverforeningen Gennem 50 Aar, Copenhagen, 1946.
Dansk Arbejdsgiverforening, Annual Reports, 1900–1950.
——— Proceedings of General Assemblies, 1900–1950.

INDEX